CLOUD COMPUTING 2019

The Tenth International Conference on Cloud Computing, GRIDs, and Virtualization

May 5 - 9, 2019

Venice, Italy

CLOUD COMPUTING 2019 Editors

Bob Duncan, University of Aberdeen, UK

Yong Woo Lee, University of Seoul, Korea

Magnus Westerlund, Arcada University of Applied Sciences, Finland

Andreas Aßmuth, Technical University of Applied Sciences OTH Amberg-Weiden, Germany

Printed from e-media with permission by:

Curran Associates, Inc.
57 Morehouse Lane
Red Hook, NY 12571

Some format issues inherent in the e-media version may also appear in this print version.

Printed by Curran Associates, Inc. (2019)

International Academy, Research, and Industry Association (IARIA)
412 Derby Way
Wilmington, DE 19810

Phone: (408) 893-6407
Fax: (408) 527-6351

petre@iaria.org

Additional copies of this publication are available from:

Curran Associates, Inc.
57 Morehouse Lane
Red Hook, NY 12571 USA
Phone: 845-758-0400
Fax: 845-758-2633
Email: curran@proceedings.com
Web: www.proceedings.com

Table of Contents

Monitoring and Managing IoT Applications in Smart Cities Using Kubernetes 1
Shapna Muralidharan, Gyuwon Song, and Heedong Ko

The Weaponization of Cloud-based Social Media: Prospects for Legislation and Regulation 7
Barry Cartwright, George Weir, Lutfun Nahar, Karmvir Padda, and Richard Frank

Invisible Ubiquity - Cloud Security in UK Corporate Annual Reporting 13
Bob Duncan and Mark Whittington

Investigating the Tension Between Cloud- Related Actors and Individual Privacy Rights 19
Bob Duncan, Karen Renaud, and Beverley Mackenzie

EU General Data Protection Regulation Compliance Challenges for Cloud Users 25
Bob Duncan

Cloud Compliance Risks 31
Bob Duncan and Yuan Zhao

Towards Trustworthy Financial Reports Using Blockchain 37
Van Thanh Le, Gianfranco D'Atri, Nabil El Ioini, and Claus Pahl

Version Control Using Distributed Ledger Technologies for Internet of Things Device Software Updates 43
Magnus Westerlund, John Wickstrom, and Goran Pulkkis

Governance in Decentralized Ecosystems: A Survey of Blockchain and Distributed Ledger White Papers 49
Petri Honkanen, Magnus Westerlund, and Mats Nylund

Blockchain Challenges for Cloud Users 55
Yuan Zhao and Bob Duncan

Cloud Security and Security Challenges Revisited 61
Fabian Suss, Marco Freimuth, Andreas Assmuth, George Weir, and Robert Duncan

UnCle SAM: Modeling Cloud Attacks with the Automotive Security Abstraction Model 67
Markus Zoppelt and Ramin Tavakoli Kolagari

Fighting Disinformation Warfare with Artificial Intelligence: Identifying and Combating Disinformation Attacks in C 73
Barry Cartwright, George Weir, and Richard Frank

PLASMA – Platform for Service Management in Digital Remote Maintenance Applications 78
Natascha Stumpp, Doris Aschenbrenner, Manuel Stahl, and Andreas Assmuth

Risk Analysis of the Cloud Infrastructure of Smart Grid and Internet of Things 82
Katrin Neubauer, Sebastian Fischer, and Rudolf Hackenberg

Security of Cloud Services with Low-Performance Devices in Critical Infrastructures 88
Michael Molle, Ulrich Raithel, Dirk Kraemer, Norbert Grass, Matthias Sollner, and Andreas Assmuth

Performance Comparision between Scaling of Virtual Machines and Containers using Cassandra NoSQL Database 93
Sogand Shirinbab, Lars Lundberg, and Emiliano Casalicchio

BalloonJVM: Dynamically Resizable Heap for FaaS 99
Abraham Chan, Kai-Ting Amy Wang, and Vineet Kumar

Efficient Virtual Machine Consolidation Approach Based on User Inactivity Detection 105
Jan Fesl, Vineet Gokhale, and Marie Feslova

Anomaly Detection and Analysis for Clustered Cloud Computing Reliability 110
Areeg Samir and Claus Pahl

Relational Algebra for Heterogeneous Cloud Data Sources 120
Aspen Olmsted

Building Trust in Cloud Computing – Isolation in Container Based Virtualisation 127
Ibrahim Alobaidan, Michael Mackay, and Nathan Shone

Cloud-RAIR: A Cloud Redundant Array of Independent Resources 133
Abdelhamid Khiat

CLOUD COMPUTING 2019

Forward

The Tenth International Conference on Cloud Computing, GRIDs, and Virtualization (CLOUD COMPUTING 2019), held between May 5 - 9, 2019 - Venice, Italy, continued a series of events targeted to prospect the applications supported by the new paradigm and validate the techniques and the mechanisms. A complementary target was to identify the open issues and the challenges to fix them, especially on security, privacy, and inter- and intra-clouds protocols.

Cloud computing is a normal evolution of distributed computing combined with Service-oriented architecture, leveraging most of the GRID features and Virtualization merits. The technology foundations for cloud computing led to a new approach of reusing what was achieved in GRID computing with support from virtualization.

The conference had the following tracks:

- Cloud computing
- Computing in virtualization-based environments
- Platforms, infrastructures and applications
- Challenging features

Similar to the previous edition, this event attracted excellent contributions and active participation from all over the world. We were very pleased to receive top quality contributions.

We take here the opportunity to warmly thank all the members of the CLOUD COMPUTING 2019 technical program committee, as well as the numerous reviewers. The creation of such a high quality conference program would not have been possible without their involvement. We also kindly thank all the authors that dedicated much of their time and effort to contribute to CLOUD COMPUTING 2019. We truly believe that, thanks to all these efforts, the final conference program consisted of top quality contributions.

Also, this event could not have been a reality without the support of many individuals, organizations and sponsors. We also gratefully thank the members of the CLOUD COMPUTING 2019 organizing committee for their help in handling the logistics and for their work that made this professional meeting a success.

We hope that CLOUD COMPUTING 2019 was a successful international forum for the exchange of ideas and results between academia and industry and to promote further progress in the area of cloud computing, GRIDs and virtualization. We also hope that Venice provided a pleasant environment during the conference and everyone saved some time for exploring this beautiful city.

CLOUD COMPUTING 2019 Chairs

CLOUD COMPUTING 2019 Steering Committee

Carlos Becker Westphall, Federal University of Santa Catarina, Brazil
Yong Woo Lee, University of Seoul, Korea
Christoph Reich, Furtwangen University, Germany
Hong Zhu, Oxford Brookes University, UK
Bob Duncan, University of Aberdeen, UK
Aspen Olmsted, College of Charleston, USA
Alex Sim, Lawrence Berkeley National Laboratory, USA

CLOUD COMPUTING 2019 Industry/Research Advisory Committee

Antonin Chazalet, Orange, France
Sören Frey, Daimler TSS GmbH, Germany
Mohamed Mohamed, IBM, Almaden Research Center, USA
Raul Valin Ferreiro, Fujitsu Laboratories of Europe, Spain
Uwe Hohenstein, Siemens AG, Germany
Bill Karakostas, VLTN gcv, Antwerp, Belgium
Matthias Olzmann, noventum consulting GmbH - Münster, Germany
Ze Yu, Google Inc, USA

CLOUD COMPUTING 2019

Committee

CLOUD COMPUTING 2019 Steering Committee

Carlos Becker Westphall, Federal University of Santa Catarina, Brazil
Yong Woo Lee, University of Seoul, Korea
Christoph Reich, Furtwangen University, Germany
Hong Zhu, Oxford Brookes University, UK
Bob Duncan, University of Aberdeen, UK
Aspen Olmsted, College of Charleston, USA
Alex Sim, Lawrence Berkeley National Laboratory, USA

CLOUD COMPUTING 2019 Industry/Research Advisory Committee

Antonin Chazalet, Orange, France
Sören Frey, Daimler TSS GmbH, Germany
Mohamed Mohamed, IBM, Almaden Research Center, USA
Raul Valin Ferreiro, Fujitsu Laboratories of Europe, Spain
Uwe Hohenstein, Siemens AG, Germany
Bill Karakostas, VLTN gcv, Antwerp, Belgium
Matthias Olzmann, noventum consulting GmbH - Münster, Germany
Ze Yu, Google Inc, USA

CLOUD COMPUTING 2019 Technical Program Committee

Sherif Abdelwahed, Virginia Commonwealth University, USA
Maruf Ahmed, The University of Sydney, Australia
Onur Alparslan, Osaka University, Japan
Abdulelah Alwabel, PSA University, KSA
Er. Annappa, National Institute of Technology Karnataka, India
Sergio Antonio Andrade de Freitas, University of Brasilia, Brazil
Filipe Araujo, University of Coimbra, Portugal
Pattakou Argyro, University of the Aegean, Greece
Andreas Aßmuth, Technical University of Applied Sciences OTH Amberg-Weiden, Germany
Irina Astrova, Tallinn University of Technology, Estonia
José Aznar, i2CAT Foundation, Spain
Jorge Barbosa, Universidade do Porto, Portugal
Luis Eduardo Bautista Villalpando, Autonomous University of Aguascalientes, Mexico
Thais Batista, UFRN - CCET - DIMAp, Brazil
Carlos Becker Westphall, Federal University of Santa Catarina, Brazil
Ali Beklen, HotelRunner, Turkey
Andreas Berl, Technische Hochschule Deggendorf, Germany
Simona Bernardi, University of Zaragoza, Spain
Peter Bloodsworth, University of Oxford, UK

Rodrigo N. Calheiros, Western Sydney University, Australia
Paolo Campegiani, Università Roma Tor Vergata, Italy
Juan-Vicente Capella-Hernández, Universitat Politècnica de València, Spain
Mª del Carmen Carrión Espinosa, University of Castilla-La Mancha, Spain
Eddy Caron, ENS de Lyon, France
K. Chandrasekaran, N.I.T.K, India
Ee-Chien Chang, National University of Singapore, Singapore
Hsi-Ya Chang, National Center for High-Performance Computing, Taiwan
Ruay-Shiung Chang, National Taipei University of Business, Taipei, Taiwan
Kyle Chard, University of Chicago and Argonne National Laboratory, USA
Nadeem Chaudhary, University of Warwick, UK
Antonin Chazalet, Orange, France
Bo Cheng, Beijing University of Posts and Telecommunications, China
Claudia-Melania Chituc, Eindhoven University of Technology, The Netherlands
Enrique Chirivella Perez, University of the West of Scotland, UK
Lawrence Chung, The University of Texas at Dallas, USA
Antonio Corradi, Università di Bologna, Italy
Fabio M. Costa, Federal University of Goiás, Brazil
Noel De Palma, University Grenoble Alpes, France
Chen (Cherie) Ding, Ryerson University, Canada
Ioanna Dionysiou, University of Nicosia, Cyprus
Rim Drira, National School of Computer Science, Tunisia
Bob Duncan, University of Aberdeen, UK
Nabil El Ioini, Free University of Bozen-Bolzano, Italy
Kaoutar El Maghraoui, IBM T.J. Watson Research Center, New York, USA
Rania El-Gazzar, Universty of South-Eastern Norway, Norway
Islam Elgedawy, Middle East Technical University, Northern Cyprus Campus, Turkey
Khalil El-Khatib, University of Ontario Institute of Technology, Canada
José Enrique Armendáriz-Íñigo, Public University of Navarre, Spain
Javier Fabra, Universidad de Zaragoza, Spain
Fairouz Fakhfakh, University of Sfax, Tunisia
Qiang Fan, New Jersey Institute of Technology, USA
Sonja Filiposka, Ss. Cyril and Methodius University - Skopje, Macedonia
Stefano Forti, University of Pisa, Italy
Sören Frey, Daimler TSS GmbH, Germany
Somchart Fugkeaw, Thai Digital ID Co. Ltd., Thailand
Javier García Blas, Universidad Carlos III De Madrid, Spain
Filippo Gaudenzi, Università Degli Studi di Milano, Italy
Thiago Gene, University of Bern, Switzerland
Sandra Gesing, University of Notre Dame, USA
Zakaria Gheid, Ecole nationale supérieure d'informatique, Algeria
Rahul Ghosh, American Express Big Data Labs, Bangalore, India
Katja Gilly, Miguel Hernandez University, Spain
Spyridon Gogouvitis, Siemens AG, Germany
Jing Gong, KTH, Sweden
Nils Gruschka, Kiel University of Applied Science, Germany
Marco Guazzone, University of Piemonte Orientale, Italy
Jordi Guitart, Universitat Politècnica de Catalunya - Barcelona Supercomputing Center, Spain

Biruk Habtemariam, IBM, Canada
Jung Hae Sun, The University of Seoul, South Korea
Rui Han, Institute of Computing Technology - Chinese Academy of Sciences, China
Ronny Hans, Technische Universität Darmstadt, Germany
Ragib Hasan, University of Alabama at Birmingham, USA
Sergio Hernández, University of Zaragoza, Spain
Herodotos Herodotou, Cyprus University of Technology, Cyprus
Uwe Hohenstein, Siemens AG, Germany
Miaoqing Huang, University of Arkansas, USA
Chih-Cheng Hung, Kennesaw State University, USA
Luigi Lo Iacono, TH Köln, Germany
Anca Daniela Ionita, University Politehnica of Bucharest, Romania
Adrian Jackson, University of Edinburgh, Scotland
Saba Jamalian, kCura LLC, Chicago, USA
Eugene John, The University of Texas at San Antonio, USA
Carlos Juiz, University of the Balearic Islands, Spain
Dae-Ki Kang, Dongseo University, South Korea
Bill Karakostas, VLTN gcv, Antwerp, Belgium
Sokratis Katsikas, Open University of Cyprus, Cyprus / Norwegian University of Science and Technology, Norway
Zaheer Khan, University of the West of England, Bristol, UK
Peter Kilpatrick, Queen's University Belfast, UK
Kenichi Kourai, Kyushu Institute of Technology, Japan
Nane Kratzke, Lübeck University of Applied Sciences, Germany
Heinz Kredel, Universität Mannheim, Germany
Yu Kuang, University of Nevada, Las Vegas, USA
Alex MH Kuo, University of Victoria, Canada
Romain Laborde, University Paul Sabatier (Toulouse III), France
Yong Woo Lee, University of Seoul, Korea
Anna Levin, IBM Research, Israel
Tonglin Li, Oak Ridge National Laboratory, USA /
Dan Lin, Missouri University of Science and Technology, USA
Panos Linos, Butler University, USA
Xiaodong Liu, Edinburgh Napier University, UK
Jay Lofstead, Sandia National Laboratories, USA
Kerry S. Long, IARPA, USA
Habib Louafi, University of Regina, Canada
Xiaoyi Lu, Ohio State University, USA
Glenn Luecke, Iowa State University, USA
Min Luo, Huawei Technologies, USA
Yutao Ma, Wuhan University, China
Shikharesh Majumdar, Carleton University, Canada
Zoltan Mann, University of Duisburg-Essen, Germany
Ming Mao, University of Virginia, USA
Olivier Markowitch, Universite Libre de Bruxelles, Belgium
Attila Csaba Marosi, Institute for Computer Science and Control - Hungarian Academy of Sciences, Hungary
Keith Martin, Royal Holloway - University of London, UK

Goran Martinovic, J.J. Strossmayer University of Osijek, Croatia
Fanjing Meng, IBM Research, China
Philippe Merle, Inria, France
Anastas Mishev, University Ss Cyril and Methodius in Skopje, Macedonia
Mohamed Mohamed, IBM, Almaden Research Center, USA
Sébastien Monnet, Université Savoie Mont Blanc | LISTIC - Polytech' Annecy-Chambéry, France
Patrice Moreaux, LISTIC - Polytech Annecy-Chambéry - University Savoie Mont Blanc, France
Hassnaa Moustafa, Intel Corporation, USA
Nour Moustafa, American University of the Middle East (AUM), Kuwait
Francesc D. Muñoz-Escoí, Universitat Politècnica de València, Spain
Amina Ahmed Nacer, University of Bejaia, Algeria / University of Lorraine, France
Hidemoto Nakada, National Institute of Advanced Industrial Science and Technology (AIST), Japan
Joan Navarro, La Salle - Universitat Ramon Llull, Spain
Richard Neill, RN Technologies, USA
Paolo Nesi, University of Florence, Italy
Marco Netto, IBM Research, Brazil
Bogdan Nicolae, IBM Research, Ireland
Ridwan Rashid Noel, University of Texas at San Antonio, USA
Aspen Olmsted, College of Charleston, USA
Matthias Olzmann, noventum consulting GmbH - Münster, Germany
Aida Omerovic, SINTEF, Norway
Brajendra Panda, University of Arkansas, USA
Alexander Papaspyrou, adesso AG, Dortmund, Germany
David Paul, University of New England, Australia
Giovanna Petrone, Universita' di Torino, Italy
Dimitrios Pezaros, University of Glasgow, UK
Sabri Pllana, Linnaeus University, Sweden
Agostino Poggi, DII - University of Parma, Italy
Andreas Polze, Hasso-Plattner-Institute, Germany
Thomas E. Potok, Oak Ridge National Laboratory, USA
Evangelos Pournaras, ETH Zurich, Switzerland
Walter Priesnitz Filho, Federal University of Santa Maria, Rio Grande do Sul, Brazil
Abena Primo, Huston-Tillotson University, USA
Francesco Quaglia, Sapienza Universita' di Roma, Italy
Danda B. Rawat, Howard University, USA
Daniel A. Reed, University of Utah, USA
Damir Regvart, Croatian Academic and Research Network - CARNet, Croatia
Christoph Reich, Furtwangen University, Germany
Sebastian Rieger, Fulda University of Applied Sciences, Germany
Sashko Ristov, University of Innsbruck, Austria
Ivan Rodero, Rutgers University, USA
Takfarinas Saber, University College Dublin, Ireland
Valentina Salapura, IBM Watson Health, USA
Mohsen Amini Salehi, University of Louisiana Lafayette, USA
Elena Sánchez-Nielsen, Universidad de La Laguna, Spain
Harshad S. Sane, Intel Corporation, USA
Lutz Schubert, University of Ulm, Germany
Wael Sellami, Higher Institute of Computer Sciences of Mahdia, Tunisia

Alireza Shameli-Sendi, Ericsson security research, Montreal, Canada
Jianchen Shan, New Jersey Institute of Technology, USA
Mohammad Shojafar, Sapienza University of Rome, Italy
Altino Manuel Silva Sampaio, Escola Superior de Tecnologia e Gestão | Instituto Politécnico do Porto, Portugal
Alex Sim, Lawrence Berkeley National Laboratory, USA
Mukesh Singhal, University of California, Merced, USA
Soeren Sonntag, Intel, Germany
Cristian Stanciu, University Politehnica of Bucharest, Romania
Vlado Stankovski, University of Ljubljana, Slovenia
Hung-Min Sun, National Tsing Hua University, Taiwan
Alexey Svyatkovskiy, Microsoft / Princeton University, USA
Kwa-Sur Tam, Virginia Tech, USA
Bedir Tekinerdogan, Wageningen University, The Netherlands
Joe Tekli, Lebanese American University, Lebanon
Michele Tomaiuolo, DII - University of Parma, Italy
Orazio Tomarchio, Universita' di Catania, Italy
Adel Nadjaran Toosi, Monash University, Australia
Deepak K Tosh, University of Texas at El Paso, USA
Raul Valin Ferreiro, Fujitsu Laboratories of Europe, Spain
Michael Vassilakopoulos, University of Thessaly, Greece
Jose Luis Vazquez-Poletti, Universidad Complutense de Madrid, Spain
Simeon Veloudis, SEERC - South East European Research Centre, Thessaloniki, Greece
Massimo Villari, Università di Messina, Italy
Anne-Lucie Vion, Orange, Paris / Université Grenoble Alpes, Saint Martin d'Hères, France
Antonio Virdis, University of Pisa, Italy
Vladimir Vlassov, KTH Royal Institute of Technology, Stockholm, Sweden
Hironori Washizaki, Waseda University, Japan
Mandy Weißbach, Martin-Luther-University Halle-Wittenberg, Germany
George Weir, University of Strathclyde, UK
Tomi Westerlund, University of Turku, Finland / Wuxi Institute of Fudan University, China
Jidong Xiao, Boise State University, Idaho, USA
Ramin Yahyapour, University Göttingen/GWDG, Germany
Feng Yan, University of Nevada, Reno, USA
Chao-Tung Yang, Tunghai University, Taiwan
Hongji Yang, Bath Spa University, UK
Ustun Yildiz, University of Pennsylvania, USA
Ze Yu, Google Inc, USA
Vadim Zaliva, Carnegie Mellon University, USA
José Luis Zechinelli Martini, Universidad de las Américas, Puebla (UDLAP), Mexico
Thomas Zefferer, Secure Information Technology Center - Austria (A-SIT Plus GmbH), Vienna, Austria
Ahmed Zekri, Beirut Arab University, Lebanon
Dongfang Zhao, University of Nevada and University of California, Davis, USA
Hong Zhu, Oxford Brookes University, UK
Wolf Zimmermann, Martin Luther University Halle-Wittenberg, Germany

Copyright Information

Monitoring and Managing IoT Applications in Smart Cities Using Kubernetes

Shapna Muralidharan
Korea Institute of Science and Technology
Seoul, South Korea
Email: 023870@kist.re.kr

Gyuwon Song
Korea Institute of Science and Technology
Seoul, South Korea
Email: gyuwon@kist.re.kr

Heedong Ko
Korea Institute of Science and Technology
Seoul, South Korea
Email: ko@kist.re.kr

***Abstract*—With the rapid urbanization, cities are transforming to smart cities with core objectives to maintain a safe, healthy and livable environment for the people. The current landscape of smart cities are continuously evolving with unique challenges and gaining ground with new technology-based solutions on the Internet of Things (IoT) and cloud computing. The efficient integration of IoT and cloud computing can tackle the unprecedented growth of smart cities by supporting various smart services like healthcare, transportation systems, environment monitoring, smart grids, etc. Recent advances in cloud computing like containerization of applications are promising solutions to host, supervise and reform the diverse IoT applications in smart cities. In this paper, we have explored the possibilities to implement a secure, distributed and reliable cloud-based monitoring system for IoT applications for effective management of a smart city environment. We propose to build a container-based system with low latency, a reliable and secure communication among large scale deployment of IoT devices with a strong focus on horizontal interoperability among various IoT applications. Our experiment with Docker-based containerization techniques along with a Kubernetes container orchestration platform emphasizes an efficient way to manage and monitor the status and events in IoT applications in the scale of smart cities.**

Keywords- Smart city; Internet of Things (IoT); Cloud computing; Docker; Kubernetes; Interplanetary File System (IPFS)

I. INTRODUCTION

The current trend indicates that the urban areas are expanding massively, with predictions indicating 70% of the world's population in cities by 2020 [1]. Due to the anomalous increase in the urban population the standard quality of life is deteriorating. The concept of smart cities is put forth to improve the living standard in cities which is curbed by challenges like environmental issues, air pollution, traffic congestion, etc[2]. The countermeasures needed to tackle these issues are overwhelming owing not only to the scale of the smart cities but also the heterogeneous technologies, devices and the platforms involved in the development. Technologies like cloud computing and Internet of Things (IoT) envision the large-scale development of smart cities. Various applications like smart healthcare, intelligent transportation, smart grids, smart homes, etc., deploy many connected IoT devices which are distributed over a wide geographical area and perform various activities with a massive volume of data generated over a time period. IoT along with the cloud computing technologies has made an impact on analyzing and processing the diverse data collected from various applications to be useful to the end users [3].

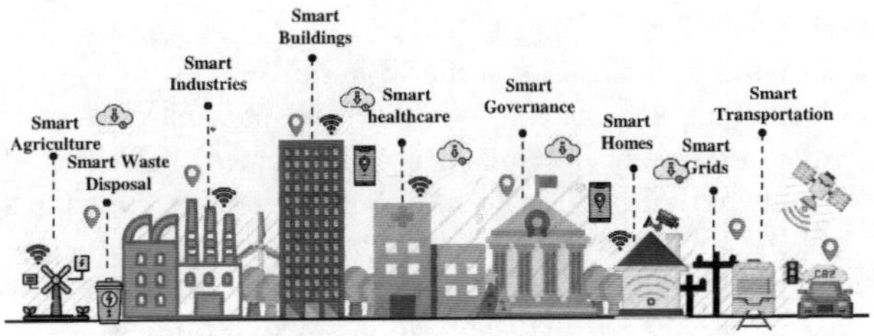

Fig. 1: A Smart City Scenario

Although IoT is the key technology to keep the smart city connected, the predictions for connected IoT devices in the future along with the traditional centralized cloud architecture might limit the horizontal development among the vertically integrated smart cities. Figure 1 shows a smart city scenario. The centralized cloud architecture is more vulnerable to increasing network loads, low latency requirements, energy issues and exposed to a single point of failure which does not suit delay-intolerant IoT applications [4][5]. To overcome these issues and to increase the efficiency of IoT applications proposals to distribute cloud architecture with edge and fog computing was introduced [6][7]. Further efforts to design frameworks based on the concept of software-defined networked systems by virtualizing IoT nodes and resources were initiated [8]. Though the distributed, hierarchical cloud architecture proved advantageous, it is challenging to implement a fully integrated approach in a hybrid smart city with its limitations.

To overcome the challenges faced by the smart city environment due to its scale and the heterogeneity of applications we need a hybrid cloud architecture managing the micro-level IoT applications. The current focus in cloud development is shifting towards containers an alternative to virtualization technique by changing the way the operations are carried out. To tackle the critical characteristics of IoT systems on its scale and data-centric nature containers make it easier to build, deploy and maintain IoT applications even when IoT devices have limited resources to support operating systems.

Containers packaged with all dependencies and software for IoT applications are portable, light and secure. Though the IoT applications are deployed at ease with containers, still the scale of the smart cities hosting multiple IoT applications makes it difficult to monitor and coordinate the containers running in different applications. A platform to orchestrate all these containers along with their varying workloads, computing, networking, and storage are in demand.

In this paper, we have created a smart city scenario and analyzed the possible options to containerize IoT applications with the help of Docker containers. Further, we have used Kubernetes an open-source platform to manage their workloads, coordinate the services providing effective monitoring and management environment. To be more precise the contributions of the paper are:

- Creating a Smart city scenario in our testbed
- Deploying IoT nodes with P2P pubsub communication model based on Interplanetary File System (IPFS)
- Containerizing IoT applications using docker containers
- Orchestrating various Docker containers in Kubernetes
- Evaluating the use of Docker containers and the Kubernetes service for IoT applications in smart cities

The remainder of this paper is structured as follows. Section II discusses the requirements of a smart city and existing related work. The enabling technologies for smart cities is illustrated in Section III. We explain the prototype implementation of our experimental framework in Section IV and results in Section V. Section VI annotates the conclusion.

II. Requirements in a Smart City & Related Work

In this section, we will describe the main requirements and challenges of an IoT-Cloud based smart city framework and the existing related works to address these issues.

A. Requirements in a Smart City

The convergence of the ubiquitous IoT technologies and the cloud resources to process, store and network data generated from IoT devices has led to the concept of a smart city. Several challenges and requirements arise from developing a smart city which include interoperability, providing efficient data management mechanisms and seamless integration of the infrastructure [9]. The essential features to develop IoT-Cloud based smart city include:

- *Reliability:* IoT devices present a range of sleep patterns and uncertainties in network connectivity can make sensitive data unavailable when needed. It is a foremost concern in safety-critical applications like healthcare.
- *Scalability:* Billions of connected devices are forecast, making it challenging to scale while ensuring its reliable data delivery.
- *Latency:* Managing latency values for delay-intolerant applications like healthcare, smart grids, demanding P2P scalability, avoiding the single point of failure by moving away from the centralized cloud-based framework.
- *Flexibility:* Providing flexibility by containerization making the IoT nodes available and inter-operate horizontally.
- *Monitoring:* Efficient monitoring is required to coordinate the IoT devices deployed in a distributed platform like smart cities.
- *Security:* Strong security measures are required to handle the data transactions among various applications.

The aforementioned challenges and requirements need to be addressed to facilitate an integrated smart city environment. The current shift in focus from virtualization to containerization can overlook and satisfy the challenges and the requirements in a smart city.

B. Related Work

The rapid development in the concept of smart cities is demanding an upgrade in a wide array of domains like IoT and cloud computing. The traditional centralized cloud-based architectures used by the IoT applications can cope with their varying storage and computing resource requirements. Existing works initially discussed the possibilities of virtualizing IoT resources with the help of Software Defined Networks (SDN) and development of an integrated IoT framework [10][11]. The solutions from virtualizing though looked promising limited the flexibility in deploying various IoT systems due to its heterogeneous nature with varying resource requirements in near real-time. To bridge this gap lightweight virtualization using containers is getting adopted. The last few years existing works have explored possibilities to use Docker containers in an IoT framework [12][13]. Container-based solutions are inherently optimized for running applications on IoT devices which have limited resources, and they are portable and lightweight, unlike virtual machines [14]. Other existing works on containerization focus their work on using containers for specific use cases even for smart cities, but there is no specific work exploring the need to orchestrate all these containers to maximize the benefits [15]-[17].

The existent works on smart cities based on IoT and cloud adopts containerization in some IoT use cases, but limited work related to the usage of containers for multiple use cases exists. Moreover, some of the issues in deploying and maintaining containers across various applications need a

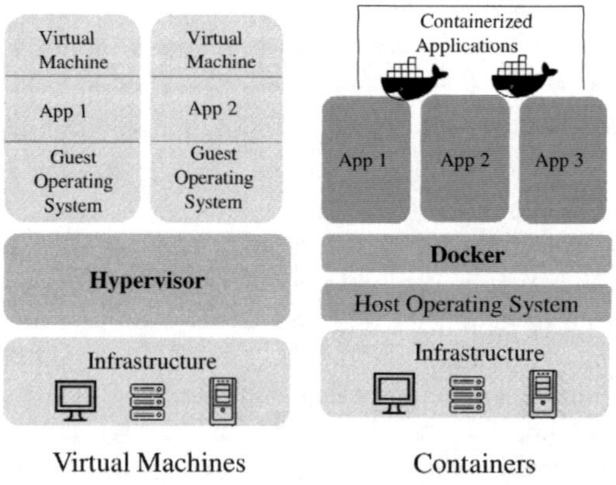

Fig. 2: Virtual Machines and Docker Container Model

monitoring platform like Kubernetes. In this paper, we have exploited the benefits of containerized IoT applications along with a monitoring platform based on Kubernetes to effectively maintain a smart city scale deployment.

III. Enabling Technologies

The paradigm focus shift from traditional virtualization to container-based virtualization solutions have gained great momentum in recent years because containers utilize kernel features to create an isolated environment of the running process. Further, they use the hardware of the host system and does not use the virtualized hardware like a hypervisor. The usage of host hardware makes the containers lightweight and able to start in milliseconds allowing it to perform well in large scale environments like in smart cities [18]. A comparison between hypervisor and docker is illustrated in Figure 2. The following explanations clearly state the reasons to choose docker to create our IoT based containers in this paper.

A. Docker

Docker is an open source project offering standardized solutions to enable the ease in implementing Linux applications inside portable containers [19]. There are a variety of system-level container services like OpenVZ and LXC available, but we chose docker since it is application oriented and it can work well with the micro-services environment like IoT [20]. Docker containers are built from base images, and they are the building blocks of docker. The images act as a template to create the containers and can be configured with the applications. Docker hub shares every change in the image with a team like a layer in git. Commands in Docker containers can be executed manually or automatically using Dockerfiles holding a series of instructions. Docker containers can be linked to each other to form a tiered application, and they can be started, stopped and terminated. There is a docker daemon that interacts with the containers through CLI or Representational State Transfer (REST) API'S. The lightweight virtualization technique is mainly used because of its features like rapid application deployment, portability, versioning of images in docker along with minimal overhead and ease in maintenance helps in building Platform as a Service(PaaS). Figure 2 shows a model of Docker container.

B. Container Orchestration

Containerization in docker expedites the feasibility to run applications that are containerized over multiple hosts in multiple clouds [21]. Cluster architecture in containers enables the need to operate multiple containers in different hosts and clouds which is inevitable in smart cities [22]. Different hosts holding same docker containers can be clustered and controlled. Further, typical applications residing in clusters are logically created from the same base images, making easier replication among various hosts. This feature of scaling the nodes can enable the vision in the scale of a smart city. The cluster-based containerization in docker creates a need to bridge the gap between the clusters and cluster management.

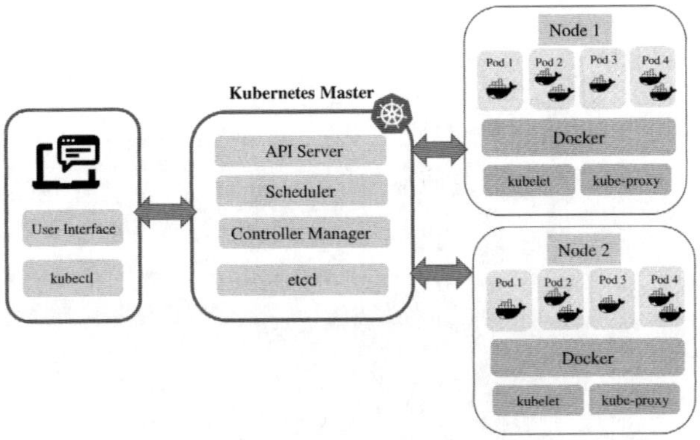

Fig. 3: Kubernetes Architecture

A cluster orchestration platform should be able to monitor the scaling, load balancing and the other services of containers residing across different hosts. It should support the scalable discovery and orchestration of the containers and provide communication in the clusters. Among various available orchestration platforms in this paper, we have used Kubernetes for monitoring and managing IoT applications.

C. Kubernetes

Kubernetes is a multihost container management platform, which uses a master to manage Docker containers over multiple hosts [23]. A sample of the Kubernetes architecture is shown in Figure 3. As mentioned before we need an orchestration platform for the clusters and Kubernetes can dynamically monitor the applications running in containers and can perform the resources provisioning along with auto-scaling support with its built-in features [24]. We have exploited this feature of Kubernetes to invigilate the nodes residing in various IoT application containers in a smart city based scenario. Kubernetes creates pods the basic deployment units, which holds one or more grouped containers. The Kubernetes master can assign each pod a virtual IP. A node agent called Kubelet monitors the pod, and it reports the pod status, its resource

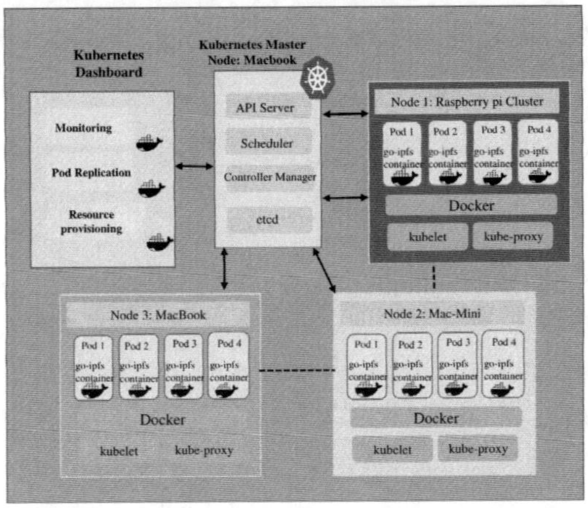

Fig. 4: Proposed Experimental Framework

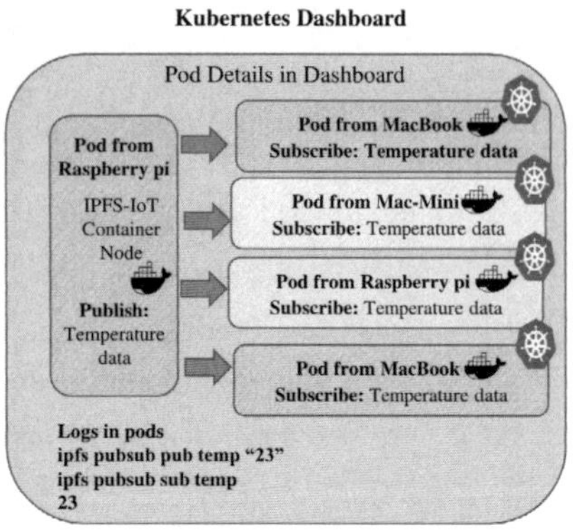

Fig. 5: A Model IoT application enabled among the pods

utilization, and events to the master. The Kubernetes master controls a scheduler, storage component, an API manager and the controller manager. Kubernetes provisions namespaces separately to enable each application to be partitioned and prevent them from affecting each other. In this paper, we have used the Kubernetes platform to monitor docker containers in the smart city scenario.

IV. Proposed Experimental Framework

- *Cluster Setup:* To replicate the smart city scenario hosting various applications, we deployed a similar prototype and evaluated the scenario experimentally. The setup consisted of a set of three different machines of different capacities hosting the docker images to imitate the different specifications of IoT nodes. The whole experimental setup is shown in Figure 4. We have used a set of five Raspberry Pi 3 nodes with Quad Core 1.2 GHz Broadcom BCM 2837, 64 bit CPU and 1 GB RAM, Mac Mini with processor i5 – 2410M, RAM 2GB 1333MHz, CPU 2.3 GHz and Mac book with processor i5 RAM 8GB for the experiments. To begin with, we have installed the docker base images of go-ipfs in all the three different sets of devices [25]. IPFS is a well-known P2P file system with inherent capabilities like clustering, pubsub model and distributed storage. We have used ipfs images so that it can emulate our IoT nodes enabled with the IPFS development Stack. So each device holds a set of containers holding go-ipfs based images packaged in it. We have mainly used the pubsub protocol in IPFS for data exchange among the IPFS-IoT nodes.
- *Cluster Orchestration:* After creating the docker images now to orchestrate these containers created we have installed Kubernetes 1.13 in all the machines and enabled a master node in the Macbook. The master node is the principal node controlling the rest of the machines which ran as container execution nodes. The IPFS daemon was initiated after enabling the IPFS based containers as pods in Kubernetes. The IPFS Daemon was initiated with the pubsub mode to enable communication among the different containers. Each container is perceived to perform a different IoT application like monitoring temperature, humidity, air quality, and many more. Each container hosting different IoT applications might need the data from another container running diverse applications in smart city scenario needing interoperability. The data exchange is enabled with the pubsub model with subscribers receiving data from publishers for a particular subscribed topic.
- *Monitoring:* To enable monitoring of the IoT applications clustered under one platform in Kubernetes we have used Heapster v.0.19.1. Heapster enables a web GUI-based Kubernetes Dashboard in the master node which helps in monitoring the system resource metrics. It can collect the resource utilization information of each node, and the gathered information can be viewed in the Kubernetes dashboard. Heapster queries the master for a list of nodes in the system using Kubernetes API, and it is possible to determine whether the node is still active or down due to some issues. Furthermore, we can visualize the information concerning the nodes, pods and the services

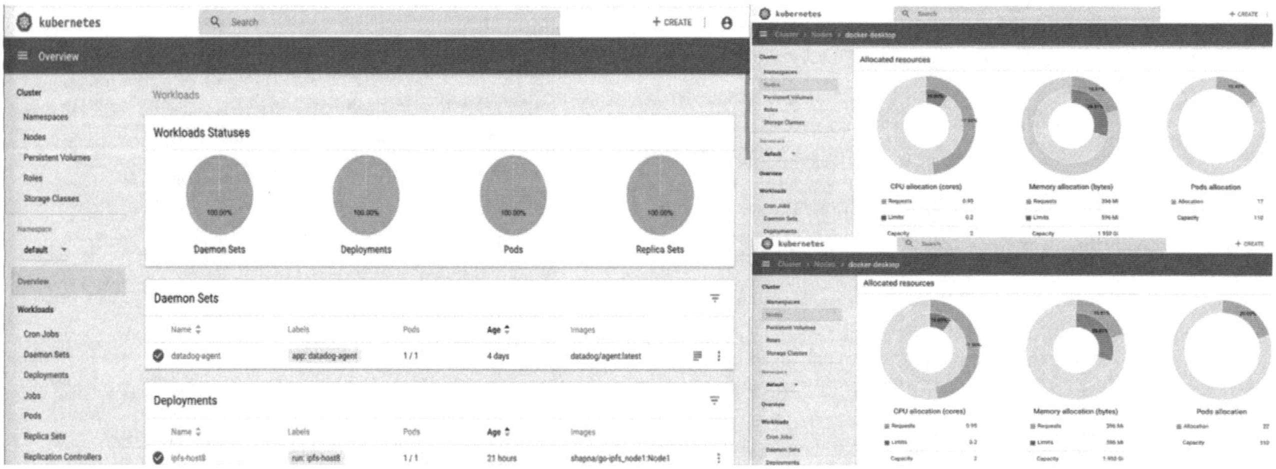

Fig. 6: Monitoring Pods in Kubernetes dashboard

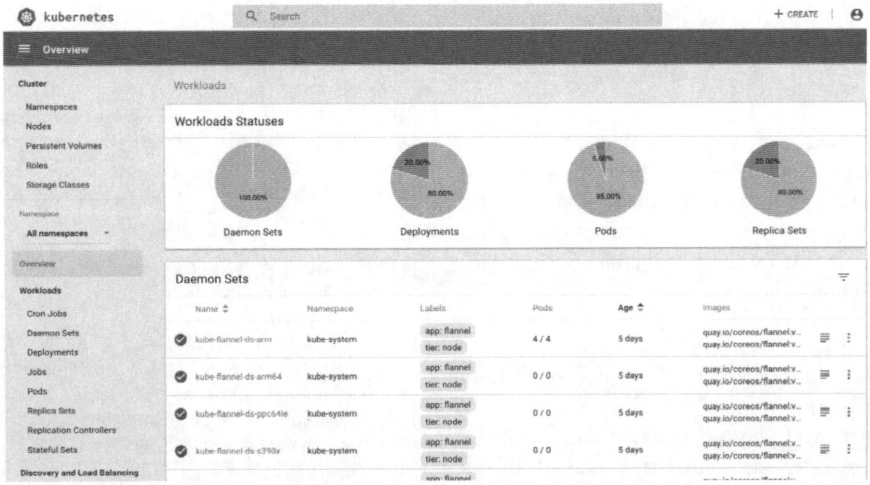

Fig. 7: Event log and Affected Pod Detection

and the data related to the deployments from the dashboard. In this paper, we have tried to establish the smart city scenario with diverse IoT applications and evaluate the docker containerized solutions along with Kubernetes orchestration platform for practical monitoring purposes. We have limited the number of containers in the pod to one to understand the Kubernetes healing action when the pod fails.

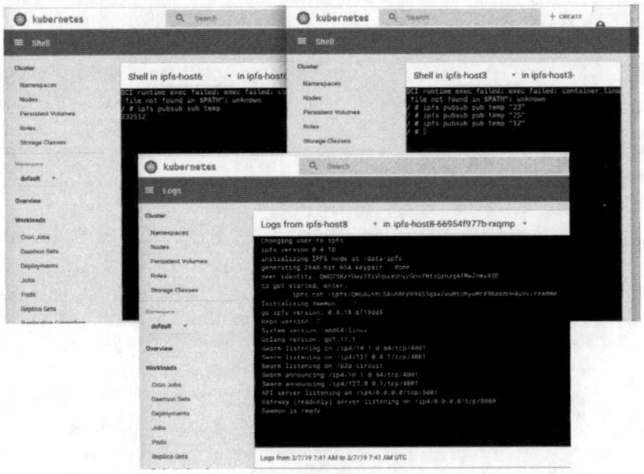

Fig. 8: Data Exchange among pods using IPFS Pubsub Mechanism

V. Evaluation of Experimental Framework

We have utilized the setup as mentioned earlier to evaluate the proposed smart city scenario. Each pod had a different schedule for publishing its data similar to an IoT application and the subscribers subscribed to a particular topic were immediately notified when there is a new update based on the IPFS pubsub model. A model setup for recording temperature data using a temperature sensor and pods subscribing for it is shown in Figure 5.

- *Monitoring:* Over this experimental setup to begin with the containers were started and the starting time was recorded in the time of milliseconds suiting IoT applications. The CPU and memory usage for the whole deployment as well as individual pod details from the time of creation is enlisted in the dashboard enabling complete details of the running pods. Then we were able to to see each log and event executed in the pods. Message logs in one dashboard logging each pubsub event happening across nodes residing in different machines made pod monitoring easier. This monitoring system hugely helps applications in large scale like IoT deployed in smart cities to locate the affected pods. The start of the entire deployment along with the pods CPU usage shown in the dashboard is illustrated in Figure 6.
- *Pod Failures:* The Kubernetes dashboard can efficiently show the pod failures by indicating the infected pods in red and the working pods in green. To try detecting this pod failure scenario, we manually terminated one of the nodes in one of the machines using the commands in Command-Line Interface (CLI). When one of the pods goes down, Kubernetes has 30 seconds to create a replication of the same pod, and this is one of the reasons we have tried to limit the number of containers in the pod to one in number to visualize the reaction of Kubernetes engine when one of the pod goes down. Figure 7 shows the self-healing capability in Kubernetes to increase the reliability and flexibility in the smart city ecosystem along with event logging.
- *Resource Scheduling:* Another important experimentation feature is the resource scheduler in Kubernetes engine. The trials are done to keep the CPU utilization of the pod within its limit. We have tried to flood many messages at a particular time from a pod to mimic this scenario. When the CPU limits cross a particular threshold, then the application is considered to be in heavy load and the Kubernetes engine can autoscale its pod to increase by one. This resource scheduling can efficiently manage real-time applications like IoT, where some of the applications

are event-driven and can considerably increase the CPU and memory usage. Efficient data exchange for a temperature sensor using the IPFS pubsub model among pods is shown in Figure 8.

From the experimental results discussed above, we can see that the docker containers enabled with Kubernetes orchestration can prove to be a comprehensive monitoring mechanism and has an ease in deployment and is flexible. This experimental setup to validate smart city scenario with containerizing IoT application proved to be advantageous.

VI. Conclusion

In this paper, we provide a container-based IoT application in a smart city scenario for efficient monitoring and management. The experiment showed efficient data exchange among the pods. Moreover, the active deployment of the application is monitored using the state of the pods. The Kubernetes dashboard helps in reviewing the system resource usage as well as the event logging in the pods which can satisfy the scalability issues in smart cities. We have also reviewed the self-healing nature of Kubernetes platform, an essential factor to ensure the reliability of the model. For further experimentation, we are trying this scenario in real life deployment at an elderly-care facility with 320 elderly in Seoul. From this work, we expect to demonstrate combining IoT applications in containers with a cloud management platform like Kubernetes would be indispensable in IoT deployment in a smart city.

ACKNOWLEDGEMENT

This research was supported by the Korea Institute of Science and Technology (KIST) under the Institutional Program (Grant No. 2E29450), and National Research Council of Science and Technology (NST) grant by the Korea government (MSIT) (No. CMP-16 − 01-KIST).

References

[1] "United Nations, Population Division", 2017, Available: http://www.un.org/en/development/desa/population/ [Accessed: 2019-02-25]

[2] T. Nam and T. A. Pardo, "Conceptualizing smart city with dimensions of technology, people, and institutions", in *Proc. ACM dg.o'11, College Park, Maryland, USA*, pp. 282–291, Dec. 2017.

[3] C. Zhu, V. C. M. Leung, L. Shu, and E. C.-H. Ngai, "Green Internet of Things for smart world," *IEEE Access*, vol. 3, pp. 2151–2162, 2015.

[4] S. Sarkar, S. Chatterjee, and S. Misra, "Assessment of the suitability of fog computing in the context of Internet of Things", *IEEE Trans. Cloud Computing*, 46-59, 2018.

[5] D. Bouley, "Estimating a data center's electrical carbon footprint," *Schneider Elec., USA, White Paper* 66, 2015.

[6] F. Bonomi, R. Milito, J. Zhu, and S. Addepalli, "Fog computing and its role in the Internet of Things," in *Proc. 1st Ed. MCC Workshop Mobile Cloud Computing, New York, NY, USA*, pp. 13–16, 2012.

[7] H. Chang, A. Hari, S. Mukherjee, and T. Lakshman, "Bringing the cloud to the edge," in Proc. IEEE Conf. Comput. Commun. Workshops (INFOCOM WKSHPS), pp. 346–351, May 2014.

[8] S. Nastic, S. Sehic, D. H. Le, H. L. Truong, and S. Dustdar, "Provisioning software-defined IoT cloud systems," in *Proc. Int. Conf. Future Internet Things Cloud (FiCloud)*, pp. 288–295, Aug. 2014.

[9] M.Vögler, J.M. Schleicher, C. Inzinger, S. Dustdar, and R. Ranjan, "Migrating smart city applications to the cloud", *IEEE Cloud Computing*, 3(2), pp.72-79, 2016.

[10] C. Buratti et al., "Testing protocols for the Internet of Things on the EuWIn platform," *IEEE Internet Things J.*, vol. 3, no. 1, pp. 124–133, Feb. 2016.

[11] T. Taleb, A. Ksentini, and R. Jantti, "'Anything as a service' for 5G mobile systems," *IEEE Netw.*, vol. 30, no. 6, pp. 84–91, Dec. 2016.

[12] T. Renner, M. Meldau, and A. Kliem, "Towards container-based resource management for the Internet of Things," in *Proc. Int. Conference Software Networking (ICSN)*, pp. 1–5, 2016.

[13] R. Morabito, "A performance evaluation of container technologies on Internet of Things devices," in *Proc. IEEE INFOCOM Demo San Francisco, CA, USA*, pp. 999–1000, 2016.

[14] C. Pahl and B. Lee, "Containers and clusters for edge cloud architectures–a technology review," in *Future Internet of Things and Cloud (FiCloud), 2015 3rd International Conference on. IEEE*, pp. 379–386, 2015.

[15] J. Rufino, M. Alam, J. Ferreira, A. Rehman, and K. F. Tsang, "Orchestration of containerized microservices for IIoT using Docker," in *Industrial Technology (ICIT), 2017 IEEE International Conference on IEEE*, pp. 1532–1536, 2017.

[16] R.G. Chesov, V. N. Solovyev, M. A. Khlamov, and A. V. Prokofyev, "Containerized cloud based technology for smart cities applications," *Journal of Fundamental and Applied Sciences*, vol. 8, no. 3S, pp. 2638–2646, 2016.

[17] M. Kovatsch, M. Lanter, and S. Duquennoy, "Actinium: A RESTful runtime container for scriptable Internet of Things applications," in *Internet of Things (IOT), 3rd Intl. Conf. on the IEEE*, pp. 135–142, 2012.

[18] M.Eder, "Hypervisor-vs. container-based virtualization." *Future Internet (FI) and Innovative Internet Technologies and Mobile Communications (IITM)*, 2016.

[19] "Docker", https://www.docker.com/ [Accessed: 2019-02-20]

[20] A. Sill, "The design and architecture of microservices," *IEEE Cloud Comput.*, vol. 3, no. 5, pp. 76–80, Sep 2016.

[21] B. Satzger, W. Hummer, C. Inzinger, P. Leitner, & S. Dustdar, "Winds of Change: From Vendor Lock-In to the Meta Cloud," *IEEE Internet Computing*, vol. 17, no. 1, pp. 69–73, 2013.

[22] V. Koukis, C. Venetsanopoulos, and N. Koziris, okeanos: "Building a Cloud, Cluster by Cluster," *IEEE Internet Computing*, vol. 17, no. 3, pp. 67–71, 2013.

[23] "Kubernetes", https://kubernetes.io/ [Accessed: 2019-02-01]

[24] C. C. Chang, S. R. Yang, E. H. Yeh, P. Lin, and J. Y. Jeng. "A kubernetes-based monitoring platform for dynamic cloud resource provisioning", *IEEE Global Communications Conference, pp. 1-6. IEEE*, 2017.

[25] "Docker-IPFS", https://hub.docker.com/r/ipfs/go-ipfs/ [Accessed: 2019-02-10]

The Weaponization of Cloud-based Social Media:

Prospects for Legislation and Regulation

Barry Cartwright
School of Criminology
Simon Fraser University
Burnaby, Canada
Email: bcartwri@sfu.ca

George R S Weir
Department of Computer & Information Sciences
University of Strathclyde
Glasgow, Scotland, UK
Email: george.weir@strath.ac.uk

Lutfun Nahar
Department of Gender, Sexuality, and Women's Studies
Simon Fraser University
Burnaby, Canada
Email: lutfun_nahar@sfu.ca

Karmvir Padda
Richard Frank
School of Criminology
Simon Fraser University
Burnaby, Canada
Email: {karmvir_padda; rfrank}@sfu.ca

***Abstract*—The 2016 U.S. Presidential election and the 2016 U.K. Brexit referendum are notable for the contemporaneous efforts by Russian-based trolls to manipulate public opinion through Cloud-based social media. Such disinformation warfare raises serious concerns about the risk of negatively influencing democratic processes, as well as the need for viable defensive measures. Responses are required in terms of technical means to detect and counter such "fake news," as well as legal proscriptions that can serve to control such threatening activities. The present paper addresses this disinformation warfare scenario, describes our current research and technical work in this area, and reviews legal precedents that shed light on the complexities and pitfalls that legislators and regulators encounter when seeking to remediate the threat.**

Keywords-Cloud-based social media; disinformation warfare; "fake news"; legislation.

I. INTRODUCTION

Legislators and government regulatory agencies worldwide face a serious challenge when it comes to the regulation of emerging online threats, such as the type of weaponization of Cloud-based social media that was witnessed in connection with the U.S. Presidential election [1] and the U.K. Brexit referendum [2], [3]. The Internet Research Agency, often referred to as the Russian troll army, deliberately distributed so-called "fake news" stories via social media accounts that had been set up for that express purpose. In the U.S., for example, these "fake news" stories heavily favored Donald Trump over Hillary Clinton in the U.S. Presidential election [2], [4], [5]. According to Special Counsel Robert S. Mueller III's recently released report into Russian interference in the U.S. Presidential election [5], these Facebook and Twitter accounts targeted certain groups, such as Blacks (through the Blacktivist Facebook page), Southern Whites (through the Patriototus Facebook page), and the right-wing anti-immigration movement (through the Secured Borders Facebook page), as well as through Twitter feeds such as @TEN_GOP (which claimed to have a connection to the Republican Party of Tennessee), and @America_1st (an anti-immigration account). In the U.K., the "fake news"—which largely stoked Islamaphobic and anti-immigration passions—made extensive use of Twitter, employing Twitter handles such as ReasonsToLeaveEU, or #voteleave [3], [6], [7].

Social network platforms themselves are coming under increasing pressure from legislators and government regulatory agencies to create and put into action their own in-house policies, practices and procedures for dealing with this issue. To illustrate, Mark Zuckerberg, the CEO of Facebook, was grilled by the U.S. Congress in April 2018 regarding the (witting or unwitting) involvement of Facebook and Instagram in the Russian hostile influence campaign during the run-up to the 2016 U.S. Presidential election [8], [9]. At almost the same time, Mike Schroepfer, the chief technology officer of Facebook, faced a similar hearing in front of a Parliamentary Committee in the U.K. regarding fake accounts, political advertising, and the role of Cambridge Analytica in voter-targeting [10]. In Canada, Robert Sherman, who was the deputy privacy officer for Facebook, and Kevin Chan, who was in charge of Facebook's public policy for Canada, were questioned about the role that Facebook and Cambridge Analytica played in both the U.S. election and the Brexit referendum, and about possible violations of Canadian privacy law [11], [12]. On all three occasions, it was indicated that failure on the part of Facebook and its executives to regulate themselves could result in future government action.

While the term "fake news" is commonly used to describe the content of these Russian-sponsored disinformation campaigns, our textual analysis of 2,500 Facebook items posted by the Internet Research Agency—from January 2015 through December 2017, i.e., during the period leading up to, during, and following the U.S.

Presidential election—indicates that an appreciable number of these stories was actually grounded to one extent or the other in "real news" events that had been reported by mainstream media sources [3]. Presumably, these "real news" stories were selected by the Internet Research Agency so as to enflame passions (or to intimidate or otherwise suppress voter turnout) amongst the targeted groups, and that they were deliberately distributed and re-distributed through automated amplification, with the intention of maximizing the potential audience [2], [13]. Nevertheless, the question remains: "how can Western-style democracies enact legislation against and effectively regulate the expression of personal opinion, or for that matter, the dissemination of what in many cases amounts to something approximating 'real news'"?

In Section II, we proceed by outlining the nature of the "fake news" problem. Section III addresses the problem of identification for "fake news". The challenges facing legislation and regulation are considered in Section IV, while we draw preliminary conclusions in Section V.

II. FRAMING THE PROBLEM

Much has been said in recent years about "fake news" and the "post-truth" era [14]. Indeed, some have erroneously attributed the term "fake news" to U.S. President Donald Trump, who is wont to label anything that runs contrary to his own narrative (especially when it comes from traditional news sources such as *CNN* or *The Washington Post*) as "fake news" [15]. However, propaganda—in the form of fake news and other types of disinformation—has been around for millennia, and has been employed with varying degrees of success by political leaders, military leaders and insurgents throughout history [16], [17]. Indeed, it has been argued that contemporary journalistic norms of balance and objectivity are the end product of a backlash against unabashed use of journalistic propaganda during both World Wars, and the manner in which such propaganda has been put to further use by large corporations [18].

Estimates vary, but it has been stated that 44 percent of the U.S. population gets its news from Facebook, whilst 12 percent gets its news from Twitter [19]. In the U.K., 27 percent of the population gets its news from Facebook, and 14 percent from Twitter [20]. In view of the relatively high percentage of individuals who apparently rely on Cloud-based social media for their news, there is reason for concern with respect to the potential for manipulation of sentiment in this environment. In particular, evidence clearly indicates that the Russians made maximum use of social media bots in their 2016 assaults on the U.S. Presidential election and the U.K. Brexit referendum [1], [2], [21], thereby amplifying the content in order to influence a much wider audience.

In 2017, the Central Intelligence Agency, the Federal Bureau of Investigation and the National Security Agency combined forces to produce an intelligence community assessment of Russian efforts to influence the U.S. Presidential election, concluding that Russia deliberately set out to denigrate and discredit Hillary Clinton whilst promoting the candidacy of Donald Trump, pointing a finger directly at Russia's Internet Research Agency (the Russian troll army), and their use—amongst other attack vehicles—of social media [22]. In February 2018, U.S. Special Counsel Robert Mueller, who was appointed to investigate Russian interference in the U.S. election, obtained a grand jury indictment against Russia's Internet Research Agency (which was bankrolled by Yevgeniy Prigozhin, often referred to as "Putin's chef"), Concord Management and Consulting LLC and Concord Catering (both operated by Yevgeniy Prigozhin), Yevgeniy Prigozhin himself, plus a dozen Russian "trolls" who were employed by the Internet Research Agency. The indictment stated that the accused had "operated social media pages and groups designed to attract U.S. audiences," with the accused falsely claiming that those pages and groups were controlled by American activists, and had used social media platforms such as Facebook, Twitter, YouTube and Instagram to advance divisive issues and create dissension [23].

Similar allegations about Russian interference in the Brexit referendum have surfaced, with as many as 150,000 Twitter bots alleged to have been linked back to Russia [24]. British Prime Minister Theresa May has directly accused Russia of planting fake news stories and seeking to sow discord in Western nations [25]. However, the U.K. government does not appear to have pursued this matter as vigorously as the U.S. government, perhaps because they have been more preoccupied with sorting out the actual ramifications of Brexit.

Evidently, the disinformation attacks by Russia on the U.S. Presidential election and the Brexit referendum were able to achieve results that likely would not have been attainable through more conventional military tactics, such as invading or bombing another country. The disinformation tactics employed by the Russians seemingly succeeded in fragmenting the European Union, testing the strength of the North Atlantic Treaty Organization (NATO), and installing an unabashedly pro-Russian figure in the White House, all without firing a single shot. This could be construed as an all-out assault on Western-style democracy.

III. IDENTIFYING "FAKE NEWS"

The difficulty in detecting hostile disinformation attacks on Cloud-based social media lies in the subtleties between fake news and traditional, "trusted" news. Whereas traditional news has the goal of reporting what happens, albeit sometimes with bias, the purpose of fake news is essentially to insert itself into the same discussion, but to twist the facts in such a way that it incites dissension and distrust. While occasionally relying upon and using the same facts, fake news is thought to focus on nuances that are designed to evoke strong sentiments in the reader. Therefore, the differences between fake news and traditional news may not be so much in the facts or the keywords, which are easier to detect, but rather, in the nuances and sentiment present, both of which are more difficult to detect. It has also been thought that these fake news items are crafted in such a way that they spread six times faster than the truth [26]. Thus, the assumption is that there must be a discernible difference between them.

Our ongoing research involves the analysis of 2,500 "fake news" messages posted on Facebook by Russia's Internet Research Agency between 2015 and 2017, juxtaposed with 2,500 "real news" items which were derived from 87,157 political news articles from October 2015. The data set of "fake news" posts from the Internet Research Agency was collected and assembled by two professors at Clemson University, Darren Linvill and Patrick Warren [27], and made available by data.world.

The 2,500 "fake news" posts were first read and provisionally analyzed in NVivo, a software tool for qualitative analysis. NVivo facilitates codification and visualization of data, and allows for data queries and automatic provisional coding of the entire dataset. It is anticipated that our ongoing NVivo analysis will lead to the detection of finer nuances and hidden meanings in the data set, which might otherwise not be detected through Posit analysis, or through sentiment analysis (once the matching "real news" data set has been assembled). The Posit toolkit generates frequency data and Part-of-Speech (POS) tagging, producing extensive statistics based on textual content such as social media posts. Posit has proven effective in developing machine learning classification applications [28], [29].

The research team is presently assembling an additional matching set of 2,500 "real news" items from 2015 through 2017, using a set of search terms derived from a careful reading and re-reading of the 2,500 "fake news" items in NVivo, particularly as they pertain to real news events reported in more traditional media sources during that time period. However, the lengthy process involved in assembling a matching "real news" data set did not prove itself amenable to automation. Thus, it was decided that the set of 2,500 "real news" articles from October 2015 would suffice for the purposes of preliminary investigation.

A first round of analysis in NVivo indicated that an appreciable number of the so-called 2,500 "fake news" messages posted on Facebook by Russia's Internet Research Agency were actually grounded in real news. To illustrate, the second message in the data set, posted under the Facebook name "Patriototus," referred to the removal of a statue of Confederate General Robert E. Lee in New Orleans. The removal of this statue was reported widely by traditional news sources, including such outlets as *CNN*, *The Washington Post* and the *New York Times*. The second message in the data set, posted under the Facebook name "Blacktivist," talked about 14-year-old Royce Mann and his slam poem on white privilege and police brutality. The twenty-ninth message, posted under the Facebook name "United Muslims for America," discussed Kadra Mohamed, the first hijab-wearing policewoman in Minnesota. Again, while the Facebook posts sought to target and agitate certain groups, and were selective in the information they recounted and how they presented it, these events described in Facebook were also reported in traditional, "trusted" news sources.

From the first round of NVivo analysis, a set of search terms (key words and key phrases) was generated, based upon a careful comparison of the Facebook posts to actual events that had been reported in mainstream news sources. Apart from being used to inform ongoing coding in NVivo, and to assist in the assembly of an additional matching set of 2,500 "real news" items, these search terms were matched against the "fake news" data set, to investigate the prevalence of "fake news" items that were in fact grounded in "real news." In particular, the use of uniquely identifiable, named entities, such as people, places, dates and events indicated that at least 13.5 percent of the so-called "fake news" posts were based to one degree or another on these named entities.

This does not mean that the remainder of the "fake news" posts were entirely fictional. Rather, the posts that did not match these named entities were often vague, or quite short, and contained insufficient information to determine whether they were informed by real news events. A case in point would be the message posted in the Facebook group "Secured Borders," which asked: "Why there's so many privileges and benefits for refugee kids, but American kids forced to grow up in poverty? That's absolutely unacceptable!!" This could conceivably have been informed by real news events, but it would be a stretch of the imagination to arrive at that conclusion. Nevertheless, it is important to recognize that the term "fake news" is likely a misnomer, which in turn has implications when it comes to the legalities surrounding the suppression of such social media activities.

To secure a source of "real news" data for our comparison with the Facebook "fake news", we obtained a large set of news posts from webhose.io. This set of 87,157 political "real news" articles, all from October 2015, was derived from a wide variety of Web-based news posts. Sources represented include the *WorldNews (WN) Network*, *Independent Television*, *Philadelphia Daily News*, the *Buffalo News*, the *Press of Atlantic City*, *The Wall Street Journal*, *The Washington Times*, *WCAX News*, Vermont, *KFMB-TV*, *Seattle PI*, *The Boston Herald*, *The Chicago Sun Times*, *The New York Times*, *Fox News* and the *BBC*. Following a process of random selection from the full data source, this "real news" set was reduced to 2,500 data items, found to be derived from a total of 172 news sources.

In order to reduce the original "real news" data to the required 2,500 items, several steps were taken: 1) all news items with duplicate content in the text were removed; 2) the maximum character length of the Facebook "fake news" posts was determined to be 2,006 characters, so all "real news" items with a number of characters greater than 2,006 were removed; 3) the average character length of the Facebook "fake news" posts was found to be 280 characters, whilst the initial average character length for the "real news" data was found to be 1,778 characters; thus, some "real news" items with character lengths greater than 1,000, were expunged from the data set in order to bring the average character length closer to that of the "fake news" posts; and 4) the remaining "real news" data were randomized and a sample of 2,500 items was extracted as the final "real news" set, to serve as a comparator for the 2,500 Facebook "fake news" items. The average character size for the 2,500 "real news" items was 376. A visual inspection of character lengths across the two sets of 2,500 items suggested a similar shaped distribution curve.

Initial comparisons of the "fake news" and "real news" items were conducted using a Posit analysis of their message content. On the basis of a character content analysis, a set of features, including the manual classification of positive or negative for "fake news" was generated for each of the 5,000 data items. Using WEKA [30], and the Random Forest tree-based classifier [31], we achieved a surprisingly high 99.8 percent classification success. While these results are preliminary, and may change when the "fake news" data set is juxtaposed with the second "real news" data set that we are presently assembling, this suggests that we may be able to develop an artificial intelligence tool that can harvest relevant information from social media sources, thereby providing government regulatory agencies with scope for the regulation of the weaponization of Cloud-based social media that was witnessed in connection with the U.S. Presidential election and the Brexit referendum.

IV. PROSPECTS FOR LEGISLATION AND REGULATION

While there have been discussions about the potential for government regulation of the dissemination of "fake news" through social media, the issue is far too "new" to have produced any legislation. Therefore, for enlightenment, we must turn to previous efforts to legislate and regulate analogous activities.

The United Nations' *Universal Declaration on Human Rights* states that "everyone has the right to freedom of opinion and expression," including the right to "impart information and ideas through any media...regardless of frontiers" [32]. That said, legal positions regarding "acceptable speech" vary widely from country-to-country, and from continent-to-continent [33]. A number of European countries, such as the U.K. and Germany, have enacted (and enforced) laws that are consistent with the European Council's 2008 Framework Decision on *Combating Certain Forms and Expressions of Racism and Xenophobia by Means of Criminal Law*, which prohibits expressions that promote hatred or deny crimes of genocide [33], [34], [35]. On the other hand, some European nations, such as Italy, Lithuania and France have grappled with the definition of "hate crime," and have been more lax when it comes to legal enforcement [36].

Unlike the U.S. and Canada, the U.K. does not have a written *Constitution* or *Charter of Rights and Freedoms* [36]. However, the U.K. attempts to comply with E.U. laws that forbid expressions of racism and xenophobia. A recent example would be the 2018 case of *PF v Mark Meechan*, wherein a Sheriff's Court in Airdrie, Scotland, fined Meechan £800 for posting a "grossly offensive or threatening" video online, to wit, a video that repeated the phrase "Gas the Jews," and depicted a dog that had been trained to raise its paw in a Nazi salute [37]. Interestingly, the *Meechan* case generated considerable controversy, with an article in *The Guardian* opining that "giving offence is inevitable and often necessary in a plural society," and that the judge made an error in conflating offensive material with fomenting hatred [38], and another article in the *American Spectator*, declaring that "free speech is dead in Britain" [39]. As well, a high court decision in the 2011 case of *Abdul v DPP* upheld a lower court conviction of five men who shouted slogans such as "burn in hell," "baby killer" and "cowards" at a parade of British soldiers, determining that the right to "freedom of expression" under Article 10 of the European Convention on Human Rights did not apply, as the prosecution was "necessary and proportionate" [40].

Although the First Amendment of the U.S. *Constitution* does not protect speech that involves threats, targeted harassment, and imminent danger through incitement of violence, it does protect freedom of speech, no matter how offensive, distasteful or bigoted that speech might be. In fact, under U.S. law, there is no legal definition of unpatriotic speech [41]. Moreover, Section 230 of the 1996 U.S. *Communications Decency Act* offers significant protections to social media platforms, stating that "no provider or user of an interactive computer service shall be treated as the publisher or speaker of any information provided by another information content provider" [42], meaning that platforms such as Facebook, Twitter, YouTube and Instagram cannot be held liable for user-generated content. In other words, it could prove difficult for the U.S. to criminalize the type of activity conducted by the Russian Internet Research Agency, without some major amendments to long-standing American legislation, and dramatic changes to legal precedent.

In Canada, the *Charter of Rights and Freedoms* states that individuals have the right to "freedom of thought, belief, opinion and expression, including freedom of the press and other media of communication" [43]. While actions such as defamatory libel and hate propaganda are prohibited by the *Canadian Criminal Code* [34], [44], the courts have gone to considerable lengths to protect freedom of expression. For example, in *Crouch v. Snell* [45] a case involving adult cyberbullying and the Province of Nova Scotia's *Cyber-safety Act* [46], the judge confirmed that the right to freedom of expression "extends to any number of unpopular or distasteful expressions, including some forms of defamatory libel, hate propaganda and false news" [47]. *R. v. Elliott* [48], heard in 2016, was a criminal harassment case in which the accused repeatedly communicated with (and allegedly harassed) two feminist activists via Twitter, both at hashtags which they had created, and at hashtags with which they were affiliated. The judge opined that Twitter was like a "public square," observing that creating a hashtag where people could follow you was similar to "announcing a public meeting," further stressing that the fact that some opinions may be "morally offensive" to some people is *not* criminal.

Evidently, contentious issues involving freedom of expression and freedom of opinion can be expected to limit any effort to regulate the publication of "fake news" on social media. To be effective, regulatory agencies may need to target the creation of fraudulent Facebook pages and Twitter feeds, and in addition, the use of social bots that amplify messages in order to create the false impression that the messages have more followers and interactions than they do in reality.

V. CONCLUSION

With democracy under threat from the intentional (and perhaps criminal) manipulation of Cloud-based social media, and the resultant digital wildfires [49], legislators, regulators and service providers are eagerly seeking solutions and defenses against disinformation warfare. We have described the brazen attempts by the Russian Internet Research Agency to manipulate public opinion in the U.S. and U.K., wherein the use of so-called "fake news" sought to influence democratic processes across international boundaries. Looking ahead to technological responses, we anticipate developing tools that will permit agencies to filter and identify suspicious social network content. While subject to further research and verification, our reported 99.8 percent accuracy in classifying "fake news" demonstrates the feasibility of this objective. Yet, in turn, such developments may infringe upon the privacy and personal rights of the individual. Free speech and data privacy need to be balanced against the requirements for management and control of disinformation threats, but such balance is not easily achieved. Indeed, there is a fine line between the monitoring of social media and the potential abrogation of the right to privacy, to the extent that such privacy rights are believed to exist in the public domain. This conflict is evident from the legislative efforts that we have considered from the U.K, Europe, the U.S. and Canada. In each jurisdiction, there is a marked tension between these conflicting rights under the law. The clear conclusion is that responses from legislators and regulators to the type of weaponization of Cloud-based social media witnessed during the U.S. Presidential election and the Brexit referendum will impact widely upon the liberty of individuals, and give rise to much contentious litigation in the years to come.

ACKNOWLEDGMENT

This research project would not have been possible without funding from the Cyber Security Cooperation Program, operated by the National Cyber Security Directorate of Public Safety Canada. We would also like to thank our research assistants, Soobin Rim and Aynsley Pescitelli for their assistance with the data.

REFERENCES

[1] W. L. Bennett and S. Livingston, "The disinformation order: Disruptive communication and the decline of democratic institutions," *European Journal of Communication*, 33(2), pp. 122-139, 2018.

[2] A. Badawy, E. Ferrara and Lerman, K., "Analyzing the Digital Traces of Political Manipulation: The 2016 Russian Interference Twitter Campaign, *arXiv* preprint arXiv:1802.04291, 2018.

[3] M. T. Bastos and D. Mercea, "The Brexit botnet and user-generated hyperpartisan news," *Social Science Computer Review*, 0894439317734157, 2017.

[4] H. Allcott and M. Gentzkow, "Social Media and Fake News in the 2016 Election," *Journal of Economic Perspectives*, 31(2), pp. 211-236, 2017.

[5] R. S. Mueller III, "Report on the Investigation into Russian Interference in the 2016 Presidential Election, pp. 1-448, 2019. URL: www.justsecurity.org/wp-content/uploads/2019/04/Muelller-Report-Redacted-Vol-II-Released-04.18.2019-Word-Searchable.-Reduced-Size.pdf [Last Accessed: 2019.04.22]

[6] M. Field and M. Wright, "Russian trolls sent thousands of pro-Leave messages on day of Brexit referendum, Twitter data reveals: Thousands of Twitter posts attempted to influence the referendum and US elections," *The Telegraph*, 2018. URL: www.telegraph.co.uk/technology/2018/10/17/russian-iranian-twitter-trolls-sent-10-million-tweets-fake-news/ [Last accessed: 2019.04.8]

[7] G. Evolvi, "Hate in a Tweet: Exploring Internet-Based Islamophobic Discourses," *Religions*, *9*(10), pp. 37-51, 2018.

[8] T. Romm, "Facebook's Zuckerberg just survived 10 hours of questioning by Congress," *Washington Post*. URL: www.washingtonpost.com/news/the-switch/wp/2018/04/11/zuckerberg-facebook-hearing-congress-house-testimony/?utm_term=.f06997434776, April 11, 2018. [Last accessed: 2019.04.8]

[9] Politico Staff, "Full text: Mark Zuckerberg's Wednesday testimony to Congress on Cambridge Analytica," April 9, 2018. URL: https://www.politico.com/story/2018/04/09/transcript-mark-zuckerberg-testimony-to-congress-on-cambridge-analytica-509978 [Last accessed: 2019.04.8]

[10] A. Satariano, "Facebook Faces Tough Questions in Britain That It Avoided in the U.S.," 2018. URL: www.nytimes.com/2018/04/26/business/facebook-british-parliament.html [Last accessed: 2019.04.8]

[11] J. P. Tasker, "'We are sorry': Facebook execs grilled by Canadian MPs over Cambridge Analytica scandal: For 2 years, Facebook knew personal info of thousands of Canadians may have been in hands of a third party," *CBC News*, April 2018. URL: www.cbc.ca/news/politics/facebook-execs-house-of-commons-sorry-1.4626206 [Last accessed: 2019.04.8]

[12] D. Ebner and C. Freeze, "AggregateIQ, Canadian data firm at centre of global controversy, was hired by clients big and small," *Globe and Mail*, April, 2018. URL: www.theglobeandmail.com/canada/article-aggregateiq-canadian-data-firm-at-centre-of-global-controvery-was [Last accessed: 2019.04.8]

[13] C. Shao, P. M. Hui, L. Wang, X. Jiang, A. Flammini, F. Menczerand and G. L. Ciampaglia, "Anatomy of an online misinformation network," PloS one, 13(4), e0196087, 2018.

[14] H. Berghel, "Lies, damn lies, and fake news," *Computer*, 50(2), pp. 80-85, 2017.

[15] J. E. Kirtley, "Getting to the Truth: Fake News, Libel Laws, and 'Enemies of the American People,'" 2018. URL: www.americanbar.org/groups/crsj/publications/human_rights_magazine_home/the-ongoing-challenge-to-define-free-speech/getting-to-the-truth/ [Last accessed: 2019.04.8]

[16] N. W. Jankowski, "Researching fake news: A selective examination of empirical studies," Javnost-The Public, 25(1-2), pp. 248-255, 2018.

[17] E. C. Tandoc Jr, Z. W. Lim and R. Ling, "Defining 'fake news': A typology of scholarly definitions," *Digital Journalism*, 6(2), pp. 137-153, 2018.

[18] D. M. Lazer, M. A. Baum, Y. Benkler, A. J. Berinsky, K. M. Greenhill, F. Menczer and M. Schudson, "The science of fake news," *Science*, *359*(6380), pp. 1094-1096, 2018.

[19] E. Shearer and K. E. Matsa, "News Use Across Social Media Platforms 2018: Most Americans continue to get news on social media, even though many have concerns about its accuracy," Pew Research Center, 2018. URL: www.journalism.org/2018/09/10/news-use-across-social-media-platforms-2018/ [Last accessed: 2019.04.8]

[20] N. Newman, R. Fletcher, and A. Kalogeropoulos, Reuters Institute Digital News Report 2018. URL: http://media.digitalnewsreport.org/wp-content/uploads/2018/06/digital-news-report-2018.pdf?x89475 [Last accessed: 2019.04.8]

[21] C. Shao, P. M. Hui, L. Wang, X. Jiang, A. Flammini, F. Menczer and G. L. Ciampaglia, "Anatomy of an online misinformation network," *PloS one*, *13*(4), e0196087, 2018.

[22] Central Intelligence Agency, Federal Bureau of Investigation and National Security Agency, "Assessing Russian Activities and Intentions in Recent US Elections," 2017. URL: www.dni.gov/files/documents/ICA_2017_01.pdf [Last accessed: 2019.04.8]

[23] United States v. Internet Research Agency LLC, Case 1:18-cr-00032-DLF, The United States District Court for the District Of Columbia, February 26, 2018. URL: www.justice.gov/file/1035477/download [Last accessed: 2019.04.8]

[24] V. Narayanan, P. N. Howard, B. Kollanyi and M. Elswah, "Russian involvement and junk news during Brexit," (2017). URL: comprop.oii.ox.ac.uk/wp-content/uploads/sites/93/2017/12/Russia-and-B rexit-v27. pdf [Last accessed: 2019.04.8]

[25] The Economist, "Russian Twitter trolls meddled in the Brexit vote. Did they swing it?," 2017. URL: www.economist.com/britain/2017/11/23/russian-twitter-trolls-meddled-in-the-brexit-vote-did-they-swing-it [Last accessed: 2019.04.8]

[26] M. Fox, "Fake News: Lies spread faster on social media than truth does," *NBC News*, 2018. URL: www.nbcnews.com/health/health-news/fake-news-lies-spread-faster-social-media-truth-does-n854896 [Last accessed: 2019.04.8]

[27] D. L. Linvill and P. L. Warren, "Troll factories: The Internet Research Agency and state-sponsored agenda-building," Resource Centre on Media, 2018.

[28] G. Weir, R. Frank, B. Cartwright and E. Dos Santos, "Positing the problem: enhancing classification of extremist web content through textual analysis," International Conference on Cybercrime and Computer Forensics (IEEE Xplore), June 2016.

[29] G. Weir, K. Owoeye, A. Oberacker and H. Alshahrani, "Cloud-based textual analysis as a basis for document classification," *International Conference on High Performance Computing & Simulation (HPCS)*, pp. 672-676, July 2018.

[30] M. Hall, E. Frank, H. Geoffrey, B. Pfahringer, P. Reutemann and I. Witten, "The Weka data mining software: an update," *SIGKDD Explorations*, vol. 11, pp. 10-18, 2009.

[31] L. Breiman, "Random Forests," *Machine Learning*, vol. 45, pp. 5-32, 2001.

[32] UN General Assembly. *Universal declaration of human rights*. 1948. URL: http://www.un.org/en/udhrbook/pdf/udhr_booklet_en_web.pdf [Last accessed: 2019.04.8]

[33] J. Walker, *Hate Speech and Freedom of Expression: Legal Boundaries in Canada*, Library of Parliament, 2018. URL: lop.parl.ca/sites/PublicWebsite/default/en_CA/ResearchPublications/201825E [Last accessed: 2019.04.8]

[34] Council of the European Union, *Council Framework Decision 2008/913/JHA of 28 November 2008 on Combating Certain Forms and Expressions of Racism and Xenophobia by Means of Criminal Law*, 2008. URL: publications.europa.eu/en/publication-detail/-/publication/f015ed06-b071-41e1-84f1-622ad4ec1d70 [Last accessed: 2019.04.8]

[35] Article 19, *United Kingdom (England and Wales): Responding to 'hate speech,'* 2018. URL: www.article19.org/wp-content/uploads/2018/06/UK-hate-speech_March-2018.pdf [Last accessed: 2019.04.8]

[36] J. Garlandand N. Chakraborti, "Divided by a common concept? Assessing the implications of different conceptualizations of hate crime in the European Union," *European Journal of Criminology*, *9*(1), pp. 38-51, 2012.

[37] Judiciary of Scotland, *PF v Mark Meecham*, 2018. URL: http://www.scotland-judiciary.org.uk/8/1962/PF-v-Mark-Meechan [Last accessed: 2019.04.8]

[38] K. Malik, "The 'Nazi pug': giving offence is inevitable and often necessary in a plural society," *The Guardian*, March 2018. URL: www.theguardian.com/commentisfree/2018/mar/25/being-offensive-should-not-be-illegal-in-society-that-defends-free-speech [Last accessed: 2019.04.8]

[39] E. McGuire, "Free Speech is Dead in Britain," *The American Spectator*, March 2018. URL: spectator.org/free-speech-is-dead-in-britain/ [Last accessed: 2019.04.8]

[40] L. J. Gross and J. David, *Munim Abdul and Others v Director of Public Prosecutions*, EWHC 247 (Admin), 2011. URL: swarb.co.uk/abdul-and-others-v-director-of-public-prosecutions-admn-16-feb-2011/ [Last accessed: 2019.04.8]

[41] American Library Association, "Hate speech and hate crime" nd. URL: http://www.ala.org/advocacy/intfreedom/hate [Last accessed: 2019.04.8]

[42] *Communications Decency Act*, 47 U.S.C. §230, 1996. URL: http://www.columbia.edu/~mr2651/ecommerce3/2nd/statutes/CommunicationsDecencyAct.pdf [Last accessed: 2019.04.8]

[43] *Canadian Charter of Rights and Freedoms*, s8, Part 1 of the *Constitution Act*, 1982, being Schedule B to the Canada Act 1982 (UK), c 11, 1982.

[44] *Criminal Code*, RSC 1985, c C-46, s 318(1)(a), 1985.

[45] G. G. McDougall, *Crouch v. Snell*, vol. 2015 NSSC 340, 2015.

[46] Nova Scotia Government, *Cyber-Safety Act: An Act to Address and Prevent Cyberbullying*, vol. 61, 2013.

[47] B. Cartwright,"Cyberbullying and 'The Law of the Horse': A Canadian viewpoint," *Journal of Internet Law*, *20*(10), pp. 14–26, 2017.

[48] B. Knazan, *R. v. Elliott*, vol. [2016] ONCJ 310, 2016.

[49] H. Webb, P. Burnap, R. Procter, O. Rana, B. C. Stahl, M. Williams, ... M. Jirotka., "Digital Wildfires: Propagation, Verification, Regulation, and Responsible Innovation," *ACM Transactions on Information Systems*, *34*(3), pp. 15:1–15:23, 2016.

Invisible Ubiquity - Cloud Security in UK Corporate Annual Reporting

Bob Duncan*, Mark Whittington†
Business School
University of Aberdeen
Aberdeen, UK
Emails: *robert.duncan@abdn.ac.uk, †mark.whittington@abdn.ac.uk

Abstract—**The cloud is embedded in the operations of large businesses, who will understand the incentives in terms of cost reduction but also need to recognise, accept and mitigate the risks that come with adoption of an approach that brings in more actors and more opportunities for rogue interventions. We address the extent to which the five quoted UK banks, as an interesting sample of UK quoted corporates, inform their shareholders of the benefits and risks of cloud use through the traditional official medium of the annual report. There has been a rise in pressure, whether legal, quasi-legal or perceived best practice, to report significant risks to the business and it would be reasonable to assume that using the cloud might be such a risk. A study of the banks' lengthy reports, with over 1,600 pages across the five reports for 2017, shows minimal mention of cloud as a risk, but the use of "cyber" as the term for, it seems, internet and computer risks of all kinds. The reports focus on directors overseeing and making themselves aware of risks with much of the language vague with key terms not defined. Standard Chartered, however, seems to take a different and, it is suggested, a more constructive approach than their peers.**

Keywords–FTSE100 companies; GDPR compliance; cloud forensic problem.

I. INTRODUCTION

Large corporates have always been interested in embracing outsourcing technologies [1], and in particular IT. With many decades of experience, they have become very good at it, and understand the risks well. They also understand the value of using the best of technology for their business and were quick to realise the added value that outsourcing gave them, allowing them to access better and faster technology, without having to invest inordinately high sums of money to achieve their objectives.

With cloud now into its second decade of evolution, it is no longer the novelty architectural solution to corporate IT problems, but has rather become an accepted part [2] of the process of doing business. The rapid scalability of cloud resources allows expanding resource requirements for even the largest of corporates to now be considered an everyday event. Indeed, it is so ubiquitous that you will be hard pressed to find any large corporate who does not enjoy its benefits in a multiplicity of ways today.

That does not mean the inherent security issues of cloud are now a thing of the past. Indeed, many of these risks remain to this day [3]. However, it is clear that with many decades of experience in outsourcing IT behind them, large corporates have developed a much deeper understanding of many of the risks involved, with more of a "can do" approach than many smaller companies seem to be able to manage.

Achieving information security with conventional distributed network computer systems continues to present a significant challenge, and cloud still continues to present difficulties towards achieving this end. The principal reason for the difficulty of this challenge remains the not yet fully resolved "Cloud Forensic Problem" [4]. This arises once an attacker gains a foothold in a cloud system and becomes an intruder. Once this happens, there is little to prevent the intruder from helping themselves to any amount of data, either by viewing, modifying, deleting or ex-filtrating it from the victim system. Worse still, there is nothing to prevent the intruder from gaining sufficient privileges to completely delete all trace of their attack. While there is still no bulletproof solution, where appropriate mitigatory steps are taken, the risk can be significantly reduced. It is clear that serious monitoring must take place continuously.

Large corporates also understand well the need to achieve legislative and regulatory compliance, as well as the potential penalties for failure to deliver such compliance. They do have the advantage of having adequate resources at their disposal, meaning they have no difficulty in accessing the best expertise to deal with any situation. They certainly are aware of both the financial and reputational consequences of compliance failure.

Thus they have a clear view of the incentives, both for compliance and the benefits to their business by ensuring that all the people they deal with are also in a position to achieve compliance. Knowing who you are dealing with and understanding that they too are compliant, ensures a far higher level of trust, which in turn ensures there are less likely to be issues surrounding compliance failures.

We start in Section II, by considering the cloud specific issues that present a barrier to good security and privacy with cloud use. In Section III, we consider IT and cloud risk reporting to shareholders in large corporates and in Section IV, we consider how this is approached by the 5 largest UK banks listed on the FTSE100 Index. In Section V, we look at the requirement UK banks have to report to shareholders. In Section VI, we discuss our findings, and in Section VII, we discuss our conclusion and make our recommendations.

II. CLOUD RISK AND SECURITY ISSUES

IT risk has become a more prominent feature of risk reporting in many jurisdictions, including the UK [5]. Over and above the other risk and security issues with IT, cloud adds a further level of issues and of questions that need answers. There are a great many additional risk vectors which come into play once cloud computing is deployed. It is not just a case of getting past the corporate firewall and through the internal defence network of the organisation, but in addition, attackers do not even have to get inside corporate systems. They can attack network traffic to and from the cloud instances. They can attack the Cloud Service Provider (CSP) direct, or through side channel attacks from their own, or other compromised systems. They can attack third party service providers, they can attack through compromised Internet of Things (IoT) networks, which are notoriously insecure.

Cloud systems are generally multi tenanted, with a range of other users. Proper partitioning between different clients can present non trivial challenges within the cloud environment. Achieving and maintaining proper access controls is another challenging area. Cloud systems can be vulnerable to Denial of Service (DoS) or Distributed Denial of Service (DDoS) attacks. Achieving and maintaining proper configuration of client based systems to use the cloud from within the corporate network systems can also present a huge challenge.

Why would large corporates want to use outsourced resources for their IT? What is the incentive for large corporates to use cloud? All major cloud service providers make much of the benefits of using cloud for businesses. We believe the following would be the most appropriate incentives for large corporates to use cloud:

- Access Anywhere, Anytime;
- Cost-Effectiveness;
- High Scalability;
- Improved Disaster Recovery;
- Improved Uptime;
- Multiple Migration Options;
- Sophisticated Security.

What kind of cloud deployments would they be interested in? Here are some examples of the most appropriate cloud deployments for use in large corporates:

- Accounting systems;
- Business to Business (B2B) systems;
- Corporate eMail systems;
- Corporate forecasting tools;
- Customer Relationship Management (CRM) systems;
- Enterprise Resource Planning (ERP) systems;
- Human Resources (HR) systems;
- Online web systems for both information and trading;
- Supply Chain Management (SCM) systems.

What kind of issues would they be likely to face in using cloud for these cloud deployments? Here are some examples of the kind of challenging issues they might face:

- Abuse of Cloud Systems;
- Account or Service Traffic Hijacking;
- Data Breaches;
- Data Loss;
- Denial of Service;
- Insecure APIs;
- Insufficient Due Diligence;
- Malicious Insider;
- Malware Injection;
- Shared Vulnerabilities.

Why would these present a particular challenge? The primary security goal of all companies is to achieve Confidentiality, Integrity and Availability (CIA) of their data. For cloud use, the CIA objective must still be met. We will briefly look at each of these issues in turn:

A. *Abuse of Cloud Systems*

Attacking encrypted systems, for example, is a difficult task to complete computationally. Some attackers will abuse cloud systems by gathering significant cloud resources to carry out malicious attacks on others. This is not easy to detect, unless particular attention is paid to high volume activity through log analysis.

B. *Account or Service Traffic Hijacking*

If account details are stolen, often through phishing, vishing, social engineering, and other non-technical attacks, as well as through technical means, including cross site scripting and traffic attacks, this can give an attacker a solid base from which to attack the overall system. It also allows the attacker a base from which to gain access to other systems more easily, as well as an opportunity to insert malware into the system.

C. *Data Breaches*

A data breach is the result of an intrusion which is most likely to be both malicious and intrusive. Because of the communication speed of cloud resources, any breach can result in mass data becoming exposed. This means data breaches are a particularly worrying attack, which can have devastating legislative and regulatory compliance consequences.

D. *Data Loss*

Data loss can arise for a number of different reasons. The data owner could lose the encryption key rendering the data useless. An authorised user might delete data accidentally. An intruder might maliciously delete data. There could be a physical failure of storage media, which if not properly backed up could result in data loss. Where proper backups are not in place, all these examples have the same result — the data is irretrievably lost.

E. *Denial of Service*

This is an old attack which attempts to disrupt business by flooding the system with hundreds, thousands or millions of automated requests for service. If not detected and dealt with, this brings the system to a halt, effectively closing down the availability of the system. It is like being caught in a rush hour traffic jam — you can neither go forward to your destination, not backwards to try to find an alternative route through, meaning you have to sit there doing nothing until the traffic clears.

F. *Insecure APIs*

Cloud computing brings with it the dichotomy of trying to make services available to millions yet keep systems secure at the same time — two incompatible goals. That solution has been the public facing Application Programming Interface (API). OAuth, and open authorisation service for web services which control third party access has been developed to help with this task.

G. Insufficient Due Diligence

Many companies fail to perform adequate due diligence to understand the full implications of using cloud before they embark on using cloud. Often companies expect well protected internal systems to work really well when they push them to cloud and fail to grasp the subtle differences between the two environments, leading to introducing weaknesses to their system.

H. Malicious Insider

Where a company depends solely on the cloud service provider for their security — they are at increased risk of exposure to malicious user attacks. This is especially problematic where the encryption keys are kept in the cloud, rather than securely in the company's own internal systems. Consider the damage caused by the Edward Snowden leaks.

I. Malware Injection

Malware injections are scripts or code embedded into cloud services, which then purport to provide valid SaaS instance services to cloud servers. This allows the code to perform malicious actions to eavesdrop on company traffic, compromise the integrity of sensitive areas, exfiltrate sensitive data, or perform any number of malicious actions on behalf of the attacker to the detriment of the company.

J. Shared Vulnerabilities

Cloud security is a function that must necessarily be shared between provider and client. Each party has the responsibility to take appropriate action to safeguard and protect the data. This means the provider must provide a secure environment in which to operate, but equally, the user must take responsibility for ensuring that they take proper precautions to secure user passwords and access restrictions to both data and devices, preferably by the use of multi-factor authentication.

III. IT and Cloud Risk Reporting to Shareholders in the UK

Quoted UK companies have a significant responsibility to report on their performance and, increasingly, their risks to their shareholders as well as other stakeholders. This responsibility is partly legally defined and necessary and partly voluntary. Some content falls between these two neat categories as the law might dictate a heading to be covered and then the approach and the level of detail to adequately address this is determined by the company with the oversight of their auditor. Risk is an area in this mezzanine category with paragraph 414c of The Companies Act 2006 (Strategic report and Directors' Report) Regulations 2013, No 1970 [6] stating that the strategic report for the company, which is the main descriptive part of the annual report, must contain "(a) a fair review of the company's business and (b) a description of the principal risks and uncertainties facing the company". This legislation reflects a growing trend towards the encouragement of more non-financial reporting such as the EU non-financial disclosure directive (2014) [7].

Companies, of course, face many risks of which cloud is only one. As we have seen, however, it is becoming a risk concerning not just known, narrowly defined problems but a more pervasive background to the entirety of "doing business". In this context, it is interesting to address the question of how much companies feel they need to tell their shareholders concerning their reliance on the cloud and the risks their business consequentially has embedded in it.

IV. Introduction to Banks

In order to focus our investigations into this question, we will consider the five banks quoted in the FTSE100 index as at October, 2018. These were Barclays, HSBC, Lloyds, RBS and Standard Chartered. Banks, perhaps more than any other industry, have layer upon layer of required reporting — some nationally determined, some internationally — some general, some very bank specific. Banks are a particularly interesting sector as, it is often argued, the rest of the economic system is dependent on the survival of the systemic or "too big to fail" members of the sector. It could be argued that in seeking to address the problems highlighted by the 2008 financial crisis, banks have been more regulated than they have been reduced to sizes that might solve the too big to fail issue. Hence, now banks report to, and are monitored by, their "host" government and by global banking supervisory bodies, for example the Financial Stability Board, as well as their traditional owners and masters — their shareholders. On top of this other stakeholders (customers, creditors, employees, etc.) are increasingly recognised by corporate governance codes, as the Financial Times [8] puts it "When only shareholders matter, there is only one constituency to disappoint. As capitalism tilts slowly to recognise other shareholders, General Motors is showing the way in how to let multiple interested parties down." So, for this sector in particular, there are many concerned overseers and it will be interesting to see what general or narrow cloud risk gets through the filter to reach the owners (aka shareholders).

Banks have often been in the eye of the news websites for disappointing IT related performance and, in a business model that relies more on web-enabled software than traditional branches or face-to-face contact, they are a key focus of the dependability and trustworthiness of IT systems remembering that disappointed customers may well take actions that will lead to disappointed shareholders. Whilst the engagement with cloud is often implicit and assumed rather than stated, there is no doubt that cloud is critical and will be become more so as the banks seek to increase efficiency by becoming more virtual and less physically accessible. This shift inevitably changes the risk profile of the banks and, while potentially reducing some risks (physical stealing of actual notes, for example), it will mean a raised level for online risks that any organization might struggle to keep up with.

V. Banks' Requirement to Report to Shareholders

There is a logic to risk reporting being less clearly defined than, say, the reporting of financial statements. Whilst all companies have sales and costs, the types and level of threat posed by differing risks will vary considerably by industry, as would the importance of various environmental issues between a bank and an oil company. There is a developing literature focused on risk reporting (see [9] for a literature review) and a concern that the idea of risk itself is not clearly conceptualised [9](pp 54). Whilst directors have a requirement to report issues of material and strategic importance or threat to the company, it is clear that they would also wish to give the impression that they are indeed "managing" the company and that risks are under control and mitigated. Banking, in particular, has developed a multi-dimensional set of risk frameworks for bank-specific risks (credit risk, liquidity risk, market risk — see the annual reports of our case companies for more details) and, perhaps this leaves little room for the more mundane "normal risks" that face other businesses from their operations and systems. Nevertheless, it would seem that a cursory glance at the popular press and IT industry news feeds would suggest there might be much to make sure shareholders are aware of.

The methodology used here is that of content analysis an approach that seeks to examine qualitative information by turning it into quantitative data. This approach can address many questions the tone and style of reports, the relative importance through comparing quantities of mentions on differing topics, highlighting which topics merit graphs or pictures as opposed to just words, would be just three of many angles one might take. Such studies have looked at environmental, social, governance, risk and other areas of corporate reporting. The issue of confusing the measurable "quantity" with the less definable "quality" presents many issues and problems. Repeated mentions of the same information may show some recognition of importance, but does not impart more knowledge. One truth is that whilst "quantity does not mean quality", "no quantity means no quality". We find, perhaps surprisingly few (and oft repeated) direct mentions of "cloud" or even the broader "cyber" within the long five reports we examine. Hence our approach is adapted to become more discursive and less numerically focused as we seek to modify our methods to fit the data that presents itself. This highlights a further issue in studies such as this; that statistical sophistication, whilst desirable, is only possible when there is plenty of data, yet there are many topics that might be even more important but without the data quantities to satisfy the number-crunching desires of top academics.

VI. Cloud in the Banks' Annual Report

Banks do not only report using their "Annual Report". Like any other large, listed company there will be interim or quarterly reports along with a regularly updated website. Producing a "Corporate Citizenship" report, however titled, is usual and, if there is a share quote on a USA exchange, then a US reporting format referred to as a 20-F. Specific banking rules also require a Pillar 3 report covering their approach to having adequate capital. Focusing on the Annual report, banks have much to include, yet there is no word or page limit. Table I below shows the pages in each of the latest (October, 2018) annual reports for the 5 banks and the number of pages specifically in the risk section — of course, risk will probably also appear elsewhere in the report.

TABLE I: BANK PAGE STATS 2017 ©2019 Duncan and Whittington

Bank	AR Date	Length AR pp	(pages) Risk pp	% Risk
Barclays Bank	31/12/2017	328	87	27%
HSBC Holdings	31/12/2017	274	57	21%
Lloyds Banking Group	31/12/2017	278	50	18%
Royal Bank of Scotland Group	31/12/2017	419	80	19%
Standard Chartered	31/12/2017	344	74	22%

In a review of risk reporting in another UK industry (food producers), Abraham and Shrives [10] found a majority of general rather than specific disclosures and that content was repetitive over time They took this to imply that the companies were showing a concern to disclosure (symbolic) rather than offering substantive content. Such an approach may be more difficult for companies to achieve in 2017/2018 as audit coverage is somewhat broader than in the years 2002-2007 used in their survey and now includes the auditor having a check of much of the discursive section of the report. As stated above, there are many categories of risk that banks are required to take account of before they might turn to consider areas where reporting might be more voluntary and would have similarities with non-financial businesses. These are usually referred to as "operational risk" disclosures. Only one paper has considered banking operational risk disclosures in Europe [11] and this makes no specific reference to cloud, IT or internet risk issues. A critical flaw in the use of content analysis is that there needs to be some relevant content that is available for analysis and, hence, perhaps, the approach taken did not focus on such details.

Reviewing the five lengthy reports reveals some differing approaches. Whilst all five are "banks", they are not the same and do not face the same risks. Lloyds is a UK-focused retail bank whilst the other four include the wide breadth of investment banking too. RBS is still recovering from the financial crisis and continuing government ownership of a majority stake. Different activities will lead to different risks and therefore direct comparison may not be meaningful. Also, there is significant repetition in some of the reports which, a common issue with content analysis, can lead to statistics which show a great deal of disclosure when there is actually one disclosure ten times. Hence, a more discursive rather than numerical approach has been adopted.

"Cloud" rarely appears in any of the reports and not in a risk context. HSBC and Standard Chartered do not mention cloud once in their reports. Barclays launched a customer product called "Cloudit" and, more usefully, Lloyds states: "To support our transformation and deliver further efficiency savings, we will simplify and modernise our IT architecture while deploying new technologies such as cloud computing to enhance our capabilities and increase resilience." (Page 16, Lloyds — Digitising the group — Leveraging new technologies) This is confirmation of our expectation of "cloud behind the scenes". RBS, in a similar vein, states: "Faster repositioning of the bank's existing distribution network and technology platforms towards mobile, cloud based platforms and virtualisation." (Page 13, RBS)

"Cyber", on the other hand, either by itself or as the initial part of a word or phrase (cybersecurity, cyber-attack, cybercrime, etc.) is used to cover most information systems, internet and distributed computing concerns and solutions. The RBS quote below shows such an example: "Delivering appropriate digital infrastructure is important to ensure a 'technically-able' bank that supports its long-term future. Cyber security is also a vital part of providing a safe and secure banking service. Banks need to proactively identify and manage risks and efciencies in their operations and facilities" (Page 39, RBS)

The tables below (Tables II, III, IV, V and VI) show some of the key content in each of the reports — there seems a focus on showing that the directors have cyber covered in their board and risk committee structures. Interestingly, some banks have cyber risk mostly within operating risk, whereas Lloyds and, more prominently, Standard Chartered now have it as a primary risk category on its own. Two banks had directors who might be seen to be experts in this field, a third had developed a system of named specialist external advisors to make sure there was such expertise. Three banks mentioned cyber within bonus objectives for one or more of the directors. Heavy investment in resilience and technology was mentioned frequently but without financial numbers. The audit row of the table shows the variety of length of the audit reports and also that there appears to be a bespoke approach with different cyber risks being highlighted by the audit firm, or, indeed, with HSBC, none at all. Despite the number of data breaches suffered by banks in previous years, the GDPR (General Data Protection Regulations) makes few explicit appearances in these reports, even though implementation was only a few months away when the reports were written. Only Lloyds has more than two mentions within their lengthy reports, with Barclays the only one to highlight the size of potential fines.

TABLE II: BARCLAYS BANK 2017 [12]

Item	Description
Key Point	New Centre of excellence for cyber security as part of restructuring
Comments in introductory pages	Investing in digital and mobile capabilities with an awareness of the cyber risk management
Risks highlighted	Cyber crime as a risk to the bank's business model. Model is stress tested with cyber attacks) Increased compliance costs as regulators focus on cyber risk
Directors	CEO has a target of strengthening cyber readiness
Committees	Risk committee sees the cyber theme as part of operational risk Cyber has reputational risk
Audit KPMG 6pp	User access management. Some concerns about developers, but found no reason to investigate further

TABLE III: HSBC HOLDINGS 2017 [13]

Item	Description
Key Point	"dominant threat"
Comments in introductory	rising cyber threat risk
Risks highlighted	Cyber threat Unauthorised systems access
Directors	Non-exec director is a security expert CEO has a cyber personal objective
Committees	Also a Financial Systems Vulnerability Committee
Audit PWC 5pp	No comments

TABLE IV: LLOYDS BANKING GROUP 2017 [14]

Item	Description
Key Point	" near term challenges new threats from data and cyber security" (P2)
Comments in introductory pages	"UK's largest digital bank" (P9) Information and cyber security policy are also included as part of the Human Rights commitment
Risks highlighted	IT infrastructre, cyber risk, 3rd party reliance Operational risk has cyber as a secondary section. List of potential cyber damage on page 135
Directors	Chief Operating Officer is assessed on mitigating evolving risks, including cyber
Committees	Board risk committee report separates out "IT and cyber risk" from operational risks
Audit PWC 8pp	Highlights access concerns, but additional testing found this to be secure

Uniquely, at least in this small data set, RBS provide a section of "additional information" from page 357 which extends for 50 pages which includes further risk factors. Whilst one cannot be entirely sure, this approach may well put this section beyond the reviewing eye of the external audit team. We will focus on the aspects of Standard Chartered's reporting that would appear to differentiate it from the other banks. The additional information includes more detail on dependency on IT systems, reputational damage of loss of customer data, potential for fines, cost-saving focus undermining resourcing improved security amongst others. On page 389, a cyber act as part of a geopolitical event is mentioned as a further potential problem.

TABLE V: ROYAL BANK OF SCOTLAND GROUP 2017 [15]

Item	Description
Key Point	"a key operational competence"
Comments in introductory	Refers to a multi-layered defence to cyber security , systems enhancements and training
Risks highlighted	Financial malware
Directors	No comment
Committees	Risk Committee receives bi-annual Resilience and Security report where cyber is highlighted Simulated cyber attack scenarios undertaken
Audit EY 14pp	Review of IT systems and controls mentioned, but no concerns found

TABLE VI: STANDARD CHARTERED 2017 [16]

Item	Description
Key Point	Not complacent. Further enhancing cyber security (P6)
Comments in introductory	We have made significant progress in our work to combat financial crime and have increased focus on our cyber risk management capabilities (p33) Mentions cyber security industry working bodies that it sits on
Risks highlighted	Information and cyber security raised to principal risk level
Directors	Directors joined by specialist external advisor on risk committee and subcommittee
Committees	Board Financial Crime Risk Committee Committees on Cyber Security and Cyber Threat Management mentioned
Audit KPMG 8pp	IT risk highlighted with discussion of controls and access - in relation to financial reporting found acceptable

Apart from this RBS appendix, Standard Chartered would seem to have the most thorough and structured discussion of cyber risk. It stands out by giving a definition of information and cyber security risk as: "the potential for loss from a breach of confidentiality, integrity or availability of the Group's information systems and assets through cyber attack, insider activity, error or control failure" (page 162, Standard Chartered). It would seem the other banks take for granted the assumption that the reader's understanding of cyber security risk as matching their own.

Standard Chartered also uniquely further describes its management approach to the risk: "The Group seeks to avoid risk and uncertainty for our critical information assets and systems and has a low appetite for material incidents affecting these or the wider operations and reputation of the bank" (page 34, Standard Chartered)

And finally gives an overview of its "risk appetite" for cyber security: "The Group seeks to avoid risk and uncertainty for our critical information assets and systems and has a low appetite for material incidents affecting these or the wider operations and reputation of the Group" (page 177, Standard

Chartered)

Page 177 explains Standard Chartered's approach to cyber risk including roles, committee structure and monitoring in a more accessible way, as well as defining terms when other banks just use words and spread any content throughout the report.

There is, of course, much that of necessity needs to be left out of an annual report. However, it is easy enough for a vigilant analyst or shareholder to find the evidence presented earlier in the paper from a variety of sources and form their own view of the banks' ability to get to grips with "cyber". The task of the annual report perhaps, would seem to be to present a calm assurance that all is under control or at least controllable. As the audit reports do not directly address the broader cyber risks, it is for the shareholder to decide whether presentation truly matches the reality they gather from elsewhere.

VII. Conclusion

We can see from Section II, that there are a great many possible additional threats to achieving proper security once cloud is introduced to the provisioning of IT resources for large corporates. Many of these are not trivial to resolve. Increased vigilance becomes one of the most important elements of any defensive plan, without which the business will be exposed to further risk.

In an industry with so many risks and where other risks are heavily regulated and require extensive coverage and reporting, it might seem unreasonable to expect depth and detail on cyber security. However, it is rising in prominence as a risk category and is mentioned as a threat to the integrity of the business model on at least two occasions. However superficial coverage of ill-defined terms appears the norm.

The comments and statements in these annual reports do not give great insight or detail, some of the banks appear to be emphasising a big picture that they are doing whatever they can to not only recognise but also match the cyber challenges that they face. There is only the briefest glimpse into what this means below the surface, apart from page 177 in Standard Chartered's report. Standard Chartered might be held up as a role model in the clarity of their reporting such response to peer pressure is a recognized feature of the analysis of corporate reporting. The recognition that terms need to be explained, especially when the term "cyber" seems so frequent and vague, and the attempt to bring together the information on the topic rather than spreading it through the report gives the impression of seeking to inform the reader rather than just ticking boxes in a structure designed to report on committees rather than subjects. Whilst impression management is another key theme within discursive reporting research, this awareness in itself is to be credited.

The annual report is the authorised vehicle for informing shareholders specifically about the success and risks of the business they own. The banks tend to focus on banking risk categories, and this might squeeze the word count available for more usual business risks. Banks, due to their size and importance, as well as their reliance on IT, including cloud, could do more to inform their owners about more than the committee structures and broad themes. Perhaps this traditional report structure is not the best way of doing this, yet Standard Chartered seem to have provided a higher degree of clarity and sharpness by defining terms and focusing a little more on topic than corporate structure.

References

[1] R. Babin, S. Briggs, and B. Nicholson, "Corporate Social Responsibility and Global IT Outsourcing," Commun. ACM, vol. 54, 2011, p. 28.

[2] J. Gubbi, R. Buyya, and S. Marusic, "1207.0203," Futur. Gener. Comput. Syst., vol. 29, no. 1, 2013, pp. 1–19.

[3] B. Duncan and Y. Zhao, "Risk Management for Cloud Compliance with the EU General Data Protection Regulation," in 7th Int. Work. Secur. Priv. Perform. Cloud Comput. (SPCLOUD 2018), Orleans, France, 2018, p. 8.

[4] B. Duncan, M. Whittington, and V. Chang, "Enterprise security and privacy: Why adding IoT and big data makes it so much more difficult," in Proc. 2017 Int. Conf. Eng. Technol. ICET 2017, vol. 2018-Janua, 2018.

[5] B. Duncan, Y. Zhao, and M. Whittington, "Corporate Governance, Risk Appetite and Cloud Security Risk: A Little Known Paradox. How Do We Square the Circle?" in Cloud Comput. 2017 Eighth Int. Conf. Cloud Comput. GRIDs, Virtualization, Athens, 2017, pp. 1–6.

[6] U. Gov, "The Companies Act 2006 (Strategic report and Directors' Report) Regulations 2013," 2013. [Online]. Available: https://www.legislation.gov.uk/ukdsi/2013/9780111540169/part/2 Accessed: 28/03/2019

[7] EU, "(2) EU (2014) Directive 2014/95/EU of the European Parliament and of the Council of 22 October 2014 amending Directive 2013/34/EU as regards disclosure of non-financial and diversity information by certain large undertakings and groups." 2014.

[8] FT, "General Motors: Cruzing for a bruising," 2019.

[9] T. Elshandidy, P. J. Shrives, M. Bamber, and S. Abraham, "Risk reporting: A review of the literature and implications for future research," J. Account. Lit., vol. 40, 2018, pp. 54–82.

[10] S. Abraham and P. J. Shrives, "Improving the relevance of risk factor disclosure in corporate annual reports," Br. Account. Rev., vol. 46, no. 1, 2014, pp. 91–107.

[11] A. Barakat and K. Hussainey, "Bank governance, regulation, supervision, and risk reporting: Evidence from operational risk disclosures in European banks," Int. Rev. Financ. Anal., vol. 30, 2013, pp. 254–273.

[12] B. Bank, "Barclays Bank 2017 Annual Reort," Tech. Rep., 2017. [Online]. Available: https://home.barclays/investor-relations/reports-and-events/annual-reports/2017/{\%}0A Accessed: 28/03/2019

[13] HSBC, "HSBC Holdings 2017 Annual Report," Tech. Rep., 2017. [Online]. Available: https://www.hsbc.com/-/files/hsbc/investors/hsbc-results/2017/annual/hsbc-holdings-plc/180220-annual-report-and-accounts-2017.pdf Accessed: 28/03/2019

[14] Lloyds, "Lloyds Bank 2017 Annual Report," Tech. Rep., 2017. [Online]. Available: https://www.lloyds.com/investor-relations/financial-performance/financial-results/annual-report-2017 Accessed: 28/03/2019

[15] RBS, "Royal Bank of Scotland Group 2017 Annual Report," Tech. Rep., 2017. [Online]. Available: https://investors.rbs.com/{~}/media/Files/R/RBS-IR/annual-report-2017/royal-bankof-scotland-annual-report-and-accounts2017.pdf Accessed: 28/03/2019

[16] S. Chartered, "Standard Chartered 2017 Annual Report," Tech. Rep., 2017. [Online]. Available: https://www.sc.com/annual-report/2017/ Accessed: 28/03/2019

Investigating the Tension Between Cloud-Related Actors and Individual Privacy Rights

Bob Duncan
Business School,
Aberdeen University, Scotland
robert.duncan@abdn.ac.uk

Karen Renaud
Division of Cyber Security,
Abertay University, Scotland
k.renaud@abertay.ac.uk

Beverley Mackenzie
Division of Cyber Security
Abertay University, Scotland
1705191@abertay.ac.uk

***Abstract*—Historically, little more than lip service has been paid to the rights of individuals to act to preserve their own privacy. Personal information is frequently exploited for commercial gain, often without the person's knowledge or permission. New legislation, such as the EU General Data Protection Regulation Act, has acknowledged the need for legislative protection. This Act places the onus on service providers to preserve the confidentiality of their users' and customers' personal information, on pain of punitive fines for lapses. It accords special privileges to users, such as the right to be forgotten. This regulation has global jurisdiction covering the rights of any EU resident, worldwide. Assuring this legislated privacy protection presents a serious challenge, which is exacerbated in the cloud environment. A considerable number of actors are stakeholders in cloud ecosystems. Each has their own agenda and these are not necessarily well aligned. Cloud service providers, especially those offering social media services, are interested in growing their businesses and maximising revenue. There is a strong incentive for them to capitalise on their users' personal information and usage information. Privacy is often the first victim. Here, we examine the tensions between the various cloud actors and propose a framework that could be used to ensure that privacy is preserved and respected in cloud systems.**

***Index Terms*—Cloud, Cloud actors, Privacy, Confidentiality**

I. INTRODUCTION

In the decade since the introduction of the cloud computing paradigm, we have seen a significant shift in cloud capabilities. In 2011, NIST [1, p.2] provided an updated definition of what cloud computing is, explaining that the essential characteristics of the cloud are (1) on-demand self service, (2) broad network access, (3) resource pooling, (4) rapid elasticity, and (5) measured service

Since this definition was formulated, the capabilities of cloud, and the uses to which it can be put, have evolved considerably. It is perhaps inevitable that hackers have turned their attention to cloud as well, with some success as recent attacks demonstrate [2]. Successful hacks leak data, and privacy violations become a huge concern. We have to take a close look at the parameters of this problem, to consider how to formalise better mechanisms for preserving the privacy of everyone using the cloud.

Of interest, here, is the number of different actors involved in the cloud ecosystem. This has rendered the environment far more complex than traditional distributed network systems. The number of actors has increased considerably, to include both programmatic and human actors. The number of bad actors carrying out attacks has increased exponentially [3], [4], [5], [6], [7]. We can see that the time between breach and discovery has been steadily falling between 2012 and 2016. This can be attributed in some way to the impact of efforts of companies to improve security in light of the need to comply with the General Data Protection Regulation (GDPR). This momentum was rather lost when some serious lobbying resulted in a change from the requirement to report a breach within 72 hours of occurrence to *within 72 hours of discovery*, as evidenced by the 2017 breach report [8], where the time between breach and discovery returned to near 2012 levels in the space of a year. Of significance throughout this period is the alarming increase in attack volume throughout, yearly.

While cloud users have been quick to exploit the opportunities offered by cloud, so too have bad actors been keen to exploit its inherent vulnerabilities. Hackers are now specifically targetting the cloud [9] so all stakeholders really cannot afford to neglect cloud security. This is not a simple task, as [10] points out. He refers to the "The Inevitability of Combinatorial Risk" due to technical interdependencies and the multiple actors involved in the system.

In addition, we have seen a significant change in the way governments approach security and privacy concerns. Of particular interest is the new EU GDPR [11], which brings to bear very significant penalties for non-compliance in the event of a security breach. Furthermore, jurisdiction is now global, instead of EU-wide only. This is likely to encourage other jurisdictions to strengthen their own security and privacy legislation, which, to date, have been rather poorly framed.

In Section II, we present the core principles of privacy. In Section III, we consider the range of vulnerabilities in cloud ecosystems that must be addressed in order to ensure a high level of security and privacy can be achieved. Then, in Section IV, we look at how the actors involved in cloud ecosystems have evolved during the past decade. In Section V, we develop a framework to address how to defend against such vulnerabilities. In Section VI, we consider the anticipated manner in which the framework might be deployed, and in Section VII, we discuss our conclusions.

II. Privacy and the Cloud

Privacy researchers have expressed concerns about computer users divulging too much information [12], not appreciating or valuing their personal information and giving it away unthinkingly, unwittingly sacrificing their privacy [13]. As governments move to put all their citizens' details online [14], utilizing cloud services to do so, the potential for privacy invasion increases the consequences disastrous [15].

Privacy is undoubtedly a complicated concept [16]. Solove explains that privacy is *"an umbrella term, referring to a wide and disparate group of related things"* [17, p.485]. Privacy, according to Privacy International, who are more specific, is a multidimensional concept, which is related to four components: (1) body, (2) communications, (3) territory, and (4) information. When it comes to the cloud, our interest is in the second and fourth of these.

Privacy is a human right in Europe, and the United Kingdom is a signatory of the European Convention of Human Rights. Article 8 of the Convention [18] states that EU citizens have the right to respect for private and family life. In particular, the State may only interfere with this right proportionally, in accordance with law and in the interests of national security, public safety, and for the prevention of crime. Yet the public at large seems to accept widespread privacy violations, seemingly without protesting [19], [20], [21].

Yet the UK government itself does not seem to respect their citizens' privacy rights. The UK government recently passed the Investigatory Powers Act (IPA). Part 4 of the Act requires web and phone companies to retain all data logs pertaining to their customers' activities for two years. They are required, upon request, to provide these to official bodies without judicial oversight, not respecting privacy.

Privacy and confidentiality are aligned yet conceptually different terms, which are often conflated. For example, Meriam Webster defines privacy as "freedom from unauthorized intrusion", "seclusion" and "secrecy". Confidentiality is defined as "private, secret". Yet these concepts are very different. The ISO/IEC 29100 [22] provides a more specific definition of the privacy principle: *"specific choices made by a personally identifiable information (PII) principal about how their PII should be processed for a particular purpose"*. The ISO/IEC 27001 [23] definition of confidentiality is: *"that information is not made available or disclosed to unauthorized individuals, entities, or processes"*. This distinction is important when we start considering privacy and the cloud.

The introduction of the GDPR is said to be *"the most important change in data privacy regulation in 20 years"* [11]. The legislation came into force on the 25th May 2018, and replaced the existing Data Protection Directive 95/46/EC. Organisations that fail to comply will be subject to significant fines. GDPR is essentially linked to confidentiality; the requirement for cloud service providers is to ensure that personal data provided, or stored, by their users is secured and not leaked.

This means that cloud providers have to start taking confidentiality seriously, but little advice is offered to cloud providers in this respect. The Information Commissioner's website offers advice to the man and woman in the street, but not to cloud service providers [24]. In this paper, we propose a framework that will fill this gap.

III. Range of Vulnerabilities in Cloud Ecosystems

Due to the nature of the cloud ecosystem, and the various actors involved in the provision of cloud services, cloud users are at risk from cloud-specific threats and vulnerabilities. A cloud-based attack can have huge economic ramifications, comparable to that of a major natural disaster [25]. The range of vulnerabilities can be demonstrated by looking at the OWASP Top 10 risk tables for 2017. The first one addresses Web based weaknesses:

- A1:2017 — Injection
- A2:2017 — Broken Authentication
- A3:2017 — Sensitive Data Exposure
- A4:2017 — XML External Entities (XXE)
- A5:2017 — Broken Access Control
- A6:2017 — Security Misconfiguration
- A7:2017 — Cross-Site Scripting (XSS)
- A8:2017 — Insecure Deserialization
- A9:2017 — Using Components with Known Vulnerabilities
- A10:2017 — Insufficient Logging & Monitoring

The next Top 10 list considers Cloud specific risks:

- Accountability & Data Risk;
- User Identity Federation;
- Legal & Regulatory Compliance;
- Business Continuity & Resiliency;
- User Privacy & Secondary Usage of Data;
- Service & Data Integration;
- Multi-tenancy & Physical Security;
- Incidence Analysis & Forensics;
- Infrastructure Security;
- Non-production Environment Exposure.

We should also consider potential IoT weaknesses, since many cloud systems have enabled IoT use, and therefore are exposed to IoT vulnerabilities:

- Insecure Web Interface;
- Insufficient Authentication/Authorization;
- Insecure Network Services;
- Lack of Transport Encryption;
- Privacy Concerns;
- Insecure Cloud Interface;
- Insecure Mobile Interface;
- Insufficient Security Configurability;
- Insecure Software Firmware;
- Poor Physical Security.

Since mobile communication also forms an intrinsic part of the Cloud and IoT — we should also take account of the potential impact of Mobile vulnerabilities. To this end, we consider the OWASP top 10 of Mobile Vulnerabilities:

- M1 — Improper Platform Usage;
- M2 — Insecure Data Storage;

- M3 — Insecure Communication;
- M4 — Insecure Authentication;
- M5 — Insufficient Cryptography;
- M6 — Insecure Authorisation;
- M7 — Client Code Quality;
- M8 — Code Tampering;
- M9 — Reverse Engineering;
- M10 — Extraneous Functionality.

In the UK, the Information Commission Office (ICO) is the body that is responsible for the provision of individual rights with respect to data privacy. But, over the last decade cloud computing has been afforded little attention from this body. Yet, in 2015, the ICO's 'Annual Track Report' reported that it was established that out of a survey sample of 2,465 respondents, 60% stated that they had some apprehension with respect to cloud computing [26]. Such apprehension is well grounded, as demonstrated by some recent attacks [2]. Insurance companies like Lloyds are warning of the possibility of huge losses related to cloud attacks [27].

Cloud security issues were also identified by the Cloud Security Alliance (CSA), in their list of the cloud computing notorious nine security risks [28] with the cloud ecosystem being considered susceptible to: data loss, data breach, account hijacking, insecure API's, denial of service, malicious insider, insufficient due diligence, cloud abuse and share technology.

There is also a very important point to take into account here. We have looked at a range of "top 10" vulnerabilities. It is vitally important to realise that there are far more than the ten vulnerabilities in each of these areas. For example, in the case of IoT vulnerabilities, OWASP has identified a total of 94 IoT vulnerabilites that remain to be resolved. Thus, in every single case, it will be vital to not just consider the top 10 vulnerabilities, but to address all potential vulnerabilities to which the company will be exposed.

Due to the nature of cloud, mitigation of these risk is often outside the control of a cloud user. Hence, on occasions when security breaches and security failures do occur, it may be impossible for a client to identify the responsible actor, which, in turn, could lead to tension between actors.

There is a particular issue that must be taken into account with cloud systems, and that is the so called Cloud Forensic Problem [29], [30]. This arises when an attacker gains even a small foothold in a cloud system. Once there, the attacker seeks to escalate privileges to gain access to the forensic logs, which allows them to modify or delete all traces of their incursion into the cloud system. This allows the attacker to become a more permanent intruder, resulting in their capability to access considerably more information over the longer term, while remaining hidden. There is nothing within a cloud system to prevent this from occurring.

We need also to consider the damage insiders can cause from within the company, due to poorly updated processes, poorly configured IT resources and vulnerabilities [31].

Other issues are poorly defined policies, lack of attention to server logs and other aspects that are relatively easy things to police if only the cloud provider takes the time to do so. Finally, there are the malware attacks, such as the Mirai virus attack on cheap Internet of Things (IoT) devices [32]. It subsequently spread to corporate Windows desktops [33], thus facilitating the leveraging of compromised IoT networks into other more valuable corporate systems.

IV. Actors Involved in Cloud Ecosystems

Once cloud started to gain traction just over a decade ago, it offered some interesting opportunities to companies in terms of the ease with which they could provision IT resources. Many assumed it was just the cloud user and the cloud service provider who were the solo actors in the equation, but there were far more than that even 10 years ago. Cloud Service Providers (CSPs) made much of how committed they were to vetting all their staff members properly. However, little was said about the need to hire in temporary staff on an emergency basis, where often such agency companies were much less rigorous in their vetting processes [34].

Similarly, many of the services offered were not actually provided by the CSPs themselves. Often third party providers were used who had much less rigorous approaches to issues of security, privacy and confidentiality. CSPs were often less than transparent about where the data in their cloud offerings would reside, and even less transparent about who access it.

This would give rise to significant issues for European companies who were using cloud, since EU legislative and regulatory recommendations were to only use cloud provided by companies resident within the EU. The European base for Amazon Web Services (AWS) is in Ireland, a European company, so it might be assumed that anyone using such a service would be compliant. However, that would not necessarily be the case, as AWS also have data centres on the East and West coasts of the USA as well as data centres in the Far East[35].

In the interests of availability, AWS frequently would place copies of both software systems and data in other data centres in the interests of resilience, to ensure that recovery from any possible breakdown of services, or a major cyber breach, would be instantaneous. No mention of the possibilities that security standards in each physical location would be of the same high standard. An unwelcome byproduct of this arrangement would be a possible unexpected and unwelcome exposure to foreign legal jurisdiction, even where the company does not trade in that jurisdiction. In US legislation, for example, running software on a US based system automatically extends their jurisdiction over that company and exposes them to the full penalties of the law.

Contractors, consultants and many other parties will also be involved in a cloud ecosystem. Likewise, within a cloud user company, there will also be the need for temporary staff, contractors and consultants, many of whom will, of necessity, have direct access to cloud systems. This introduces a significant degree of complexity to the management of such systems and opens up a huge range of potential exposure and vulnerability to attack.

However, the problem does not end there. Cloud was instrumental in energising the take up of Big Data, and both have been great enablers for the Internet of Things (IoT). This means that there are now a considerable range of software actors to add to the mix. IoT systems require access to cloud systems where data is stored, processed, analysed and so on. In addition, many of these systems are highly insecure and vulnerable to a range of attacks.

IoT services such as: Domestic and Home Automation, eHealth, Industrial Control, Logistics, Retail, Security and Emergencies, Self Driving Cars and Trucks, Smart Agriculture, Smart Animal Farming, Smart Cities, Smart Environment, Smart Water, Smart Metering, Smart Transport and Smart Utilities have all placed additional stresses on cloud computing. As dumb (and sometimes not so dumb) actors, these can also open up more and more vulnerabilities [36].

This also means that the complexity of handling cloud systems has increased exponentially in the decade since the cloud paradigm really started to gain serious traction. That increase in complexity presents a considerable increase in the risks associated with trying to ensure that a proper and secure environment can be developed to safeguard the security and privacy of customers and enable companies to be compliant with legislation and regulation.

V. Developing a Cloud Security and Privacy Framework

In developing a framework suitable for ensuring that an adequate level of security can be achieved by a cloud-using organisation, we need to consider three separate layers.

The **first layer** we must consider is our security and privacy goals, which will comprise the traditional triad of Confidentiality, Integrity and Availability, along with any new goals we would care to add, such as Audit and Forensic Trails.

The **second layer** we must consider is the systems architecture of the company, which comprises any traditional systems, services and applications, plus cloud services, such as IaaS, PaaS and SaaS.

The **third layer** is the Business Architecture of a company, which comprises a combination of (a) People, (b) Process and (c) Technology [37].

We illustrate this in Figure 1, where each of the layers is described as an axis point on the model. Where any point of confluence between the three axes occurs, we can very clearly articulate what we seek to address for our security and privacy concerns. Thus, at any particular intersection we can identify what the specific goal will be.

This first stage of developing the framework will allow us to set the declared policies the business will seek to achieve by addressing each of the confluence points.

However, this represents the goals at a high level of abstraction. We can subdivide each of the axes into smaller components. Thus, for example, Z1 could be broken down to identify each individual in the company using their ID code. Y6 can be broken down into each specific application in use. X4 can be broken down into the Audit trail requirement for each application, and so on. By this means, we can increase the granularity of addressed details, retaining essential details.

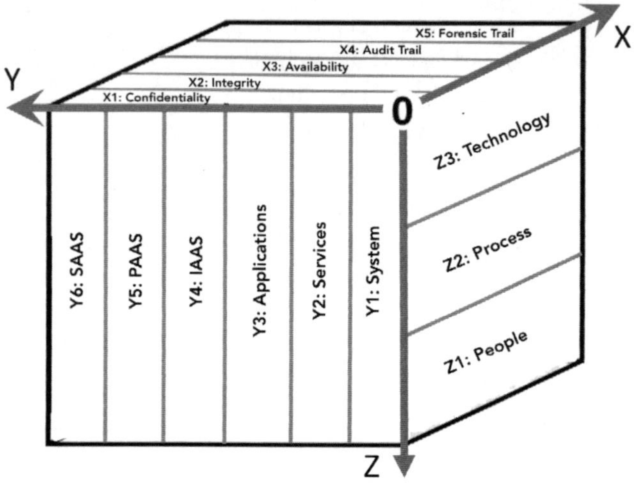

Figure. 1. A Cloud Three-Dimensional Policy Framework Matrix. (X=Security Properties; Y=System Architecture; Z=Business Architecture; 0=Origin)

The next stage will be to consider all known vulnerabilities against each area on the matrix. Thus social engineering attacks would principally relate to Z1, database injection attacks would relate to all instances which use databases on the Y axis, and so on. For each of these attacks, we can collect signatures to identify how each attack can be perpetrated, and can utilise these later for attack detection purposes.

We could also consider adding a risk layer to quantify our perception of risk attaching to each coordinate in the matrix, thus allowing us to evaluate the potential adverse impact of any consequential breach.

For the high-level matrix, we can also borrow from economic utility theory, for example [38], [39], which would allow us to incorporate a simple utility model into these relationships to provide a weighting to express the preferences of the business. This will allow us to develop a simple means of tailoring the model to suit any business.

Thus, to represent the policy of the business at an initial high level of abstraction, there would be three main aims for each of the relationships defined in the model: 1) to provide a mechanism for measurement; 2) to define a target position; 3) to define a utility preference over the target.

To illustrate this point: if we consider coordinate (X3, Y3, Z2): representing "availability for applications to run processes".

For each such component of the policy framework model, as specified in Figure 1, that is of interest — let's assume we index these components by a variable i — we associate a component U_i of a utility function, as follows:

- Measure: M_i; for example, % uptime of systems hardware; in this case, expressed as an average over time;
- Target: m_i, the declarative target for this operation;
- A function f_i expressing how utility depends on deviation from target. For example, a Linex function [40], usually

expressed in the form $g(z) = (exp(\alpha z) - \alpha z - 1)/\alpha^2$, is used to capture a degree of asymmetry that is parameterized by α;
- The weight w_i (between 0 and 1, and $\sum_i w_i = 1$) expressing the managers' weighting/preference for the ith security component of interest;
- This can be expressed thus: $U_i = w_i f_i(M_i - m_i)$;
- System equation $M_i = s_i(x_i)$, where x_i is a vector of control variables and s_i describes M_i's dependency upon them.

Thus the overall utility function is

$$U = \sum_i U_i = \sum_i w_i f_i(M_i - m_i).$$

We can obtain a treatment of the expected utility of the system by introducing suitable stochastic processes into the system functions s_i. In general, such treatment of a system's properties will be too complex to have analytic solutions for the control variables, thus simulations must be used. By evaluating each co-ordinate in the policy framework layer, the business can define their position on the security risks they face and the resulting utility model of the whole will reflect the level of utility they seek, while ensuring compliance with any legislation, regulation and standards. It will also be possible to place constraints on the targets. For example, in the above example, the target may be 99.99%, but the constraint may be that availability should never fall below 98%. In analysing all the co-ordinates of this model, it may be that some threats are subsidiary to others, and that by securing the main threat, this eliminates the subsidiary threats, although this may not always be the case. Each business can take a view on whether they cover these threats individually, or as related groups, depending on what would be appropriate to suit particular needs.

VI. Anticipated Usage of the Cloud Security and Privacy Framework

Now that we have developed a framework to address our needs, we need to understand how we might anticipate its usage in practice. The framework allows us to define what our cloud security and privacy goals are, and to identify how important they are to the company. As it is the company that is responsible for ensuring the security and privacy of PII, on pain of potentially significant fines, the company is therefore accountable for its actions.

Having identified what the security and privacy goals are, we have a good starting point to begin using the framework. In order to understand and measure the degree to which a company using this framework would be compliant, we need to examine our systems to see what has actually transpired during the period under examination. We can examine audit trails, forensic trails, system logs and carry out whatever other analytics are necessary to identify what exactly has been happening during the period under scrutiny. By compiling the metrics we seek to use to reflect real events, we can now compare those against the targets we have set for compliance. Again, to use an example from the previous section, in looking at that example, if our target is 99.99% and the constraint is a minimum of 98%, then if our actual figure shows 95%, then we will have failed our minimum compliance test. With a result of 98.5%, we would have passed our minimum compliance target of 98%, but failed our ultimate goal of 99.99%.

In the event that we fail on any part of the framework, we can then investigate to understand whether the failure arises due to an as yet unidentified attack, or from some other performance failure. In this way, we can identify where our weaknesses lie and take corrective action to ensure these failures do not arise again. If, on the other hand, we discover that an attack has occurred, then we will be in a good position to effect immediate action. Given the average time between breach and discovery of 200 days [41], we will find ourselves in a much stronger position than we otherwise might.

This will give us the comfort that we can identify poor performance and can quantify what that might be, also that we might identify any attack that has been perpetrated, and pick up the fact considerably in advance of the time in which we might otherwise be able to detect it.

For those users who do not have a high level of understanding of cyber security issues, there is an alternative, simpler approach to take. The user can make a list of all the known vulnerabilities already listed by the CSA and OWASP, to which they can add vulnerability lists from any other sources. Each vulnerability can be classified according to the framework matrix. As new vulnerabilities are discovered, these can be added, thus building up a more complete framework over time. Once they have specified their performance targets, they can no run their systems through the various open source tools to see which vulnerabilities are present in their systems, which they can then address. By regularly measuring performance using the framework matrix, they will be able to ensure they are addressing all the most important vulnerabilities.

However, these are not the only ways we can use the framework. Should we decide to implement an intrusion detection system, we will have identified the main known vulnerabilities to which our systems architecture are vulnerable, and can implement the necessary patterns into the intrusion detection software, meaning that we will be better placed to discover the occurrence of such attacks. While that will still leave us exposed to new attacks, which would be the case regardless of whether we operated the framework or not, there is a possibility that something uncharacteristic will show up somewhere in the system as a consequence of the intrusion.

VII. Conclusion

Thus we can see that using this framework, it will be possible to improve our security and privacy posture in the business. We will be able to detect where poor performance impacts on security and privacy compliance, but more importantly, where a breach does occur, we will have an advanced warning of that fact and will be able to do something constructive about it long in advance of what might be possible otherwise.

It is certainly the case that the sooner we are in a position to discover the incidence of an attack having arisen, the sooner we can take defensive and corrective action. If we have take a sensible approach to holding data in encrypted form, then we are likely to be significantly mitigate the impact of any potential breach. There is no doubt that breaches will arise, but the more we can do to mitigate the impact, the better it will be for all concerned, and in particular the users who have no real control over what might happen to their PII.

Given the misalignment of the agendas of all the actors in cloud ecosystems, it is likely that the use of our proposed framework will provide a much more secure environment for retaining users' PII, and thus reducing the impact of any breach we sustain to a considerable extent.

REFERENCES

[1] P. Mell, T. Grance, and Others, "The NIST Definition of Cloud Computing," National Institute of Standards and Technology, Tech. Rep., 2011.

[2] N. Goud, "Cyber attack on cloud computing company makes france news websites go dark," 2017, https://www.cybersecurity-insiders.com/cyber-attack-on-cloud-computing-company-makes-france-news-websites-go-dark/.

[3] Verizon, "2012 Data Breach Investigation Report: A study conducted by the Verizon RISK Team in cooperation with the United States Secret Service and Others," Tech. Rep., 2012, http://www.verizonenterprise.com/resources/reports/rp_data-breach-investigations-report-2012_en_xg.pdf.

[4] Verizon, "2013 Data Breach Investigation Report: A study conducted by the Verizon RISK Team in cooperation with the United States Secret Service and Others accessed 28/03/19," Tech. Rep., 2013, http://www.verizonenterprise.com/resources/reports/rp_data-breach-investigations-report-2013_en_xg.pdf.

[5] Verizon, "2014 Data Breach Investigations Report," Tech. Rep. 1, 2014. [Online]. Available: \url{http://www.verizonenterprise.com/resources/reports/rp_Verizon-DBIR-2014_en_xg.pdf}Accessed28/03/19

[6] Verizon, "2015 Data Breach Investigation Report," Tech. Rep., 2015, https://iapp.org/media/pdf/resource_center/Verizon_data-breach-investigation-report-2015.pdf Accessed 28/03/19.

[7] Verizon, "2016 Verizon Data Breach Report," Tech. Rep., 2016, http://www.verizonenterprise.com/resources/reports/rp_DBIR_2016_Report_en_xg.pdf Accessed 28/03/19.

[8] Verizon, "Verizon Security Breach Report 2017," Tech. Rep., 2017, https://www.verizondigitalmedia.com/blog/2017/07/2017-verizon-data-breach-investigations-report/ Accessed 28/03/19.

[9] D. Pudles, "Hackers target cloud services," 2018, https://www.forbes.com/sites/steveandriole/2018/09/10/cyber-apocalypse-now-how-bad-what-to-do/\#687b4a611638, Accessed 14/4/2019.

[10] S. Andriole, "Cyber apocalypse now - how bad? what to do," 2018, https://www.forbes.com/sites/steveandriole/2018/09/10/cyber-apocalypse-now-how-bad-what-to-do/ Sept 10.

[11] EU Parliament, "Home Page of EU GDPR," 2018, https://www.eugdpr.org/(Accessed 14/4/2018).

[12] S. Barnes, "A privacy paradox: Social networking in the United States," *First Monday*, vol. 11, no. 9, 2006.

[13] P. A. Norberg, D. R. Horne, and D. A. Horne, "The privacy paradox: Personal information disclosure intentions versus behaviors," *Journal of Consumer Affairs*, vol. 41, no. 1, pp. 100–126, 2007.

[14] T. Marceddo, "The battle of the cloud: The digital front," 2018, https://www.cso.com.au/article/646311/battle-cloud-digital-front/06 September, Accessed 14/4/2019.

[15] N. Ntuli, "No help for victim of identity theft," 2018, https://www.news24.com/SouthAfrica/News/no-help-for-victim-of-identity-theft-20180117 Accessed 10/4/2019.

[16] S. T. Margulis, "Conceptions of privacy: Current status and next steps," *Journal of Social Issues*, vol. 33, no. 3, pp. 5–21, 1977.

[17] D. J. Solove, "A taxonomy of privacy," *University of Pennsylvania Law Review*, vol. 154, p. 477, 2005.

[18] European Convention, "Article 8 of the European Convention on Human Rights," 2012, http://www.equalityhumanrights.com/sites/default/files/documents/humanrights/hrr_article_8.pdf.

[19] Amnesty International, *Dangerously disproportionate: The ever-expanding national security state in Europe*. Amnesty International, 2017.

[20] Liberty International, "The people vs. the snoopers charter part 2," 2018, https://www.crowdjustice.com/case/snooperscharterpart2/ Accessed 14/4/2019.

[21] K. Renaud, S. Flowerday, R. English, and M. Volkamer, "Why don't UK citizens protest against privacy-invading dragnet surveillance?" *Information & Computer Security*, vol. 24, no. 4, pp. 400–415, 2016.

[22] ISO/IEC 29100, "Privacy Framework, International Organization for Standardization (ISO) and the International Electrotechnical Commission (IEC)," 2011, https://www.iso.org/obp/ui/fr/#iso:std:iso-iec:29100:en Accessed 14/4/2019.

[23] ISO/IEC 27001, "Information Security Management Systems, International Organization for Standardization (ISO) and the International Electrotechnical Commission (IEC)." 2013, https://www.iso.org/isoiec-27001-information-security.html Accessed 14/4/2019.

[24] ICO, "Information commissioner's office (results for 'cloud')," https://icosearch.ico.org.uk/s/search.html?query=cloud&collection=ico-meta&profile=_default accessed 12/4/2019.

[25] D. Palmer, "Cloud computing: Why a major cyber-attack could be as costly as a hurricane," 2018, https://www.zdnet.com/article/cloud-computing-why-a-major-cyber-attack-could-be-as-costly-as-a-hurricane/.

[26] SPA Future Thinking, "Report on Information Commissioner's Office Annual Track 2012/13," online, 11 2014, https://ico.org.uk.

[27] S. Barlyn, "Insurance giant Lloyd's of London: Global cyber attack could trigger $53 billion in losses the same as Hurricane Sandy," 2017, https://www.businessinsider.com/r-global-cyber-attack-could-spur-53-billion-in-losses-lloyds-of-london-2017-7 Jul. 17 Accessed 14/4/2019.

[28] Cloud Security Alliance, "The notorious nine–cloud computing top threats in 2013," 2013, https://downloads.cloudsecurityalliance.org/initiatives/top_threats/The_Notorious_Nine_Cloud_Computing_Top_Threats_in_2013.pdf Accessed 14/4/2019.

[29] B. Duncan, "FAST-CFP: Finding a Solution To The Cloud Forensic Problem," in *The Ninth International Conference on Cloud Computing, GRIDs, and Virtualization*. Barcelona: IARIA, 2018, p. 3.

[30] I. Ferguson, K. Renaud, and A. Irons, "Dark Clouds on the Horizon: The Challenge of Cloud Forensics," *Cloud Computing*, p. 61, 2018.

[31] McAfee, "Cloud adoption and risk report," 2019, https://www.skyhighnetworks.com/cloud-report/ Accessed 14/4/2019.

[32] J. Fruhlinger, "The Mirai botnet explained: How teen scammers and CCTV cameras almost brought down the internet," 2018, mAR 9 https://www.csoonline.com/article/3258748/security/the-mirai-botnet-explained-how-teen-scammers-and-cctv-cameras-almost-brought-down-the-internet.html Accessed 14/4/2019.

[33] M. Mimoso, "Windows Botnet Spreading Mirai Variant," 2017, https://threatpost.com/windows-botnet-spreading-mirai-variant/123805/ 21 February, Accessed 14/4/2019.

[34] E. Meelhuysen, "Danger within: Defending cloud environments against insider threats," 2018, https://www.cloudcomputing-news.net/news/2018/may/01/danger-within-defending-cloud-environments-against-insider-threats/ 1 May, Accessed 14/4/209.

[35] Datacenters.com, "Locations," https://www.datacenters.com/locations/aws Accessed 12/4/2019.

[36] C. O'Donoghue and E. Brooks, "UK: Security Challenges Arising Out Of The Convergence Of Internet Of Things And Cloud Computing," 2018, http://www.mondaq.com/uk/x/739914/Security/Security+Challenges+Arising+Out+Of+The+Convergence+Of+Internet+Of+Things+And+Cloud+Computing 26 Sept, Accessed 14/4/2019.

[37] PWC, "UK Information Security Breaches Survey - Technical Report 2012 accessed 14/4/2019," PWC, Tech. Rep. April, 2012.

[38] R. Keeney and H. Raiffa, *Decisions with multiple objectives - preferences and value*. Cambridge University Press, 1994, vol. 39, no. 2.

[39] B. Duncan, D. J. Pym, and M. Whittington, "Developing a Conceptual Framework for Cloud Security Assurance," in *Cloud Computing Technology and Science (CloudCom), 2013 IEEE 5th International Conference on (Volume 2)*. IEEE, 2013, pp. 120–125.

[40] A. Zellner, "Bayesian Estimation and Prediction Using Asymmetric Loss Functions," *Journal of the American Statistical Association*, vol. 81, no. 394, pp. 446–451, 1986.

[41] OWASP, "OWASP home page," 2017, https://www.owasp.org/index.php/Main_Page Accessed 14/4/2019.

EU General Data Protection Regulation Compliance Challenges for Cloud Users

Bob Duncan
Business School
University of Aberdeen, UK
Email: bobduncan@abdn.ac.uk

***Abstract*—The EU General Data Protection Regulation (GDPR) has been with us now since the 25th May 2018. It is certainly the case that in many of the 28 EU countries, regulators were not all properly resourced by the starting deadline. However, progress has been made since then. We review the challenges faced by cloud users, and consider whether all the compliance challenges existent then have persisted, and whether there are any other challenges that have evolved. We examine the most serious risks faced by cloud users and consider how users might mitigate their exposure to these hard problems. We provide a series of practical solutions which might help them to keep abreast with these issues while proper long term solutions can be found.**

***Keywords*-EU GDPR; Compliance; Cloud computing; cloud forensic problem; unresolved vulnerabilities.**

I. Introduction

It is certainly the case that the new EU General Data Protection Regulation (GDPR) [1], has some serious teeth, with maximum fine levels for each breach being the greater of €20million or 4% of global turnover. It is also the case that a number of cloud vulnerabilities are still unresolved, and are frequently exploited by attackers. This results in a potential nightmare scenario for cloud users where they are unable to ensure compliance with the regulation. In May last year, 17 out of 24 regulators polled in a Reuters survey [?], claimed they would not be ready in time for the new regulation. However, in addition, other jurisdictions are now taking a lead from the EU to implement regulations or legislation of their own.

In the US, the State of California introduced their own version of the EU GDPR within a month of it going live [2]. Currently, the White House is working on introducing stringent data protection legislation based on the model of the EU GDPR. It is likely to be only a matter of time before other jurisdictions follow suit. For global corporates in particular, this is likely to present a serious challenge to their ability to demonstrate compliance with these regulations and other legislation. Make no mistake, there is no doubt that these regulators have a serious intent, and there is little doubt that they will exercise their considerable powers to bring unwilling cloud users into line.

We start by looking at the most serious challenges highlighted by two cloud security organisations — the Cloud Security Alliance (CSA) [3], and the Open Web Application Security Project (OWASP) [4]. The CSA were set up specifically to examine cloud security issues. The OWASP project was initially set up to examine Web based vulnerabilities, but over time extended their remit to incorporate mobile, internet of things and cloud vulnerabilities as well. Both organisations collect data on vulnerabilities and make good suggestions to help mitigate these issues. Both issue a report every three years which brings attention to their understanding of the most serious vulnerabilities.

Achieving information security is a big challenge already for all companies who use conventional distributed network systems, but once cloud systems are involved, the challenge increases exponentially. This mainly arises due to the complexity that the many issues of additional relationships and agendas of different participant companies involved brings to cloud ecosystems. Much research has been carried out to attempt to resolve these problems e.g., [5]–[14].

One of the most challenging, and as yet, still not properly unresolved issue is the cloud forensic problem [15]. Many are aware of it, but no-one seems to be prepared to discuss it, let along try to properly resolve the problem. It is of course a technical problem to address, but that does not mean it can be left unresolved. Regulators will quite rightly expect some mitigating steps be taken to address the issue, rather than allowing companies to trust to luck.

If any company using cloud is unable to resolve the cloud forensic problem, we suggest this will present such a fundamental issue that it will be impossible for that company to comply with this new regulation. As far back as 2011 and in subsequent years [16]–[22], a great deal of research was focussed on trying to resolve this issue, yet it is clear from looking at regulatory fines for breaches that the message is not getting though.

In 2012, Verizon estimated that a total of 174 million data records were compromised [23]. Yahoo disclosed a 1 billion compromised account breach in the 2013 attacks, yet when Verizon took over Yahoo two years ago, it turned out that **ALL 3 billion accounts** had been compromised [24]. By 2017, records compromised had increased to an estimated 2 billion records lost or compromised in the first half of 2017 alone [25]. In the last year, it is estimated by Gemalto in their Breach Level Index, that over 4.5 billion data records were lost or stolen in the first half of 2018 [26], an increase of 133% on the same period in 2017. The current level of data records lost is running at 6.4 million records per day [27], of which only 4% were encrypted. It is clear that data breaches are continuing at an alarming rate. Of particular concern is the 96% of unencrypted records compromised being exposed.

In Section II, we look at the top cloud vulnerabilities identified by both the CSA and OWASP. In Section III, we look at what the Cloud Forensic Problem is, and address why it is such a challenging problem to overcome. In Section IV, we address the minimum requirements necessary to achieve compliance. In Section V, we look at whether this approach will ensure good security and privacy is possible. In Section VI, we consider future developments of this work, and in Section VII, we discuss our conclusions.

II. THE MOST SERIOUS CLOUD VULNERABILITIES

We start by looking at the most recent vulnerability list for the CSA and OWASP. Their most recent list was published in 2017, and is based on the most damaging vulnerabilities for the 2016 year. We can see the comparison in the Tables below.

TABLE I: CSA TOP 12 CLOUD VULNERABILITIES 2017 [28]

Priority	CSA Top 12 Vulnerabilities
1	Data Breaches
2	Insufficient Identity, Credential and Access Management
3	Insecure Interfaces and APIs
4	System Vulnerabilities
5	Account Hijacking
6	Malicious Insiders
7	Advanced Persistent Threats
8	Data Loss
9	Insufficient Due Diligence
10	Abuse and Nefarious Use of Cloud Services
11	Denial of Service
12	Shared Technology Vulnerabilities

TABLE II: OWASP TOP 10 CLOUD VULNERABILITIES 2017 [29]

Priority	OWASP Top 10 Vulnerabilities
1	Accountability & Data Risk
2	User Identity Federation
3	Regulatory Compliance
4	Business Continuity & Resilience
5	User Privacy & Secondary Usage of Data
6	Service & Data Integration
7	Multi-Tenancy & Physical Security
8	Incidence Analysis & Forensics Risk
9	Infrastructure Security
10	Non-Production Environment Exposure

It is clear that each has taken a completely different approach to the perceived vulnerabilities, thus expanding the range of the most important vulnerabilities to a total of 22. In the case of the CSA, they have take the approach of identifying the 12 most important technical challenges faced by cloud users. On the other hand, OWASP have completely changed their approach by shifting to the Behaviour Driven Development (BDD) process, which shifts the focus away from technical issues alone to encompass all the stakeholders in cloud and in particular the business procedural oriented aspects. They further develop this by taking a risk-based approach, and have identified the 10 most dangerous risks facing cloud users.

While technical challenges are vitally important to address, it is equally important to address the risks which address mostly the non-technical element of cloud use. When we realise that the business architecture of a company comprises a combination of people, process and technology [30], and not technology alone, we can start to see how combining these two different approaches will have value. However, we have only considered two aspects of the foundational triad of business architecture. We must also consider the impact of people challenges.

People have long proved to be a serious security weakness in organisations. It is clear that criminals have long realised that the easiest way to successfully attack any system is through the weakest link — and that is invariably always people. We list here some 16 extremely successful social engineering attacks. We must add a proviso that these attacks are not specific to cloud users only, but they are common indeed. In fact, social engineering became the most successful attack vector in 2015 [31].

TABLE III: 16 SUCCESSFUL SOCIAL ENGINEERING ATTACKS ©2019 Duncan

Attack Name	Attack Description
Phishing	These are the most common type of attacks leveraging social engineering techniques. Attackers use emails, social media, instant messaging, and SMS to trick victims into providing sensitive information or visiting a malicious URL in an attempt to compromise their systems.
Watering Hole	A "watering hole" attack consists of injecting malicious code into the public Web pages of a site that the targets are known to visit. Once a victim visits the page on the compromised website a backdoor trojan is installed on their computer
Whaling Attack	This is an extension of a Phishing attack, used to steal confidential information,personal data, access credentials to restricted services/resources and specifically information with relevant value from an economic and commercial perspective. This is targeted at executives of private companies and government agencies, hence the use of whaling to describe the "big fish"
Pretexting	This term describes the practice of pretending to be someone else, such as an external IT services operator in order to obtain private information.
Baiting & Quid Pro Quo Attacks	Baiting exploits the user's curiosity, with the promise of some good that the attacker uses to deceive the victim, often with a malicious file disguised as a 'security' update. The Quid Pro Quo or 'something for nothing' attack offers a service or benefit to the victim in exchange for information, or facilitation of an attack
Tailgating	This is where an attacker gains physical entry to a restricted area in contravention of security policy by walking through behind an authorised person when they enter a secure area
Deceptive Phishing	Arises when attackers attempt to replicate a legitimate company email account to elicit information from the victim
Spear Phishing	These attacks are specially tailored for a single victim using knowledge obtained from social media profiles and other public sources of information, exposing the victim to identity theft, malware, credit card fraud and even blackmail
Whaling / CEO Fraud	In this attack, victims are asked to provide information or to authorise payment urgently at the behest of the CEO
Vishing	This is where an attack is perpetrated by Voice over IP (VoIP). Becasue the VoIP server can be made to look like anything, it can appear that the call is coming from an important outside entity such as a bank or the Inland Revenue
SMiSHing	This attack purports to come via SMS, and asks the victim to respond by clicking on a malicious link, or calling the attacker's phone, who then tries to extract information
W2 Phishing	This is where the attacker pretends to be a senior executive or an external service like the Inland Revenue in order to obtain personal information such as NI numbers
Pharming	This is more sophisticated than Phishing, whereby the attacker used cache poisoning to purport to come from an official web site.
Ransomware Phishing	This Phishing variant contains a link to download malware usually in the form of ransomware
Dropbox Phishing	This Phishing variant purports to come from Dropbox and seeks to obtain private files and photos usually leading to blackmail
Google Docs Phishing	This variant of Phishing spoofs the Google Docs login page and seeks to collect the victim's userid and password

These attacks are particularly well crafted and have proved to be exceptionally successful in tricking victims into giving up sensitive information, passwords and so on. Often, they look every bit as good as official communications, despite the fact that sometimes they are poorly constructed, or use poor English grammar and spelling. While it is fair to say that the social engineering attacks equally relate to non-cloud environments, nevertheless, they still present a serious challenge to the cloud environment.

Now, we can see that it is clear that not only is the business architecture of any company comprised of a combination of people, process and technology, but so too are attacks crafted to attack each of these sectors.

III. The Cloud Forensic Problem (and Why it is Such a Hard Problem)

While all computing systems are constantly under attack, this can present a far more serious issue for users of cloud systems. Once an attacker gains a foothold in a cloud system and becomes an intruder, there is little to prevent the intruder from helping themselves to any amount of data, especially that which is covered by the GDPR, either by viewing it, modifying it, deleting it or ex-filtrating it from the victim system [32]–[34]. Worse, should the intruder gain sufficient privileges, they are then able to completely delete all trace of their incursion, perhaps deleting far more records than they need to in the process, leading to further problems for business continuity.

After the intruder has removed every trace of the intrusion, the forensic trail will have little left to follow, which means many companies will be totally unaware that the intrusion has taken place, let alone understand what records have been accessed, modified, deleted or stolen. This leads to a serious issue for companies who believe they have retained a full forensic trail in their running instance. They frequently fail to realise that without special measures being taken to save these records off-site [8], everything will vanish when the instance is shut down, often by the intruder. In such a case, there will be no mitigating factor that the company can use, rendering them liable to the full force of the penalties under the regulation.

In any cloud based system, there is a need to ensure a complete and intact audit trail is stored off cloud in order for the breached organisation to be able to tell which records have been accessed, modified, deleted or stolen. Otherwise, if the audit trail and all forensic records have been deleted, there will be no physical means for any organisation to be able to tell which records have been accessed, modified, deleted or stolen, putting these organisations immediately in multiple breaches of the GDPR. This will also pose a serious impediment to using business continuity plans for recovery.

Thus, in addition to the 38 attacks discussed in the previous section, we must now add this difficult challenge to the list.

IV. What do we Need to do to Achieve Compliance with the GDPR?

Simply address the above 39 points and we will be compliant, yes? Sadly, the reality is that those actions alone will not guarantee compliance, and we will explain the reason in the following subsections.

A. Cloud Security Alliance

It is not as simple as dealing with our 39 identified vulnerabilities. If we start with the CSA top 12 vulnerabilities, this represents just the 12 most damaging vulnerabilities. The CSA maintains a full list of all known cloud vulnerabilities, which is known as the Common Vulnerabilities and Exposures (CVE) list [35]. The list comprises all known vulnerabilities which are, or are expected to become public. The CVE Numbering Authority (CNA) [36], assigns all such identified CVEs with a unique number, which are then published in the MITRE CVE database [37]. Workarounds and fixes, as they are developed, are associated with the appropriate CVE number.

This list also feeds the National Vulnerability Database (NVD) [38], which was launched by the National Institute of Standards and Technology (NIST) [39], in 2005. NIST provide a range of enhanced information about each vulnerability including such information as fix information, severity scores and impact ratings. The NVD also offers this information by Operating System (OS); by vendor name; product name, and/or version number; as well as by vulnerability type, severity, related exploit range and impact. NIST also offer the Common Vulnerability Scoring System (CVSS) [40]. The first version, released in 2005, following feedback was updated to V2 in 2007, and following further feedback was updated to V3 in 2015.

The following website provides a list of 12 free online tools to test your website to scan for website security vulnerabilities and malware.

TABLE IV: 12 FREE TEST SITES FOR CSA VULNERABILITIES [41]

No	Site Address
1	Scan My Server
2	Sucuri
3	Qualys SSL Labs, Qualys FreeScan
4	Quttera
5	Detectify
6	SiteGuarding
7	Web Inspector
8	Acunetix
9	Netsparker Cloud
10	UpGuard Web Scan
11	Tinfoil Security
12	Observatory

B. The Open Web Application Security Project

Likewise for the OWASP issues. These represent only the top 10 issues. OWASP also provide suggestions to address or mitigate each issue.

There is also another organisation, WAVSEC [42], who have compiled a list of 51 companies who provide both proprietary and open access tools to test your website for OWASP and other vulnerabilities.

C. Social Engineering

Since social engineering attacks are attacks on people, there are no software tools available to test for the presence of such attacks on any system, making the job of defence rather more challenging. It is therefore necessary to ensure that companies keep on top of the ever increasing range of new attacks being developed, so that proper training can be made available for every single employee in the company. It will also be important to ensure that adequate training is provided to ensure that actors who are not employees of the company, such as suppliers, customers and others are made aware of the dangers surrounding these attacks. Additional security provisions and monitoring may be necessary to ensure a higher level of protection is available.

D. The Cloud Forensic Problem

We have seen that to do nothing would not be a viable option as far as GDPR compliance is concerned. Attacks will continue unabated. We must therefore be prepared and armed with whatever tools we can develop to ensure we achieve as high a level of compliance as we possibly can. For a pragmatic approach to helping resolve this problem Duncan and Whittington [43], make some practical suggestions to mitigate this potential problem.

We therefore need to consider what the absolute minimum technical requirement might be to attain our objective of GDPR compliance. We know that under the GDPR the organisation must be able to:

- provide a Right of Access (under Article 15) to personal data by data subject, if requested;
- provide the means to comply with a Right to Erasure (under Article 17) by data subject, subject to the appropriate grounds being met;
- provide privacy by design;
- in the event of a data breach, report the breach to the Supervisory Authority within 72 hours after having become aware of the data breach (Article 33). The breach must also be reported to the controller without undue delay after becoming aware of a personal data breach;
- in the event of a data breach, notify the data subject if adverse impact is determined (under Article 34), unless the data was encrypted;

To meet the first requirement, we must ensure the provenance and veracity of the contents of the database. For the second requirement, if appropriate, the same provision would apply.

For the third requirement, the cloud system must be designed in accordance with the recommendations of the Article 29 Working Party [44], which suggests the reports produced by ENISA should be followed. This report [45], specifies that encryption and decryption operations must be carried out locally, not by remote service, because both keys and data must remain in the power of the data owner if any privacy is to be achieved. Furthermore, it specifies that outsourced data storage on remote clouds is practical and relatively safe, as long as only the data owner, not the cloud service, holds the decryption keys. ENISA have also produced a stream of other relevant reports, including a Cloud Risk report in 2009 [46], and recommendations for certification in 2017 [47].

For the fourth requirement, we would require to ensure the provenance and veracity of the contents of the database. For the fifth requirement, where the data is not yet encrypted, the same provision would also apply. However, it should be stressed that it will always be preferable to ensure data is encrypted before it leaves the control of the data owner.

It is clear that where no steps have been taken to ensure the cloud forensic problem has been mitigated, the organisation will fail on every count. Thus, as a minimum, we need to ensure the following steps are taken:

- all personal data should be encrypted, and this should be performed locally;
- the encryption and decryption keys should not be maintained on the cloud instance;
- a full audit trail of the entire database must be maintained off-site;
- full forensic records of all users having accessed the database and carried out any commands on the database must be collected and stored off-site.

V. Will this Approach Provide Good Security and Privacy?

The business architecture of a company comprises a combination of people, process and technology [30], not technology alone. As we have seen in Section III, all three aspects of the business architecture are subject to attack. We saw how social engineering attacks in Table III, could be used effectively against people in the business. From the OWASP weaknesses list in Table II, we see how effectively processes can be attacked, and from the technical attacks in Table I, how a wide range of effective attacks can be perpetrated agains the technological systems of the company.

We must, of course, understand that we cannot simply address each of the three areas in isolation, but must instead be prepared to consider the possibility that an attack could end up compromising the company more easily through combining attacks from two or more of the three sectors to develop an even more effective attack.

Thus, we must take a multi-pronged approach to keeping our cloud systems secure:

- People
  - Keep abreast of evolving social engineering attacks
  - Train the people in the organisation regularly to recognise these attacks and deal with them properly
- Process
  - All processes must be properly documented and kept up to date
  - All processes must be checked for potential vulnerabilities
- Technology
  - Test continually for vulnerabilities
  - Monitor constantly
  - Analyse logs regularly
  - Constantly review for new evolving vulnerabilities and exploits
- Cloud Forensic Problem
  - Encrypt all data
  - Ensure data is backed up off-cloud
  - Ensure encryption/decryption keys are stored off-cloud

In addition, we should regularly check all systems to ensure no new vulnerabilities or weaknesses have appeared. We should regularly check for evolving threats and take appropriate mitigatory action. We should perform continuous monitoring and analytics on all systems to ensure they are as up to date and secure as possible. Adding an Intrusion Detection System (IDS) and an Intrusion Prevention System (IPS) would also be a prudent measure to take.

There are two essential tasks that must be performed to ensure the effectiveness of this approach. Persistent storage in the running cloud instance cannot retain data beyond its currently running lifetime [8], so we need to ensure that all necessary logs and data is stored securely elsewhere. Also, since the default settings for the majority of all database software involves logging being turned off by default [32], it is essential that we turn it on in all running cloud instances, with the data being stored securely elsewhere.

All of these measures will give us a much higher chance of achieving a good level of security and privacy, as well as the means to deliver a compliant system from the point of legislative and regulatory requirements.

VI. Future Work

We need to understand what data we require to keep. To meet our legislative and regulatory compliance requirements, we need to understand the 5 W's — namely: Who is accessing our system? Where have they come from? What are they looking for? When is this happening? From this data, we should be able to infer the Why? Are they authorised to be in the system, to enter the system the way they have, to look at the data they are trying to access, and at the time they are trying to access it? Deducing the Why can give an indicator of anomalous behaviour.

We plan to construct a working model based on the ideas outlined in this paper with which to test this solution over the next 6 months, which will allow us to confirm how well it might work in the real world. It is not overly complicated to be able to do this, which means even the smallest business would have the means to ensure proper compliance can be achieved.

VII. Conclusion

As each of the EU countries gets their regulators properly in place and responding to breaches, and as their expertise starts to grow, there is no doubt that the level of fines will start to grow.

Once serious fines start to be levied, it is likely that many companies will start to get the message, and will finally wake up to the seriousness of this particular regulation. The forthcoming GDPR fines will certainly get some serious attention. In this paper, we have considered whether it is possible to achieve regulatory compliance where any organisation is using cloud computing. It is clear that without suitable precautions being put in place, the answer is a resounding "No!".

We have outlined the key requirements from the GDPR to which all organisations falling under its jurisdiction must comply. We have identified the currently unresolved "Cloud Forensic Problem" as presenting the largest obstacle to achieving compliance. We have proposed how this challenging problem may be approached to ensure that cloud users can be fully compliant with this new regulation, with little more than being sensibly organised. Clearly, additional cost will require to be incurred, and there may be a small impact on latency, but these costs could significantly mitigate the possibility of a huge regulatory fine in the event of a breach. It is also likely that this approach will ensure faster discovery of the occurrence of a breach, thus minimising the potential impact on business continuity.

References

[1] EU, "EU General Data Protection Regulation (GDPR)," 2017. [Online]. Available: http://www.eugdpr.org/ [Retrieved: March 2019]

[2] Reuters, European Regulators, 2018. [Online]. Available: https://www.reuters.com/article/us-europe-privacy-analysis/european-regulators-were-not-ready-for-new-privacy-law-idUSKBN1I915X. [Retrieved: March 2019]

[3] California, "The California Consumer Privacy Act of 2018." [Online]. Available: https://www.caprivacy.org/ [Retrieved: March 2019]

[4] CSA, "Cloud Security Alliance," 2019. [Online]. Available: https://cloudsecurityalliance.org/ [Retrieved: March 2019]

[5] OWASP, "Open Web Application Security Project," 2019. [Online]. Available: https://www.owasp.org/index.php/OWASP_Cloud_Security_Project [Retrieved: March 2019]

[6] M. Felici, "Cyber Security and Privacy: Trust in the Digital World and Cyber Security and Privacy EU Forum 2013 Brussels, Belgium, April 18-19, 2013 Revised Selected Papers," in Commun. Comput. Inf. Sci. Springer International Publishing, 2013, vol. 182 CCIS, pp. 77–88.

[7] Y. Y. Haimes, B. M. Horowitz, Z. Guo, E. Andrijcic, and J. Bogdanor, "Assessing systemic risk to cloud-computing technology as complex interconnected systems of systems," Syst. Eng., vol. 18, no. 3, 2015, pp. 284–299.

[8] C. Millard, I. Walden, and W. K. Hon, "Who is Responsible for 'Personal Data' in Cloud Computing? The Cloud of Unknowing, Part 2," Leg. Stud., vol. 27, no. 77, 2012, pp. 1–31.

[9] R. K. L. Ko, P. et al., "TrustCloud: A framework for accountability and trust in cloud computing," Proc. - 2011 IEEE World Congr. Serv. Serv. 2011, 2011, pp. 584–588.

[10] R. K. L. Ko, B. S. Lee, and S. Pearson, "Towards achieving accountability, auditability and trust in cloud computing," Commun. Comput. Inf. Sci., vol. 193 CCIS, no. PART 4, 2011, pp. 432–444.

[11] N. Papanikolaou, S. Pearson, and M. C. Mont, "Towards Natural-Language Understanding and Automated Enforcement of Privacy Rules and Regulations in the Cloud: Survey and Bibliography," Analysis, 2011, pp. 1–9. [Online]. Available: http://www.springerlink.com/index/T63266U4407458T5.pdf [Retrieved: March 2019]

[12] S. Pearson, "Taking account of privacy when designing cloud computing services," Proc. 2009 ICSE Work. Softw. Eng. Challenges Cloud Comput. CLOUD 2009, 2009, pp. 44–52.

[13] S. Pearson, "Towards Accountability in the Cloud," IEEE Internet Comput., vol. 15, no. 4, jul 2011, pp. 64–69.

[14] D. Pym and M. Sadler, "Information Stewardship in Cloud Computing," Int. J. Serv. Sci. Manag. Eng. Technol., vol. 1, no. 1, 2010, pp. 50–67.

[15] T. Takahashi, Y. Kadobayashi, and H. Fujiwara, "Ontological Approach toward Cybersecurity in Cloud Computing Categories and Subject Descriptors," in Sci. Technol., 2010, pp. 100–109.

[16] B. Duncan, M. Whittington, and V. Chang, "Enterprise security and privacy: Why adding IoT and big data makes it so much more difficult," in Proc. 2017 Int. Conf. Eng. Technol. ICET 2017, vol. 2018-Janua, 2018.

[17] K.-K. Choo and A. Dehghantanha, "Contemporary Digital Forensics Investigations of Cloud and Mobile Applications," in Contemp. Digit. Forensic Investig. Cloud Mob. Appl. Elsevier, 2017, pp. 1–6.

[18] N. Papanikolaou, S. Pearson, M. C. Mont, and R. Ko, "A Toolkit for Automating Compliance in Cloud Computing Services," Int. J. Cloud Comput., vol. x, no. x, 2014, pp. 45–68.

[19] K. Ruan, J. James, J. Carthy, and T. Kechadi, "Key terms for service level agreements to support cloud forensics," in IFIP Adv. Inf. Commun. Technol., 2012, vol. 383 AICT, pp. 201–212.

[20] K. Ruan, J. Carthy, T. Kechadi, and I. Baggili, "Cloud forensics definitions and critical criteria for cloud forensic capability: An overview of survey results," Digit. Investig., vol. 10, no. 1, 2013, pp. 34–43.

[21] J. Singh and J. M. Bacon, "On middleware for emerging health services," J. Internet Serv. Appl., vol. 5, no. 1, 2014, p. 6.

[22] J. Singh, J. Bacon, and D. Eyers, "Policy Enforcement Within Emerging Distributed, Event-based Systems," Proc. 8th ACM Int. Conf. Distrib. Event-Based Syst. - DEBS '14, 2014, pp. 246–255.

[23] J. Singh, J. Powles, T. Pasquier, and J. Bacon, "Data Flow Management and Compliance in Cloud Computing," Cloud Comput., no. Special Issue on Legal Clouds., 2015, pp. 1–12.

[24] Verizon, "2012 Data Breach Investigations Report," Verizon, Tech. Rep., 2012. [Online]. Available: https://www.wired.com/images_blogs/threatlevel/2012/03/Verizon-Data-Breach-Report-2012.pdf [Retrieved:March 2019]

[25] S. Khandelwal, "Its 3 Billion! Yes, Every Single Yahoo Account Was Hacked In 2013 Data Breach," 2017. [Online]. Available: https://thehackernews.com/2017/10/yahoo-email-hacked.html [Retrieved: March 2019]

[26] Verizon, "Verizon Security Breach Report 2017," Tech. Rep., 2017.

[27] GDPR.Report, "Gemalto Breach Level Index data records lost or stolen in the first half of 2018," 2018. [Online]. Available: https://gdpr.report/news/2018/10/09/data-breaches-compromised-4-5-billion-records-in-first-half-of-2018/ [Retrieved: March 2019]

[28] Gemalto, "Data Breach Statistics," 2019. [Online]. Available: https://breachlevelindex.com/ [Retrieved: March 2019]

[29] CSA, "CSA Top 12 Cloud Vulnerabilities," Tech. Rep., 2017.

[30] OWASP, "OWASP Top 10 Web Application Security Risks for 2017," 2017. [Online]. Available: https://https//www.owasp.org/index.php/Top_10-2017_Top_10 [Retrieved: March 2019]

[31] PWC, "UK Information Security Breaches Survey - Technical Report 2012," London, Tech. Rep. April, 2012. [Online]. Available: www.pwc.com www.bis.gov.uk [Retrieved: March 2019]

[32] W. Ashford, "Social engineering confirmed as top information security threat in 2015," 2015. [Online]. Available: https://www.computerweekly.com/news/4500273577/Social-engineering-confirmed-as-top-information-security-threat [Retrieved: March 2019]

[33] B. Duncan and M. Whittington, "Enhancing Cloud Security and Privacy: The Power and the Weakness of the Audit Trail," in Cloud Comput. 2016 Seventh Int. Conf. Cloud Comput. GRIDs, Virtualization, no. April. Rome: IEEE, 2016, pp. 125–130.

[34] G. Weir, A. Aßmuth, M. Whittington, and B. Duncan, "Cloud Accounting Systems, the Audit Trail, Forensics and the EU GDPR: How Hard Can It Be?" in Br. Account. Financ. Assoc. Scottish Area Gr. Annu. Conf.relax Aberdeen: BAFA, 2017, p. 6.

[35] P. Tobin, M. McKeever, J. Blackledge, M. Whittington, and B. Duncan, "UK Financial Institutions Stand to Lose Billions in GDPR Fines: How can They Mitigate This?" in Br. Account. Financ. Assoc. Scottish Area Gr. Annu. Conf., BAFA, Ed., Aberdeen, 2017, p. 6.

[36] CSA, "Common Vulnerability and Exposure List," 2018. [Online]. Available: https://cve.mitre.org/cve/ [Retrieved: March 2019]

[37] CSA, "CVE Numbering Authorities," 2019. [Online]. Available: https://cve.mitre.org/cve/cna.html [Retrieved: March 2019]

[38] Mitre, "CVE Database," 2019. [Online]. Available: https://cve.mitre.org/ [Retrieved: March 2019]

[39] NIST, "National Vulnerability Database," 2019. [Online]. Available: https://nvd.nist.gov/ [Retrieved: March 2019]

[40] NIST, "NAtional Institute of Standards and Technology," 2019. [Online]. Available: https://www.nist.gov/ [Retrieved: March 2019]

[41] NIST, "Common Vulnerability Scoring System (CVSS)," 2019. [Online]. Available: https://www.nist.gov/publications/common-vulnerability-scoring-system-cvss

[42] C. Kumar, "12 Online Free Tools to Scan Website Security Vulnerabilities & Malware," 2019. [Online]. Available: https://geekflare.com/online-scan-website-security-vulnerabilities/ [Retrieved: March 2019]

[43] WAVSEC, "Evaluation of Web Application Vulnerability Scanners in Modern Pentest/SSDLC Usage Scenarios," 2018. [Online]. Available: http://sectooladdict.blogspot.com/ [Retrieved: March 2019]

[44] B. Duncan and M. Whittington, "The Complexities of Auditing and Securing Systems in the Cloud is there a Solution and will the GDPR move it up the Corporate Agenda?" Int. J. Adv. Secur., vol. 11, no. 3&4, 2018, pp. 232–242.

[45] D. M. Thompson, D. B. Ligon, J. C. Patton, and M. Pape, "Effects of life-history requirements on the distribution of a threatened reptile," 2017. [Online]. Available: http://eur-lex.europa.eu/LexUriServ/LexUriServ.do?uri=SWD:2012:0271:FIN:EN:PDF [Retrieved: March 2019]

[46] ENISA, "Article 4 Technical Report," ENISA, Tech. Rep., 2011.

[47] ENISA, "Cloud Risk," ENISA, Tech. Rep., 2009. [Online]. Available: https://www.enisa.europa.eu/publications/cloud-computing-risk-assessment [Retrieved: March 2019]

[48] ENISA, "Recommendations on European Data Protection Certification," Tech. Rep., 2017.

Cloud Compliance Risks

Bob Duncan*, Yuan Zhao†
Business School
University of Aberdeen, UK
Emails: *robert.duncan@abdn.ac.uk, †y.zhao@abdn.ac.uk

***Abstract*—In the current business climate, there is an ever growing need for companies to comply with a range of legislation, regulation and standards. There is also a need for companies to be transparent in demonstrating that they are in compliance and due to the nature of certain cloud weaknesses, this can prove to be problematic. Given the potential magnitude of fines for non-compliance, there is a strong incentive for companies to be able to clearly demonstrate full compliance. In this paper, we investigate what these challenges are, and suggest a means to resolve these issues so that cloud users stand a better chance of achieving compliance and reducing the risk of exposure to huge fines.**

Keywords–Risk management; Cloud vulnerabilities; GDPR compliance.

I. INTRODUCTION

It is very much the case today that all computing systems are continuously under attack. Due to the multi-tenancy nature of cloud computing, this presents additional challenges with respect to achieving a good level of security and privacy for all cloud users. Of course this is not the only challenge they face. Over and above the need to achieve and maintain a high level of security and privacy for good business reasons, there is an additional requirement that most are subject to. That requirement stems from the need to be transparent to a range of legislative, regulatory and standards bodies, depending on the industry in which they operate. This requirement is usually satisfied by achieving compliance with the legislation and regulatory rules they must comply with in order to provide assurance to the relevant regulators.

We have seen some change in these areas over recent years. For example, with the ISO Security Standards in the ISO 27000 series, they have quietly been effecting a shift away from the old "Plan, Do, Check, Act" approach to a new risk based approach. This seeks to better understand the risks faced by users wishing to adopt the standards in order to ensure they adopt the right mitigatory approaches, or at least understand better the risks they face and are prepared to accept. The Cloud Security Alliance (CSA) has long being identifying and recording all cloud vulnerabilities and has been recommending technical solutions, but now also provide an identification of both the risk faced, as well as the potential impact that a breach might have on the company.

Regulatory authorities have been evolving in the range and scope of regulations being implemented across the globe, and the new EU General Data Protection Regulation (GDPR), which became live on 26 May 2018, now has some serious teeth to ensure compliance by all companies who fall under its scope.

There are already a huge range of legislative Acts, which have been passed across the globe in different jurisdictions to try to safeguard shareholders and other stakeholders from the effects of losses arising from poor security. While many of these are outdated when considering their effectiveness against cloud issues, there is no doubt that many are going through an updating process, and there are many more new pieces of legislation in the pipeline. Many governments are reactive, rather than proactive, so are often running behind the evolution of technology.

In Section II, we consider a number of legislative, regulatory and standards compliance requirements to provide a flavour of the scale of the problem faced by cloud users, while in Section III, we consider what kind of challenges are faced by cloud users when seeking to achieve compliance with these requirements. In Section IV, we consider how to address these challenges, and how best to attempt to mitigate the substantial risks cloud users face. In Section V, we discuss our findings, and in Section VI, presents our conclusions.

II. COMPLIANCE REQUIREMENTS (LEGISLATION, REGULATION, STANDARDS)

Legislation, Regulation and Standards — are they not all the same? The answer to that is no, they are not. We will use the UK to illustrate the differences. Legislation comes from Acts of Parliament, which are passed by Government to ensure behaviour across society as a whole is controlled on pain of penalty, to ensure the country is run properly and that all citizens and companies behave in an appropriate manner.

Legislation can include criminal proceedings for the worst cases, which can include large fines and even jail sentences. This can cover the behaviour of citizens, companies, indeed even other countries who might have belligerent intent. There will also be legislation to organise how government will perform certain duties, such as the Taxes Acts, which are regularly updated to reflect the changing resource needs of the country as a whole. Compliance is mandatory under force of law.

Regulation has long been used for the control of regulated industries, such as accounting and audit, advertising, agriculture, charities, competition and markets authority, direct marketing authority, education, engineering council, environment agencies, equality and human rights commission, film classification, financial industries, including banks, insurance, investments and so on, food production, forensic science, fundraising, gambling commission, gaming board, gangmasters licensing authority, health, information commissioners office, legal system, other professional organisations, planning inspectorate, press regulation, Scottish housing regulator, security industry authority, social care, transport, such as air, rail, road and sea transportation and, utilities, such as power generation, petroleum, oil and gas, water and sewage industries.

For each of these industries, regulators were appointed under statute to oversee the industry, and were granted certain powers to ensure each industry behaved in an appropriate way. Some had very little power, relying instead on companies "doing the right thing" rather than using enforcement. Of course in many cases it became necessary to have additional powers to ensure proper compliance with the regulations in place. Sometimes the regulator can only suggest a course of action, sometimes they have the right to levy sanctions and fines, and in worst cases, can withdraw the license for the company to operate within that regulated industry. Compliance is mandatory under the terms of the regulations, which are implemented under the guidance of the regulator.

Standard setting has been around a very long time. It is intended to provide a blueprint for, in this case, companies to carry out processes and activities to a common standard agreed by all to adhere to. Compliance is nowadays a voluntary process. The incentive for companies to adhere to common standards is that where large companies are compliant, there is a knock on impact to the supply chain, which encourages them to be compliant in order to gain business contracts from the larger companies. The gain for the larger companies is that they can trade easily with their peers, and where smaller companies in the supply chain are also compliant, the large compliant company gains better comfort in doing business with the smaller companies, leading to a win win situation for all who become compliant. This is usually also good news for the customer, since such compliant companies usually always perform to a much higher standard than those who are not compliant.

There is also the possibility of compliance being required with industry best practice. Some industries have set up their own body to conduct research into providing 'best practice' guidelines for all industry members. In this way, the industry can be seen to be transparent in its approach to ensuring all industry body members adhere to high standards of behaviour.

For some companies, this means they will face a raft of compliance requirements across a broad range of legislation, regulation, standards and best practice requirements. This means they will require to implement a means of tracking their compliance with each measure. This will be an ongoing requirement.

Of course, all these compliance challenges will not only be restricted to business issues relating to the industry within which they operate. Nowadays, there is a huge increase of compliance requirements arising from business use of computer systems, and in particular the storing of sensitive information, or data.

If we consider the security and privacy of data, then compliance in the UK would be required with the Data Protection Act, the EU GDPR, and possibly the ISO/IEC 27000 series of standards, and perhaps even industry standards, such as the PCI/DSS industry standard for online payment systems.

Compliance with each will be mandatory. Penalties for non-compliance can be significant. In a recent breach of privacy, the Information Commissioners Office (ICO) — the regulatory body for the UK, fined Newham Council in London £145,000 for a privacy breach of a small amount of data on 203 individuals whose un-redacted data records, collected by the Metropolitan Police legally in their fight against crime, was distributed by the council to 44 groups in contravention of the Data Protection Act . The French GDPR regulator recently fined Google $57 million for lack of transparency on giving clear instructions to new users on what they are signing up for.

The impact of a compliance breach of the ISO/IEC 27000 series will be more subtle. If compliance cannot be maintained, then the company may not use the ISO/IEC 27000 compliance logo on all their stationary and websites. The impact from this will be that other ISO/IEC 27000 compliant companies, will be less inclined to trade with such a company, which could result in the loss of significant revenues over time. A breach of say the PCI/DSS industry standard could in a worst case result in that company having the ability to accept payment cards to collect cash from customers withdrawn, resulting in a potential adverse impact on cash flow.

III. Cloud Compliance Challenges

Computer systems are continuously under attack, and cloud systems are no exception. No computer system is immune to attack, and that is certainly the case for cloud systems. During the past decade, a great many research papers, such as [1]–[14], have made many suggestions, which have improved the level of security and privacy offered in cloud systems. Despite these efforts, no complete solutions have yet been found to resolve the cloud forensic problem.

After an attacker breaches a cloud system, gaining even a small foothold, and becoming an intruder, their next task is usually to try to escalate privileges until they can access and modify, or delete, the forensic log trail to hide all trace of their incursion into the system. This gives them the means to dig deep in order to retain a long term foothold within the system, which allows them to help themselves to whatever data they wish over time. Their primary goal is to achieve this as quickly as they possibly can. They are often able to achieve this task within a very short time frame. This presents a major compliance challenge.

These attackers and intruders are often aided by the lack of scrutiny of server logs evident in many corporate systems. Often, companies neither retain records of which database records have been accessed, nor by whom. This means that once breached, the company will no longer have the ability to understand which records have been accessed, copied, modified, deleted or ex-filtrated from the system, meaning they will be unable to report this incursion to the necessary people or authorities. This will result in an immediate state of non-compliance with the GDPR, resulting in a potential exposure to sanctions or fines. In order to achieve compliance with the GDPR, companies must be able to report a breach within 72 hours of discovery.

Globally, the average time for all companies between breach and discovery in 2012 was an average of 6 months [15] [16]. This had improved to some 4 weeks by 2016 [17] — still far short of what is needed to understand what has been going on with the intruders while they were undiscovered. However, because the EU changed the requirement to report from within 72 hours of breach arising, to within 72 hours of discovery of the breach, companies stopped trying so hard, resulting in time between breach and discovery in 2017 returning to almost as high as 2012 levels, at just under 6 months [18]. This relaxation misses the point that the longer an intruder remains in a system undetected, the more damage or harm they can cause. Considering the fact that encryption is not a requirement of the GDPR, then in a case where a company chooses not to encrypt, the damage caused by undetected mass leakage will very much mean there will be little leeway to claim mitigation when it comes to the eventual inevitable fine by the regulator.

When a company uses cloud, and particularly, where any Internet of Things (IoT) use is included, this raises the question as to just how feasible compliance might really be. Compliance within such a tight time schedule could be all but impossible. Where a company using cloud is breached, and particularly where no special arrangements to ensure the safety of forensic and audit trail data has been made, the 72 hour deadline is moot. With no means of knowing that the company has been breached, there will be nothing to report, exposing the company to huge potential fines. Naturally, ignorance of the fact that a breach has arisen will not be accepted as a mitigatory factor. Once discovery eventually does occur, usually through third party sources, there will be no prospect of ever finding out precisely which records have been compromised, as once they are gone, the forensic and audit trails are gone forever.

In the case where a company uses IoT devices, this can present additional security issues. Most IoT devices are cheaply made, with minimal resources, and frequently with insufficient or no security. The biggest issue is not really the loss of the IoT device data, rather it is the fact that a skilled intruder can easily leverage these compromised devices to gain access to other more sensitive systems. Bear in mind that the Mirai virus started as a simple attack on individual IoT devices, which progressed to seeking out and leveraging other higher powered devices at scale to perpetrate massive Distributed Denial of Service (DDoS) attacks, and from there, once Mirai had been ported to be able to attack Windows machines, to then penetrate sensitive PC networks. Thus, any company utilising IoT devices will have a range of additional compliance risks to face. We do not specifically address the IoT issues here, but recognise that any company using any IoT devices must take special measures to ensure GDPR compliance can be achieved.

Of course, there are additional vulnerabilities to consider. The business architecture of a company comprises a combination of people, process and technology [15], not technology alone. It will be no surprise to learn that attackers have developed approaches to attack each of these three elements of the business architecture. People attacks are generally undertaken through social engineering attacks, which while often relatively simple to perpetrate, are frequently very successful. Attacks on business processes have become more of a problem, and this has been recognised by the Open Web Application Security Project (OWASP) [19]. They regularly identify weaknesses in web based systems, mobile systems, cloud systems and IoT systems. They recommend techniques to mitigate these weaknesses. Naturally, there are a great many attacks perpetrated on the technology of businesses, and the Cloud Security Alliance (CSA) [20] also maintain a full list of these attacks, what to do to mitigate them, what the likely impact might be and thus, how serious the effect on the company.

Every company that does not take special measures to safeguard their forensic and audit trail data will be at much greater risk of becoming non-compliant, thus exposing them to the inevitable breach occurring, leading to the possibility of huge fines. Their ability to discover that a breach has occurred, will be very slim indeed. In the event that they do discover the breach, they would struggle to understand what they need to report. This is very likely to be a factor in raising the level of the fine to which they would be liable.

There is no doubt that the longer an intruder remains hidden inside a company system, the more damage they are likely to be able to carry out. Where the company is unable to discover the breach within 72 hours of occurrence, it is highly unlikely that they will ever be in a position to discover the breach, let alone understand which records have been compromised. With no forensic or audit trails to follow, it will be completely impossible to determine what to report. However, as will inevitably happen, the breach becomes public knowledge, at which point, the regulator will become involved. If it can be shown that the company was negligent in its approach to safeguarding this Personally Identifiable Information (PII) of data subjects, the penalties will doubtless be significant. There is no requirement specified in the GDPR to encrypt data. However, there is certainly a very strong recommendation that this should happen, and within a reasonable time. The regulation also suggests that encryption and decryption keys should not be stored on the cloud instance. Failure to implement encryption properly will certainly lead to stiffer fines in the event of a breach.

Thus, we need to consider addressing the following risk areas:

- Credit Risk
- Liquidity Risk
- Market Risk
- Operational Risk
    - Cloud Operational Risk
    - Cloud Forensic Problem Risk
    - IoT Operational Risk
    - Monitoring Failure Risk
    - No Encryption Risk
    - Business Architecture Risk
        - People Risk
        - Process Risk
        - Technology Risk

Thus, in the next section, we shall take a look at how cloud users should address these risks, and will consider whether this will be adequate for cloud compliance with the GDPR.

IV. How to Address and Mitigate Cloud Compliance Risks

Taking a risk based approach is an excellent way to identify potential exposure to risks. This requires the proper identification of the risks faced by the business, the probability of the risk materialising, the cost of mitigation against the financial impact should the risk materialise. Identifying and recognising all the relevant areas of potential exposure is the first step in the process. Companies do not necessarily have to mitigate every risk, as they might choose to accept any risk if they believe the have the appetite to do so. We can see that there will now be a considerable number of categories of risk to address. We will consider each in turn, with our suggestions on what should be done to ensure compliance.

1 Credit Risk Credit risk is more frequently an issue in financial institutions where banks, for example, lend money to companies and individuals. Credit risk is the risk that the borrower will default on their payment. However, all companies provide lending to their customers in the form of trade accounts, which offer credit terms, with many using cloud based accounting systems, and this can add an additional element of risk to the equation. In addition, where the customer is an EU resident, the company is required to achieve GDPR compliance. Also, many companies provide loans to other companies when they have a huge cash surplus, as they can often obtain far greater rates of return than currently on offer from their banks.

2 Liquidity Risk Liquidity risk is the risk that a company or bank may be unable to meet short term financial demands, otherwise known as 'running out of money.' This can arise due to the difficulty of converting some security or hard asset into cash, from poor management of debtors, or over-extending through poor cash management. There can be many other factors which can cause this risk, but the effects can be catastrophic.

3 Market Risk Market risk is more frequently seen in financial institutions, where banks, for example, experience losses due to failings in the overall performance of the financial markets in which they are involved. Companies may also experience losses due to the way they make both short term and longer term investments of surplus business funds.

4 Operational Risk This area generally addresses all remaining risks and it is clear that the risks in this area are growing significantly.

4.1 Cloud Operational Risk

- **4.1.1 CSP Risk** The use of market leading, experienced cloud service providers familiar with legal and regulatory requirements for safeguarding customer data and other sensitive data;
- **4.1.2 Backup and Recovery Risk** Backup, redundancy, and recovery are at the core of the decision to use an outsourcing vendor with highly redundant and resilient data centres designed for mission-critical applications;
- **4.1.3 Internal Control Risk** Internal controls and security processes must ensure customer information is appropriately segregated and protected by industry-standard compliance policies;
- **4.1.4 CSP Hardware Environment Risk** Leading cloud providers continuously improve their hardware environments to ensure the latest versions of operating systems are installed and use agile software development to deploy feature/function releases on an accelerated basis;
- **4.1.5 Tailored Cloud Deployment Risk** The use of tailored cloud deployment options to meet your specific needs including private clouds solely deployed on your behalf, or a hybrid cloud consisting of shared hardware but segregated data storage would be a prudent move;
- **4.1.6 IT Outsourcing Risk** Outsourcing portions of your information technology infrastructure can free up internal IT resources to focus on strategic initiatives and new product development;
- **4.1.7 Financial Services Risk** Providers with financial services domain expertise reduce complexity and risk for Financial Institutions with their extensive knowledge of global standards, communications protocols and file formats;
- **4.1.6 CSP Global Support Center Risk** Cloud providers with global support centres can provide 24 x 7 support in multiple languages, ensuring your international clients and regional offices have access to the support resources required as problems arise.

- **4.2 Cloud Forensic Problem Risk** This is a huge potential problem unless special arrangements are in place, e.g., a secure forensic and audit trail is maintained using a high security immutable database [21]–[24], and examination of all system access requests to determine the authority of all users to have authorised access to the system. Use of intrusion detection and authentication technology to automate the monitoring for attack attempts is also necessary [25];
- **4.3 IoT Operational Risk** IoT devices used for any purpose by cloud users present a considerable risk, mainly due to the often cheaply made devices with little or no security, often vulnerable to the Mirai virus, which can allow attackers to gain access to systems and to further compromise the main PC and server network due to the porting of the Mirai virus to be able to attack Windows computers [26][18];
- **4.4 Monitoring Failure Risk** We need to understand the 5 Ws – Who, from Where, When did they access the database, What did they see, modify, delete or exfiltrate from the system [27][28]? This allows us to infer the Why so that we can understand their motivation. Simple monitoring and analysis of system logs will go a long way to mitigate the well known exploits currently in active use by attackers [24]. Some, like [29]–[31] propose the use of data provenance to ensure the integrity of data, with others proposing a new method of cloud forensic audit to assure the provenance of the data [32];
- **4.5 No Encryption Risk** Encryption is a good thing to consider [33], but there are caveats – first, the encryption and de-cryption keys must not be kept on the cloud instance. The encryption should be carried out offline in the cloud users' own systems before being transferred to cloud. Done properly, this can provide serious mitigation to the new EU GDPR fine levels, because if an intruder does get into the cloud system, all they get is meaningless data. With strong levels of encryption, it becomes practically impossible to crack [34] (of course, all this could change with the development and evolution of quantum computing, although there is little doubt that once quantum computing becomes an everyday reality that CSPs will introduce quantum cloud to address this issue).
- **4.6 Business Architecture Risk**
  - **4.6.1 People Risk** People are generally seen as the weakest link in any company, and are particularly prone to social engineering attacks. The company needs to keep abreast of these attacks and ensure all people in the company are regularly trained to understand the risks.

- **4.6.2 Process Risk** Processes are often well documented, but also can be woefully out of date. Attackers know to exploit these areas, sometimes in conjunction with social engineering attacks. OWASP are taking a more informed view of dealing with these kinds of attacks.
- **4.6.3 Technology Risk** This is where companies are exposed to highly technical attacks. The CSA has done some good work on identifying these risks, as well as offering good strategies to mitigate the risks.

Many of these issues have been around for many years. In 2011, NASA [35] were one of the early organisations to recommend using a risk based approach for identifying, recognising and dealing effectively with operational risk, particularly where complex IT systems are in use.

Failure to deal properly with the above risks could lead to very serious compliance breaches, which can trigger punitive levels of the fines imposed by the regulator. However, these risks can generate further risks in regard to business diminution; loss of share value; reputational damage risk; an emerging era of potentially serious regulatory fines, the serious expense of forensic investigations after a breach, and the impact on business continuity.

V. Discussion

As is now becoming clear, GDPR compliance will be far from easy to achieve, and for cloud this will be especially problematic and challenging. For a great many organisations, the GDPR brings a great many risks to bear when considering compliance with the GDPR. They come from a great range of sources, and the biggest risk of all is likely to come in the form of failure to recognise just how important it is to identify and mitigate these risks properly.

There are a great many companies will not be able to recognise these risks, particularly where they do not have the financial clout to provide the right level of expertise. The result is that they will be even more exposed than those who do have the means to recognise and address these risks. There can be no doubt that these risks are significant, and potentially devastating for the company should they fail to achieve compliance with the GDPR. A law firm, Cleary Gottlieb [36], provide a GDPR watch service, where they try to clarify how successful breaches might be dealt with.

We hope this paper might provide them with a starting point to consider what is required to achieve compliance, and what the implications might be for compliance failure. The steps outlined here are straightforward to implement. The most important point being that in order to deal with a risk, the company must first recognise the risk, and in order to do that, must have an understanding of what these risks are and how they might go about mitigating the potential impact of these risks.

Companies will need to carry out some serious testing in order to find a satisfactory equilibrium between security, privacy, performance, reliability, accessibility and the accountability we require for GDPR compliance. We plan to conduct a pilot case study on how the technical aspects might be implemented in order to meet all the required goals to ensure compliance can be achieved. This will run around a miniature cloud system, offering both cloud-based and non-cloud based systems to assess what the optimum configuration might be. This will allow us to ascertain how well the cloud-based solution can match the capability of the non-cloud based system, after taking into account the impact of the cloud forensic problem.

VI. Conclusion

For any company using cloud, it is clear that it will prove impossible to achieve compliance with the GDPR in the event of a security breach where they have not at least dealt properly with the as yet unresolved, cloud forensic problem. Claiming ignorance of this problem following a cyber breach will not be sufficient grounds for mitigation of the fine by the regulator after the fact. It will certainly be too late by then. Thus, cloud users who must be compliant with the GDPR will have to take steps now to be thoroughly prepared ahead of time.

We have looked at traditional cloud operational risks and the new risks relating to coping with these unresolved problems and discussed how to go about resolving them, using wherever possible simple, yet effective, approaches to ensure a robust solution that will be both easy to implement and easy to maintain. By this means, we can eliminate a large amount of the risk. We accept that all risk will not be entirely removed, but there is the possibility to make a significant reduction in risk levels involved. More importantly, it will be possible to demonstrate a high level of compliance with the GDPR to the regulator in the event of breach arising.

Implementing these proposals should ensure that a healthy level of compliance can be achieved, without the need for expensive, complex solutions that could prove highly expensive to implement and maintain.

References

[1] M. Felici, "Cyber Security and Privacy: Trust in the Digital World and Cyber Security and Privacy EU Forum 2013 Brussels, Belgium, April 18-19, 2013 Revised Selected Papers," in Commun. Comput. Inf. Sci. Springer International Publishing, 2013, vol. 182 CCIS, pp. 77–88.

[2] Y. Y. Haimes, B. M. Horowitz, Z. Guo, E. Andrijcic, and J. Bogdanor, "Assessing systemic risk to cloud-computing technology as complex interconnected systems of systems," Syst. Eng., vol. 18, no. 3, 2015, pp. 284–299.

[3] C. Millard, I. Walden, and W. K. Hon, "Who is Responsible for 'Personal Data' in Cloud Computing? The Cloud of Unknowing, Part 2," Leg. Stud., vol. 27, no. 77, 2012, pp. 1–31.

[4] R. K. L. Ko et al., "TrustCloud: A framework for accountability and trust in cloud computing," Proc. - 2011 IEEE World Congr. Serv. Serv. 2011, 2011, pp. 584–588.

[5] R. K. L. Ko, B. S. Lee, and S. Pearson, "Towards achieving accountability, auditability and trust in cloud computing," Commun. Comput. Inf. Sci., vol. 193 CCIS, no. PART 4, 2011, pp. 432–444.

[6] N. Papanikolaou, S. Pearson, and M. C. Mont, "Towards Natural-Language Understanding and Automated Enforcement of Privacy Rules and Regulations in the Cloud: Survey and Bibliography," Analysis, 2011, pp. 1–9.

[7] S. Pearson, "Taking account of privacy when designing cloud computing services," Proc. 2009 ICSE Work. Softw. Eng. Challenges Cloud Comput. CLOUD 2009, 2009, pp. 44–52.

[8] S. Pearson, "Towards Accountability in the Cloud," IEEE Internet Comput., vol. 15, no. 4, jul 2011, pp. 64–69.

[9] D. Pym and M. Sadler, "Information Stewardship in Cloud Computing," Int. J. Serv. Sci. Manag. Eng. Technol., vol. 1, no. 1, 2010, pp. 50–67.

[10] T. Takahashi, Y. Kadobayashi, and H. Fujiwara, "Ontological Approach toward Cybersecurity in Cloud Computing Categories and Subject Descriptors," in Sci. Technol., 2010, pp. 100–109.

[11] L. J. Sotto, B. C. Treacy, and M. L. Mclellan, "Privacy and Data Security Risks in Cloud Computing," World Commun. Regul. Rep., vol. 5, no. 2, 2010, p. 38.

[12] J. Bacon et al., "Information Flow Control for Secure Cloud Computing," IEEE Trans. Netw. Serv. Manag., vol. 11, no. 1, 2014, pp. 76–89.

[13] N. Papanikolaou, S. Pearson, M. C. Mont, and R. Ko, "A Toolkit for Automating Compliance in Cloud Computing Services," Int. J. Cloud Comput., vol. x, no. x, 2014, pp. 45–68.

[14] C. Chang and M. Ramachandran, "Towards Achieving Data Security with the Cloud Computing Adoption Framework," IEEE Trans. Serv. Comput., vol. 9, no. 1, 2016, pp. 138–151.

[15] PWC, "UK Information Security Breaches Survey - Technical Report 2012," London, Tech. Rep. April, 2012. [Online]. Available: www.pwc.com www.bis.gov.uk [Retrieved:March 2019]

[16] Trustwave, "2012 Global Security Report," Tech. Rep., 2012. [Online]. Available: https://www.trustwave.com/Resources/Library/Documents/2012-Trustwave-Global-Security-Report/ [Retrieved:March 2019]

[17] Verizon, "2016 Verizon Data Breach Report," Tech. Rep., 2016.

[18] Verizon, "Verizon Security Breach Report 2017," Tech. Rep., 2017.

[19] OWASP, "Open Web Application Security Project," 2019. [Online]. Available: https://www.owasp.org/index.php/OWASP_Cloud_Security_Project [Retrieved:March 2019]

[20] CSA, "Cloud Security Alliance," 2019. [Online]. Available: https://cloudsecurityalliance.org/ [Retrieved:March 2019]

[21] B. Duncan and M. Whittington, "Cloud cyber-security: Empowering the audit trail," Int. J. Adv. Secur., vol. 9, no. 3 & 4, 2016, pp. 169–183.

[22] B. Duncan and M. Whittington, "Creating and Configuring an Immutable Database for Secure Cloud Audit Trail and System Logging," Int. J. Adv. Secur., vol. 10, no. 3&4, 2017, pp. 155–166.

[23] B. Duncan, "Can EU General Data Protection Regulation Compliance be Achieved When Using Cloud Computing?" in Cloud Comput. 2018 Ninth Int. Conf. Cloud Comput. GRIDs, Virtualization, no. February. Barcelona, Spain: IARIA, 2018, pp. 1–6.

[24] B. Duncan, A. Happe, and A. Bratterud, "Using Unikernels to Address the Cloud Forensic Problem and help Achieve EU GDPR Compliance." in Cloud Comput. 2018 Ninth Int. Conf. Cloud Comput. GRIDs, Virtualization, no. February. Barcelona, Spain: IARIA, 2018, pp. 1–6.

[25] M. Neovius and B. Duncan, "Anomaly Detection for Soft Security in Cloud based Auditing of Accounting Systems," in Closer 2017 - 7th Int. Conf. Cloud Comput. Serv. Sci., Porto, Portugal, 2017, pp. 1–8.

[26] B. Duncan and M. Whittington, "Cyber Security for Cloud and the Internet of Things: How Can it be Achieved?" Cybersecurity Inst. Eng. Technol., vol. Cybersecur, no. September, 2017, pp. 1–39.

[27] B. Duncan, M. Whittington, M. G. Jaatun, and A. R. R. Zúñiga, "Could the Outsourcing of Incident Response Management Provide a Blueprint for Managing Other Cloud Security Requirements?" in Enterp. Secur. Springer B. 2016, V. Chang, M. Ramachandran, R. Walters, and G. Wills, Eds. Springer, 2016, pp. 1–22.

[28] B. Duncan, A. Bratterud, and A. Happe, "Enhancing Cloud Security and Privacy: Time for a New Approach?" in Intech 2016, Dublin, 2016, pp. 1–6.

[29] T. F. J. Pasquier, J. Singh, J. Bacon, and D. Eyers, "Information Flow Audit for PaaS Clouds," in 2016 IEEE International Conference on Cloud Engineering (IC2E), 2016, pp. 42–51.

[30] N. Papanikolaou, T. Rübsamen, and C. Reich, "A Simulation Framework to Model Accountability Controls for Cloud Computing," CLOUD Comput. 2014, Fifth Int. Conf. Cloud Comput. GRIDs, Virtualization, no. c, 2014, pp. 12–19.

[31] T. F. J. M. Pasquier and J. E. Powles, "Expressing and Enforcing Location Requirements in the Cloud using Information Flow Control," Proc. - 2015 IEEE Int. Conf. Cloud Eng. IC2E 2015, 2015, pp. 410–415.

[32] B. Duncan and M. Whittington, "Can Forensic Audit Help Address the Cloud Forensic Problem in Light of the Requirements of the Forthcoming European Union General Data Protection Regulation?" in Cloud Comput. 2018 Ninth Int. Conf. Cloud Comput. GRIDs, Virtualization, no. February. Barcelona, Spain: IARIA, 2018, pp. 84–89.

[33] V. Chang, M. Ramachandran, Y. Yao, Y. H. Kuo, and C. S. Li, "A resiliency framework for an enterprise cloud," Int. J. Inf. Manage., vol. 36, no. 1, 2016, pp. 155–166.

[34] T. Pasquier, B. Shand, and J. Bacon, "Information Flow Control for a Medical Records Web Portal," Cl.Cam.Ac.Uk, 2013, pp. 1–8.

[35] M. Stamatelatos and H. Dezfuli, "Probabilistic Risk Assessment Procedures Guide for NASA Managers and Practitioners," NASA, Tech. Rep. December, 2002. [Online]. Available: http://www.hq.nasa.gov/office/codeq/doctree/praguide.pdf [Retrieved:March 2019]

[36] Cleary, "Cleary Cybersecurity and Cyber Watch," Cleary Gottlieb, 2019. [Online]. Available: https://www.clearycyberwatch.com/2018/01/notification-data-breaches-gdpr-10-frequently-asked-questions/. [Retrieved:March 2019]

Towards Trustworthy Financial Reports Using Blockchain

Gianfranco D'Atri

Department of Mathematics and
Computer Science,
Calabria University,
Rende, Cosenza, Italy
Email: gdatri@mat.unical.it

Van Thanh Le, Claus Pahl , Nabil El Ioini

Faculty of Computer Science,
Free University of Bolzano,
Bolzano, Italy
Email: {vanle,cpahl,nelioini}@unibz.it

***Abstract*—The need to develop a system for dealing with the transparency analysis of financial reports has pushed companies to look for possible solutions to store their data in a reliable and trustworthy database, that enables all authorized entities to access and check financial data of their partners. The eXtensible Business Reporting Language (XBRL) is the digital format of financial reports that provides data and rules to perform different analysis following a number of techniques: (1) consistency calculation, (2) rates between debts and interests, (3) checking the Benford's law, (4) financial item value comparison. In this paper, we propose a blockchain based solution where all reports analysis activities and results are recorded into a shared ledger to guarantee their integrity and consistency. Specifically, we have designed and implemented a prototype to validate and store financial statements using Ethereum blockchain. Additionally, we have performed an initial set of tests based on a set of Italian financial reports.**

Keywords–Blockchain; XBRL; Financial Reports; DLV; ASP.

I. INTRODUCTION

Financial statements are formal records of the financial activities that companies use to provide an accurate picture of their financial history. Their main purpose is to offer all the necessary data, which allows for an accurate assessment the economic situation of a company and its ability to attract investors.

In the Italian context, financial statements start with business accounting collecting all the relevant financial data, processing and validating its consistency, then generating a standard eXtensible Business Reporting Language (XBRL) format report (i.e., XBRL is a standard digital format for financial reports). The report is then sent to the Chambers of Commerce (a.k.a board of trade, an association or network of businesspeople designed to promote and protect the interests of its members [1]). After a series of checks (e.g., checking consistency between inputs and outputs), the Chamber of Commerce publishes the reports in a publicly accessible domain (i.e., registroimprese.it).

Two of the issues that arise in the current approach for report evaluation is its incompleteness in terms of evaluation method (e.g., checking the format) and its lack of traceability in report updates, which might prove to inconsistency and lack of trust among business organizations, in other words, in many jurisdictions, the reliability and consistency of published data is not yet assured by public bodies. To this end, our goal is to investigate how blockchain can be used to address these limitations to restore trustworthiness in the published financial reports. Our contribution is two fold (i) provide a methodology to automatically evaluate and validate the consistency of the generated reports, *(ii)* use Ethereum smart contract to store financial reports and track all updates that might take place in the future. Additionally, an initial set of experiments is presented to illustrate the cost factor of the proposed approach.

The remaining of this paper is organized as follows: Section II provides background information about the used technologies. Section III discusses the main related work studies connected to our work. Section IV describes the system architecture. Section V presents the implementation details. Section VI experimentally evaluates the cost and performance of our approach and Section VII gives our conclusions.

II. BACKGROUND

The following section introduces the different technologies used in the definition of the proposed architecture.

A. XBRL

Financial reports contain sensitive data that might have a huge impact on organization's future in terms of investments and collaborations, which mandates careful management and control mechanisms able to capture any inconsistencies or manipulation of the published reports. The first step towards this goal started with the introduction of the eXtensible Business Reporting Language [2], which is the world leading standard for financial reporting. It facilitates inter-organizations communication and enables automatic reports processing and analysis. XBRL relies on XML and XML based schema to define all its constructs. Its structure consists of two main parts:

1) XBRL instance, containing primarily the business facts being reported (see figure 1).

```
<rp:RevenueTotal unitRef="EUR">5000</rp:RevenueTotal>
<rp:CostOfSales unitRef="EUR">3000</rp:CostOfSales>
<rp:GrossProfit unitRef="EUR">2000</rp:GrossProfit>
```

Figure 1. Facts example

2) XBRL taxonomy, a collection of arcs which define metadata about these facts and their relationship with other facts (see figure 2).

Figure 3 depicts XBRL structure and the relations between the different components.

```
<loc xlink:type="locator"
  xlink:href="taxonomy#rp_RevenueTotal" />
<loc xlink:type="locator"
  xlink:href="taxonomy#rp_CostOfSales" />
<loc xlink:type="locator"
  xlink:href="taxonomy#rp_GrossProfit" />
<calculationArc xlink:type="arc"
  xlink:from="rp_GrossProfit" xlink:to="rp_RevenueTotal"
  weight="1" />
<calculationArc xlink:type="arc"
  xlink:from="rp_GrossProfit" xlink:to="rp_CostOfSales"
  weight="-1" />
```

Figure 2. XBRL Linkbase example

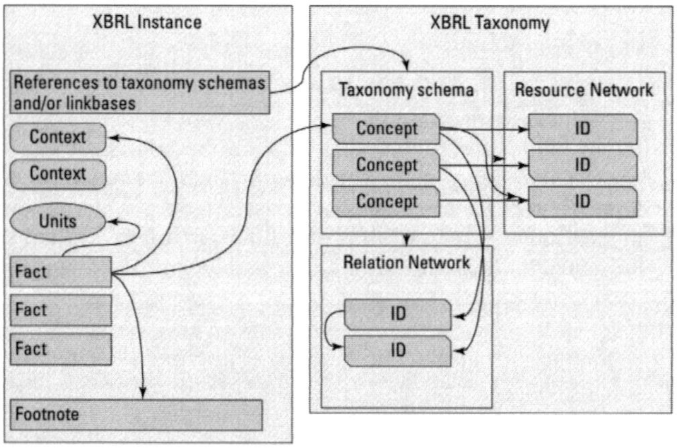

Figure 3. XBRL Structure

B. I-DLV

As the complexity of XBRL structure increases, it could reach a high number of definitions, which makes it impractical to check and validate manually. Thus, a number of tools have been developed to automate the validation process, Answer Set Programming (ASP) is a form of declarative programming oriented towards difficult search problems, highly used in both academia and industry.

The possible use of an ASP language for analyzing XBRL financial reports was explored by Gianfranco d'Atri in [3]. The tokenization and standardization of data supported by the XBRL Consortium allow an extensive and meaningful use of AI techniques to support economic analysis and fraud detection.

I-DLV [4] is a new intelligent grounder of the logic-based Artificial Intelligence system DLV [5], it is an ASP instantiator that natively supports the ASP standard language. Beside ASP features, external computation in I-DLV is achieved by means of external atoms, whose extension is not defined by the semantics within the logic program, but rather is specified by means of externally defined Python programs, the so-called external atom in the rule bodies, which are also one of the most outstanding of I-DLV. Because of these features, in the paper, we applied DLV queries to analyze and absorb valuable knowledge from financial reports.

C. Blockchain

Blockchain is a distributed, decentralized ledger to store transactions and addresses the double-spending problem in a trust-less peer-to-peer network, without the need for a trusted third party or an administrator. Blockchain is maintained by a network of computers called nodes. Whenever a new transaction arrives, the nodes verify its validity and broadcast it to the rest of the network. The main building blocks of a Blockchain are [6]:

- Transactions, which are signed pieces of information created by the participating nodes in the network then broadcast to the rest of the network.
- Blocks, that are collections of transactions that are appended to the blockchain after being validated.
- A blockchain is a ledger of all the created blocks that make up the network.
- The blockchain relies on Public keys to connect the different blocks together (similar to a linked list).
- A consensus mechanism is used to decide which blocks are added to the blockchain.

Generally, there are three types of blockchain platforms: public , consortium, and private [7]. In the public blockchain all participants can execute and validate transactions. In consortium blockchain, the identity of the participants is known, but they do not necessarily trust each other. The network is moderated by one or more participants to keep access under control. Different participants might have different roles. In a private blockchain instead, the whole network is managed by one single organization. In our context, we apply public blockchain to publish financial reports to the public, where all participant could check business working status.

In our case, Ethereum [8] is the best candidate, since it is an open source blockchain platform that enables developers to build and deploy decentralized applications. The platform runs smart contracts, a computer protocol running on top of a blockchain, performing as a contract. Smart contracts can include data structures and function calls that are executed in a centralized fashion. This guarantees the fact that the contract execution will persist on the chain.

III. RELATED WORK

Providing trustworthy financial data is a challenging endeavor. Over the years different tools have been developed to analyze the financial information generated by companies to in order to check its consistency and integrity. However, since most of the proposed tools rely on third party organizations, issues related to trustworthiness and privacy still need to be solved.

Recently blockchain has found applications in different domains including IoT [9] [10], finance [11], health care [12] and others. In the literature, a number of studies considered the implication of blockchain on financial services and accounting. Byström [13] argues that blockchain can help corporate accounting in many ways, especially in terms of trustworthiness in accounting information and data availability in a timely manner. In [14], the authors discuss how blockchain can be an enabler technology for accounting ecosystem auditing and transparency. In [15], Colgren discusses the advantages that blockchain can bring to companies by allowing a fast and public access to companies financial statements. In [11], Bussmann has given a more general overview on the potential disruption of blockchain on the Fintech market. For banking services, Ye Guo [16] suggests that blockchain is able to replace the banking industry as external and internal issues like economic deceleration and increasing credit risk and non-performing assets. Thus, blockchain could synchronize and verify financial transactions to eliminate the problems of subsequent reconciliation. Applying blockchain as a storage, Sven Helmer et al. built MongoDB database functions into Ethereum in [17], that separates the driver and database to reduce the cost transactions. The main goal of their approach is to keep all data on-chain.

In terms of tools related to XBRL, a number of tools are in use, however, they are not able to guarantee the long term trustworthiness of the reports on produced. With regard to analysis of financial report in XBRL format, Arelle [18] is an open source platform for XBRL financial reports format analysis. Users can view the structure of a document and use features with a GUI. Arelle provides many services that can be integrated with other technologies. Altova [19] is also well-known based on the XML development. With the help of Altova, users can present XBRL maps and relationships inside, including facts, context and arcs. These tools have their own evaluation tools but just check with basic concept even with some specific documents, so the result is not consistent. Moreover, considering the transparent characteristics of financial documents, we need a better approach that guarantees transparency of the whole validation process.

IV. System Architecture

The goal of the proposed architecture is to provide an end to end solution that leverages different technologies for managing financial reports and a trustworthy publishing and updating.

Figure 4 depicts an overview of the proposed architecture. It is divided into three main components: XBRL Reader, XBRL Evaluator and XBRL Storage.

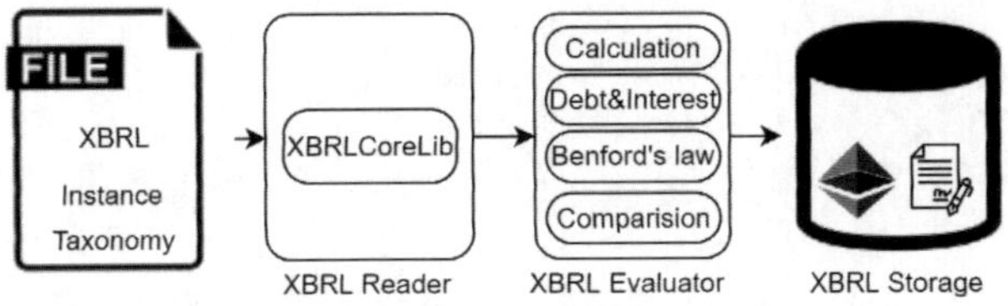

Figure 4. Architecture

A. XBRL Reader

XBRLReader is responsible for validating the XBRL formatting by checking that all the schema is fully described. It takes as input an XBRL Instance that contains facts and a link to the taxonomies to be used.

The output of XBRLReader is a list of facts and arcs that are given to the XBRL Evaluator.

B. XBRL Evaluator

Facts and arcs from the first step are evaluated following these aspects:

- Calculation consistency will check each value of facts, even if the value is aggregated from other asset's values like the example $GrossProfit = RevenueTotal - CostOfSales$, we will compare the result of $RevenueTotal - CostOfSales$ and $GrossProfit$ value with a threshold, the check applies for all the assets in the report, this kind of check also shows the errors inside reports where the difference between the actual value and the calculated value is greater than the threshold.
- The rate between interest and debt: a financial report normally shows data in 2 consecutive years, it could calculate changes of $interest/debt$ ratio during the years, if the index is too high, an alert is crucial for the company because it could be a potential sign for bankruptcy.
- Financial item comparison: From many reports in a year, we also compare financial item values among businesses to find, for example, the company has the highest revenue, or even filter companies do not have cost of warehouse.
- Benford's law checking: Benford's law [20] is an observation about the frequency distribution of leading digits in real-life data sets. The law states that a set of numbers is said to satisfy Benford's law if the leading first digit d ($d \in 1, .., 9$) occurs with probability (see figure 5):
  $P(d) = \log_{10}(d+1) - \log_{10}(d) = \log_{10}(\frac{d+1}{d})$

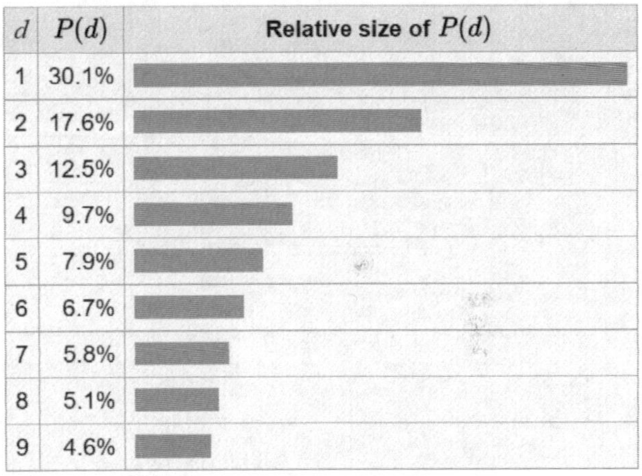

Figure 5. Benford's law for the first digit

The complicated formula are explained in [21] about stock prices example with distributions. Benford's law could check the whole data set or each financial reports.

We note that the evaluation process can result in valid reports meaning that they satisfy all the pre-defined evaluation criteria or invalid reports that violate one or more requirements. At this point, it is up to the report owner to decide whether to publish the report or not. We also note that if invalid reports are published, they can be updated subsequently (e.g., add more information) to a valid state.

C. XBRL Storage

Storing financial data in a trusted location is a necessity to keep data safe and to be able to trace all the updates occurring over time. The main pieces of data of interest in our scenario are the financial facts and arcs. Blockchain is used as the back-end storage where each fact and arc are stored in separate transactions. Once transactions are validated (i.e., added to the blockchain), the data becomes available to the users of the network who can view them, and any updates can be traced.

D. Use cases

To illustrate the interaction between the different components, we have defined a set of use cases addressed by the proposed architecture. All scenarios assume that the user has a company registered in the system, the user then chooses an XBRL file and the evaluator shows four possible outcomes. Fig. 6 depicts a sequence diagram that covers most of the scenarios.

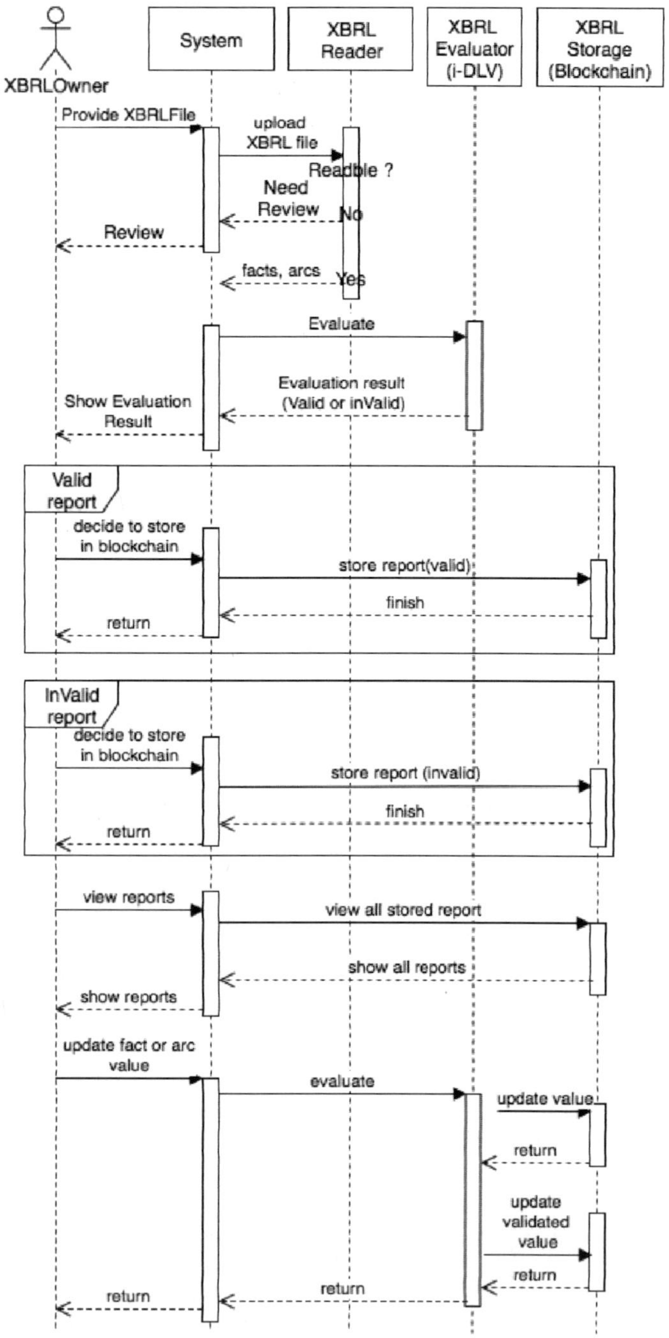

Figure 6. Report evaluation sequence diagram

- If all aspects are satisfied (valid), the user publishes the data into the blockchain.
- If one of evaluation criteria is violated, the user is advised to review the report and submit it later.
- If one of the evaluation criteria is violated, the user can still publish it into the blockchain but it will be flagged as invalid.
- Invalid reports already in the blockchain can be updated by their owners (e.g., update report values). The evaluator will check them again, if the updated report is accepted, the flag will change to valid. We note that if valid reports are updated with incorrect values they will be also flagged invalid.
- Other users or any third party organizations could view and evaluate any reports.

V. IMPLEMENTATION

The implementation of the proposed approach is conducted using a three layer architecture. Each of the layers is detailed in the following sub sections. The current implementation is a standalone application that interacts with the blockchain network. For the Etherum network, we rely on Blockchain network instance deployed at the University of Calabria, Italy called Unical coin [22] with the following configuration: (difficult:y "0x90000", gasLimit : "0x2fefd8", running nodes: 4). The full implementation of the proposed approach can be found in our Github repository [23].

A. XBRL Reader

XBRL Reader uses XBRLCore [24], a library to read and extract data. It receives as input an XBRL file and extracts all the relevant information for the validation process, which include both XBRL instances and XBRL taxonomies (arcs) according to the XBRL 2.1 Specification. XBRLCore also has it own validation but it does not fit to the newest taxonomy (for example with group of item). For example, facts: $RevenueTotal \ : \ 5000EUR$, and $CostOfSales \ :$ $3000, GrossProfit \ : \ 2000$ and arcs: $GrossProfit \ =$ $RevenueTotal - CostOfSales$, could be presented as figure 7

```
fact(revenueTotal, "5000", eur).
fact(costOfSales, "3000", eur).
fact(grossProfit, "2000", eur).
arc(grossProfit, costOfSales, "-1").
arc(grossProfit, revenueTotal, "1").
```

Figure 7. Facts and Arcs example

B. XBRL Evaluator

XBRL Evaluator stores facts and arcs together with the queries in a query file to examine indices in the reports, also report where there is the error by i-DLV by calling from Java Runtime:

```
idlv xbrlFile.dlv calculation.py
```

xbrlFile.dlv includes the list of facts and arcs, queries (see figure 8), and calculation.py includes utility functions such as real numbers operations and list functions (see figure 9). After running the command above, it prints "invalidDocument" if the data is not correct otherwise it prints "validDocument". The code computes the assets' values by *i)* choosing each fact and its relation (arc) *ii)* multiple weight with asset value of each arc, and *iii)* sum these values to get expected asset value to compare with the actual value from fact. If they are not equal, $checkFact$ returns $false$ and $isValidDocument$ is also $false$, in other words, the document is not valid, otherwise, it is accepted.

```
chooseArc(F1, F2, V) :- fact(F2,V2,U), arc(F1,F2,W),
    &times(F1,V2,W;V).
invalidFact(F) :- chooseArc(F, _, V), &checkFact(F,V
    ;"False").
invalidDocument :- &checkDocument(;"False").
validDocument :- &checkDocument(;"True").
```

Figure 8. Query example

```
listFacts = {};
isValidDocument = True
def times(F, X, Y):
    fx = float(X)
    fy = float(Y)
    if F not in listFacts:
        listFacts[F] = 0
    listFacts[F] += fx * fy
    return str(fx * fy)
def checkFact(F,X):
    fx = float(X)
    if fx == listFacts[F] :
        return True
    else :
        isValidDocument = False
        return False
def checkDocument():
    return isValidDocument
```

Figure 9. Calulcation.py example

C. XBRL Storage

Financial data from evaluator are published into blockchain via web3js and built smart contract. Smart contract will make the skeleton to store data of a report, a company has many reports, each reports has its own facts and arcs (see figure 10).

```
struct Fact {
    string concept;
    string context;
    string value;
    string unit;
    string factgroup;
}
struct Arc {
    string conceptFrom;
    string conceptTo;
    string weight;
    string calLinkBase;
}
struct Report {
    string reportId;
    string date;
    string validated;
    Fact[] facts;
    Arc[] arcs;
}
struct Company {
    address companyAddress;
    string companyName;
    Report[] reports;
}
Company[] public companies;
```

Figure 10. Companies structure

Functions facilitate users to fill data into the structure (see figure 11).

```
function ownCompany();
function ownReport( reportId);
function registerNewCompany();
function getCompany();
function addReport(report);
function addFact(fact);
function addArc(arc);
function updateFact(fact);
function updateArc(arc);
```

Figure 11. Functions

VI. EVALUATION

Two important aspects to evaluate when considering blockchain based solutions are cost and performance. Running computations onchain might result to be costly and impractical in many scenarios. The cost is associated with smart contracts execution and transactions recording and it is generally determined by two parameters: the amount of gas used by the execution of contract and the gasPrice associated with the transaction. The first one depends on the needed computation to perform the task, since every instruction executed by the Ethereum Virtual Machine has a certain gas cost. The second instead represents the cost in Ether of one gas unit, which depends on the blockchain network state when the transaction is performed. The general rule is that when a high number of transactions are pending, those with higher gasPrice have higher probability of being executed by a miner and be therefore added to the chain. In terms of performance since increasing the number of transactions increase the application latency.

A. Cost evaluation

We tested our system using 200 valid XBRL files, 22 invalid files (valid in calculation consistency) provided by different business providers and are annual financial reports. The tests consider all the implemented functions of the smart contract. These tests have been run on a test blockchain network and can be reproduced by calling a set of REST endpoints. Endpoint return the amount of gas consumed by while executing transactions. The amount of gas used is multiplied by the gasPrice to obtain the costs in Ether. The Ethereum to Euro conversion factor to these prices allows to compute the monetary cost. Table I presents the cost of executing the various contract functions.

TABLE I. COSTS OF SMART CONTRACT FUNCTIONS EXECUTION

Function	*Ether cost (GWei)*	*Euro cost (€)*	*Avg Time (ms)*
registerNewCompany	0,00032	0,059	7022
addFact	0,01	1,83	7579
addArc	0,01	1,83	7579
addReport	0,0012	0,22	11705
updateFact	0,01	1,83	7579
updateArc	0,01	1,83	7579
updateValidatedValue	0.0012	0,22	12325

We note that on average an annual report contains around 129 facts and 122 arcs (251 transactions) which would cost approximately 2.5124 ETH (183 EUR at 9 November 2018 followed by [25]).

B. Performance evaluation

In terms of performance, we simulated the main scenario used in our approach, that is the process of publishing reports (addReport, addFact, addArc, updateValidatedValue). Figure 12 shows the average execution time for the whole process. The x axis represents the total number of facts and arcs as used in the process.

The results depicted show that the execution time is linear relative to the number of transactions. However, there are other factors that affect the execution time, mainly the variation of gas price which affects what transactions will be picked by the miners first and the size of the network (i.e., how fast the transactions are broad casted).

VII. CONCLUSION AND FUTURE WORK

In this paper, we have presented the design and a prototype implementation of a blockchain based financial reports ledger. The main goal of the proposed approach is to increase trust

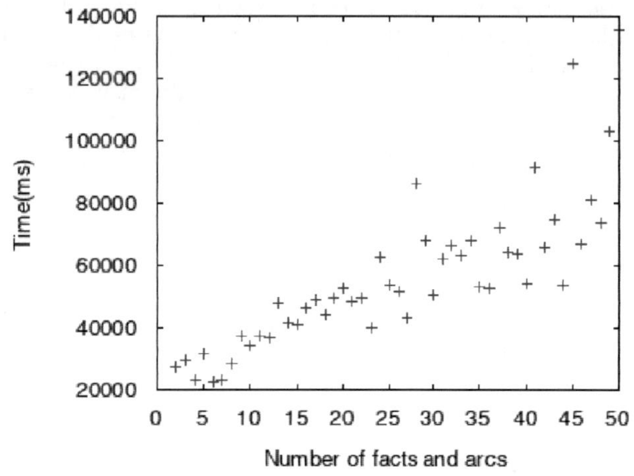

Figure 12. Main scenario average execution time.

and transparency in published financial reports, which can have great impact on inter-organizational transactions.

Using ASP in the first prototype makes flexible and easy to maintain. However in the next version, we will move all computations into be on-chain, and compressing technologies are also considered to reduce transaction weight, so the execution time can be reduced.

Although the study is limited to the Italian context and does not provide a cross analysis with other systems, the goal here is to shed some light on the great potential of using distributed ledger technologies in financial reports validation, storage and traceability. The proposed approach has been applied to the niche area of financial reports, but the same approach may have much wider applications in numerous contexts.

For future work, we are investigating the automatic correction of invalid XBRL documents such as typing mistakes and facts missing value. Moreover, financial statements should be based on the cash flow statements from organization to organization. When we have all data flow, we can provide end to end trustworthiness and reliability.

REFERENCES

[1] Investopedia, "Chamber of Commerce," 2018, URL: https://www.investopedia.com/terms/c/chamber-of-commerce.asp [accessed: 2019-04-10].

[2] XBRLOrganization, "An Introduction to XBRL," 2001, URL: https://www.xbrl.org/the-standard/what/an-introduction-to-xbrl/ [accessed: 2019-04-10].

[3] G. D'Atri, "Logic-based consistency checking of xrbl instances," IJACT, vol. 3–6, 2014, pp. 126–131.

[4] J.Zangari, "idlv," 2018, URL: https://github.com/DeMaCS-UNICAL/I-DLV/wiki [accessed: 2019-04-10].

[5] W. T. Adrian, M. Alviano, F. Calimeri, B. Cuteri, and e. a. Dodaro, "The asp system dlv: Advancements and applications," KI-Künstliche Intelligenz, 2018, pp. 1–3.

[6] C. Cachin, "Architecture of the hyperledger blockchain fabric," 2016, workshop on Distributed Cryptocurrencies and Consensus Ledgers.

[7] N. El Ioini and C. Pahl, A Review of Distributed Ledger Technologies: Confederated International Conferences: CoopIS, C&TC, and ODBASE 2018, Valletta, Malta, October 22-26, 2018, Proceedings, Part II, 10 2018, pp. 277–288.

[8] EthereumFoundation, "Ethereum," 2013, URL: https://www.ethereum.org/ [accessed: 2019-04-10].

[9] C. Pahl, N. El Ioini, S. Helmer, and B. Lee, "An architecture pattern for trusted orchestration in iot edge clouds," in Fog and Mobile Edge Computing (FMEC), 2018 Third International Conference on. IEEE, 2018, pp. 63–70.

[10] C. Pahl, N. EL Ioini, and S. Helmer, "A Decision Framework for Blockchain Platforms for IoT and Edge Computing," Proceedings of the 3rd International Conference on Internet of Things, Big Data and Security, no. IoTBDS, 2018, pp. 105–113.

[11] O. Bussmann, "The future of finance: Fintech, tech disruption, and orchestrating innovation," in Equity Markets in Transition. Springer, 2017, pp. 473–486.

[12] M. Mettler, "Blockchain technology in healthcare: The revolution starts here," in e-Health Networking, Applications and Services (Healthcom), 2016 IEEE 18th International Conference on. IEEE, 2016, pp. 1–3.

[13] H. Byström, "Blockchains, real-time accounting and the future of credit risk modeling," Lund University, Department of Economics, 2016.

[14] J. Dai and M. A. Vasarhelyi, "Toward blockchain-based accounting and assurance," Journal of Information Systems, vol. 31, no. 3, 2017, pp. 5–21.

[15] T. D. Colgren, "Xbrl, blockchain, and new technologies," Strategic Finance, vol. 99, no. 7, 2018, pp. 62–63.

[16] Y. Guo and C. Liang, "Blockchain application and outlook in the banking industry," Financial Innovation, vol. 2, no. 1, 2016, p. 24. [Online]. Available: https://doi.org/10.1186/s40854-016-0034-9

[17] S. Helmer, M. Roggia, N. El Ioini, and C. Pahl, "Ethernitydb – integrating database functionality into a blockchain," 09 2018, pp. 37–44, aDBIS.

[18] H. Fischer and D. Mueller, "Open source & xbrl: the arelle® project," in 2011 Kansas University XBRL Conference, 2011, pp. 29–30.

[19] Altova, "XBRL Development Tools," 2018, URL: https://www.altova.com/xbrl-tools [accessed: 2019-04-10].

[20] W. contributors, "Benford's law — Wikipedia, The Free Encyclopedia," 2019, URL: https://en.wikipedia.org/w/index.php?title=Benford%27s_law&oldid=885125880 [accessed: 2019-04-10].

[21] L. Pietronero, E. Tosatti, V. Tosatti, and A. Vespignani, "Explaining the uneven distribution of numbers in nature: the laws of benford and zipf," Physica A: Statistical Mechanics and its Applications, vol. 293, 2001, pp. 297–304.

[22] UnicalCoinTeam, "Unicalcoin," 2017, URL: https://github.com/marcuzzu/UnicalCoin [accessed: 2019-04-10].

[23] V. T. Le, "Trustable system for XBRL," 2001, URL: https://github.com/levanthanh3005/TrustableSystem-for-XBRL [accessed: 2019-04-10].

[24] Y.seki, "XBRL Core," 2006, URL: https://sourceforge.net/projects/xbrlcore/ [accessed: 2019-04-10].

[25] S. ltd, "Currencio — Cryptocurrency Converter," 2001, URL: https://currencio.co [accessed: 2019-04-10].

Version Control Using Distributed Ledger Technologies for Internet of Things Device Software Updates

Magnus Westerlund
Department of Business Management and Analytics
Arcada University of Applied Sciences
Helsinki, Finland
magnus.westerlund@arcada.fi

John Wickström
Department of Business Management and Analytics
Arcada University of Applied Sciences
Helsinki, Finland
wickstjo@arcada.fi

Göran Pulkkis
Department of Business Management and Analytics
Arcada University of Applied Sciences
Helsinki, Finland
goran.pulkkis@arcada.fi

Abstract—**The number of installed Internet of Things (IoT) devices is growing rapidly and securing these IoT installations is an important task that may require technical knowledge that the owners of these devices do not always possess. Although experts have pointed out, that security should always be a priority when creating IoT products, the challenges are numerous and security solutions are not always targeted to decentralized or distributed architectures. In this paper, we explore the mechanisms for creating a method for a distributed IoT software update service that utilize distributed ledger technologies, such as Ethereum smart contracts and the InterPlanetary File System (IPFS). Our aim is to present a method that offers a more transparent version control of updates than current solutions, which are mostly conceptually centralized. We also aim to avoid relying on a central node for distributing updates and to create a fully secured and automated process for update management.**

Keywords-IoT; distributed ledger; blockchain; version control; software update.

I. INTRODUCTION

Version control has been an integral part of software development for a long time. Common techniques and methods for provisioning IT-services (incl. configuration, deployment, orchestration and management) depend on formalizing a process for handling changes made to files and data. Version Control Systems (VCS) became commonplace in the late 1990s and initially catered mostly to intra-organizational software development (internally) and a well-known system was Rational ClearCase [1]. As software development matured and inter-organizational development (between organizations), became commonplace through, e.g., open source development, new distributed VCS, such as Git [2], emerged. These VCS have distributed features primarily from the perspective of access, who can collaborate and contribute to a project hosted on a web-based Git repository (such as Gitlab). Although it is possible to mirror Git repositories, these services have no proper distributed features in terms of inherent trustless consensus and guarantee for service availability. Such fears among developers were quite evident when Microsoft acquired GitHub [3], another Git-based repository many open source projects are relying on.

Traditionally, version control has strictly meant tracking changes in text-based files. To store binary files in a VCS offers mainly a stored version path. For some binary files, plugins exist that will allow a diff to executed, but often this would be an exception. However, there are new use cases for version control that go beyond the initial ability of performing a comparison between file versions. These use cases are coming from new technologies, such as machine learning (incl. Artificial Intelligence (AI)) and Internet of Things (IoT). For an AI-enabled service, version control extends to, that the process must include training data, network initialization, parameter settings, and serialization of the trained network to a file. Often, other types of metadata should be stored as well, e.g., statistical properties of training data, output quality metrics and naturally if the model is updated online it requires further measures. Any autonomous AI-based service aimed for production use will need continuous catering for forensic investigations during the longevity of the service.

This paper focuses on the IoT use case, to extend the understanding for what purposes version control is usable and how to implement a Proof of Concept (PoC) of a VCS for IoT software updates using Distributed Ledger Technology (DLT), such as blockchain, smart contracts, and the InterPlanetary File System (IPFS) [4]. This paper adopts a methodology intended to identify single case mechanisms through an exploratory approach [5]. Our long-term research aim is to develop a new methodology for fully secured and automated IoT device updates. This process must also be transparent in terms of who has created updates and be auditable in case there are detected vulnerabilities. We limit the scope for this paper to the backend architecture utilizing IPFS, Ethereum smart contracts, and browser-based Distributed Applications (DApp).

This paper has the following structure: Section II describes the problem setting of reliability in IoT devices. Section III presents relevant IoT policies and standardization efforts. Section IV discusses DLT-based update services. Section V surveys other proposals for distributed update services and presents our PoC. Section VI contains conclusion and proposal for future development

II. Problem Setting for IoT Device Reliability

The proliferation of IoT devices and services based on these are helping to digitize the physical landscape. IoT enabled devices have been introduced into almost any setting and convey large volume of data and varieties of data, e.g., in the format of video, sound, and potentially any data type that can be measured with a sensor that converts analogue measurements into a digital data flow. We can anticipate the technological progress will continue to shape new domains in our lives and within the coming decades, extending to include many new areas, e.g., personal healthcare and home automation. These new domains will introduce a myriad of highly sensitive information sources, information that must be processed, and often stored for an indefinite and sometimes an infinite period for the digitization of these areas. By embedding information-sharing electronics into everyday physical objects, we will create a "global cyber-physical infrastructure" [6]. IoT uses standardized communication protocols and merges computer networks into a "common global IT platform of seamless networks and networked "Smart things/objects"" [7]. From the perspective of platform and service innovation, by utilizing IoT technology, the focus will be on creating AI-enabled services that are able to draw inferences from the data collected from IoT devices. This will offer users descriptive answers, predict future behavior and needs, and eventually provide prescriptive suggestions for improving daily life. We here define AI-enabled services as based on machine learning techniques that infer decision support or decisions based on the collected IoT data. Therefore, relying on data veracity becomes crucial for the trustworthiness of these services.

Network and information security are often more challenging for IoT systems than for traditional networks. Cloud resources used by many IoT systems are publicly accessible and thereby, through this availability, increase the risk of intrusion. The increase in the processing of sensitive data in IoT systems makes security challenges more noteworthy, particularly in light of legal issues around cross-border transfers and data protection [8]. The debate regarding a sustainability problem in IoT security has resulted in some experts calling for a halt to IoT deployments and innovations [9] and that IoT devices should come with public safety warnings [10]. This paper takes the position that there is currently a sustainability problem in IoT security and we should innovatively address this problem with new secure IoT management methods designed specifically for the distributed architecture of IoT networks.

III. Current IoT Policy Situation

In a traditional IoT architecture, IoT devices are network nodes, which transmit their data (incl. logs) to a data store through some proxy. IoT device management for enterprise-level devices is often a manual process, whereas consumer devices may query a manufacturer-defined end-point for software updates, which typically are impossible to validate for origin or content. Device administrators have local credentials for authentication, but an Identity and Access Management (IAM) solution is often missing. Only authenticated users should have authorization to access IoT devices and to update device firmware from device deliverers' databases. A system log stored on a respective node would require device access for collection (pull) of data. Storage space is often very limited so only the most recent activities may be stored on the device. Hence, continuous collection to an external data store is required.

From an accountability perspective, continuous delivery of new updates to a node is also a necessity, something that often requires a manual process by a system administrator. The manufacturer should also provide new software (e.g., firmware) security updates for the lifetime of said IoT devices. For this process to be complete, traditional IoT systems require many manual process steps that are often not possible to ensure in today's environment. Hence, we find it motivated to propose a new type of architecture better suited to a decentralized or distributed network topology.

A secure IoT system is one that can fulfil the following criteria [11]:

- does not contain any hardware, software, or firmware component with any known security vulnerabilities or defects,
- relies on software or firmware components capable of accepting properly authenticated and trusted updates from the vendor,
- uses only non-deprecated industry-standard protocols and technologies for functions such as communication, encryption, and intercommunication with other devices, and
- does not include any fixed or hard-coded credentials used for remote administration, the delivery of updates, or communication.

The Cloud Security Alliance (CSA) [12] IoT Working Group published in 2018, 10 security recommendations for IoT firmware updates [13]. The recommendations focus on device integrity and the use of a conceptually centralized service backend.

A. *IoT Device Software Update Standardization Efforts*

The Internet Engineering Task Force (IETF) has a currently active Security Area Working Group called Software Updates for Internet of Things (suit) [14]. The focus is on secure firmware update solutions, which include a mechanism for transporting firmware images to compatible devices, a digitally signed manifest containing firmware image meta-data and the firmware image(s).

A recent informational Internet-Draft [15] defines that the purpose of an IoT firmware update is to fix vulnerabilities, to update configuration settings, and to add new functionality for improved security. A firmware update must ensure firmware image authentication and integrity protection. In certain cases, prevention of the use of modified firmware images or images from unknown sources may be necessary. Here, it is important to understand the dilemma of potentially installing vulnerable software, versus an informed operator installing a trusted open source-based alternative. Encryption based confidentiality protection can prevent unauthorized access to and modification of the plaintext binary of a firmware image. However, encryption may decrease transparency in some cases.

Firmware updates can be client-initiated by polling for new firmware images or server-initiated by status tracking of IoT devices. A firmware update in an IoT device consists of following steps [15]:

- the device is notified that an update exists,
- a pre-authorization verifies if the manifest signer is authorized to update device firmware. IoT device decide on acceptance of the new firmware image,
- dependency resolution is needed when more than one firmware component can be updated,
- a local copy of the firmware image is downloaded,
- the image is processed into a format the IoT device can recognize and install. Thereafter, the bootloader boots from the installed firmware image.

IV. Distributed update Services Based on DLT Concepts

As discussed in the previous section, traditional IT-architectures, incl. cloud computing based Software-as-a-Service, rely mainly on a conceptually centralized service provision model, while IoT networks and DLT originate from decentralized or distributed architectures. The Bitcoin blockchain [16] introduced a cryptographically secured and distributed ledger. The ability to append transactions to an otherwise immutable ledger comes from a distributed and pseudonymous consensus mechanism, i.e., Nakamoto consensus [16]. Bitcoin's consensus protocol includes both a validity check of a certain transaction and an information sharing protocol, where accepted transactions are stored in blocks chained together in a chronological order. The ledger is an immutable transactional database, thus, the blockchain only stores transactional changes and thereby stays immutable by not forcing an update on pre-existing variable values. In [17], this represents the first generation of DLT. The second DLT generation is in [17] defined to be based on smart contracts, which not only perform an authentication of users and verification of transactions, but may also involve more advanced logical condition states for authorization and automated continuous verification of these condition states.

DLT-based protocol extensions to the web software stack have inter alia provided a new distributed approach to provisioning web services. IPFS provides a Peer-to-Peer (P2P) hypermedia protocol [4] that makes it possible to distribute high volumes of data with high efficiency. IPFS is a distributed file system that utilizes content addressing to fetch static information, rather than location addressing like most traditional file systems. Hashing the content of files or the entire directories achieves this. A resulting hash string works as a link, which also makes IPFS immune to duplicate files. IPFS file versioning based on the generated content identifier (hash) is directly usable for a known latest revision. However, an InterPlanetary Name System (IPNS) [18] identifier exists based on the node peer ID that provides a mutable resource link to the IPFS file hash which when published can be bound to the IPNS. Accessing a file through the IPNS link allows the revision of the IPFS file to change, by republishing the new hash of the file to the IPNS; see Fig. 1 for an illustration.

The data structure behind IPFS is the Merkle Directed Acyclic Graph (DAG), whose links are hashes. Users are the individual peer nodes in a larger swarm. All hashed content published in that particular swarm is retrievable for any participating user. Each IPFS node utilizes a Public Key Infrastructure (PKI) based identification that generates an IPNS, which is a self-certifying PKI namespace (IPNS). This provides all objects in IPFS some useful properties:

- authenticated content,
- permanent cached content,
- a universal data structure, a Merkle DAG,
- a decentralized platform for collaboration.

V. Version Control DLT Solutions

This paper focuses on a new extended VCS use case for fully secured and automated IoT device updates and related management. The first sub-section presents the existing literature of other proposed DLT-based solutions to version control of IoT software updates. The following sub-sections presents initial results of our study on how to implement a fully secured and automated architecture for handling IoT software updates. As stated, the aim of this research is to bring transparency into the process of maintaining IoT devices, by utilizing the earlier mentioned beneficial properties of IPFS and smart contracts executed on the Ethereum blockchain and the Ethereum virtual machine. The benefit of these distributed ledger technologies is that they are, often similarly to the architecture for IoT devices, based on an automated process and can be configured to construct a decentralized platform. Therefore, combining these technologies in a system architecture should improve the reliability, maintainability, and forensic abilities in IoT network supervision.

A. *Proposed DLT-Based Solutions to Version Control of IoT Software Updates.*

Several authors have accentuated the data structure similarities between Git and DLT, and that it is possibly usable for some form of DLT-based version control, e.g., "blockchain can be seen as a Peer-to-Peer (P2P) hosted Git repository" [19].

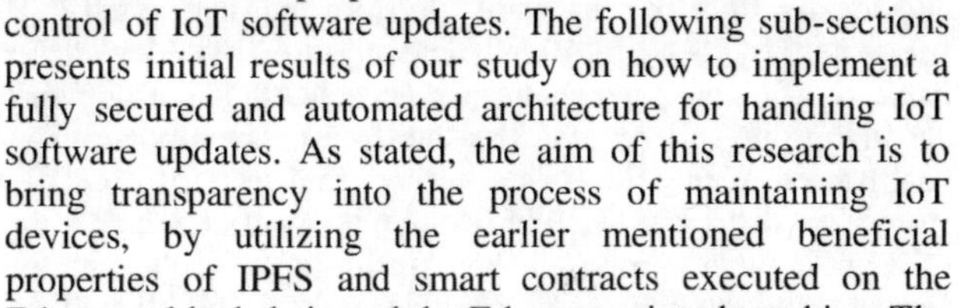

Figure 1. IPFS addressing process flow.

Feature wise Git repository branches are blockchains according to the definition “A blockchain is a sequence of blocks of data in which each block, other than the first, is cryptographically linked to its predecessor” [20]. A blockchain network definition is “a Peer-to-Peer network in which peers collaborate to achieve a common goal by using a blockchain” [20]. According to this definition, a Git repository is a blockchain network, the Git repository peers are developers in a software development project, and the blockchain is the master branch. Git peers often fork the master branch when new versions are stored in the repository, collaborate on the master branch, and strive to merge other branches with the master branch. A Git repository is permission-based and consensus is trust-based on some Git hosting service.

In a proposed setup for IoT device firmware updates, a device manufacturer provides a master update node and configures all IoT devices from the manufacturer as nodes in the same blockchain network [21]. The setup deploys a smart contract for storing the hash of the latest firmware update as a transaction record in a blockchain and for retrieving the latest stored transaction record. The corresponding firmware file is stored in a distributed P2P file system such as IPFS. The manufacturer’s blockchain node stores new firmware updates. IoT devices can find hashes of new firmware updates by querying the smart contract and then to request and locally store the firmware file from the distributed P2P file system by its hash. An IoT device joining the blockchain network after the manufacturer’s node has left the network can therefore still retrieve the latest firmware update. The hash stored of the blockchain verifies that the firmware file stored in a distributed P2P file system is untampered

For another proposed blockchain-based solution for secure firmware updates in IoT devices [22], the blockchain network consists of normal nodes, which are IoT devices and verification nodes, which store firmware files and hash values of firmware files called verifiers in their databases. Outside the blockchain network are firmware vendor nodes. A vendor node maintains a secure communication channel to a verification node for delivery of new firmware updates. A normal node requests a firmware update by broadcasting a version check message to other blockchain network nodes, which respond to the message. If the first response comes from a verification node, then the verification node checks whether the firmware of requesting normal node already is up-to-date. If the firmware is up-to-date, then the verification node checks integrity of the firmware. If the requesting normal node’s firmware is not up-to-date, the responding verification node downloads the latest firmware version to the requesting normal node. If the first response comes from another normal node, then the responding normal node compares the version of its firmware with the requesting node’s firmware version. If the firmware versions are the same, then a lightweight Proof-of-Work mining procedure in blockchain network checks the correctness of the verifier of the requesting node’s firmware. Six confirmations from other blockchain network nodes prove the correctness of the verifier. If the firmware versions are different, then a verification node downloads an up-to-date firmware file to the normal blockchain node whose firmware version is older. The proposed firmware update scheme uses a blockchain block scheme, where each block has a header and a verification field. In the header is stored the size and version of the block, a hash of the header of the previous block, and the root of the Merkle hash tree in the verification field.

The CSA Blockchain/Distributed Ledger Technology Working Group published in 2018 a report “Using Blockchain Technology to Secure the Internet of Things” [23]. In a preferred communication model, each IoT device is a blockchain network node hosting the full ledger of transactions and is capable of participating in blockchain transaction validation and mining. Because of the limited processing, storage, and power resources of most IoT devices, the report proposes a communication model where IoT devices are clients with Application Programming Interfaces (APIs) to blockchain nodes in a cloud based blockchain network service. An IoT device sends digitally signed data from its API to a blockchain network node for processing. A trusted secure communication channel is required between the IoT device and the blockchain network node. The blockchain ledger can store the last version of validated IoT firmware or its hash. An IoT device requests its blockchain network node to deliver, from the transaction ledger, the latest firmware version or the hash of this version. If the blockchain network node delivers a hash, then the IoT device retrieves the latest firmware version from a cloud service and checks if the hash of the retrieved version matches the hash delivered by the blockchain network node.

B. Development of PoC for our Solution

The literature review on the security of IoT software updates shows that research on this topic area has yet to receive the focus it deserves. Although several expressed opinions exist, a universal method (de-facto standard) for solving the problem does not yet exist. That secure IoT device updates and management is problematic or even unsustainable has been established, still very few, if any, solutions exist for either the open source community or for commercial manufacturers to automate and secure software updates to IoT devices in a transparent fashion. The papers reviewed provide several good ideas for further study to identify single case mechanisms for providing IoT update services utilizing DLT-based version control. We proceed through an exploratory approach aimed at understanding the engineering demands of such systems by constructing a PoC backend as an initial step [5].

In our distributed IoT architecture proposal, shown in Fig. 2, IoT nodes transmit their log data to a distributed and replicated data store. The data store exists outside the limited nodes and utilizes a P2P protocol. Utilization of different data stores depend on requirements, such as scalability, speed, or post-processing. A suitable batch-based solution may be the IPFS or a proprietary P2P data transfer protocol. If a streaming solution is required, then the use of a decentralized data and analytics marketplace such as Streamr [24] is an option. Smart contracts executed on top of a DLT implementation may authorize IoT devices and furthermore offer device management, e.g., issue management commands. Implementation of an automatic service for IoT device firmware updates may be similar. Storing the latest version of a binary update file in IPFS and in a smart contract store an IPFS immutable content address that allows the node to query correct IPFS file and firmware signature to confirm file integrity. This tells the IoT node how to access IPFS files and how to perform verification of the needed update. A different solution is to make use of an IPNS hash that points to the latest IPFS hash. The third solution is to mix both approaches. As these systems require two different logins for a manufacturer to share an update, 2-step verification is achievable by using both techniques (smart contract and IPFS) in combination and then compare the content hashes to the downloaded file update hash.

For the future, we consider it important that a manufacturer may want to offer a service contract to any IoT system maintainer/owner. Currently, a significant problem is that IoT nodes have no long-term support as the manufacturer often fails to get financial compensation for updating firmware once the product enters a maintenance/archival phase. A smart contract providing the manufacturer with a decentralized platform for selling firmware updates could implement this business model. An automated update function and contract resolution can be provided to any IoT node maintainer, either on a node basis (number of nodes) or on a network basis (maintaining organization).

C. *Explored Mechanisms and Methods*

This section is devoted to reviewing the technical mechanisms used for the implementation of the frontend interface for the software update manufacturer and the backend. The frontend utilizes a DApp that allows the software developer to deploy new software releases to the platform. A DApp is a stateless web application stored on IPFS and is executable without any dedicated server. This is possible by creating a web application that is self-contained and run within a browsing session initiated by a user. Hence, no server-side processing is required as the client downloads and executes the application. Routines in a JavaScript API library [25] push data to and pull data from IPFS node storage.

The DApp can be, while it is running, as dynamic as a traditional web application; however, from the statelessness follows, that no collected data is normally sent back to a server and stored when the browser is shutdown. Naturally, in the future, there will be more advanced use cases as well, but the idea of decentralized platforms such as ours is to avoid centralized processing that introduces dependencies, bottlenecks and transparency concerns. User authentication occurs before publishing new updates through the IPFS node and through Ethereum [26]. In addition to maintaining the latest content update in IPNS we also propose to store it in a smart contract. The main reason for this is that dual verification can ensure either a two-factor authentication or that the development team can share the IPFS node key for administration purposes, while the final software update release will require the Ethereum key as well. The smart contract is also usable for auditing purposes, as each published directory hash (i.e., a combined hash taken of all files in a directory each time it changes) is stored on the blockchain. In Fig. 3, we present an information flow for the backend of the DApp for releasing software updates. The PoC proposal makes use of a smart contract for guaranteeing revision history and IPFS for file update distribution and file history record.

VI. CONCLUSIONS AND FUTURE DEVELOPMENT

An important task in keeping devices secure in IoT systems, is by ensuring automatic and secure delivery of updates. These challenges involve version control of the software intended to run on the edge nodes, confirming installed software and hardware versions, and linking the versioning data to usage data that may reveal patterns and storing the data that allows auditing of the system. Because IoT networks are distributed/decentralized (depending on network topology choices), we find that not only new technologies, but also new methods for securing IoT devices are needed.

Our paper presents an initial PoC and explores some of the important mechanisms involved in creating a method that offers a more transparent version control of updates than today's services that are conceptually centralized. Our solution does not rely on a central node for distributing updates as IPFS handles file distribution and Ethereum smart contracts handle version management. Our continued development will focus on creating a fully secured and automated process for management of IoT software updates management and on verifying this process with IoT device integration.

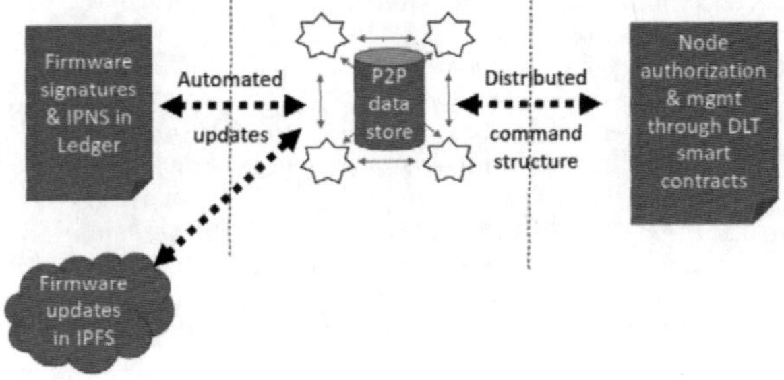

Figure 2. Proposed architecture solution, integrating IoT and DLT.

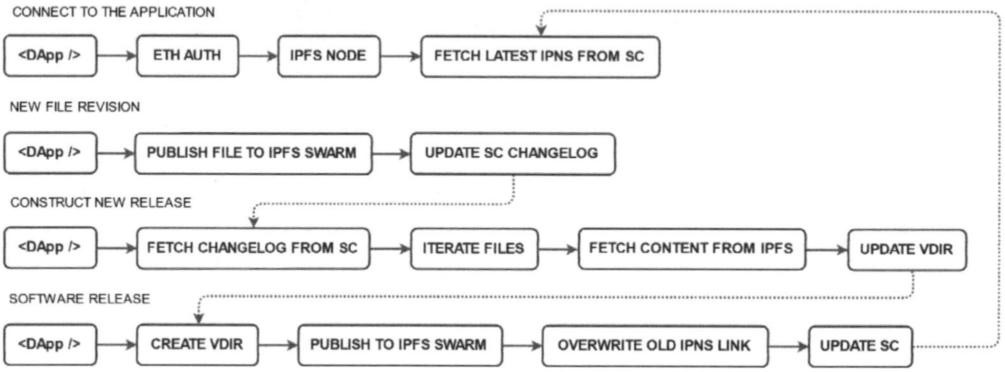

Figure 3. DApp information flow.

REFERENCES

[1] IBM Rational ClearCase. [Online]. Available from: https://www.ibm.com/fi-en/marketplace/rational-clearcase 2019.04.08

[2] Git–fast-version-control. [Online]. Available from: https://git-scm.com 2019.04.08

[3] Built for developers. [Online]. Available from: https://github.com/ 2019.04.08

[4] IPFS. *IPFS is the Distributed Web*. [Online]. Available from: https://ipfs.io/ 2019.04.08

[5] R. J. Wieringa, Design Science Methodology for Information Systems and Software Engineering. Berlin, Heidelberg: Springer-Verlag, 2014

[6] D. Miorandi, S. Sicari, F. De Pellegrini, and I. Chlamtac, "Internet of things: Vision, applications and research challenges" Ad Hoc Networks, vol. 10, no. 7, pp. 1497-1516, 2012.

[7] O. Vermesan and P. Friess, Internet of Things - Global Technological and Societal Trends From Smart Environments and Spaces to Green ICT, Denmark: River Publishers, 2011.

[8] M. Westerlund, "A study of EU data protection regulation and appropriate security for digital services and platforms," Doctoral Dissertation, Åbo Akademi University, Åbo, Finland, 2018.

[9] M. Giles. *For safety's sake, we must slow innovation in internet-connected things*. [Online]. Available from: https://www.technologyreview.com/s/611948/for-safetys-sake-we-must-slow-innovation-in-internet-connected-things/ 2019.04.08

[10] J. Condliffe. *Should IoT Devices Come with Public Safety Warnings?* [Online]. Available from: https://www.technologyreview.com/the-download/609124/should-iot-devices-come-with-public-safety-warnings/ 2019.04.08

[11] M. Westerlund, M. Neovius, and G. Pulkkis, "Providing Tamper-Resistant Audit Trails with Distributed Ledger based Solutions for Forensics of IoT Systems using Cloud Resources." International Journal on Advances in Security, vol.11, no. 3 and 4, pp. 288-300, 2018

[12] CSA cloud security alliance. [Online]. Available from: https://cloudsecurityalliance.org 2019.04.08

[13] CSA cloud security alliance. *Recommendations for IoT Firmware Update Processes*. [Online]. Available from: https://downloads.cloudsecurityalliance.org/assets/research/internet-of-things/recommendations-for-iot-firmware-update-processes.pdf 2019.04.08

[14] IETF. *Software Updates for Internet of Things (suit)*. [Online]. Available from: https://datatracker.ietf.org/wg/suit/about/ 2019.04.08

[15] B. Moran, M. Meriac, H. Tschofenig, and D. Brown. *A Firmware Update Architecture for Internet of Things Devices. draft-ietf-suit-architecture-02*. [Online]. Available from: https://datatracker.ietf.org/doc/draft-ietf-suit-architecture/ 2019.04.08

[16] S. Nakamoto, "Bitcoin: A Peer-to-Peer Electronic Cash System," 2008. [Online]. Available from: https://bitcoin.org/bitcoin.pdf 2019.04.08

[17] M. Westerlund and N. Kratzke, "Towards Distributed Clouds," Proc. 16th International Conference on High Performance Computing & Simulation (HPCS), IEEE Press, July 2018, pp. 655-663, doi:10.1109/HPCS.2018.00108.

[18] Data done differently. [Online]. Available from: https://www.streamr.com/ 2019.04.08

[19] J. Ramos. *Blockchain: Under the Hood*. [Online]. Available from: https://www.thoughtworks.com/insights/blog/blockchain-under-hood 2019.04.08

[20] E. Feig, "A Framework for Blockchain-Based Applications," arXiv:1803.00892 [cs.CY], 2018. [Online]. Available from: https://arxiv.org/abs/1803.00892 2019.04.08

[21] K. Christidis and M. Devetsikiotis, "Blockchains and smart contracts for the Internet of Things," IEEE Access, vol 4, pp. 2292–2303, 2016, doi: 10.1109/ACCESS.2016.2566339.

[22] B. Lee and J.-H. Lee, "Blockchain-based secure firmware update for embedded devices in an Internet of Things environment," The Journal of Supercomputing, pp. 1–6, 2016, doi: 10.1007/s11227-016-1870-0.

[23] CSA cloud security alliance. *Using Blockchain Technology to Secure the Internet of Things*. [Online]. Available from: https://downloads.cloudsecurityalliance.org/assets/research/blockchain/Using_BlockChain_Technology_to_Secure_the_Internet_of_Things.pdf 2019.04.08

[24] IPFS Documentation - IPNS [Online]. Available from: https://docs.ipfs.io/guides/concepts/ipns/ 2019.04.08

[25] A client library for the IPFS HTTP API, implemented in JavaScript. [Online]. Available from: https://github.com/ipfs/js-ipfs-http-client 2019.04.08

[26] Ethereum JavaScript API. [Online]. Available from: https://github.com/ethereum/web3.js/ 2019.04.08

Governance in Decentralized Ecosystems:

A Survey of Blockchain and Distributed Ledger White Papers

Petri Honkanen
Department of Business Management and Analytics
Arcada University of Applied Sciences
Helsinki, Finland
petri.honkanen@arcada.fi

Magnus Westerlund
Department of Business Management and Analytics
Arcada University of Applied Sciences
Helsinki, Finland
magnus.westerlund@arcada.fi

Mats Nylund
Department of Business Management and Analytics
Arcada University of Applied Sciences
Helsinki, Finland
mats.nylund@arcada.fi

Abstract—**For organizations of today, Information Technology (IT) governance is an important part of managing IT investments. To understand how governance is handled in blockchain projects, we surveyed a large body of project white papers to understand the level of organizational maturity in the field. The results show that governance has yet to receive a similar stance in blockchain projects as compared to IT governance in general. We introduce a discussion around implicit versus explicit governance, as to highlight the challenges in simplifying the debate around a level of distributedness, in terms of premissionless (public) and permissioned (private) blockchains.**

Keywords-governance; blockchain; distributed ledger technology; decentralized platforms; decentralized ecosystems.

I. INTRODUCTION

Over the last two decades, companies have begun understanding the importance of accountability in IT decision making. Today IT governance is part of any mature organization's toolset to determine that IT decisions truly provide a return on investment and that managers of IT-systems are accountable for the organizations decision making on investing in new and in maintaining legacy systems. An organization without a formalized approach to IT governance will have to rely on the individual system operator or manager to resolve issues as they arise and perhaps most importantly that this isolated decision making is also beneficial long-term to the company [1] [2].

Traditional IT systems are usually under the direct influence of the system owner, meaning that this system can receive updates and that the service can potentially be terminated in case a catastrophic error is detected. IT system decision making is also conceptually centralized around a system owner that may to a certain degree take input from users and customers, but the final decision is always in the hands of the owner. As IT architectures have moved over to a cloud provisioned model that may utilize a loosely coupled and fine-grained microservice architecture the control has become more difficult and may thus require an even deeper focus on IT governance.

The new type of distributed architectures based on technologies, such as public (permissionless) distributed ledgers and blockchains introduces a new set of problems that require an increased understanding of governance. The distributed nature of execution means that a system owner no longer has the full control over who uses the system or even for what usage purpose. For decentralized ecosystems, based on Distributed Ledger Technology (DLT), it may even become difficult to determine who the system owner is. Here, the decentralized ecosystem becomes the inherent infrastructure to build new systems and services upon, and the original ecosystem creator may no longer be a relevant party to the continued development and maintenance of said ecosystem and services. Still, this does not mean that governance of the ecosystem is no longer required, rather this suggests that in accordance with open source software development this becomes a group effort.

A core tenant of these decentralized ecosystems is that they offer users a certain amount of pseudonymity and this is something that often contrasts them from open source development. Architectures for decentralized ecosystems are based on the principal of achieving consensus based on trustless transactions. This can best be understood as that Alice and Bob can perform a transaction securely without the need for them to first establish trust towards each other. This is ensured by a consensus from the network peers that validate the transaction on behalf of Alice and Bob. Therefore, to enable anonymity in governance for decentralized ecosystems, the governance mechanisms should be distributed and arguably be based on the same trustless procedures as for other transactions.

In this paper, we survey white papers from DLT and blockchain projects, and related proposals to understand how they intend to deal with governance. The initial survey aims to select those white paper proposals that raise the subject of governance and then to further expand on the maturity of these approaches. We limit the scope of the survey to a focus on the long-term benefits for users of these ecosystem. We acknowledge that there is an argument for a developer and investor viewpoint as well, but due to length constraints we have chosen this focus for our present study.

The structure of the paper is the following, first data gathering is described and from this material, we provide general observations and then describe models and challenges discovered. We then introduce the abstractions of implicit and explicit governance, to deliver an analysis of the implications of a lack of governance. Finally, we present conclusions and future work.

II. Data Gathering and Research Aim

For the survey, we have examined 241 white papers, which all cover and describe blockchain- or distributed ledger technology-based projects. These white papers include different types of projects, for example protocols, platforms or applications, which we refer to in a common term as "ecosystems". The range of scanned white papers is wide and aims to select those papers that make a direct mention of governance for further study. The corpus was selected through non-probabilistic and discretionary sampling from various sources, that were found through search engines and various websites that report on relevant matters. Due to the inexistence of an all-inclusive global registry of DLT ecosystems, discretionary sampling remained our only alternative.

The role of releasing white papers has become the de-facto norm when projects and ecosystems are conceptualized, and design views, abilities and features are explained, and staff introduced. In this survey, we present the first results of our study. We start from the general findings and follow the path to explain what these results could mean in the larger context of institutions, actors, structures and organizations. Further research concentrates on the relevance of decentralization by analyzing potential institutional and organizational changes, in order to capture and understand current and future developments occurring in the society at large.

III. General Observations

The survey had a wide scope as to amass a large enough research body to examine. We start by discussing the common position and role of governance that is found in the whitepapers and then in consequent sections drill down into specific projects and their solutions.

Governance, decision-making structures, and the inner processes (human activity) of the decentralized ecosystem as an explicit standpoint are missing in a large part of the examined whitepapers. This does not mean though, that there would be no governance, decision-making structures, or processes in these ecosystems. Structures and processes of governance can also exist implicitly and can be assessed through various scales, e.g., centralization vs. decentralization, explicated vs. hidden, dynamic vs fixed, and technocentric vs. human oriented. There are commonly no explicit explanations for the absence of governance structures and processes in white papers nor is there a standardized format the white paper should adhere to, therefore in this study, the reason for absence can only be conjectured.

Potential reasons can be traced by considering the setting of white paper producers. Most of the white papers have been written by/for a company or other legal entity (e.g., foundation), whose main interest lays in initiating, developing and launching an ecosystem, but also to collect financing for the ecosystem through an Initial Coin Offering (ICO) or Security Token Offering (STO). Due to this latter target, some entities might want to hold quorum among the immediate beneficiaries of the project and are not prepared to discuss about the notion of distributing governance.

Other reasons for absence of governance structures can signal various features of organizational structure, incompleteness of the planned ecosystem, planned unimportance of decentralization, forgetfulness of writers, or intended mischievous behavior. Another possibility is a misconception concerning an audience. Those who have produced the white papers may have had beliefs, that by describing an implicit technical solution of governance, they would not need to give any further explanation of how it works. This type of minimalism can be found for example in the Bitcoin white paper [3]. As such, today it can be considered delusional in a sense, that as the white paper paves the way for the first blockchain and the first successful cryptocurrency ever, the ecosystem should be able to function without any other governance structure than incentives for mining. Since the launch of Bitcoin, we have observed how this minimalistic model has led to deep contradictions and hard forks, because of a lack of consensus around decision-making and governance concerning the continued development of the bitcoin protocol. Concerning the Bitcoin white paper, which was written 2008, it is understandable that governance was not understood and consequently described in more detail. In the more recent white papers we examined, which were published during 2017-18, the absence of a governance structure is more peculiar.

Altogether, for an ecosystem to seem genuinely decentralized, the absence of a governance standpoint in a white paper may indicate some long-term issues the ecosystem will have to face. However, there are also white papers in which governance is described in detail and in these white papers conditions of governance have been scrutinized profoundly and it is sometimes clear that problems of a technical or human design are attempted to be solved by using certain models of governance. Due to these differences in attitudes, one may ask if there is something to conceal in the ecosystem projects, which do not openly describe and justify their governance model or even worse do not mention a governance standpoint at all. Due to this lack of clarity, we find that continued research into the role of governance for building sustainable decentralized ecosystems is well merited.

IV. Governance Models and Challenges

In the following sub-section, we start with a brief examination of what primary and secondary sources discuss on the topic of blockchain governance. The following sub-section then highlights findings from some of the blockchain projects surveyed.

A. Literature survey

Governance studies in academic literature is still sparse, particularly surveys of how blockchain projects view and implement governance. Some literature sources examine the philosophical aspects of decentralized governance and others consider how trust emerges towards a decentralized project. Others examine a specific case, such as the DAO project [4], but to the authors best knowledge none examined a multitude of projects as we do in this survey.

Secondary sources such as open blog posts have so far been the foremost place for fostering a discussion about how governance should be implemented and approached. The discussion and openings originating from influential blockchain researchers such as Nick Szabo and Vlad Zamfir focus on definition [5]. The former, Szabo has provocatively classified blockchain governance into three categories [6] 1. "Lord of Flies" [edit. disastrous attempt of self-governance], 2. Lawyers, 3. Ruthlessly minimized. His categorization gives an impression of frustration for governance choices and discussion about governance. However, all governance analysis does not remain as superficial as that. Zamfir has underlined the political aspect of governance and presented a "Blockchain governance outcome" model with five visions for the future [7]. These five visions are: Autonomous Blockchains, Blockchain Governance Capture, Internet Censorship as Blockchain Governance, Governance via Public International Law or Diplomacy, and Governance via International Private Cooperation. However, despite profound argumentation, Zamfir's view is validating the setting in which the general blockchain governance model is still very incomplete and even the definition is controversial.

CleanApp foundation has brought a more analytical grasp to the discussion about governance. In their continuation of Zamfir's five views, they introduced a "vocabulary for blockchain governance", which can be interpreted to be based on at least six layers or operational contexts [8]. The six layers are: Intra-blockchain governance, Inter-blockchain governance, Pan-blockchain governance, Supra-blockchain governance, Private-off-chain governance and Global governance. As a result of their analysis CleanApp concluded that "today's blockchain governance mechanisms are broken because it's almost impossible to access today's blockchain governance mechanisms" and "today's blockchain governance feedback mechanisms are either non-existent or grossly under-developed". To make governance easier to approach and understandable the concepts in-chain and off-chain governance is used. This categorization elucidates the differences between traditional and automated (voting and execution) features of governance [9].

By following commentaries about on-chain and off-chain governance, it can at times be an inflammatory theme of discussion. It seems that many writers do advocate the role of off-chain governance as a primary source of order and power in ecosystems. A good example of this genre is the title of Vlad Zamfir's blog article. "Against on-chain governance" [10]. Also, Haseeb Qureshi has promoted the ideology that "Blockchains should not be democracies" [11]. He has argued that governance process should be built around the expertise of capable technologists, who can "get shit done". However, his thesis is anchored to the phase of (radical) development of blockchain technology as he has stated himself: "Perhaps someday blockchains will be robust and stable enough to no longer need the guiding hand of capable technologists."

B. White paper survey

In Table I, we present a classification of the white papers surveyed. General refers to broad DLT projects such as the Bitcoin blockchain. Others mean projects that could not be categorized under our classification. In the leftmost column, we list the types of projects included. In the following four columns, we have categorized the papers on a scale of 0-3 defining the level of governance found. Here, 0 means that an explicit mentioning of governance is missing, while 3 means that governance is thoroughly described. We intentionally included a larger sample of media and content type projects as there was a higher ratio of white papers that described governance.

In the white papers, an explicit on-chain or off-chain conceptualization is not common. Still, the NEO [12] white paper [13] provides an exception and governance for on-chain/off-chain governance is briefly defined as following:

*"**Chain governance:** NEO token holders are the network owners and managers, managing the network through voting in the network, using the GAS generated from NEO to utilize the functions in the network. NEO tokens can be transferred.*

***Off-chain governance:** NEO Council consists of the founding members of the NEO project, under which the management committee, technical committee and the secretariat, respectively, are responsible for strategic decision-making, technical decision-making and specific implementation. The NEO Council is responsible to the NEO community for the promotion and development of NEO ecosystem as its primary objective."*

As we see, there are obvious reasons to ask if NEO is a centralized and not a decentralized ecosystem. Even though on-chain processes are enabled in NEO, crucial decision making is located in a predefined off-chain governance structure.

TABLE I - A SUMMARY AND CLASSIFICATION OF SURVEYED WHITE PAPERS

Types	Explicit governance missing	Vague reference	Brief description	Governance described	Total
General	31	3	5	15	54
Data	13	3	2	2	20
Energy	7	0	0	0	7
Finance	8	0	2	1	11
Media&content	42	7	5	11	65
Professional	6	0	1	3	10
Sharing&reputation	14	3	2	2	21
Tools	9	0	2	2	13
Health	5	1	1	2	9
Commerce	5	1	1	1	8
Others	18	2	1	2	23
Total	158	20	22	41	241

Essentially, the off-chain committees should be responsible for proposals and decision making and very little information exists on NEO's website on who belongs to these committees, the nomination and expulsion process of these individuals/institutions. The financial decision making is also centralized as this comes from reserved NEO tokens during the launch and according to the white paper from the GAS generated from the NEO transaction processing.

Recently, the NEO Council acknowledged the issue as well and have proposed a plan to instigate a decentralization of consensus nodes. Part of this process will be to rethink financing of the development work once the reserved tokens are consumed.

"NEO Council had been spending the reserved NEO tokens to accelerate development, reward community, and foster ecosystem. Decreasing amount of NEO held by NEO Council means decreasing voting power, and eventually all NEO tokens aka governance power will be distributed to the community." [14]

For a project to explicate their own governance model in a white paper format, seems to be a challenging task for the organization responsible for blockchain- or other DLT-based ecosystems. Although the study found dozens of white papers with some sort of explicit approach to the governance issue, pervasive and integrated (in-chain) models of governance were rare. One explanation for the difficulties may lie in the incompleteness of ecosystems. As the ecosystem has not been launched or exists in a very early phase, real life tests are not possible to experience how the ecosystem functions in a real-life context. However, in some white papers, the ecosystem defines a clearly articulated process, including roles and positions of governance and there are clear signs of an endeavor to decentralize the ecosystem in these projects.

Furthermore, the few whitepapers in which governance models are profoundly detailed, tend to be advancing decentralization at least on a discursive level as desirable and as the intended final state of the ecosystem.

As mentioned in the beginning, without exception, all the white papers have some sort of – although sometimes hidden - agenda for governance. However, the governance model does not have to be decentralized, it can be centralized or very minimalistic, but it exists. Dan Larimer [15] has described this as:

"Every blockchain that has a "process for upgrading" has a governance structure that is capable of changing the rules, rolling back stolen funds, etc. It is the good-old-boy network of Github admins, exchange connections, and mining pool operators. The problem is that these processes are informal and less predictable and even less accountable than the governmental structures we hope the blockchains would replace."

Even projects with a target of very thin governance can openly admit that some sort of governance is needed. In the white paper of Mixin [16] Network is stated:

"We try our best to make Mixin Network just work without any governance, but there are still situations the program can't handle" (p.27).

In order to find solutions for the in-chain/off-chain challenge, some ecosystems have been created with a written constitution. For example, EOS [17]and media platform Civil [18] attempt to base their operations on this type of model. In the constitution there are established rules and principles that should govern the continued operation of these ecosystems. Qureshi has used Blockchain 3.0. to define on-chain based ecosystems, *"On-chain governance is central to many "blockchain 3.0" projects, such as Tezos* [19], *DFINITY* [20], *and Cosmos* [21]. *Others, such as 0x* [22]*and Maker* [23], *are planning to eventually implement on-chain governance through a more gradual transition."*

V. GOVERNANCE ABSTRACTIONS

The traditional classification of blockchain types has been based on a technical distinction whether they are private or public. This usually refers to access control, determining, e.g., who may perform transaction validations and what incentive is offered to the nodes to stay honest. Below we consider the two main abstractions that we have found in the white-paper review.

A. *Implicit governance*

The most common governance abstraction found is implicit governance. Implicit governance refers to the lack of an explicated well-formed process that deal with decision-making and the governance of those humans that still make decisions in relation to the ecosystems. Implicit governance is used both by Bitcoin and Ethereum and refer to a model that is based on human expertise to make decisions when they arise. Often these decisions are of a technical nature, e.g., when advancing the protocol. Such measures may require a deep level of technical knowledge that few people behold, and the obvious choice is to delegate the decision-making to this group. However, the dilemma arises when the changes are not only of a technical nature but may also change the dynamics of the ecosystem.

An example of such a situation occurred when the Ethereum developer group decided to switch away from a pure Proof of Work (PoW) consensus model towards a Proof of Stake (PoS) model. The technical decision-making of such a change may require that a small group of physically identified and trusted people make the necessary design decisions, but the lack of an explicit governance model means that the users of Ethereum have as much input in the decision-making process as they would have with a private chain. In this case, the change means that the mining process is altered so that miners are no longer compensated and that mining hardware is not needed as before. Please, note that we are not taking the position that either PoW or PoS is either good or bad, this is merely an example of the conundrum.

Another example of implicit governance and lack of any institutionalized governance occurred in 2017 when there was a dispute over the 'segwit2x' hard fork and doubling of the block size among Bitcoin stakeholders. Due to the disagreement over doubling the block size, it led to that Bitcoin Cash was created and forked from the original Bitcoin. This could also have occurred, had a formally defined governance protocol existed, but for a characteristically decentralized ecosystem the latter system seems to be more effective, transparent, and foreseeable for all of the potential stakeholders. Implicitness – trust without reservations and doubts – may entice conflicts when significantly upgrading the ecosystems, even when they are needed for the ecosystem to stay relevant in the market.

In time of change, implicit governance leaves the stakeholders with three options, accept the modifications, exit the ecosystem, or in some cases do a hard-fork. Some would argue that these options provide a technocratic society with minimalistic regulation, while still functioning. However, a critical view is to ask how mature such thinking is and if this is inclusive enough for mainstream users to place their trust in such technology.

B. *Explicit governance*

Explicit governance arises from a well-formed process for decision-making, oversight, and stakeholder participation. Explicit governance is therefore not a purely technological solution, but rather something that resembles real life. An explicit governance ecosystem must strive to embrace the occurrence of conflict through resolution, rather than to state a take-it/leave-it implication. A technocratic society may view this as a 'disastrous attempt of self-governance' and they may be correct in such an assumption, still for a more human-centric society, the aim is often not an autonomous ecosystem, but rather an automated ecosystem that increases peer participation in the decision-making process.

In addition to the operative and strategic decision-making process, explicit governance also seeks to define the development process. In IT governance we often see that the development process is defined through a maturity model, meaning that the initial stage (level 1) would likely be developer based, as we also often find in the case for implicit governance. The Capability Maturity Model Integration (CMMI) model [24] define five maturity levels, described in Table II. Considering our review of the white papers, we can characterize most governance models to be on a maturity level of one or two. To achieve explicit governance, we consider that it requires that the CMMI level is also raised to three or higher. As most blockchain development projects are still in an early stage, we should perhaps not be too surprised with these findings.

However, there may also be influences present from the traditional open source community that have often refuted commercial interests as a driving force for development. The question then becomes, moving beyond open source products towards online services and platforms based on various value instruments, such as coins and tokens, should this not be reflected in the maturity level of processes?

TABLE II - CMMI MATURITY LEVELS

Level	Description
5	Optimizing the process continously
4	Process is quantitatively managed
3	Process is defined and proactive
2	Development is managed, but process is often reactive
1	Unpredictable and poorly controlled

The level of decentralization cannot only be measured in a technical context (e.g., node distribution), but also needs to reflect the participation rate of human peers. Thus, a blockchain project may consider themselves decentralized, but without a communicated explicit governance structure this should not be understood as anything different to a centralized model around a private chain. As shown, the differentiation between private and public chains only serves to communicate whom its intended target group is.

VI. IMPLICATIONS FOR DECENTRALIZED ECOSYSTEMS

In consequence of the absence of clearly defined governance in the project white papers and especially the lack of explanations for this omission, it may lead to a dubious effect on the decentralization discussion and over time slowly reduce the trust for the ecosystems, incl. connected companies and foundations responsible for the development of these ecosystems. An ecosystem without open access for all stakeholders to participate in a transparent way on agenda setting and decision making may from a decentralized point of view be considered distrustful. In addition, given a highly speculative project (high Return on Investment (ROI) potential), if a party can become a project stakeholder (decision maker) by acquiring coins/tokens of the ecosystem, it suggests that a centralization of power will eventually occur as the financial incentives would likely outcompete other incentives in the long-term. Then at least from an ideology perspective, but likely also from a perspective of influence, the project will become more centralized than equally distributed among participants.

We cannot comprehensively know how the qualities of a governance model affect decisions of potential users when they choose between different alternative ecosystems. Nevertheless, these kinds of questions may arise in the near future if adaption of decentralized ecosystems takes place en masse. The relevance of governance as criteria for potential adopters should be elucidated through independent research.

A peculiar feature concerning claims for decentralized ecosystems, is that a decentralized ecosystem by default also embodies a conceptually decentralized governance structure. However, in our view, ecosystems without decentralized governance are not properly decentralized ecosystems and based on some project white papers it can be difficult to understand if or even how people are poised to operate in that kind of an ecosystem.

In this research, we have primarily considered white papers as research data when searching for the existence and features of governance models for DLT ecosystems. However, this does not denote that all aims of ecosystems and their governance have been documented in the white papers.

There may also be reservations concerning the transparency of ecosystems. Because of local regulations of raising funds for DLT ecosystems, governance may restrict, e.g., the potential rights of the token holders. Ultimately, this could mean that in some cases the genuine goal of the ecosystem and its governance structure has been hidden to enable the development and launch of ecosystem. However, without further research into these types of potential distortions, we can only convey an expression of uncertainty.

VII. Conclusions and Future Work

As we have remarked, considering the size of the amassed research data we are yet to be aware of what governance features an ecosystem must have. Part of the problem is due to that there are more white papers without any explicit reference to governance than those that mentions the concept explicitly. The idea of a company, foundation or other organization as "owner" or "ultimate decision maker" of the ecosystem (through, e.g., initial token allocations), as the case is in quite many white papers, creates this enigma. Ultimately, if there is no mention of future aims of an ecosystem, i.e., to advance and deploy decentralization in governance, this kind of ecosystem refers to centralized governance without real commitment for decentralization. Hence, the traditional division of ecosystems as permissioned or permissionless, needs to be extended into a more complex framework that evaluates the current and future potential level of decentralized governance in the ecosystem.

Our future work will focus on elaborating on the project white papers that mention governance and to examine some of these in-depth to understand if they have implemented the said governance structure and to examine if they have gone beyond what they promised in their white papers. Additionally, we aim to extend the scope from the user perspective to the developer perspective.

Acknowledgment

The authors wish to thank the Lindstedt foundation for the financial grant that made this work possible.

References

[1] P. Weill, and J. Ross, "A matrixed approach to designing IT governance, ". MIT Sloan Management Review, 46(2), 26, 2005.

[2] S. De Haes, and W. Van Grembergen, "IT governance and its mechanisms, " Information Systems Control Journal, 1, 27-33, 2004.

[3] S. Nakamoto, Bitcoin: A Peer-to-Peer Electronic Cash System. Available from: https://bitcoin.org/bitcoin.pdf 2008. Accessed 14th of April 2019

[4] C. Jentzsch, Decentralized Autonomous Organization To Automate Governance. Available from: https://download.slock.it/public/DAO/WhitePaper.pdf 2016 Accessed 14th of April 2019

[5] A. Breitman (Tezos), J. Benet (Filecoin) and T. McConaghy (Ocean Protoco), In: A. Hamacher, Blockchain's "founding fathers" talk governance. Available from: https://decryptmedia.com/3853/blockchains-founding-fathers-talk-governance 2018.10.29 Accessed 14th of April 2019

[6] N. Szabo, "Blockchain governance". Available from: https://twitter.com/nickszabo4/status/1009996445280169985 2018.06.22 Accessed 14th of April 2019

[7] V. Zamfir, Blockchain Governance 101. Available from: https://blog.goodaudience.com/blockchain-governance-101-eea5201d7992 2018.09.30 Accessed 14th of April 2019

[8] CleanApp, Blockchain Governance 102- Response to Vlad Zamfir's Blockchain Governance 101. Available from: https://medium.com/cryptolawreview/blockchain-governance-102-9912a88da91d 2018.10.02 Accessed 14th of April 2019

[9] B. Curran, What is Blockchain Governance? Complete Beginner's Guide. Available from: https://blockonomi.com/blockchain-governance/ 2018.09.21 Accessed 14th of April 2019

[10] V.Zamfir, Against on-chain governance. Available from: https://medium.com/@Vlad_Zamfir/against-on-chain-governance-a4ceacd040ca 2017.12.01 Accessed 14th of April 2019

[11] H.Qureshi, Blockchains should not be democracies. Available from: https://haseebq.com/blockchains-should-not-be-democracies/ 2018.04.16 Accessed 14th of April 2019

[12] Currently the NEO coin is the 14th largest measured in market cap ($464,296,905). According to https://coinmarketcap.com/coins/. Accessed 5th of February 2019.

[13] NEO, NEO White paper. Available from: https://docs.neo.org/en-us/whitepaper.html Accessed 14th of April 2019

[14] See the following for more information. NEO, A Statement from NEO Council. Available from: https://neo.org/blog/details/3067 2018.06.03. See sub-section on "Facts about NEO's plan to decentralize Consensus Nodes", point 3. Accessed 5th of February 2019.

[15] D. Larimer, Decentralized Blockchain Governance. Available from: https://medium.com/@bytemaster/decentralized-blockchain-governance-743f0273bf5a 2018.06.20 Accessed 14th of April 2019

[16] Mixin Network, Mixin Network White paper. Available from: https://mixin.one/assets/Mixin-Draft-2018-07-01.pdf 2018.07.01 Accessed 14th of April 2019

[17] D. Larimer, EOS.io White paper. Available from: https://github.com/EOSIO/Documentation/blob/master/TechnicalWhitePaper.md 2017 Accessed 14th of April 2019

[18] Civil, The Civil Constitution. Available from: https://civil.co/constitution/#constitution Accessed 14th of April 2019

[19] LM. Goodman, Tezos — a self-amending crypto-ledger White paper. Available from: https://tezos.com/static/white_paper-2dc8c02267a8fb86bd67a108199441bf.pdf 2014 Accessed 14th of April 2019

[20] T. Hanke; Movahedi M. & Williams D. DFINITY Technology Overview Series Consensus System. Accessed 14th of April 2019

[21] J. Kwon & Buchman E. Cosmos A Network of Distributed Ledgers. Available from: https://github.com/cosmos/cosmos/blob/master/WHITEPAPER.md Accessed 14th of April 2019

[22] W.Warren, White Paper - 0x. Available from: https://0x.org/pdfs/0x_white_paper.pdf 2017 Accessed 14th of April 2019

[23] Maker, White Paper - Maker DAO. Available from: https://makerdao.com/whitepaper/ Accessed 14th of April 2019

[24] CMMI Product Team, "CMMI for Development, Version 1.3," Software Engineering Institute, Carnegie Mellon University, Pittsburgh, Pennsylvania, Technical Report CMU/SEI-2010-TR-033, 2010. http://resources.sei.cmu.edu/library/asset-view.cfm?AssetID=9661

Blockchain Challenges for Cloud Users

Yuan Zhao*,Bob Duncan†
Business School
University of Aberdeen, UK
Emails: *y.zhao@abdn.ac.uk,†robert.duncan@abdn.ac.uk

Abstract—**Blockchain presents a new paradigm for delivering a very robust audit trail through the use of distributed ledger technology. There is the potential to provide a high level of security while keeping costs under control. There are, of course, many challenges, which are specific to cloud computing, and these must be identified and addressed before the right level of security can be achieved. Failure to achieve proper security will negate the benefits of the technology and also expose companies to massive potential fines. We investigate what these challenges are and suggest a means of ensuring how these challenges can be met in order to mitigate any potential exposure of cloud users. We address this in the context of a company who wishes to use a cloud based accounting system and must be compliant with the European Union General Data Protection Regulation.**

Keywords–Cloud forensic problem; GDPR; Blockchain/bitcoin technology.

I. Introduction

All computer systems are the subject of continuous attack, no matter to which market sector they might belong. No system is immune to attack. For traditional networked computer systems, this presents a serious challenge to ensure a high level of security and privacy can be maintained, but for cloud systems, these challenges increase exponentially, due to the increase in complexity in software, and the multiplicity of layers and actors involved in modern cloud ecosystems. There are many challenges to address in order to be able to ensure compliance can be achieved.

Yet, there remains one serious, and as yet unresolved challenge, namely the Cloud Forensic Problem [1], which is likely to prove a serious barrier to achieving any robust level of security and privacy for any company. When an attacker succeeds in gaining even a temporary foothold in a cloud based system, their primary goal will be to escalate privileges until they are able to eliminate the forensic trail, which logged their incursion into the system, thus, allowing them to bury themselves deep so as to become a more permanent intruder, lying undetected inside the victim's system. With cloud systems, there is nothing to prevent this from happening. The intruder is usually perfectly happy to remain hidden in the system, where they can carry on stealing information for as long as they wish with relative impunity. Formerly, the intruder was usually happy to get in and out quickly, but now, long term surveillance can be a far more lucrative proposition for them.

This presents a particularly problematic dilemma for companies who fall under the jurisdiction of, and, therefore, require to be compliant with, the European Union (EU) General Data Protection Regulation (GDPR) [2], and where they also use cloud. By default, those who use cloud will be unable to meet the stringent compliance requirements. With the maximum punitive level of possible fines for non-compliance being up to the greater of €20million or 4% of last year's global turnover [2], this will certainly have a considerable potential impact on those companies who are unable to meet the compliance requirements.

With the widespread convenience, instant access to resources, relatively low operating cost, and no requirement for capital expenditure, cloud systems provide companies with a huge incentive for cloud use. Many companies have already committed substantially to this paradigm, thus, exposing them to the impact of non-compliance. One option would be to convert back to conventional distributed network systems, but taking into account the long lead time needed, the massive costs involved, and the level of expertise that will be required to securely set up such systems, this move back to distributed network systems is unlikely to be either an economic or even a viable option. Equally, it is also not an option to do nothing.

Thus, it is imperative for all cloud users that an alternative solution be found in the meantime, as quickly as possible, and preferably one that might be as simple as possible to implement. In this paper, we look at the use case of a company trading throughout the EU, who wish to use a cloud based accounting software programme and will be subject to and required to comply with the GDPR. They will quite rightly be concerned about the implications of non-compliance this plan might have on their ability to comply with the GDPR.

We are interested in examining the potential offered by Blockchain - the underlying technology that provides the secure backbone of crypto-currencies. We start by examining the potential weaknesses in the use of blockchain in cloud environments in Section II. Next, we consider the potential impact of those weaknesses for cloud users in Section III. In Section IV, we consider how to resolve those cloud blockchain weaknesses, while in Section V, we consider how to set up a robust architecture to address the use case scenario we just introduced. In Section VI, we discuss our findings, and in Section VII, we present our conclusions.

II. Blockchain Weaknesses for Cloud Users

It is certainly the case that no computing system is immune to attack, with this being particularly relevant for cloud based systems. During recent years, some really good research from authors on accountability [3], compliance [4], privacy [5]–[8], risk [9], security [10]–[13], and trust [14]–[16], which has ensured that a far greater level of security and privacy has been achieved in cloud systems. Despite all these good efforts, no solution has yet been developed and implemented to properly address the cloud forensic problem.

Every attacker seeks to compromise a cloud system to gain even a small foothold. They will then attempt to escalate privileges to allow them to access forensic and audit trails, to allow them to delete or modify such records as they need to hide their route into the system. At this point the attacker becomes an intruder, allowing them to remain hidden and lie undetected for long periods of time, free to help themselves to any data they choose. To achieve compliance with the GDPR, companies must be able to report a breach within 72 hours of discovery. The global average time for all companies between breach and discovery in 2012 was an average of 6 months [17] [18]. This had improved to some 4 weeks by 2016 [19] — still far short of what is needed to understand what has been going on with the intruders while they remained undiscovered.

It is obvious that the longer an intruder can remain hidden inside a company system, the more information they can acquire, or the greater the potential damage they can perpetrate. During 2017, following some serious lobbying, the GDPR was changed from "... within 72 hours of a breach occurring..." to a much less stringent "... within 72 hours of discovery ...", this rather misses the point that if a company cannot discover a breach within 72 hours of the breach occurring, how can they possibly discover it has arisen at all, let alone what data has been compromised after the intruder has deleted all forensic and audit trails? The reality of this backward step in the regulation, was that companies suddenly 'switched off' their attentions to improving cyber security, and this is evidenced by the fact that average times between breach and discovery had by the end of 2017, rather sadly returned to the levels of five years ago [20]. Unfortunately, many companies do not retain the access records that record which database records have been accessed, since many database configurations routinely turn off such functions by default in order to minimise the need for storage. This results in the situation whereby, once a breach occurs, the company will no longer have the means to be able to report which records have been accessed, copied, modified, deleted or ex-filtrated from their system. This means non-compliance with the GDPR, which in turn means exposure to potentially punitive levels of fines by the regulator.

Taking into account the high data volumes associated with cloud use, and in particular the Internet of Things (IoT), this raises the question of just how feasible complying with such a time threshold might be. For cloud users where the company is breached, and where it has made no special arrangements to ensure the safety of forensic and audit trail data, the 72 hour deadline becomes a moot point as it will have no means of knowing that it has been breached. Also, once discovery is made occur, there will be no realistic prospect of that company ever finding out just which records have been compromised. Once the forensic and audit trails are gone — they are gone forever.

A greater concern is likely to emerge where IoT is used, bringing a new range of problems to bear, not least being the general insecure level of devices, their small resource level, yet capable of generating high levels of data throughput. some of which may be lost in transit. Each device may be quite small, yet once the volume is scaled up with thousands of other devices, the impact they can create can rise exponentially. A good example of this is the mass Distributed Denial of Service (DDoS) attack perpetrated using surveillance cameras compromised by the Mirai virus [21][20]. The problem is not so much with the data lost from these IoT devices, rather than the fact that attackers can so easily compromise the devices, allowing them access via corporate networks to other more valuable devices in the system. Where a company does not take special measures to safeguard their forensic and audit trail data, they will be less likely to be able to discover the occurrence of the breach. If, by chance, they should manage to discover the breach, they would certainly be in a position to report it within 72 hours of discovery, but will simply struggle to be able to report what has been compromised, meaning they will be liable for some higher level of fine.

The general attitude by corporates now seems to be that they can forget about screening for the presence of intruders, and simply deal with the reporting once discovery takes place. Again they miss the point of the benefit that comes from rapid discovery - the longer the intruder remains inside the system, the more the damage they can do, and the greater the level of fine the regulator can levy. This means that non-compliance will necessarily become far more serious, thus, enlarging their exposure to the risk of much steeper fines.

While, under the GDPR there is no specific requirement to encrypt data, there is a very strong recommendation that this should take place, be carried out properly and completed within a reasonable time. Encryption and decryption keys should not be stored on the cloud instance. Failure to address these issues will certainly provide grounds for a much increased level of fines in the event of a breach. Thus, cloud use imposes the above weaknesses on the use of any cloud based system before considering any use of software.

As all firms involved in financial services are generally subject to a much greater level of attack than many other market sectors, it is worth taking a look at how they address security requirements. We believe there may be some merit in considering the approach taken with crypto-currencies, since as a new entrant to the market, there is more likelihood that their security approach, having security designed in from the beginning, might offer better prospects for success, as opposed to the approach taken by more traditional financial institutions.

Turning to crypto-currencies, vulnerabilities relating to crypto-currencies are mostly found in operator errors and security flaws. Equally, the Bitcoin platform also faces potential vulnerabilities from protocol designs. Moore and Christin addressed operational insecurity in [22], who suggest that fraudulence is an issue among crypto-currencies. Exchanges act as de facto banks, but almost half of them ceased operation due to the impact of security breaches, failing to reimburse their customers after shutting down. As an alternative approach, other users instead deposited their Bitcoins in a digital wallet. Naturally, these too became a target for cyber-criminals.

A small number of theoretical papers have been written by computer scientists, which address mining pool protocols and anonymity. Miners opted out of the pool in long rounds, where a potential block would be shared with large groups. Babaioff et al. [23], based on a peer-to-peer network layer, argued that the current Bitcoin protocols do not provide any incentive for nodes to broadcast transactions. This is problematic, since the whole system is based on the assumption that this incentive will form a core element. Eyal and Sirer [24], focus instead on the block mining protocol and demonstrate that mining is not incentive-compatible. They further suggest that so-called "selfish mining" can result in higher revenue for miners who collude against others. Houey [25] observed that larger blocks are not as likely to win a block race where new transactions are included into blocks.

Protection of online privacy and anonymity is an issue and both are addressed in the literature. Christin [26] examined anonymity in the online marketplace in crypto-currencies. Böhme et al. [27] examined Internet protocol adoption to see what could be learned from Bitcoin. Many of these studies analysed the public bitcoin transaction history. They were able to find a set of heuristics that can help to link a Bitcoin account with real word identities. Androulaki et al. [28] quantified anonymity in a simulated environment and found that almost half of the users can be identified by their transaction patterns. Using two examples, Bitcoin and Linden Dollars, their report focuses on the impact of digital currencies on the use of fiat money. Gans and Halaburda [29] analysed the economics of private digital currencies, but their explicit focus was on currencies issued by platforms like Facebook or Amazon (that retain full control), and not decentralized currencies like Bitcoin. Dwyer [30] provided institutional details about digital currency developments. The security, privacy and anonymity issue related to Bitcoin has been addressed by Krombholz et al. [31], in which they surveyed 990 Bitcoin users to determine Bitcoin management strategies and identifies how users deploy security measures to protect their keys and Bitcoins. They found that about 46% of participants use web-hosted solutions to manage Bitcoins, and over 50% use such solutions exclusively.

The denial-of-service attack is the one of the most prominent forms addressed by Böhme et al. [27], which entails the attacker swamping a target firm with messages and requests in such volume that either mining pools or exchanges become very slow and unusable. This type of attack is especially effective on the Bitcoin ecosystem because of its relative simplicity of monetising the attacks.

Karame, Androulaki and Capkun [32] looked at using Bitcoin for fast payments and after analysis, found that double-spending attacks on fast payments succeed with overwhelming probability and could be mounted at lower cost unless appropriate detection techniques were integrated in the current Bitcoin implementation. With regard to the double-spending and selfish mining attacks, Kogias et al. [33] proposed the use of ByzCoin as a novel protocol to optimise transaction commitment and verification under normal operation, while guaranteeing safety and liveness under Byzantine (it leveraged scalable collective signing to commit Bitcoin transactions irreversibly within seconds) faults.

There is also some attention from the literature focusing on the price dynamics and speculative bubbles in crypto-currency markets. Cheah and Fry [34] claimed that crypto-currencies are prone to substantial speculative bubbles, and they found that the fundamental value of Bitcoin is zero, by examining the daily clothing prices of Bitcoin from 2010 to 2014. A more recent study is conducted by Blau [35], which emphasised that high volatility of Bitcoin is not related to the speculative activities in this period. The volatility of Bitcoin has been analysed by Katsiampa [36]), Cheah and Fry [34], and many others.

There is no conclusive finding on whether Bitcoin is a speculative investment asset or a currency. Glaser et al. [37] suggest users treat Bitcoin as speculative assets rather than a type of currency. The diversification benefits offered by Bitcoin is also studied by Briére, Oosterlinck and Szafarz [38]. They found Bitcoin can offer diversification benefits after looking into the correlation between Bitcoin and other asset classes. Gandal and Halaburda [39] examined the exchange rates of different virtual currencies to observe the co-movement and identify the opportunities or triangular arbitrage. But they found little opportunity based on daily closing prices. Yermack [40] analysed changes in Bitcoin price against fiat currencies and concludes that its volatility undermines its usefulness as currency. To be qualified as a currency, Bitcoin needs to serve as an intermediary of exchange, as a unit of account and store value. Also, they have been proved not to be able to function as those by Bariviera et al. [41].

In [42]–[44], we considered the possible use of distributed ledger technology as a means of providing a robust mechanism for securing cloud applications. We examined the largest successful crypto-currency attacks and concluded that the link with crypto-currencies attracted greater attention from attackers than would otherwise be the case. In every case of these successful attacks, the inherent strength of the blockchain algorithm behind these companies was never in question. Rather, the success of the attacks came down to successful exploitation of mostly human weaknesses, poor decisions, poor management, neglect and sheer inexperience.

While not a blockchain specific risk, cloud operational weaknesses need to be considered, especially if we wish to include any element of cloud in our solution. We can consider these items in Table II:

TABLE I: CLOUD OPERATIONAL WEAKNESSES ©2019 ZHAO and DUNCAN

Item	Description
CSP	Using an inexperienced CSP can introduce unexpected weaknesses
Backup, Redundancy and Recovery	These issues should be at the core of any CSP decision
Internal Control Weaknesses	Proper internal control is vital to minimise access weaknesses
CSP Hardware & Environment	CSP needs to keep hardware up to date as well as software running on them
Tailored Cloud Deployment	Using "off the shelf" cloud solutions can leave weaknesses
Use of standard CSP offerings for Specilised industries such as Financial Services	Use of a standard cloud offering where the business is highly specialised presents a weakness

We cannot simply decide to use cloud in any solution without first examining their inherent weaknesses and addressing them properly.

We concluded that by removing the link to any crypto-currency, that the underlying blockchain technology could be a very robust way to secure cloud use through the provision of extremely robust audit trails. However, by removing the link to crypto-currencies, this also removes the incentive for "data miners" to spend time and resources on carrying out the necessary work to make the technology work. We suggested an alternative to this would be to create and utilise a 'paid service' to have this work carried out professionally to ensure the strength of the public distributed ledger is preserved.

There might also be an alternative to that solution, whereby a company in effect provides its own 'professional service' to maintain a secure record of the audit trail, and we will consider this as a possibility here. To conclude this section, it is clear that the weaknesses lie, not in the blockchain process, but in the use of cloud systems themselves, and we will consider what the impact of these weaknesses will be in the next section.

III. Impact of Weaknesses for Cloud Users

It is likely that by removing the crypto-currency element, leaving only the blockchain element, we can at one fell swoop eliminate the vast majority of weaknesses from the equation, and at the same time remove the attraction and incentive for attackers. This will leave us to address the cloud weaknesses that will need to be dealt with.

The Cloud Forensic Problem This is a huge potential problem unless special arrangements are in place, e.g., a secure forensic and audit trail is maintained. Failure to do this means there is nothing to prevent an attacker becoming a resident intruder, after which, they will have access to all data. This could lead to huge potential fines in the event of a breach.

The Internet of Things IoT devices used for any purpose by cloud users present a considerable risk, mainly due to the often cheaply made devices with little or no security, often vulnerable to the Mirai virus, which can allow attackers to gain access to systems and to further compromise the main PC and server network due to the porting of the Mirai virus to be able to attack Windows computers [20], [21]. This can expose many other systems to attack, leading to potentially huge fines.

The Need for Proper Monitoring Simple monitoring and analysis of system logs will go a long way to mitigate the well known exploits currently in active use by attackers. Failure to carry out this essential task can result in the company failing to spot attacks, leading to non-compliance and subsequent fines.

Not Using Encryption Under the EU GDPR, the use of encryption is not mandatory. That does not mean it is a good idea not to use it. In the event of a breach where any unencrypted data is leaked, the fine level will be very high. In addition, there is a requirement to notify every single data subject whose data has been compromised. For a large data leak, this could be very time consuming to do, and in the event that the company cannot determine what data details have been compromised, then a higher fine could apply.

Cloud Operational Weaknesses

Each of these cloud operational weaknesses, if not properly addressed, can lead to attackers gaining entry to important systems, leading to non-compliance and huge fines.

Thus, we can see that leaving these weaknesses unaddressed is not an option. In the next section, we consider how we might address these issues in a simple and straightforward way to substantially reduce the exploitation rise.

IV. How We Might Resolve These Weaknesses

There is no doubt that these weaknesses must be addressed, and we advocate doing so in as straightforward a manner as possible.

The Cloud Forensic Problem There has been some interest in addressing the cloud forensic problem [43]–[50], with some easy to implement and use suggestions. The key suggestions are the need for a solid and permanent audit trail and system logs through installing an off-cloud immutable database to store a tamperproof record of the required transactions.

The Internet of Things Great care will need to be taken if IoT devices are to be used. Strong authentication, and robust Intrusion Detection and Intrusion Protection systems should be installed. It would also be prudent to block access by default to all requests originating from the IoT devices and network.

The Need for Proper Monitoring A permanent monitoring system needs to be in place, which can carry out appropriate analytics to detect any anomalous behaviour that occurs on a day to day basis.

The Need to Use Encryption Encryption is a good thing to consider [51], but there are caveats – first, the encryption and de-cryption keys must not be kept on the cloud instance. The encryption should be carried out offline in the cloud users' own systems before being transferred to cloud. Done properly, this can provide serious mitigation to the new EU GDPR fine levels, because if an intruder does get into the cloud system, all they get is meaningless data. With strong levels of encryption, it becomes practically impossible to crack [52]. The regulator will not require data subjects to be notified where the data leak is in encrypted format.

Cloud Operational Weaknesses Resolution

TABLE II: CLOUD OPERATIONAL WEAKNESSES RESOLUTION ©2019 ZHAO and DUNCAN

Item	Description
CSP	Using a market-leading well established CSP who are familiar with legal and regulatory requirements for safeguarding customer data and other sensitive data
Backup, Redundancy and Recovery	Backup, redundancy, and recovery are at the core of the decision to use an outsourcing vendor with highly redundant and resilient data centres designed for mission-critical applications
Internal Control Weaknesses	Internal controls and security processes must ensure customer information is appropriately segregated and protected by industry-standard compliance policies
CSP Hardware & Environment	Leading cloud providers continuously improve their hardware environments to ensure the latest versions of operating systems are installed and use agile software development to deploy feature/function releases on an accelerated basis
Tailored Cloud Deployment	The use of tailored cloud deployment options to meet your specific needs including private clouds solely deployed on your behalf, or a hybrid cloud consisting of shared hardware but segregated data storage would be a prudent move
Use of standard CSP offerings for Specialised industries such as Financial Services	Providers with financial services domain expertise reduce complexity and risk for Financial Institutions with their extensive knowledge of global standards, communications protocols and file formats
CSP Global Support Centre	Cloud providers with global support centres can provide 24 x 7 support in multiple languages, ensuring your international clients and regional offices have access to the support resources required as problems arise

Outsourcing portions of your information technology infrastructure can free up internal IT resources to focus on strategic initiatives and new product development

Conventional Cloud weaknesses Naturally, conventional cloud weaknesses must not be forgotten. These revolve around the Business Architecture of a company, which comprises a combination of People, Process and Technology [17].

- **People Risk Mitigation** People are generally seen as the weakest link in any company, and are particularly prone to social engineering attacks. The company needs to keep abreast of these attacks and ensure all people in the company are regularly trained to understand the risks.

- **Process Risk Mitigation** Processes are often well documented, but also can be woefully out of date. Attackers know to exploit these areas, sometimes in conjunction with social engineering attacks. OWASP [53]are taking a more informed view of dealing with these kinds of attacks.
- **Technology Risk Mitigation** This is where companies are exposed to highly technical attacks. The CSA [54] has done some good work on identifying these risks, as well as offering good strategies to mitigate the risks.

It would certain be a prudent move to test the company cloud systems against the OWASP and CSA vulnerabilities to ensure all discovered vulnerabilities are patched. In the next section, we will look at how to address the resolution of the use case we introduced in the introduction.

V. Addressing the Use Case

Let us return to the use case we introduced at the beginning. The first requirement the company has is to properly secure their main cloud instance on which their cloud accounting system is to run, using all the recommendations we made in Section IV. That will set the scene for a robust environment in which to operate their main business. An essential part of this architecture will be to incorporate the recording of audit and forensic data in an off-cloud immutable database.

The next requirement is to decide on how many blockchain servers the company will seek for the purpose of redundancy. Each blockchain server should be set up in the same secure way as outlined for the main cloud server, but with the addition of the appropriate blockchain algorithms. The preference would be for each blockchain server to be hosted using a different CSP host, again following all the recommendations made in Section IV.

This architecture will provide the basic needs to run the accounting system software, together with an immutable audit and forensic trail. Each of the blockchain servers will have the same security and redundancy. Once the required number of blockchain servers have been set up, the whole system will offer an extremely high level of redundancy. The more robustness is required, it is simply a case of adding more blockchain servers. The more there are, the more challenging it becomes for an attacker to overturn the consensus between all the blockchain servers, and the more robust the system becomes.

VI. Discussion

Because of the major weakness posed by the cloud forensic problem, i.e., the potential to lose both the audit trail and the forensic trail means that recording the data we require to remain compliant with the GDPR becomes a vitally important task for us. The use of a distributed ledger holds great promise. The thinking behind the Blockchain approach affords us with huge redundancy, meaning that an attacker will have to compromise a great many of the distributed ledgers before they can have any impact on the ledger contents. Some would see this as too much redundancy. We would view this as just enough to provide the required assurance. This can therefore provide us with a very strong assurance that the consensus across the ledgers will deliver a high level of comfort as to the veracity of the contents. So, while this represents a big drawback for some, for us, it represents a major advantage.

Some would suggest that the huge volumes of processing generated by the Blockchain process as used in Bitcoin, would be too computationally expensive for our purposes. We disagree. Because it is a crypto-currency and highly volatile, Bitcoin is subject to transactional volumes measuring in multi-trillions per year. By stripping out the crypto-currency aspect from the equation, we also remove the need for such extreme volumes of transactional data, rendering the approach very manageable for any size of company.

VII. Conclusion

We have considered blockchain weaknesses for cloud users, and identified the fact that the major risks lie with the crypto-currencies attached to them. This risk can be eliminated by removing the crypto-currency from the equation. There are more risks attached to cloud use for users to contend with, and we have shown how to approach dealing with those risks.

Our proposal will be to use the underlying concept of a distributed ledger to ensure we are in a position to retain some element of both audit trail and forensic trail data to allow us to meet the compliance requirements of the GDPR, which would otherwise be impossible in the event of a breach. There will be a need to carry out some serious testing in order to find a satisfactory equilibrium between security, privacy, performance, reliability, accessibility and the accountability we require for GDPR compliance. However, it is clear that few current systems can offer anything close to this level of robustness.

References

[1] B. Duncan, "FAST-CFP: Finding a Solution To The Cloud Forensic Problem," in The Ninth International Conference on Cloud Computing, GRIDs, and Virtualization, 2018, p. 3.

[2] EU, "EU General Data Protection Regulation (GDPR)," 2017. [Online]. Available: http://www.eugdpr.org/ [Retrieved: March 2019]

[3] S. Pearson, "Towards Accountability in the Cloud," IEEE Internet Comput., vol. 15, no. 4, jul 2011, pp. 64–69.

[4] N. Papanikolaou, S. Pearson, M. C. Mont, and R. Ko, "A Toolkit for Automating Compliance in Cloud Computing Services," Int. J. Cloud Comput., vol. x, no. x, 2014, pp. 45–68.

[5] C. Millard, I. Walden, and W. K. Hon, "Who is Responsible for 'Personal Data' in Cloud Computing? The Cloud of Unknowing, Part 2," Leg. Stud., vol. 27, no. 77, 2012, pp. 1–31.

[6] N. Papanikolaou, S. Pearson, and M. C. Mont, "Towards Natural-Language Understanding and Automated Enforcement of Privacy Rules and Regulations in the Cloud: Survey and Bibliography," Analysis, 2011, pp. 1–9.

[7] S. Pearson, "Taking account of privacy when designing cloud computing services," Proc. 2009 ICSE Work. Softw. Eng. Challenges Cloud Comput. CLOUD 2009, 2009, pp. 44–52.

[8] L. J. Sotto, B. C. Treacy, and M. L. Mclellan, "Privacy and Data Security Risks in Cloud Computing," World Commun. Regul. Rep., vol. 5, no. 2, 2010, p. 38.

[9] Y. Y. Haimes, B. M. Horowitz, Z. Guo, E. Andrijcic, and J. Bogdanor, "Assessing systemic risk to cloud-computing technology as complex interconnected systems of systems," Syst. Eng., vol. 18, no. 3, 2015, pp. 284–299.

[10] J. Bacon et al., "Information Flow Control for Secure Cloud Computing," IEEE Trans. Netw. Serv. Manag., vol. 11, no. 1, 2014, pp. 76–89.

[11] C. Chang and M. Ramachandran, "Towards Achieving Data Security with the Cloud Computing Adoption Framework," IEEE Trans. Serv. Comput., vol. 9, no. 1, 2016, pp. 138–151.

[12] D. Pym and M. Sadler, "Information Stewardship in Cloud Computing," Int. J. Serv. Sci. Manag. Eng. Technol., vol. 1, no. 1, 2010, pp. 50–67.

[13] T. Takahashi, Y. Kadobayashi, and H. Fujiwara, "Ontological Approach toward Cybersecurity in Cloud Computing Categories and Subject Descriptors," in Sci. Technol., 2010, pp. 100–109.

[14] R. K. L. Ko et al., "TrustCloud: A framework for accountability and trust in cloud computing," Proc. - 2011 IEEE World Congr. Serv. Serv. 2011, 2011, pp. 584–588.

[15] R. K. L. Ko, B. S. Lee, and S. Pearson, "Towards achieving accountability, auditability and trust in cloud computing," Commun. Comput. Inf. Sci., vol. 193 CCIS, no. PART 4, 2011, pp. 432–444.

[16] M. Felici, "Cyber Security and Privacy: Trust in the Digital World and Cyber Security and Privacy EU Forum 2013 Brussels, Belgium, April 18-19, 2013 Revised Selected Papers," in Commun. Comput. Inf. Sci. Springer International Publishing, 2013, vol. 182 CCIS, pp. 77–88.

[17] PWC, "UK Information Security Breaches Survey - Technical Report 2012," London, Tech. Rep. April, 2012. [Online]. Available: www.pwc.com www.bis.gov.uk [Retrieved: March 2019]

[18] Trustwave, "2012 Global Security Report," Tech. Rep., 2012. [Online]. Available: https://www.trustwave.com/Resources/Library/Documents/2012-Trustwave-Global-Security-Report/ [Retrieved: March 2019]

[19] Verizon, "2016 Verizon Data Breach Report," Tech. Rep., 2016. [Online]. Available: https://regmedia.co.uk/2016/05/12/dbir$_2016.pdf[Retrieved : March2019]$

[20] Verizon, "Verizon Security Breach Report 2017," Tech. Rep., 2017. [Online. Available: https://www.ictsecuritymagazine.com/wp-content/uploads/2017-Data-Breach-Investigations-Report.pdf [Retrieved: March 2019]

[21] B. Duncan and M. Whittington, "Cyber Security for Cloud and the Internet of Things: How Can it be Achieved?" Cybersecurity Inst. Eng. Technol., vol. Cybersecur, no. September, 2017, pp. 1–39.

[22] T. Moore and N. Christin, "Beware the middleman: Empirical analysis of Bitcoin-exchange risk," in International Conference on Financial Cryptography and Data Security. Springer, 2013, pp. 25–33.

[23] M. Babaioff, S. Dobzinski, S. Oren, and A. Zohar, "On bitcoin and red balloons," in Proceedings of the 13th ACM conference on electronic commerce. ACM, 2012, pp. 56–73.

[24] I. Eyal and E. G. Sirer, "Majority is not enough: Bitcoin mining is vulnerable," in International Conference on Financial Cryptography and Data Security. Springer, 2014, pp. 436–454.

[25] N. Houy, "The economics of Bitcoin transaction fees," GATE WP, vol. 1407, 2014.

[26] N. Christin, "Traveling the silk road: A measurement analysis of a large anonymous online marketplace," in Proceedings of the 22nd international conference on World Wide Web. ACM, 2013, pp. 213–224.

[27] R. Böhme, N. Christin, B. Edelman, and T. Moore, "Bitcoin: Economics, technology, and governance," The Journal of Economic Perspectives, vol. 29, no. 2, 2015, pp. 213–238.

[28] E. Androulaki, G. O. Karame, M. Roeschlin, T. Scherer, and S. Capkun, "Evaluating user privacy in bitcoin," in International Conference on Financial Cryptography and Data Security. Springer, 2013, pp. 34–51.

[29] J. S. Gans and H. Halaburda, "Some economics of private digital currency," in Econ. Anal. Digit. Econ. University of Chicago Press, 2015, pp. 257–276.

[30] G. P. Dwyer, "The economics of Bitcoin and similar private digital currencies," J. Financ. Stab., vol. 17, 2015, pp. 81–91.

[31] K. Krombholz, A. Judmayer, M. Gusenbauer, and E. Weippl, "The other side of the coin: User experiences with bitcoin security and privacy," in International Conference on Financial Cryptography and Data Security. Springer, 2016, pp. 555–580.

[32] G. O. Karame, E. Androulaki, and S. Capkun, "Double-spending fast payments in bitcoin," in Proceedings of the 2012 ACM conference on Computer and communications security. ACM, 2012, pp. 906–917.

[33] E. K. Kogias, P. Jovanovic, N. Gailly, I. Khoffi, L. Gasser, and B. Ford, "Enhancing bitcoin security and performance with strong consistency via collective signing," in 25th USENIX Security Symposium (USENIX Security 16). USENIX Association, 2016, pp. 279–296.

[34] E.-T. Cheah and J. Fry, "Speculative bubbles in bitcoin markets? an empirical investigation into the fundamental value of bitcoin," Economics Letters, vol. 130, 2015, pp. 32–36.

[35] B. M. Blau, "Price dynamics and speculative trading in bitcoin," Research in International Business and Finance, vol. 41, 2017, pp. 493–499.

[36] P. Katsiampa, "Volatility estimation for bitcoin: A comparison of garch models," Economics Letters, vol. 158, 2017, pp. 3–6.

[37] F. Glaser, K. Zimmermann, M. Haferkorn, M. C. Weber, and M. Siering, "Bitcoin-asset or currency? revealing users' hidden intentions," 2014.

[38] M. Brière, K. Oosterlinck, and A. Szafarz, "Virtual currency, tangible return: Portfolio diversification with bitcoin," Journal of Asset Management, vol. 16, no. 6, 2015, pp. 365–373.

[39] N. Gandal and H. Halaburda, "Can we predict the winner in a market with network effects? competition in cryptocurrency market," Games, vol. 7, no. 3, 2016, p. 16.

[40] D. Yermack, "Is Bitcoin a real currency? An economic appraisal," National Bureau of Economic Research, Tech. Rep., 2013.

[41] A. F. Bariviera, M. J. Basgall, W. Hasperué, and M. Naiouf, "Some stylized facts of the Bitcoin market," Phys. A Stat. Mech. its Appl., vol. 484, 2017, pp. 82–90.

[42] Y. Zhao and B. Duncan, "Could Block Chain Technology Help Resolve the Cloud Forensic Problem?" in Cloud Comput. 2018 Ninth Int. Conf. Cloud Comput. GRIDs, Virtualization, no. February. Barcelona, Spain: IARIA, 2018, pp. 39–44.

[43] Y. Zhao and B. Duncan, "Fixing the Cloud Forensic Problem with Blockchain," Int. J. Adv. Secur., vol. 11, no. 3&4, 2018, pp. 243–253.

[44] Y. Zhao and B. Duncan, "The Impact of Crypto-Currency Risks on the Use of Blockchain for Cloud Security and Privacy," in 7th Int. Work. Secur. Priv. Perform. Cloud Comput. (SPCLOUD 2018), 2018, p. 8.

[45] B. Duncan, M. Whittington, and V. Chang, "Enterprise security and privacy: Why adding IoT and big data makes it so much more difficult," in Proc. 2017 Int. Conf. Eng. Technol. ICET 2017, vol. 2018-Janua, 2018.

[46] B. Duncan, "Can EU General Data Protection Regulation Compliance be Achieved When Using Cloud Computing?" in Cloud Comput. 2018 Ninth Int. Conf. Cloud Comput. GRIDs, Virtualization, no. February. Barcelona, Spain: IARIA, 2018, pp. 1–6.

[47] B. Duncan and M. Whittington, "Can Forensic Audit Help Address the Cloud Forensic Problem in Light of the Requirements of the Forthcoming European Union General Data Protection Regulation?" in Cloud Comput. 2018 Ninth Int. Conf. Cloud Comput. GRIDs, Virtualization, no. February. Barcelona, Spain: IARIA, 2018, pp. 84–89.

[48] B. Duncan and Y. Zhao, "Risk Management for Cloud Compliance with the EU General Data Protection Regulation," in 7th Int. Work. Secur. Priv. Perform. Cloud Comput. (SPCLOUD 2018), Orleans, France, 2018, p. 8.

[49] B. Duncan, A. Happe, and A. Bratterud, "Using Unikernels to Address the Cloud Forensic Problem and help Achieve EU GDPR Compliance."

[50] B. Duncan and M. Whittington, "The Complexities of Auditing and Securing Systems in the Cloud — is there a Solution and will the GDPR move it up the Corporate Agenda?" Int. J. Adv. Secur., vol. 11, no. 3&4, 2018, pp. 232–242.

[51] V. Chang, M. Ramachandran, Y. Yao, Y. H. Kuo, and C. S. Li, "A resiliency framework for an enterprise cloud," Int. J. Inf. Manage., vol. 36, no. 1, 2016, pp. 155–166.

[52] T. Pasquier, B. Shand, and J. Bacon, "Information Flow Control for a Medical Records Web Portal," Cl.Cam.Ac.Uk, 2013, pp. 1–8.

[53] OWASP, "Open Web Application Security Project," 2019. [Online]. Available: https://www.owasp.org/index.php/OWASP_Cloud_Security_Project Accessed: 28/03/2019

[54] CSA, "Cloud Security Alliance," 2019. [Online]. Available: https://cloudsecurityalliance.org/ [Retrieved: March 2019]

Cloud Security and Security Challenges Revisited

Fabian Süß[1], Marco Freimuth[1], Andreas Aßmuth[1], George R S Weir[2] and Bob Duncan[3]

[1]Technical University of Applied Sciences OTH Amberg-Weiden, Amberg, Germany,
Email: {f.suess | m.freimuth | a.assmuth}@oth-aw.de
[2]University of Strathclyde, Glasgow, UK, Email: george.weir@strath.ac.uk
[3]University of Aberdeen, Aberdeen, UK, Email: robert.duncan@abdn.ac.uk
4

Abstract—**In recent years, Cloud Computing has transformed local businesses and created new business models on the Internet–and Cloud services are still flourishing. But after the emphatic hype in the early years, a more realistic perception of Cloud services has emerged. One reason for this surely is that today, Cloud Computing is considered as an established and well-accepted technology and no longer as a technical novelty. But the second reason for this assessment might also be numerous security issues that Cloud Computing in general or specific Cloud services have experienced since then. In this paper, we revisit attacks on Cloud services and Cloud-related attack vectors that have been published in recent years. We then consider successful or proposed solutions to cope with these challenges. Based on these findings, we apply a security metric in order to rank all these Cloud-related security challenges concerning their severity. This should assist security professionals to prioritize their efforts toward addressing these issues.**

Index Terms*—*Cloud Security; Threat; CVSS.

I. Introduction

Cloud security risks have been widely discussed in recent publications by different security specialists, e.g., by the Cloud Security Alliance. [1] Since Cloud services are provided over the Internet, most well-known attacks against web applications are threats against Cloud services, too. In addition, the characteristics of Cloud Computing amplify such existing vulnerabilities and there exist new security challenges that arise from the properties of Cloud services. In order to provide an overview of significant security threats in Cloud Computing, we have grouped the different security issues. In this paper we consider attack vectors against:

- Cloud infrastructures,
- transportation of data to and from the Cloud and
- a client's connection to Cloud services and data.

After a brief description of these respective attack vectors in Sections III to V, we provide some hints and best practice solutions to prevent or reduce the impact of these incidents. In order to help professionals understand the severity of the associated security flaw, we rate these issues using the Common Vulnerability Scoring System (CVSS). [2] [3] For those readers who are not familiar with CVSS, a brief introduction is given in Section II. Having rated the listed attack vectors, we give a final conclusion and outlook in Section VI.

II. Common Vulnerability Scoring System

CVSS is an open framework intended to describe the properties and impact of information security threats and attack vectors. It provides standardised vulnerability scores that are used, for example, in the Common Vulnerability and Exposure (CVE) list or in the National Institute of Standards and Technology's National Vulnerability Database (NVD). To compute a score using CVSS, three metric groups have to be taken into account, Base, Temporal and Environmental, each consisting of a set of metrics. The Base metric group addresses the intrinsic characteristics of a vulnerability that are constant over time and do not depend on specific environments. Table I shows the two sets of metrics within the Base metric group, the Exploitability metrics and the Impact metrics. In the following sections, the listed abbreviations will be used for the corresponding metrics.

TABLE I. Base Metric Group. [3]

Exploitability metrics	Impact metrics
Attack Vector (AV)	Confidentiality Impact (C)
Attack Complexity (AC)	Integrity Impact (I)
Privileges Required (PR)	Availability Impact (A)
User Interaction (UI)	
Scope (S)	

The Temporal metric group describes time-dependent, but environment-independent factors of a vulnerability and consists of three metrics: Exploit Code Maturity (E), Remediation Level (RL) and Report Confidence (RC) (cf. Table II). Finally,

TABLE II. Temporal Metric Group. [3]

Exploit Code Maturity (E)	Remediation Level (RL)
Report Confidence (RC)	

the Environmental metric group addresses properties of a vulnerability that are relevant and unique to a certain environment. Using these context-specific metrics, scores of the Base metric group or Temporal metric group can be amplified or reduced according to a given setup or scenario. Since we intend to give an overview of Cloud security threats, we do not address environmental specifics and therefore just compute CVSS scores for the Base and Temporal metric groups.

When the metrics are assigned values, the equations of CVSS compute a score ranging from 0.0 (not vulnerable), 0.1 to 3.9 (low), 4.0 to 6.9 (medium), 7.0 to 8.9 (high) and 9.0 to 10.0 (critical). For more detailed information about CVSS, we refer to [2] [3].

III. Attacks against the Cloud infrastructure

A. Denial of Service

A (Distributed) Denial of Service ((D)DoS) attack against a Cloud service provider (CSP) is the cyber criminals attempt to prevent clients from accessing their data or services operated in the Cloud. This can be achieved by flooding the Cloud providers web access with nonsense requests until the servers cannot distinguish between authorised and unauthorised requests and will stop working as a result of the load that leads to the server running out of computing resources. In February 2018, Github was attacked using a so-called memcached DDoS. This means there were no botnets involved, but instead the attackers leveraged the amplification effect of a popular database caching system known as memcached. The attackers flooded memcached servers with spoofed requests and were able to generate incoming traffic for Github at the rate of 1.35 Tbps. [4] Another variant of a DoS attack could, for instance, be an unplanned shutdown of computing resources due to human error.

DDoS attacks can be started remotely, e.g., over the Internet (AV:N) (cf. Table III), without needing special privileges (PR:N) and the complexity of the attack is low (AC:L). No user interaction is needed (UI:N). Usually, DDoS attacks target one specific domain, website or service and therefore we assume the scope of the attack does not cause additional security issues (S:U). In practice, this might not be true for all DDoS attacks and depending on the kind of service under attack, other resources might be affected too. DDoS attacks do not target confidentiality or integrity (C:N, I:N), but availability (A:H).

Concerning the temporal metrics, it can be stated that this kind of attack is well-known (RC:C) and attackers know how to perform DDoS attacks (E:H). On the other hand, there are many best practice measures to deal with DDoS attacks (RL:O). Specialized firewalls, for example, can detect uncommon behaviour and block the incoming traffic from specific sources. [5] Newer implementations use techniques of artificial intelligence in order to perform anomaly detection. [6] In addition, load balancing techniques enable CSPs to distribute incoming traffic over different gateways.

TABLE III. CVSS score for DDoS attacks.

Base metrics				Score
AV:N S:U	AC:L C:N	PR:N I:N	UI:N A:H	**7.5**
Temporal metrics				Score
E:H	RL:O	RC:C		**7.2**

This leads to a Base metrics score of 7.5 and a Temporal metrics score of 7.2, which both mean severity "high".

B. Malware infection

Like any other computer system, Cloud Computing resources are vulnerable to malware infections. The impact of the infection depends on the variety of the malware. For example, an infection by ransomware where data gets encrypted by the attacker would deny users access to their own data, whereas an infection by a keylogger or a rootkit would probably lead to unauthorized access due to stolen credentials.

As the Securonix Threat Research Team reported, it only takes minutes before automated attacks against a new exposed IP address begin. The attack itself ranges from attempts to install crypto mining software to irrecoverably deleting databases after the adversary gains access to the system. Both Linux and Windows operating system machines are being attacked. [7]

The most common way to become infected by one of these types of malware is by an unpatched software vulnerability being exploited by an attacker, e.g., when a user opens the malicious attachment of an email (AV:N) that will allow the attacker access (S:C) to the victim's system. The exploit itself can be found easily (AC:L) on special databases like the CVE website. [10] In order to exploit weaknesses of the targeted system, the malware needs higher privileges (PR:H) and the user also needs to actively click and run the exploit (UI:R). After an attacker has access to a system, integrity (I:H), confidentiality (C:H) and availability (A:H) can no longer be guaranteed.

As stated before, an attacker can use pre-built malware kits (E:F) making it easy to generate the malware. Workarounds after patches have been released are usually only temporary because, first of all, they need to be implemented regularly and secondly, they can only fix known issues and are also only available for software under maintenance (RL:W). On the other hand, many of these security issues are demonstrated by security researchers in special scenarios (RC:C).

This leads to a high severity, both for the Base (8.4) and the Temporal metrics group (8.1). There are counter measures against these kinds of attacks like hardening the environment, for example, by rolling out a patch management that keeps the operating system and the application software up to date. Additionally, firewalls and anti-malware software should be the first line of defence to tackle this high threat. Isolation of highly threatened applications, e.g., by using sandboxing, is another efficient countermeasure that should be considered.

TABLE IV. CVSS score for malware infection.

Base metrics				Score
AV:N S:C	AC:L C:H	PR:H I:H	UI:R A:H	**8.4**
Temporal metrics				Score
E:F	RL:W	RC:C		**8.1**

C. Unauthorized access

In this scenario, an attacker or a user has unauthorized access to another user's data or services. This is mostly achieved by stealing (see Subsection III-B, keylogger) or cracking weak passwords. After the adversary has successfully logged in with the user's credentials, he can abuse all the user's services or steal their data. Additionally, more sophisticated attacks like virtual machine escape, when an intruder breaks out of the limitations of a virtual resource in order to get access to other users' resources, are a serious threat due to the necessary wide use of shared resources by virtualisation techniques.

To give an example, we refer to the marketing company Exactis which leaked a database containing personal information of users with about 340 million records. [8] The incident occurred because the database was publically accessible over the Internet. The relevant web server could easily be found using the search engine 'Shodan.' [11] Shodan is not specialized in finding web content but systems attached to the Internet according to, for instance, the services these provide. This makes it especially helpful for attackers when searching for vulnerable (Cloud) systems.

Since the goal of the attack is to log on remotely with a legitimate user's credentials, the attacker is not limited to physical access to a system (AV:N). The attack complexity on the other hand is considered high (AC:H) because it needs significant technical understanding of the system, e.g., in order to escape a virtual machine's limitations, or psychological skills in order to get credentials using social engineering techniques. As the scope of this attack is to get unauthorized access, it will not be changed (S:U) and user privileges are not required (PR:N) just as user interaction (UI:N). Once an attack provides access to a system, all three security goals, confidentiality (C:H), integrity (I:H) and availability (A:H), can no longer be guaranteed. This is also the reason why this attack has a high base score of 8.1, although it might by very complex to successfully run it.

A way to counter this attack on the credential side is to enforce minimum password requirements along with two-factor authentication (RL:W). Additionally, a single user should only have as limited access permissions as needed. Virtual machine escape on the other hand is harder to tackle, and the defence strategy is mainly to have different layers of security enabled, along with an up-to-date patch management.

TABLE V. CVSS SCORE FOR UNAUTHORIZED ACCESS.

Base metrics				Score
AV:N S:U	AC:H C:H	PR:H I:H	UI:N A:H	**8.1**
Temporal metrics				Score
E:F	RL:W	RC:C		**7.7**

Encrypting data stored in the Cloud and keeping the decryption key(s) stored on another platform is also a good approach to tackle unauthorized data flow. Exploitations on the social engineering or virtual machine sides have been seen in the past (E:F) and detailed reports are available (RC:C). This lowers the temporal score compared to the base score to 7.7, but this attack scenario is still a serious (high) threat.

D. Data loss

Data loss describes the event when data is irrecoverably lost by, for example, an environmental catastrophe or a mistaken user interaction. Another scenario in which data might get lost is when data is encrypted but the keys are deleted by accident.

Backups should never be accessible over the Internet, so we assume that if an attacker wants to delete data irrecoverably, he needs to have local access to the storage and backup system (AV:L). We assume the attacker does not need special privileges (PR:L). The complexity of the attack is quite low (AC:L), the scope remains unchanged (S:U) and no user interaction is needed (UI:N). Confidentiality is not affected at all (C:N), but integrity (I:H) as well as availability are highly affected as we assume that the data can not be recovered or reconstructed.

One of the most catastrophic data losses in recent years was probably the unrecoverable deletion of databases from the popular code managing platform GitLab. [12] In early 2017, an engineer wanted to test a new database model for which he set up multiple postgres SQL servers. During the test an abnormally high load occurred causing the new database to stop while performing a backup. For some technical reasons, the backup failed. In the end, only data from a later date could be recovered leading to the loss of recent pulls of about 5,000 projects.

In order to deal with data loss, services and data should be operated redundantly, whenever possible not only within the same data centre but also in different locations. A proper backup strategy that includes the testing of all backups is strongly recommended. Since this effectively and reportedly reduces the impact of data loss, we rate this as an "official fix" (RL:O). There are numerous reports of attacks that lead to data loss (E:F) and most of them can be reproduced easily (RC:C).

TABLE VI. CVSS SCORE FOR DATA LOSS.

Base metrics				Score
AV:L S:U	AC:L C:N	PR:L I:H	UI:N A:H	**7.1**
Temporal metrics				Score
E:F	RL:O	RC:C		**6.6**

This assessment leads to a score of 7.1 for the Base metrics group (high) and a temporal score of 6.6 (medium). This emphasises that well-known counter-measures, like storing data redundantly or limiting access to backups, work effectively in practice. The risk of data loss should not be underestimated though.

IV. ATTACKS ON THE TRANSPORTATION SIDE

A. Sniffing / Man in the Middle attacks

Sniffing means that the adversary is eavesdropping on the communication channel. By observing a client's communication to a Cloud service, the goal of the attacker is to retrieve valuable information. In a so-called Man in the Middle attack, communication from a client to a Cloud service is routed through the attacker. Encrypted traffic might be decrypted by the adversary in order to get the information, re-encrypted and sent to its destination. To give an example, due to misconfiguration leading to allowing public writes to S3 buckets, unauthorised persons could write content to another party's Cloud storage. [9]

Since the attack takes place between the client and the Cloud, the adversary needs access to the adjacent network (AV:A). In cases when communication is not encrypted end to end, this attack scenario is trivial. But even if mechanisms like Transport Layer Security (TLS) are enabled, an attacker is still able to trick (SSL Stripping) the client in order to disable the security efforts. We rate the attack complexity as low (AC:L). Therefore, TLS should always be used along with a technique called HTTP Strict Transport Security (HSTS), which enforces the use of encryption between client and server and makes the attack harder. As stated in the example, a misconfiguration could also lead to a Man in the Middle attack. The attack usually takes place without the user's knowledge (PR:N, UI:N). Depending on the data sniffed, the scope can change and could lead to a break in the confidentiality (C:H), as well as integrity (I:H). We assume that the attacker wants to stay

TABLE VII. CVSS SCORE FOR SNIFFING / MAN IN THE MIDDLE.

Base metrics				Score
AV:A S:U	AC:L C:H	PR:N I:H	UI:N A:N	**8.1**
Temporal metrics				Score
E:F	RL:O	RC:C		**7.5**

unnoticed and therefore does not interrupt the communication (A:N). This makes the base score 8.3 and is considered high.

There is an offical fix (RL:O) to tackle this attack scenario, namely the use of TLS along with HSTS as described above. But since there is functional exploitation code available (E:F) and detailed reports about this attack exist, the temporal score (7.7) still remains high.

B. Rerouting

This attack is similar to a Man in the Middle attack. But unlike the attack described above, the attacker usually cannot access plaintext (C:L, I:L) data. The adversary reroutes the packets either on the client or server side (AV:L) in order to prevent successful transmission. The attacker's goal is to make the services operated by the Cloud unavailable (A:H) leading to a Denial of Service. Neither special privileges (PR:N) nor user interaction (UI:N) is needed, but the goal of making the attacked service unavailable remains unchanged (S:U). Since the attacker needs access to the provider's or the customer's gateway, the complexity is considered high (AC:H).

As an example, Microsoft's Cloud services were unavailable for several days due to a failure of a public DNS provider, leading to DNS requests targeting Microsoft's Cloud server failing. [13] Putting the base values together, a medium value (6.2) shows that the effects of this attack are controllable.

Although this attack can easily be discovered (unlike the sniffing approach described above), it can be hard to overcome

TABLE VIII. CVSS SCORE FOR REROUTING ATTACKS.

Base metrics				Score
AV:L S:U	AC:H C:L	PR:N I:L	UI:N A:H	**6.2**
Temporal metrics				Score
E:F	RL:W	RC:R		**5.7**

(RL:W). The best effort would be trying to prevent an attacker from getting access to the local or adjacent network. The attacker has access to a wide range of functional exploitation code (E:F), the attacking vectors are also reasonable (RC:R). This leads to a temporal score of 5.7.

V. ATTACKS AGAINST THE CLIENT

A. Malware infection

As discussed in Subsection III-B, this attack vector is considered on both sides, the client as well as the server. The means attackers use for infection are similiar, and the same applies to potential counter measures. Since the Cloud or the Internet in general offer an easy way for multiple users to work together from all over the world, this benefit can be abused by attackers to infect a lot of clients by successfully attacking a single client (S:C).

Reports about upcoming, new malware can be seen almost daily. For example, we consider an Android malware that was reported on 15th June 2018. This malware is specialized as it is multi-functional. It exploits banking details, it stores all characters entered using the on-screen keyboard and has the ability to encrypt the complete device. [15]

The CVSS score is equivalent to the score for malware on the (Cloud) servers. An attacker only needs to send malware via email (AV:N), for example, to infect an end user's device. The attack complexity is quite low (AC:L) as there are pre-built toolkits available on the Darknet. [14] A privileged (PR:H) users' action is mandatory (UI:R), the

TABLE IX. CVSS SCORE FOR MALWARE INFECTION.

Base metrics				Score
AV:N S:C	AC:L C:H	PR:H I:H	UI:R A:H	**8.4**
Temporal metrics				Score
E:H	RL:T	RC:C		**8.1**

scope can change (S:C) based on the details exposed and all three security goals, confidentiality (C:H), integrity (I:H) and availability (A:H) have to be rated as high, leading to a base score of 8.4.

As the example above indicates, functional code exists (E:H) and numerous attacks have been seen in recent years (RC:C). Positively for the user, simple actions are available to deal with this risk at least temporarily (RL:T), like compliance rules for a required minimal security level in order to access Cloud services using a certain client, should be enforced as well as hardening the client's environment. The severity of this threat is still high as a temporal score of 8.1 indicates.

B. Unauthorised data access

Just as described above, attackers might try to steal user credentials in order to access data without permission. But there are several other examples that might lead to unauthorised access as well. A user might mistakenly be granted higher permissions or a CSP might still process customer data, even after that data has been marked to be deleted by the customer, e.g., in older backups.

On 4th September 2018, for instance, an attacker accessed the upload mechanism of the Google Chrome extension "MEGA". He added malware code to the extension to steal users' passwords and upload these to the attacker's server. The malware-embedded software was distributed by the normal update process. [16]

The metrics are similar to unauthorised data access on the Cloud side, but limited by the fact that the effects are lower, as a single user usually does not have full access to all the data stored in the Cloud. Additionally, an attacker needs access to the victim's (local) network (AV:L) and data that is stored in the Cloud can be restored more easily (A:L). This leads to a lower base score of 7.7.

In addition to that, it is also easier to protect a single client than the complete Cloud infrastructure of a CSP, although new

TABLE X. CVSS UNAUTHORIZED DATA ACCESS ATTACKS.

Base metrics				Score
AV:L S:C	AC:H C:H	PR:L I:H	UI:N A:L	**7.7**
Temporal metrics				**Score**
E:H	RL:T	RC:C		**7.4**

counter-measures have to be adopted constantly in order to deal with more advanced threats (RL:T). A simple way to reduce the attack surface of such attacks is to enforce a strong password policy or even better two-factor authentication. The maturity of the attack vector, on the other hand, has to be rated higher (E:H) since more malware exists for clients than for Cloud systems. This leads to a temporal score of 7.4.

VI. CONCLUSION

Attacks against Cloud infrastructures are multifaceted. They range from Denial of Service attacks to more complex attempts where an attack tries to get unauthorised access. In any discussion about the risk of a Cloud infrastructure, not only the Cloud provider's side should be considered but also the transportation of data as well as the security of the endpoints connected to the services and data operated by the Cloud. The CVSS scoring helps companies to identify the most critical security flaws. Based on the attack vectors and vulnerabilities described in the previous sections, we used the Temporal metrics score to rank these security challenges (cf. Table XI). This table only contains security problems for the Cloud infrastructure and the data connection between clients and the Cloud services. These are the aspects a CSP has under their sole control and from a customer's perspective, these are the most important properties that should be addressed when a contract with a CSP is negotiated. In a more specialised setting, e.g., for a Cloud-based SCADA (supervisory control and data acquisition) system, the situation might be easier because of the smaller number of potentially different clients.

TABLE XI. RANKING OF THE MOST SEVER CLOUD SECURITY CHALLENGES.

Rank	Security challenge	Score
1	Malware infection (Cloud infrastructure)	8.1
2	Unauthorised access	7.7
3	Man in the Middle attacks	7.5
4	DDoS attacks	7.2
5	Data loss	6.6
6	Rerouting	5.7

Vulnerabilities or attacks targeting specifically the client side are hard to deal with for most CSPs. The clients are usually not managed or controlled by the CSP but by the customers themselves. If a CSP offers a multi purpose Cloud service that should be usable by any customer and any device, it is hard to deal with all potential vulnerabilities of all possible combinations of client applications and operating systems. Nevertheless, it is highly recommended not to support "ancient" client software (applications as well as operating systems) for which security updates have officially been discontinued. However, the security challenges for clients described in Section V, malware infections (8.1) and unauthorised data access (7.4), both have to be considered as highly severe. Therefore, customers are advised to install security patches as soon as those are available and also to have a proper strategy for access control.

In order to obtain a scoring of the discussed security challenges for a unique environment, we suggest to add the metrics of the Environmental metric group according to the given scenario. On the Internet, there are several CVSS 3.0 calculators available, like the one provided by the Forum of Incident Response and Security Teams (FIRST) [18]), that can be used to do the calculations easily.

ACKNOWLEDGMENT

The authors would like to thank the Bavarian Research Alliance (BayFOR) for funding several visits of the partners involved in this paper. This funding definitely helped to develop joint research and teaching activities.

REFERENCES

[1] Cloud Security Alliance, Ed., The Treacherous 12, Top Threats to Cloud Computing + Industry Insights, 2017.
[2] P. Mell, K. Scarfone and S. Romanosky, "Common vulnerability scoring system", IEEE Security & Privacy, vol. 4, no. 6, 2006.
[3] FIRST.Org, Inc., 2015, "Common Vulnerability Scoring System v3.0, Specification Document", URL: https://www.first.org/cvss/cvss-v30-specification-v1.8.pdf [accessed: 2019.04.12]
[4] L. Hay Newman, "GitHub Survived the Biggest DDoS Attack Ever Recorded", wired.com, 2018.03.01 [accessed: 2019.04.12]

[5] A. Khadke, M. Madankar and M. Motghare, "Review on Mitigation of Distributed Denial of Service (DDoS) Attacks in Cloud Computing" in Proceedings of the 10th International Conference on Intelligent Systems and Control (ISCO), January 7–8, 2016, Coimbatore, India. IEEE, Nov. 2016, pp. 1–5, ISBN: 978-1-4673-7807-9.

[6] S .Alzahrani and L. Hong, "Detection of Distributed Denial of Service (DDoS) Attacks Using Artificial Intelligence on Cloud" in Proceedings of the 2018 IEEE World Congress on Services (SERVICES), July 2–7, 2018, San Francisco, USA. IEEE, Oct. 2018, pp. 36–36, ISBN: 978-1-5386-7374-4.

[7] L. Jaffee, "Cloud infrastructure exposed by multivector, multi-platform malware attacks prevalent, mass scale", SC Media, January 1st, 2019, URL: https://www.scmagazine.com/home/security-news/cloud-infrastructure-exposed-by-multivector-multi-platform-malware-attacks-prevalent-mass-scale/ [accessed: 2019.04.12]

[8] A. Greenberg, "Marketing Firm Exactis Leaked a Personal Info Database With 340 Million Records", wired.com, June 27th, 2018, URL: https://www.wired.com/story/exactis-database-leak-340-million-records/ [accessed: 2019.04.12]

[9] D. Olenick, "Misconfigured Amazon S3 Buckets allowing man-in-the-middle attacks", SC Media, November 2nd, 2017, URL: https://www.scmagazineuk.com/misconfigured-amazon-s3-buckets-allowing-man-in-the-middle-attacks/article/1473869 [accessed: 2019.04.12]

[10] CVE database, URL: https://cve.mitre.org/cve/search_cve_list.html [accessed: 2019.04.12]

[11] Shodan search engine, URL: https://www.shodan.io/ [accessed: 2019.04.12]

[12] GitLab, "Postmortem of database outage of January 31", February 10th, 2017, URL: https://about.gitlab.com/2017/02/10/postmortem-of-database-outage-of-january-31/ [accessed: 2019.04.12]

[13] G. Born, "Microsoft calls DNS-Problems solved", February 12th, 2019, URL: https://www.borncity.com/blog/2019/02/12/microsoft-meldet-dns-probleme-als-behoben-11-2-2019/ [accessed: 2019.04.12]

[14] Bruno, "DIY Ransomware Kits Accessible on the Dark Web", February 18th, 2018, URL: https://darkwebnews.com/dark-web/ransomware-diy-kits/ [accessed: 2019.04.12]

[15] D. Palmer, "This new Android malware delivers banking trojan, keylogger and ransomware", June 15th, 2018, URL: https://www.zdnet.com/article/this-new-android-malware-delivers-banking-trojan-keylogger-and-ransomware/ [accessed: 2019.04.12]

[16] C. Nguyen, "Hacked Chrome extension disguised as legitimate version steals logins", May 9th, 2018, URL: https://www.digitaltrends.com/computing/mega-cloud-storages-chrome-extension-hacked-to-steal-your-passwords/ [accessed: 2019.03.03]

[17] Westfälische Nachrichten, Ed., "Bagger legt Telekommunikation lahm" (Excavator paralyses telecommunication), May 29th, 2018, URL: https://www.wn.de/Muenster/Stadtteile/Mecklenbeck/3320424-Kein-Telefon-kein-Internet-Bagger-legt-Telekommunikation-lahm [accessed: 2019.04.12]

[18] Forum of Incident Response and Security Teams (FIRST), Ed., "Common Vulnerability Scoring System Version 3.0 Calculator", URL: https://www.first.org/cvss/calculator/3.0 [accessed: 2019.04.12]

UnCle SAM: Modeling Cloud Attacks with the Automotive Security Abstraction Model

Markus Zoppelt
Department of Computer Science
Nuremberg Institute of Technology
Nuremberg, Bavaria 90489
Email: markus.zoppelt@th-nuernberg.de

Ramin Tavakoli Kolagari
Department of Computer Science
Nuremberg Institute of Technology
Nuremberg, Bavaria 90489
Email: ramin.tavakolikolagari@th-nuernberg.de

***Abstract*—Driverless (autonomous) vehicles will have greater attack potential than any other individual mobility vehicles ever before. Most intelligent vehicles require communication interfaces to the environment, direct connections (e.g., Vehicle-to-X (V2X)) to an Original Equipment Manufacturer (OEM) backend service or a cloud. By connecting to the Internet, which is not only necessary for the infotainment systems, cars could increasingly turn into targets for malware or botnet attacks. Remote control via the Internet by a remote attacker is also conceivable, as has already been impressively demonstrated. This paper examines security modeling for cloud-based remote attacks on autonomous vehicles using a Security Abstraction Model (SAM) for automotive software systems). SAM adds to the early phases of (automotive) software architecture development by explicitly documenting attacks and handling them with security techniques. SAM also provides the basis for comprehensive security analysis techniques, such as the already available Common Vulnerability Scoring System (CVSS) or any other attack assessment system.**

Keywords–Automotive Security; Automotive Software Engineering; Security Modeling; Cloud Attacks; OTA Updates.

I. Introduction

Modern cars are interconnected networks, with potentially more than 150 Electronic Control Units (ECUs) in luxury models communicating with one another and with the environment (V2X communication). In recent years, car manufacturers produced vehicles that are connected to the Internet and are providing cloud services, e.g., Tesla's mobile app, BMW iDrive or Audi Connect. In most cases, the user can even monitor or control parts of the vehicle using a mobile application or cloud service. These convenience features are designed to attract new customers but may impede some of the security goals by downright enabling a barrage of possible attack vectors. Attackers do not target cars in the same way as they would attack standard computer systems; cars use different networks, protocols and architectures [1], [2]. Moreover, cars carry burdensome legacy mechanisms with insecure and unencrypted protocols (e.g., CAN, Controller Area Network) in their system design and were originally not designed in line with today's security principles [3], [4]. Secure automotive network architectures were not prioritized in the past due to the general preconception in the last three decades that cars are secure because of their technical complexity (security by obscurity). The goal is to establish the principle of security by design, not only for automotive software systems but for cloud services as well. However, numerous attack vectors [5], [6], [7] on cars and their network of ECUs, actuators and sensors exist. In contrast to desktop computers, human lives are at stake when these "driving computers" are the target of an attack.

In an earlier publication, we introduced SAM: a Security Abstraction Model for automotive software systems [8]. The examples discussed in [8] are direct attack vectors. In this paper, however, we will focus on remote attack scenarios in the automotive domain considering cloud attacks and over-the-air (OTA) updates. Figure 1 illustrates the difference between direct attack vectors and cloud attack vectors. Cloud attack vectors target the vehicle indirectly over cloud infrastructure, e.g., the OEM's server.

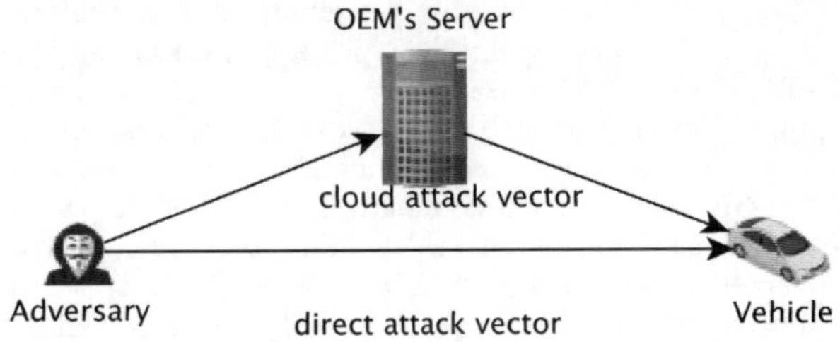

Figure 1. Direct Attack Vector vs. Cloud Attack Vector

In this paper, we show:

- A list of certain cloud attack vectors that cause major threats to automotive systems.
- A revamped version of SAM, featuring the ability to use any type of scoring system for attack rating.
- An explanation of how to use a well-known security scoring system (like CVSS) with SAM.
- A practical case study, applying the new version of SAM to the discussed cloud attacks from our list.

The rest of this paper is structured as follows: Section II reviews the state of the art on remote / cloud attacks on modern vehicles. Section III discusses possible remote attack scenarios and the security challenges of cloud attacks and OTA updates in the automotive domain. Section IV presents the current version of SAM and how to use any generic scoring system for attack rating. Section V illustrates two examples of remote and OTA update attacks using SAM for security modeling. Section VI reviews related work on security architectures for automotive software systems. Section VII concludes the paper and gives an outlook on future work.

II. State of the Art

Modern vehicles communicate critical and safety relevant commands over a shared powertrain between different types of ECUs. The most popular broadcast network used for communication is the CAN bus. CAN bus messages are unencrypted and unsigned by default, because this just wasn't an issue when CAN was designed. Remote exploitation of a single ECU item on the CAN bus causes a major security threat because it allows an attacker to send valid (and potentially harmful) messages over the bus to critical parts of the vehicle's ECU network. Various attacks [7] have shown that adversaries are able to cause serious threats by compromising a vehicle's ECU (or adding an external device) and sending malicious CAN commands to the devices listening on the bus. Once the adversary has the ability to send arbitrary CAN messages, she is able to control the braking system, engine behaviour, the air vents, (un-)locking the doors, etc. Therefore there is a strong need to secure the vehicle before the adversary even can gain access to the CAN bus. If the adversary has access to the powertrain it is already too late.

Modern vehicles have a tremendous amount of remote attack surfaces like wireless protocols, mobile application support and more. Examples of specific remote technologies are the passive anti-theft system (PATS), tire pressure monitoring systems (TPMS), remote keyless entry (RKE), Bluetooth, radio data systems (3G, 4G, LTE, 5G, etc.), Wi-Fi and telematics. Miller and Valasek describe numerous remote exploits targeting said technologies [7]. Typically, infotainment systems tend to feature Internet access and support for third-party applications. If one or some of these applications or services become vulnerable to hacking attacks over the network, an adversary might be able to control a crucial participant in the physical network of the vehicle: the CAN bus. Automotive Ethernet is a new approach in the automotive domain to connect ECUs in the vehicle, though, it is not expected to fully replace the CAN bus. CAN will continue to exist as a low-cost component, for example for connecting low-cost and computationally weak actuators and sensors with their corresponding ECUs or gateways, rather than be used as the main powertrain. As of today, the LIN-bus (Local Interconnect Network) is used for this type (low-cost, low-risk) of connection.

Although the CAN specification describes CAN as unencrypted by default, a sound solution for encryption and authentication is necessary to ensure a safe and secure distribution of critical new software over this public channel. In the automotive domain, there are not only software updates to consider, but hardware updates as well. If a workshop, for instance, replaces one of the brakes in a vehicle, they might also replace the corresponding ECU. In that scenario, how will the new cryptographic key (for message cryptography) be obtained? Common key distribution techniques like the Diffie-Hellman key exchange are difficult to implement, since many of the smaller network participants are low-cost and computationally weak ECUs. These ECUs often do not feature enough memory or CPU power to perform those cryptographic algorithms and methods. Cost is a limiting factor as well, when it comes to implementing expensive hardware into the vehicle. Automobile manufacturers prefer to spend more money on the salaries of programmers (fixed costs; used for entire fleet) rather than spending a cent more on a hardware part of a vehicle (variable costs; for each vehicle) because of the huge market scale. This means that hardware modules like TPMs (Trusted Platform Modules) are unattractive (cost, weight, space) as a key storing solution for each and every communicating part in the vehicle. Message cryptography on the CAN bus is not only hard to realize due to the strong network complexity, where key distribution is a difficult problem, but because an adversary in control of an ECU also gets access to the keys stored on that device.

III. Automotive Attack Scenarios

This section describes the motivation of our approach. This motivation is necessary to highlight the threats and dangers of automotive attack scenarios when considering cloud attack vectors. The claim of this section is to demonstrate what kinds of cloud attacks are possible and how they should be generally assessed. Section IV will describe how to assess them in more detail with SAM. A majority of remote attack vectors targeting automotive systems lead to accessing and tampering with the CAN bus, i.e., altering, sending or blocking CAN frames. Therefore it is necessary to improve the security of the remote access systems before a potential adversary even gets to the powertrain. OTA updates are most often pulled and received via the infotainment unit, which has access to a 4G, LTE or 5G broadband connection. From there, each and every ECU that needs to receive an update has to get the new firmware or software patch from the infotainment unit via the CAN bus. Rolling out sensitive data, especially new firmware or security patches in case of OTA updates over the CAN bus is incredibly critical and a major liability. OEM updates must be checked and validated before they can be deployed to the range of ECUs connected to the CAN bus. Faulty network configurations and the lack of authentication checks for OTA updates and patches can increase the risk of cloud and botnet attacks, e.g., Mirai [9].

All of this information needs to be documented in a system model that takes attack modeling for automotive software systems into account. The latest version of SAM [10] introduces new attributes for rating these kinds of attacks.

The following is a non-exhaustive list of cloud attack vectors that cause major threats to automotive software systems:

- Rolling out malicious (possibly unsigned) firmware to ECUs.
- Gaining remote control access to the vehicle using the OEMs cloud and mobile application's infrastructure.
- Infecting the system with ransomware.

The above attacks were chosen because they break the security goals integrity and authenticity. These security goals are especially important to make sure that the safety critical software of the vehicle stays untampered. Once the adversary has gained remote access to the vehicle she can start follow-up attacks as she already has access to the powertrain. The following is a list of automotive attack vectors regarding the CAN bus, assuming the adversary already has gained access via remote attack:

- Reverse engineering of CAN frames by filtering by arbitration IDs and identifying frames via tools like cansniffer or other can-utils [11].
- Injection of CAN frames from ECUs that were taken over after the remote attack (e.g., replay attacks, spamming attacks, etc.).
- Denial of Service (DoS) attacks, e.g., as shown by Palamanca et al [12].

Basically, cloud features and OTA updates have to be considered skeptical from the start. Even if the distribution source of the software is the OEM, attacks are still possible. A potential attacker might have found a way to distribute his malware over the OEM's infrastructure (e.g., their servers) and as a result a trust problem arises. It is fair to assume that any kind of roll-out (software updates, cloud data) is untrusted until the key distribution problem described earlier has been solved. Even if a solution for key distribution in heterogeneous CAN bus networks is developed, the number of remote attack vectors will rise harshly in comparison to the number of direct attack vectors. Hence, it is important to have a framework for modeling safe and secure automotive software systems with a system architecture model that takes even cloud attacks and remote attack vectors into account. The changes to the SAM meta model presented in this paper are a tangible solution for this kind of security analysis and security by design.

IV. USING GENERIC SCORING SYSTEMS FOR SAM

The current version of SAM introduces many new attributes to the modeling entities which allow for using well-known security scoring systems like CVSS [13]. In order to be able to keep SAM up-to-date and gain, some flexibility by not making a strong commitment to one particular system, we designed SAM to use any generic scoring system. When modeling attack scenarios, users of SAM can choose among their favorite. In this paper, we will use the CVSS. The latest version of SAM is available open source [10]. The architecture description has been completed to the extent that common scoring systems are now able to find the necessary information and thus perform their analyses. Inspired by the CVSS, which is an acclaimed industry standard for rating vulnerabilities in computer systems, we added new attributes to some of SAM's entities. The CVSS proposes three different metric groups for calculating the vulnerability scores. In the following, an explanation of the interplay between SAM and the metrics is given. The assignment of the attributes to the meta entities and partly their naming does not come from CVSS, but was developed by the athors.

The Base Metric Group reflects the intrinsic properties of Attack: from SAM's automotive-oriented perspective, this group therefore indicates the characteristics that result if the attack in question is aimed at the automotive domain in general. The entity AttackableProperty refers to the properties of the attacked item that are beyond the control of the attacker and must exist in order to exploit the vulnerability For example, in the case of a side channel attack, the use of shared caches within a multicore system. The attribute `conditionPrerequisiteComplexity` ("Low" and "High") in the AttackableProperty refers to the complexity of encountering or creating such conditions. For example, in the case of the side channel attack mentioned above, the `conditionPrerequisiteComplexity` is "Low" because shared caches are to be expected nowadays. It would be "High" if the attack made it necessary for all tasks on all cores to use one single common cache. When evaluating this property, all user interaction requirements for exploiting the vulnerability must be excluded (these conditions are recorded in the property `privilegesRequired` of Attack instead). If the `conditionPrerequisiteComplexity` is "Low", the attack is more dangerous than if the `conditionPrerequisiteComplexity` is "High". The property `privilegesRequired` describes the level of privileges an attacker must possess before successfully exploiting the vulnerability. This metric is greatest if no privileges are required. Also, the Attack entity has been extended with the attributes `accessRequired` and `userInteraction`. The attribute `accessRequired` describes the context in by which vulnerability exploitation is possible. Whether the user or driver of the vehicle needs to interact with the system in a certain way, e.g., by pressing a button, is captured in `userInteraction`. Attacks that do not require any user interaction increase the score of the attack. **The Temporal Metric Group** allows for adjustment of the score after more information of the exploited vulnerability is available. If, for example, `exploit code` has been published or the `report confidence` of a vulnerability is confirmed, the temporal score rises. In SAM, temporal metrics are part of the entity Vulnerability. **The Environmental Score Metrics** additionally enable the general CVSS Score (resulting from the Base Metric Group) to be adapted to the specific (automotive) company. The metrics are the modified equivalent of the base metrics weighting properties related to the concrete company's infrastructure and business risk. SAM offers a fully comprehensive basis to analyse the CVSS Base Metric Group, which means that SAM can also be used to evaluate the Environmental Metric Group. Environmental Metrics do not require any additional information beyond the Base Metrics, but merely a readjustment of the analysis perspective towards the concrete company. This means that the security scoring analysis can be carried out entirely by an analyst based on the available information provided by SAM.

The new changes to the SAM meta model (see Figure 2) allow the use of any security scoring or attack rating system, not only CVSS. This means that not all metrics and explanations of the CVSS have been transferred to SAM. This allows for more flexibility and SAM does not have to be adapted for any future CVSS updates. All attributes used for attack assessment are of the type String. This allows for SAM to be used with generic assessment techniques and is not tightly coupled with the CVSS attribute descriptions. In the model itself, or from the model itself, a CVSS score cannot be calculated automatically anyway. Doing so would happen in a behaviour model while SAM models are structure models. But if a security analyst is familiar with the CVSS, she will be able to calculate the CVSS score with all the information that is provided by the structure model. It is therefore still possible to find related information about the attribute types ("High" and "Low", etc.) in the notes of the meta model, but does not lead to problems in case of non-compliance.

V. CASE STUDY ON CLOUD ATTACKS

SAM allows for a security analysis of cloud attacks. In the following we will show two examples: a remote attack

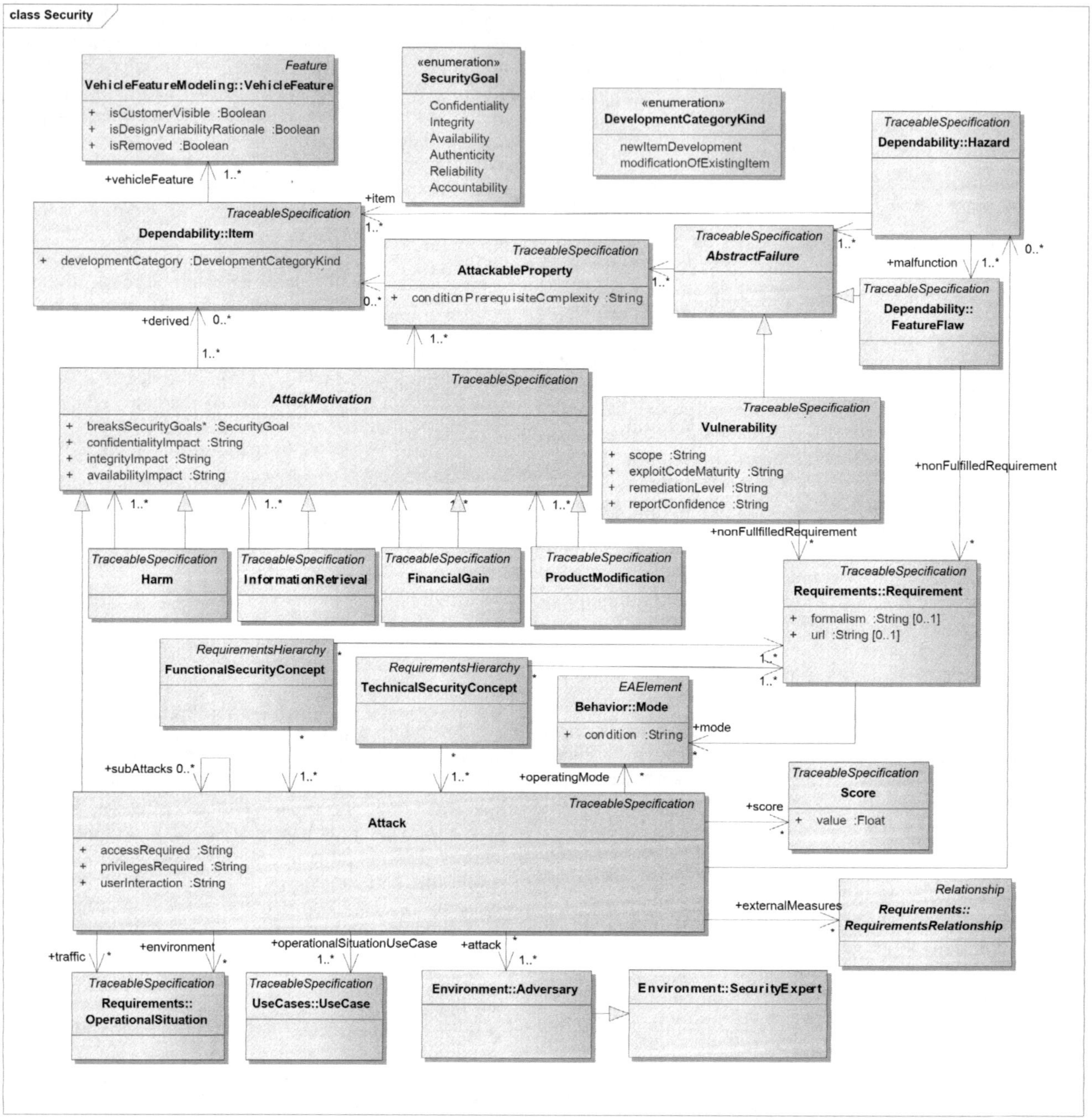

Figure 2. SAM Metamodel

to gain control of the vehicle (1) and an OTA update attack to install ransomware on the vehicle's infotainment unit (2). The attacks were chosen because they break the security goals authenticity and integrity. Cloud attack vectors often work only because of the absence of those security goals. The following examples are both in that category. (1) In the first part of the case study, we elaborate on a remote attack to gain control of a driving passenger vehicle as described by Miller and Valasek [7]. This kind of attack is one of the worst scenarios that can happen in theory and in practice, as an adversary does not need to have physical access to the target (`accessRequired` = N). Once the remote attack was successful, the adversary can perform numerous follow-up attacks as listed in Section III. Hence, the impact on the three security goals (confidentiality, integrity, availability) is *H*(igh). The adversary performing the attack is a **RemoteAttacker** and his attack motivation might be to *harm* the passengers or other road users (**CrashVehicle**). The exploited vulnerability is the **wrong D-Bus configuration**, specifically the **open D-Bus port** as the *AttackableProperty*. The vulnerability exists because of the *VehicleFeature* **BroadbandConnectivity** of the *Item* **InfotainmentUnit**. As the *Vulnerability* is already known because of the publication of Miller and Valasek and an official fix by the OEM is available, the tempo-

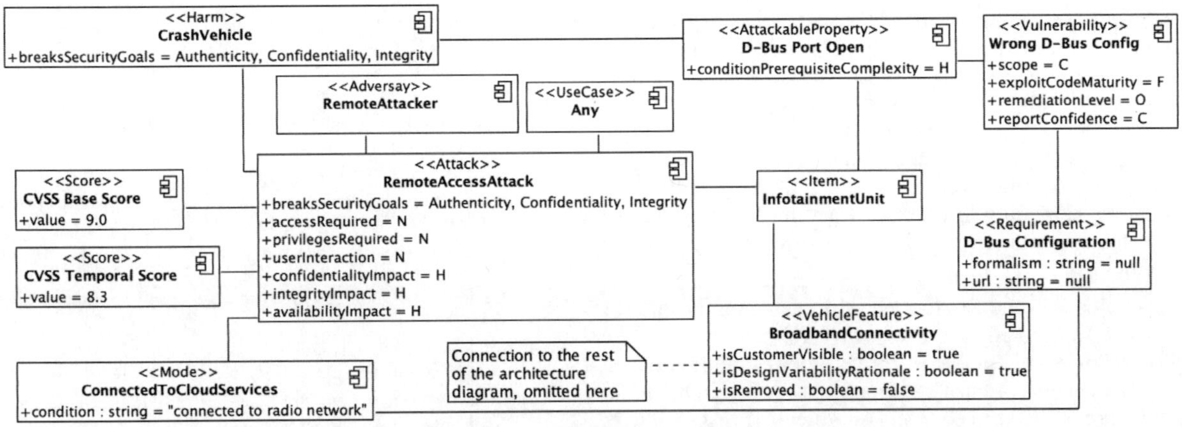

Figure 3. Exemplary architecture model for a cloud attack.
CVSS v3.0 Vector String: CVSS:3.0/AV:N/AC:H/PR:N/UI:N/S:C/C:H/I:H/A:H/E:F/RL:O/RC:C

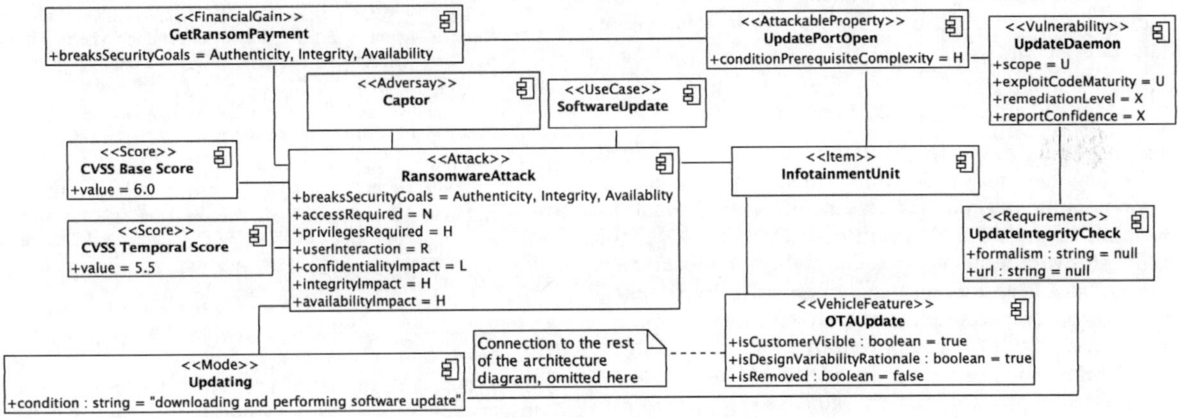

Figure 4. Exemplary architecture model for an OTA attack.
CVSS v3.0 Vector String: CVSS:3.0/AV:N/AC:H/PR:H/UI:R/S:U/C:L/I:H/A:H/E:U

ral metrics are *F*(unctional) for `exploitCodeMaturity`, *O*(fficial) Fix for `remediationLevel` and *C*(onfirmed) for `reportConfidence`. Hence, the remote attack scores a 9.0 as a **Base Score** and a 8.3 as a **Temporal Score**. This cloud attack is illustrated in Figure 3.

(2) The second part of the case study illustrates an OTA update attack using ransomware. A potential attack might compromise the OTA update interface to install an adversary's version of firmware. The ransomware would take control of the car by, e.g., by blocking or weakening the braking system until the user whose car has been infected pays a ransom to gain back full control of their vehicle. The attack motivation of such attack would be *financial gain* in the SAM context with the adversary demanding the ransom. For the update to be installed, however, the user is required to approve the update, e.g., by pressing a confirmation button on the infotainment unit. In contrast to the attack described above, this attack example is merely an unproven concept as no such attack or real scenario is known yet. However, it might be in the future and SAM is able to create a threat model for such an attack scenario. The exploit code maturity is unproven and there is no remediation level or report confidence defined. Hence, this OTA update attack scores a 6.0 as a **Base Score** and a 5.5 as a **Temporal Score**. This OTA update attack is illustrated in Figure 4.

VI. Related Work

SAM utilizes common concepts of the listed projects and related work. A non-trivial foundation includes the work of Holm [14], featuring a Cyber Security Modeling Language (CySeMoL) for enterprise architectures, Mouratidis [15] (Secure Tropos), papers, such as Ngyuyen [16], Juerjens [17], featuring UMLSec, which allows to express security-relevant information within the diagrams in a system specification, INCOSE work on integrating system engineering with system security engineering [18], NIST SP 800-160 [19] and other NIST work on cyber-physical systems [20]. SAM's unique characteristic and advantage over those existing approaches is that it is already integrated into an existing system model, (i.e. EAST-ADL [21]). SAM uses existing entities of the EAST-ADL system model (e.g., `Environment`, `Hazard`, `Item`, etc.) and is therefore tightly coupled with the system model. This enables a seamless integration of a security model into a system model that is extensively used in the automotive industry.

Some approaches deal with OTA updates in the way of hardening ECU firmware. Karamba [22] proposes a solution called "Autonomous Security" which focuses on embedding native security through static code analysis of the ECU firmware and locking it to factory settings. Multi-dimensional whitelisting might be an effective approach to vehicle cybersecurity. As manufacturers strive to limit post-deployment modifications, hardening the ECUs offers the added benefit of a more stable environment that is easier to secure over the life of the vehicle.

PRESERVE was an "EU-funded project running from 2011 to 2015 and contributed to the security and privacy of future vehicle-to-vehicle and vehicle-to-infrastructure communication systems. It provides security requirements of vehicle security architectures" [23]. The EVITA project tries to "design, verify and prototype an architecture for automotive on-board networks where security-relevant components are protected against tampering and sensitive data are protected against compromise. It focuses on V2X (vehicle to anything) communications and provides a base for secure deployment of electronic safety applications" [24].

VII. Conclusion and Future Work

In this paper, we have presented an investigation on cloud attacks in the automotive domain. Doing so, we give a glimpse on possible cloud attack vectors and attack scenarios. Moreover, we revamped the Security Abstraction Model for automotive software systems with the ability to model even more precise attack vectors and attack scenarios by enabling the use of any generic security scoring system like CVSS. We showed the feasibility of our approach by giving a case study on cloud attacks applying the new model. SAM offers robust tooling for modeling security for automotive software systems. Future work will concentrate on the bottom-up approach, i.e., improving embedded security and network security on the application layer. Next steps need to develop automotive software solutions to actually be included in the technical and functional security concept. Our research focuses particularly on a lightweight crypto approach for authentication and encryption in the vehicle network and embedded software, including a suitable keys distribution solution. Our work aims to support security by design in the automotive industry and SAM offers the necessary insights and fundamentals to continue conducting relevant research in this domain.

Acknowledgment

This work is funded by the Bavarian State Ministry of Science and the Arts in the framework of the Centre Digitisation.Bavaria (ZD.B).

M.Z. was supported by the BayWISS Consortium Digitization.

References

[1] S. Tuohy, M. Glavin, C. Hughes, E. Jones, M. Trivedi, and L. Kilmartin, "Intra-Vehicle Networks: A Review," pp. 534–545, 2015.

[2] W. Zeng, M. A. Khalid, and S. Chowdhury, "In-vehicle networks outlook: Achievements and challenges," IEEE Communications Surveys and Tutorials, vol. 18, no. 3, 2016, pp. 1552–1571.

[3] ISO/IEC, "ISO/IEC 15408-1:2009 - Evaluation Criteria for IT Security," vol. 2009, 2009, p. 64.

[4] A. Happel and C. Ebert, "Security in vehicle networks of connected cars," 15. Internationales Stuttgarter Symposium: Automobil- und Motorentechnik, no. March, 2015, pp. 233–246.

[5] C. Valasek and C. Miller, "Adventures in Automotive Networks and Control Units," Technical White Paper, vol. 21, 2013, p. 99.

[6] C. Miller and C. Valasek, "A Survey of Remote Automotive Attack Surfaces," Defcon 22, 2014, pp. 1–90.

[7] ——, "Remote Exploitation of an Unaltered Passenger Vehicle," Defcon 23, vol. 2015, 2015, pp. 1–91.

[8] M. Zoppelt and R. Tavakoli Kolagari, "SAM: A Security Abstraction Model for Automotive Software Systems," in Security and Safety Interplay of Intelligent Software Systems. Springer, 2018, pp. 59–74.

[9] C. Kolias, G. Kambourakis, A. Stavrou, and J. Voas, "Ddos in the iot: Mirai and other botnets," Computer, vol. 50, no. 7, 2017, pp. 80–84.

[10] SAM repository on Bitbucket [retrieved: April, 2019]. [Online]. Available: https://bitbucket.org/east-adl/sam

[11] can-utils repository on GitHub [retrieved: April, 2019]. [Online]. Available: https://github.com/linux-can/can-utils

[12] A. Palanca, E. Evenchick, F. Maggi, and S. Zanero, "A stealth, selective, link-layer denial-of-service attack against automotive networks," in Lecture Notes in Computer Science (including subseries Lecture Notes in Artificial Intelligence and Lecture Notes in Bioinformatics), M. Polychronakis and M. Meier, Eds. Cham: Springer International Publishing, 2017, vol. 10327 LNCS, pp. 185–206.

[13] Common Vulnerability Scoring System [retrieved: April, 2019]. [Online]. Available: https://www.first.org/cvss/

[14] H. Holm, M. Ekstedt, T. Sommestad, and M. Korman, "A Manual for the Cyber Security Modeling Language," 2013, p. 110.

[15] H. Mouratidis and P. Giorgini, "Secure Tropos: a Security-Oriented Extension of the Tropos Methodology," International Journal of Software Engineering and Knowledge Engineering, vol. 17, no. 02, 2007, pp. 285–309.

[16] P. H. Nguyen, S. Ali, and T. Yue, "Model-based security engineering for cyber-physical systems: A systematic mapping study," pp. 116–135, 2017.

[17] J. Jürjens, "UMLsec: Extending UML for Secure Systems Development," in International Conference on The Unified Modeling Language. Springer, 2002, pp. 412–425.

[18] INCOSE, "Systems Engineering Handbook," in Systems Engineering, no. August, 2000.

[19] R. Ross, M. McEvilley, and J. Carrier Oren, "Systems Security Engineering: Considerations for a Multidisciplinary Approach in the Engineering of Trustworthy Secure Systems," vol. 160, no. November 2016, 2016.

[20] J. Lee, B. Bagheri, and H.-a. Kao, "A Cyber-Physical Systems architecture for Industry 4 . 0-based manufacturing systems," Manufacturing Letters, vol. 3, 2015, pp. 18–23.

[21] H. Blom, H. Lönn, F. Hagl, Y. Papadopoulos, M. Reiser, C. Sjöstedt, D. Chen, and R. Tavakoli Kolagari, "EAST-ADL–An Architecture Description Language for Automotive Software-Intensive Systems–White Paper Version 2.1. 12," Hyperlink: http://www.maenad.eu/public/conceptpresentations/EAST-ADL_WhitePaper_M2 [retrieved: December 2018], vol. 1.

[22] D. Barzilai, "Autonomous Security [retrieved: January 2019]," 2018, pp. 1–14. [Online]. Available: https://www.karambasecurity.com/approach

[23] N. Bißmeyer, S. Mauthofer, J. Petit, M. Lange, M. Moser, D. Estor, M. Sall, M. Feiri, R. Moalla, M. Lagana, and F. Kargl, "PREparing SEcuRe VEhicle-to-X Communication Systems," 2014.

[24] O. Henniger, L. Apvrille, A. Fuchs, Y. Roudier, A. Ruddle, and B. Weyl, "Security requirements for automotive on-board networks," in 2009 9th International Conference on Intelligent Transport Systems Telecommunications, ITST 2009. IEEE, 2009, pp. 641–646.

Fighting Disinformation Warfare with Artificial Intelligence

Identifying and Combatting Disinformation Attacks in Cloud-based Social Media Platforms

Barry Cartwright
School of Criminology
Simon Fraser University
Burnaby, Canada
Email: bcartwri@sfu.ca

George R. S. Weir
Department of Computer & Information Sciences
University of Strathclyde
Glasgow, Scotland, UK
Email: george.weir@strath.ac.uk

Richard Frank
School of Criminology
Simon Fraser University
Burnaby, Canada
Email: rfrank@sfu.ca

***Abstract*—Following well-documented Russian interference in the 2016 U.S. Presidential election and in the Brexit referendum in the U.K., law enforcement, intelligence agencies and social network providers worldwide have expressed growing interest in identifying and interdicting disinformation warfare. This paper reports on a research project being conducted by the International CyberCrime Research Centre (ICCRC) at Simon Fraser University (Canada) in cooperation with the Department of Information and Computer Sciences at the University of Strathclyde (Scotland). The research project involves the development of a method for identifying hostile disinformation activities in the Cloud. Employing the ICCRC's Dark Crawler, Strathclyde's Posit Toolkit, and TensorFlow, we collected and analyzed nearly three million social media posts, examining "fake news" by Russia's Internet Research Agency, and comparing them to "real news" posts, in order to develop an automated means of classification. We were able to classify the posts as "real news" or "fake news" with an accuracy of 90.12% and 89.5%, using Posit and TensorFlow respectively.**

Keywords-Cybersecurity; Cloud-based social media platforms; disinformation; machine learning.

I. Introduction

Amongst the key challenges currently facing law enforcement agencies, intelligence agencies, cybersecurity personnel and business owners-operators around the world are how to monitor and efficiently respond to dynamic and emerging cybersecurity threats, with increasing attention being paid to hostile disinformation activities in Cloud-based social media platforms. To illustrate, on November 27, 2018, a senior executive from Facebook was grilled by a Parliamentary Committee in the U.K. regarding the (witting or unwitting) involvement of Facebook in the Russian hostile influence campaign during the run-up to the 2016 U.S. Presidential election. According to the CIA, the FBI, and the NSA, various other social media, including Twitter and Instagram, have also been implicated as (possibly unaware) participants in the hosting and dissemination of these disinformation attacks [1].

Our research, sponsored by the Canadian government's Cyber Security Cooperation Program, and conducted by the International CyberCrime Research Centre at Simon Fraser University in cooperation with the Department of Information and Computer Sciences at the University of Strathclyde, involves the development of a method for identifying hostile disinformation activities in the Cloud. The knowledge generated by this research will establish the foundation for more advanced work, eventually culminating in automatic tools which can rapidly and accurately pinpoint disinformation attacks in their very early stages.

II. Research Context

The research team has several years of collaborative experience in collecting and analyzing data from online extremist forums, child pornography websites, social media feeds and the Dark Web. Our previous experience in data classification has demonstrated that we are able, through automation, to achieve predictive accuracy in the 90-95% range when it comes to detecting the nuanced text found in extremist content on the Web [2], [3], [4]. This has been accomplished in the past by applying a combination of technologies, including the Dark Crawler, SentiStrength, and Posit. For the present study, we have employed the Dark Crawler, Posit, and TensorFlow. Additional information on these research tools is provided below. From this background, we have a methodology that is applicable to the analysis and classification of data from Cloud-based social media platforms.

A. Research Tools

The Dark Crawler is a custom-written, web-crawling software tool, developed by Richard Frank of Simon Fraser University's International CyberCrime Research Centre. This application can capture Web content from the open and Dark Web, as well as structured content from online discussion forums and various social media platforms [5]. The Dark Crawler uses key-words, key-phrases, and other syntax to retrieve relevant pages from the Web. The Crawler analyzes them, and recursively follows the links out of those pages. Statistics are automatically collected and retained for each webpage extracted, including frequency of keywords and the number of images and videos (if any are present). The entire content of each webpage is also preserved for further automated textual analysis. Content retrieved by our Dark Crawler is parsed into an Excel-style worksheet, with each data-element being identified and extracted. In previous studies of this nature, we have used this procedure to collect over 100 million forum posts from across a vast number of hacking and extremist forums for later analysis.

The Posit toolkit was developed by George Weir of the Department of Computer and Information Sciences at the University of Strathclyde. Posit generates frequency data and Part-of-Speech (POS) tagging while accommodating large text corpora. The data output from Posit includes values for total words (tokens), total unique words (types), type/token ratio, number of sentences, average sentence length, number of characters, average word length, noun types, verb types, adjective types, adverb types, preposition types, personal pronoun types, determiner types, possessive pronoun types, interjection types, particle types, nouns, verbs, prepositions, personal pronouns, determiners, adverbs, adjectives, possessive pronouns, interjections, and particles, or 27 features in all [6]. This generates a detailed frequency analysis of the syntax, including multi-word units and associated part-of-speech components.

TensorFlow, originally developed by the Google Brain Team, is a machine learning system that deploys deep neural networks [7]. This is a machine learning technique inspired by real neural systems. The learning algorithms are designed to excel in pattern recognition and knowledge-based prediction by training sensory data through an artificial network structure of neurons (nodes) and neuronal connections (weights). The network structure is usually constructed with an input layer, one or more hidden layers, and an output layer. Each layer contains multiple nodes, with connections between the nodes in the different layers. As data is fed into this neural system, weights are calculated and repeatedly changed for each connection [8].

III. METHODOLOGY

The research process commenced with an analysis of textual content from existing databases that had already assembled extensive materials from previously identified Russian disinformation attacks launched through social media platforms, including Twitter and Facebook. This paper reports on the analysis of textual content in Twitter, using Post and TensorFlow.

A. Research Sample

The research team downloaded a data set of 2,946,219 Twitter messages (tweets) from Github, which had been posted online by fivethirtyeight.com. This data set of tweets was collected and assembled by two professors at Clemson University, Darren Linvill and Patrick Warren [9]. These tweets were described as originating from the Internet Research Agency (IRA), also referred to in common parlance as the Russian troll factory, which was believed to have intentionally interfered in the 2016 U.S. Presidential election and the 2016 U.K. Brexit referendum.

A decision was made to extract only those entries that were labeled as being "English," thereby excluding languages such as Albanian, Bulgarian, Catalan, Croatian, Dutch, Estonian, French, German, Italian, Russian, Ukrainian, Uzbek, Vietnamese. Thus, 13 new Excel spreadsheets were created, with 2,116,904 English-speaking tweets remaining in the data set following the removal of all non-English cases.

Having acquired the Russian IRA Twitter data, we sought a second Twitter data set that would allow us to develop a classification model based upon comparison between "real news" and what has frequently been referred to as "fake news" [10], [11]. To this end, we analyzed the textual content from the full set of IRA tweets (or "fake news") using Posit, in order to identify frequently occurring terms, specifically nouns. The resultant "keyword" list was used with the International CyberCrime Research Centre's Dark Crawler to retrieve a set of matching "real news" Twitter posts from legitimate news sites. The Crawler harvested Twitter feeds maintained by more "traditional," mainstream news sources, such as the *Globe and Mail*, *CBC News*, *CTV News*, the *BBC*, the *New York Times*, the *Daily Telegraph*, the *Wall Street Journal*, *Asahi Shim-Bun*, *Times of India*, the *Washington Post*, the *Guardian*, and *Daily Mail Online*, collecting tweets posted between the beginning of January 2015 and the end of August 2018 (approximately the same time frame as the IRA tweets). Tweets from the "real news" data set that were posted after August 2018 were removed, as the data from the IRA tweets did not extend beyond that time frame. We started with 90,605 tweets, and the removal of 10,602 tweets that had been posted in late 2018-early 2019 left us with 80,003 individual cases or tweets that exemplified "real" or "legitimate" news sources. A research decision was made to random sample both data sets, creating two data sets of equal size, each consisting of 2,500 tweets, or roughly .001% of the larger "fake news" data set, and 3% of the "real news" data set. Unique identifiers were assigned to each of the data items, to ensure a means of fixed reference, and to permit future analysis of the data in NVivo and SentiStrength [12].

A somewhat different sample was assembled for the TensorFlow analysis. For TensorFlow to operate effectively, a larger data set is desirable. To achieve this, we combined the 2,116,904 English-speaking "fake news" tweets that remained (following the removal of all non-English cases) with the 90,605 "real news" tweets that were downloaded by the Dark Crawler (prior to removal of tweets that extended beyond the time frame of the IRA activities). This data set was supplemented with 3,000 Facebook messages posted by the IRA, plus an additional "real news" set of Twitter items. Thus, a large data set of 2,709,204 million tweets was analyzed in TensorFlow after the merging of these multiple data sets.

B. Data Analysis

1) Posit

Following the creation and cleansing of the data sets, we extracted features from the texts using Posit, which is designed to generate quantitative data at the level of word and part-of-speech content of texts. Posit analysis was applied to each of the 5,000 tweets in order to produce a 27-item feature list for each tweet. This was supplemented by an additional feature, to indicate the "real" or "fake" characteristic of each tweet.

Previous research has indicated that Posit's domain-independent meta-data can prove effective as a feature set for use in such text classification tasks [2], [4]. In the present study, the target textual data was made up of tweets. These have a limited maximum length of 280 characters, so they are inherently short and contain relatively few words. This was potentially an obstacle to Posit use.

Since Posit creates data on the basis of word-level information, the limited content of tweets means that many of the original features may have zero values. With this in mind, for the analysis of short texts, Posit has been extended to include analysis of character-level content. To this end, the system supplements the standard word-level statistics and generates an additional 44 character features for each instance of text data. These features include quantitative information on individual alphanumeric characters, and a subset of special characters, specifically, questions marks, exclamation marks, asterisks, periods and dollar signs. The extension of Posit to embrace character-level as well as word-level data maintains the domain-neutral nature of Posit analysis. As a result of this extended Posit analysis, each data item (tweet) is represented by a set of 72 features.

Thereafter, this list of tweet features was formulated as an arff file format, suitable for direct input to the Waikato Environment for Knowledge Analysis (WEKA) data analysis application [13]. In WEKA, we applied the standard J48 tree classification method and the Random Forest classification method [14], both with ten-fold validation. WEKA produced a measure of how many of the tweets were correctly classified.

2) TensorFlow

In this project, TensorFlow was adopted for processing the data with a Deep Neural Network (DNN). A large data set was initially fed into TensorFlow, in order to conduct DNN learning. The DNN results either updated an existing model or created a new model. TensorFlow then compared the same data against the constructed DNN model, and utilized that model to predict the category for each data entry.

In order to build an initial TensorFlow model, a large data set of 2,709,204 million tweets was created by merging multiple data sets. The more data that could be collected for training a model, the better the accuracy should be. However, the individual data files were inconsistent, since they were collected from various online resources, and were formatted in very different ways. Thus, in the process of combining them into a single data set, we opted for Microsoft Access, which allowed for a large, unified database table. All of the data sets were merged into the Access database, after which a class label column "*category*" was defined, denoting whether the data represented "fake" or "real" news.

The model was evaluated for its accuracy in predicting class values for the "fake" or "real" news category. To simplify the analysis, we decided to build our DNN model based on the content of the 2,709,204 tweets, without any further pre-processing. The DNN model used was a TensorFlow Estimator.DNNClassifier.

In the early stages of experimentation, we employed TensorFlow default settings for the parameters pertaining to the number of partitions, epochs, layers, learning rate, and regularization. With respect to regularization, data was partitioned into groups according to the order in which it appeared in the dataset. Thus, if the majority of "fake news" appeared in the beginning of the dataset, it would be difficult to maintain consistent accuracy when conducting X-fold cross validation. To overcome this issue, the data was randomized as it became partitioned. Furthermore, each partition maintained the same data across all X-fold cross validation tests, so that accuracy of results could be compared effectively.

Epochs refer to the number of times the dataset is processed during training. The greater the number of epochs, the higher the accuracy tends to be. The learning rate determines the rate at which the model converges to the local minima. Usually, a smaller learning rate means it takes longer for the model to converge at the local minima [15]. With a larger learning rate, the model gets closer to this convergence point more quickly. The values for these parameters— number of partitions, epochs, layers, learning rate, and regularization (L1 & L2)—were then tested to identify an optimal set of parameter values.

IV. Research Results

A. Posit

The Posit analysis produced a feature set with corresponding values for each of the 5,000 tweets (2,500 "fake news" tweets and 2,500 "real news" tweets). The feature set was loaded into WEKA as a basis for testing the feasibility of classification against the predefined "fake" and "real" news categories. Using the "standard" set of 27 Posit features—and the default WEKA settings with 10-fold cross validation—the J48 and Random Forest classifiers gave 82.6% and 86.82% correctly classified instances, respectively. The confusion matrix for the latter performance is shown in Figure 1, below.

a	b	← classified as
2190	310 |	a = negative
340	2160 |	b = positive

Figure 1. Confusion matrix for Posit: 27 features (Random Forest: default WEKA settings)

As indicated earlier, Posit was enhanced with an additional 44 character-based features. Using this extended feature set on the 5,000 tweets—and the default WEKA settings with 10-fold cross validation—the J48 and Random settings Forest classifiers gave 81.52% and 89.8% correctly classified instances, respectively. The confusion matrix for the latter performance is shown in Figure 2, below.

a	b	← classified as
2266	234 |	a = negative
276	2224 |	b = positive

Figure 2. Confusion matrix for Posit: 71 features (Random Forest: default WEKA settings)

Changing the number of instances (trees) from the default value of 100 to 211 in Random Forest provided a boost to the level of correctly classified instances to 90.12%. The confusion matrix for this performance is shown in Figure 3, below.

a	b	← classified as
2269	231 |	a = negative
263	2237 |	b = positive

Figure 3. Confusion matrix for Posit: 71 features (Random Forest: instances at 211 in WEKA settings)

Our best performance results (90.12%) were obtained from the Posit classification using the 71-feature set with Random Forest (instances at 211). The "detailed accuracy by class" for this result is shown in Figure 4.

	TP Rate	FP Rate	Precision	Recall	F-Measure	Class
	0.908	0.105	0.896	0.908	0.902	negative
	0.895	0.092	0.906	0.895	0.901	positive
Weighted Avg.	0.901	0.099	0.901	0.901	0.901	

Figure 4. Detailed Accuracy By Class for best Posit result

B. TensorFlow

In the early stages of experimentation, using default TensorFlow parameters for number of partitions, epochs, layers, learning rate, and regularization, the accuracy results yielded an average of around 60%. Many parameter values (for each parameter: number of partitions, epochs, layers, learning rate, and regularization) were then tested to identify an optimal set of parameter values. This resulted in an increase in accuracy of to 89.5%, a substantial improvement from the earlier results. These parameters are described below, with the post-training optimal values shown below in Table I.

To be able to run large numbers of experiments, we wrapped all code into a standalone function, so large numbers of various scenarios could be designed, set up, and tested continuously. These batch jobs allowed us to evaluate different combinations of parameters. The parameters of each run, and the corresponding results, are also shown below. Tests were run using 10 partitions, with training on the first 5 and testing on the last 5.

V. DISCUSSION

Given the limited number of words and word varieties in most tweets, the performance of the Posit analysis using the default 27 word-level features proved to be better than expected at 86.82% correctly classified instances using Random Forest. The addition of character-level information enhanced this performance to a creditable 90.12% correctly classified instances, again using Random Forest. This result may be surprising, given that alphanumeric details seem far removed from tweet content-level.

The natural presumption may be that establishing objective truth is the primary goal of such research. This could be an inaccurate assumption. Since the principal basis for any automated judgment will be secondary sources, objective truth is not always readily discernible. Facts as they pertain to the real world are present in first-order reports, but when confronted solely with such reports, we can only resort to authority, provenance and inherent credibility as bases for judgement.

Despite working solely from available sources, we have aimed to discriminate between several significant classes of report: 1) plausible and probably correct reflections of the facts; 2) likely, based upon the facts with evident 'observer' influence (such as colour or bias or prejudice); 3) largely 'interpreted' with some factual basis; 4) almost entirely devoid of factual content.

TABLE I. TENSORFLOW PERFORMANCE RESULTS

layers	learn rate	partition	size	time	accuracy
[500, 500]	0.003	0	674941	44.683	0.873
[500, 500]	0.003	1	675072	48.102	0.873
[500, 500]	0.003	2	674613	45.654	0.873
[500, 500]	0.003	3	675109	45.638	0.873
[500, 500]	0.003	4	9479	2.562	0.871
[700, 700]	0.003	0	674941	217.444	0.873
[700, 700]	0.003	1	675072	57.929	0.874
[700, 700]	0.003	2	674613	59.508	0.873
[700, 700]	0.003	3	675109	58.923	0.873
[700, 700]	0.003	4	9479	3.020	0.872
[500, 500]	0.03	0	674941	128.865	0.882
[500, 500]	0.03	1	675072	59.551	0.882
[500, 500]	0.03	2	674613	60.684	0.881
[500, 500]	0.03	3	675109	61.396	0.882
[500, 500]	0.03	4	9479	3.205	0.895

VI. CONCLUSION

Through the research process outlined above, we are: 1) developing typologies of past and present hostile activities in

Cloud-based social media platforms; 2) identifying indicators of change in public opinion (as they relate to hostile disinformation activities); 3) identifying the social media techniques of hostile actors (and how best to respond to them); and 4) undertaking cross-cultural analyses, to determine how hostile actors seek to fuel tensions and undermine social cohesion by exploiting cultural sensitivities.

Our current research will ultimately generate an algorithm that can automatically detect hostile disinformation content. In the longer term, we will use the knowledge generated by this research project to further expand the capabilities of the Posit toolkit and the Dark Crawler, in order to facilitate near-real-time monitoring of disinformation activities in the Cloud. Further, we plan to add a feature that will permit us to capture disinformation messages prior to their removal by social media organizations attempting to delete those accounts, and/or their removal by actors seeking to conceal their online identities.

During the research process, we also downloaded 2,500 "fake news" Facebook messages that had been posted by the IRA on Facebook pages known variously as Blacktivist, Patriototus, LGBT United, Secured.Borders, and United Muslims of America. (These 2,500 Facebook messages were included in our TensorFlow analysis.) All 2,500 of these messages have been subjected to a preliminary review in the qualitative research tool, NVivo. Early insights revealed that many of the allegedly "fake news" items were founded to one degree or another in contemporaneous "real news" events. We are presently devising a process for capturing "real news" stories that align as closely as possible with the "fake news," to better address the spectrum between "real" and "fake" news, and the nexus between them. Apart from informing ongoing NVivo analysis, we anticipate that this spectrum of "real" and "fake" news stories will serve as a basis for further discrimination in Posit, with the likely addition of sentiment analysis [12].

ACKNOWLEDGMENTS

This research project would not have been possible without funding from the Cyber Security Cooperation Program, operated by the National Cyber Security Directorate of Public Safety Canada. We would also like to thank our research assistants, Soobin Rim (TensorFlow) and Aynsley Pescitelli and Karmvir Padda (NVivo).

REFERENCES

[1] Background to "Assessing Russian Activities and Intentions in Recent US Elections": The Analytic Process and Cyber Incident Attribution, ICA 2017-01D, January 2017. URL: https://www.dni.gov/files/documents/ICA_2017_01.pdf [accessed: 2019.04.05]

[2] G. Weir, R. Frank, B. Cartwright and E. Dos Santos, "Positing the problem: enhancing classification of extremist web content through textual analysis," *International Conference on Cybercrime and Computer Forensics (IEEE Xplore)*, June 2016.

[3] G. Weir, K. Owoeye, A. Oberacker and H. Alshahrani, "Cloud-based textual analysis as a basis for document classification," *International Conference on High Performance Computing & Simulation (HPCS)*, pp. 672-676, July 2018.

[4] K. Owoeye and G. R. S. Weir, "Classification of radical Web text using a composite-based method, *IEEE International Conference on Computational Science and Computational Intelligence*, December 2018.

[5] A. T. Zulkarnine, R. Frank, B. Monk, J. Mitchell and G. Davies, "Surfacing collaborated networks in dark web to find illicit and criminal content," *Intelligence and Security Informatics (ISI)*, pp. 109-114, September 2016.

[6] G. R. S. Weir, "Corpus profiling with the Posit tools," *Proceedings of the 5th Corpus Linguistics Conference,* July 2009.

[7] M. Abadi, P. Barham, J. Chen, Z. Chen, A. Davis,J. Dean, M. Devin, S. Ghemawat, G. Irving, M. Isard, M. Kudlur, J. Levenberg, R. Monga, S. Moore, D. G. Murray, B. Steiner, P. Tucker,V. Vasudevan, P. Warden, M. Wicke, Y. Yu and X. Zheng, "TensorFlow: A system for large-scale machine learning," *12th USENIX Symposium on Operating Systems Design and Implementation*, pp. 265-283, November 2016.

[8] T. C. Kietzmann, P. McClure and N. Kriegeskorte, "Deep neural networks in computational neuroscience," *bioRxiv*, pp. 133504-133527, 2018.

[9] D. L. Linvill and P. L. Warren, "Troll factories: The Internet Research Agency and state-sponsored agenda-building," 2018. URL: http://pwarren.people.clemson.edu/Linvill_Warren_TrollFactory.pdf [accessed: 2019.04.05]

[10] L. Reston, "How Russia Weaponizes Fake News," *New Republic*, pp. 6-8, 2017.

[11] N. W. Jankowski, "Researching fake news: A selective examination of empirical studies," *Javnost-The Public* 25.1-2, pp. 248-255, 2018.

[12] M. Thelwall, K. Buckley, G. Paltoglou, D. Cai and A. Kappas, "Sentiment strength detection in short informal text," *Journal of the American Society for Information Science and Technology*, 61(12), 2544–2558, 2010.

[13] M. Hall, E. Frank, H. Geoffrey, B. Pfahringer, P. Reutemann and I. Witten, "The Weka data mining software: an update," *SIGKDD Explorations,* vol. 11, pp. 10-18, 2009.

[14] L. Breiman, "Random Forests," *Machine Learning,* vol. 45, pp. 5-32, 2001.

[15] Y. N. Dauphin, R. Pascanu, C. Gulcehre, K. Cho, S. Ganguli and Y. Bengio, "Identifying and attacking the saddle point problem in high-dimensional non-convex optimization," *Advances in neural information processing systems*, pp. 2933-2941, 2014.

PLASMA – Platform for Service Management in Digital Remote Maintenance Applications

Natascha Stumpp[1], Doris Aschenbrenner[2], Manuel Stahl[3] and Andreas Aßmuth[4]

[1]ESSERT GmbH, Ubstadt-Weiher, Germany, Email: n.stumpp@essert.com
[2]Technische Universiteit Delft, Delft, Netherlands, Email: d.aschenbrenner@tudelft.nl
[3]Awesome Technologies Innovationslabor GmbH, Würzburg, Germany,
Email: manuel.stahl@awesome-technologies.de
[4]Technical University of Applied Sciences OTH Amberg-Weiden, Amberg, Germany, Email: a.assmuth@oth-aw.de

***Abstract*—To support maintenance and servicing of industrial machines, service processes are even today often performed manually and analogously, although supportive technologies such as augmented reality, virtual reality and digital platforms already exist. In many cases, neither technicians on-site nor remote experts have all the essential information and options for suitable actions available. Existing service products and platforms do not cover all the required functions in practice in order to map end-to-end processes. PLASMA is a concept for a Cloud-based remote maintenance platform designed to meet these demands. But for a real-life implementation of PLASMA, security measures are essential as we show in this paper.**

Keywords–Remote Maintenance; Cloud Solution; IoT; Security.

I. INTRODUCTION

A major competitive factor for manufacturing companies is a high and reliable availability of their production facilities. Despite already existing technology like Augmented Reality (AR) or Virtual Reality (VR), which has the potential to improve the service processes, a lot maintenance even today happens manually involving expert personnel. The common

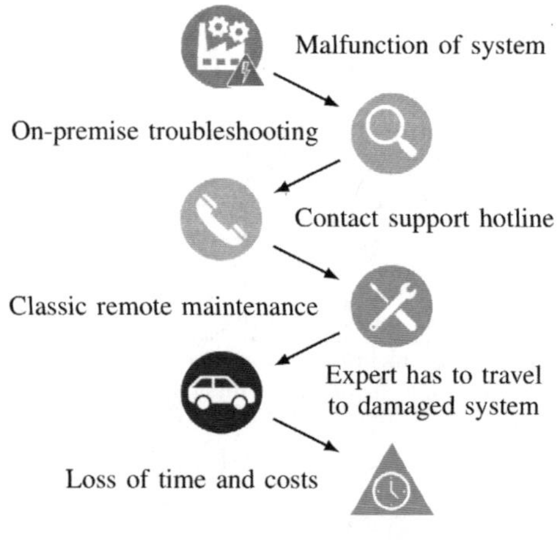

Figure 1. Course of actions without an intelligent maintenance platform.

course of actions is depicted in Figure 1. Imagine that production in a company suddenly succumbs because one of their machines stops working. At first, the workers try to find the reason for the malfunction themselves. Maybe, the company employs their own technicians for the maintenance of their systems. In this case, the workers call for one of these technicians. In most cases, these technicians do not have the same knowledge of the machine that specialists employed by the manufacturer of the machines have. In many cases, neither the technician nor the worker have all essential information or know about possible actions to solve the problem the right away. Therefore, if the technicians are not able to solve the problem, e.g., they cannot find a solution in the manual of the machine, the company contacts the manufacturer using their hotline or website. This is when classic remote maintenance comes into play. If the machine is connected to the Internet, one of the manufacturer's specialists connects to the system, e.g., via VPN, and tries to gather more information about the malfunction. There are numerous cases in which one of the specialists has to travel to a broken machine to repair it in on-site. An essential part of the machine might be physically broken and only the manufacturer is capable of installing a spare part. Assuming the manufacturer is situated in Europe and the company with the broken system is, e.g., in Australia, the travel might take days causing high costs for the company due to the outage.

A small or medium-sized company today faces the challenge to implement their whole digital service processes in their existing environment, but only the currently available solutions usually cover just a small number of isolated use cases. Additionally, even though there is a large variety of such very specialised services, encapsulated platforms or IoT solutions readily available it is difficult to choose the ones the company really needs and that can be used in combination with services for other partial tasks of their digital service processes. For a complete mapping of application-driven end-to-end processes, it is necessary to realise a combination of these different platforms for small and middle-sized businesses which could probably struggle with the implementation by themselves. And these different platforms in practice do not necessarily interact properly with each other.

A. Objective

The joint project PLASMA aims for a holistic solution, which complements existing end-to-end business processes and supports the development of new service concepts, e.g., pay-per-x or x-as-a-service. Within the project an intelligent linkage between systems and platforms will be developed to allow integrated support and innovative business models all around service for production processes and facilities.

The solution should seamlessly fit into all process models and should be integrable into existing system landscapes as well as Enterprise Resource Planning (ERP) systems. Additionally, PLASMA contains an information and knowledge management component to store and document instructions, tutorials, service reports, master data and offers a device- and location-independent visualization of it. PLASMA enables the user to handle complex machine data and real-time simulations presented in an intuitive way. With AR- and VR-support it will be possible to offer almost real guidance for maintenance and service cases. The service management platform can connect customers and suppliers and is intended to reshape the whole transparent life cycle of a product without exposing sensible data.

B. Related work

Currently, there is a vast change within automation industry which is attributed to be the "fourth industrial revolution"; although this name is mainly used in a European context, there are similar movements in the USA and Asia. [1] The goal of all these approaches is nearly the same: Whereas information and communication technology has advanced rapidly in recent years, the discovered trends and possibilities shall be transferred, so that the production industry can benefit from it. Although electronics and network infrastructure have of course been used for a long time in an industrial production setting, it is important to realise that plants and production machines are high investment goods which go together with slower innovation cycles. This means that while in the customer off-the-shelf segment, this year's "new" hardware or software will be already considered "old" in half a year (and eventually even out of stack in a very short time span), the production ecosystem has a relatively long usage period of hardware and software.

But what is exactly changing due to "Industry 4.0"? Next to individualised production, the core issues of Industry 4.0 can be formulated according to [2] as the integration of Internet and networking systems, smart objects and human machine interaction. This already emphasises the need for higher security requirements. Internet and Cloud applications [3] come with the need to integrate production systems in larger network infrastructures or even in the common Internet. The latter is strengthened by the trend to enable new kinds of human-machine interaction: Bring Your Own Device (BYOD) and remote access on industrial infrastructure with the help of mobile devices can without doubt offer new services or help to decrease costs. But they are also prone to attack scenarios.

The general challenges of cybersecurity are already widely known. According to the 2017 Global State of Information Security Survey [4], at least 80 % of companies in Europe have experienced at least one incident in 2016 and the number increased by 38 % compared to the preceding year. At the same time, approximately 69 % of European companies have either no or only basic understanding of their exposure to cyber risks and small and medium-sized companies tend to pay a higher price for this than larger companies. [5]

This topic increasingly receives the necessary political attention, for example, within the currently discussed European legislation regarding cybersecurity and vulnerability reporting. The above mentioned surveys mainly focus on "common" office and server infrastructure, although the current transition of the production industry towards "Industry 4.0" opens a large field of additional vulnerabilities. At the latest, since the Stuxnet [6] malware, the possibility of damage on industrial infrastructure through the Internet has received worldwide attention. In order to understand where additional concern of security research should focus on in the upcoming years, we provide an overview over the current changes within the production industry and the resulting possible vulnerabilities.

Due to the above explained transformation towards "Industry 4.0" a multitude of devices become connected to the common Internet; IBM estimates that the number will increase to 40 billion by 2020. [7] To conclude from the above remarks, it cannot be expected that those devices have a sufficient amount of security protection. Rather, a lot of devices might consist of old, most probably unpatched equipment, but are wired to critical infrastructures. Practical proof of this problem can be, for example, obtained with tools, which automatically detect and index Internet-facing industrial systems. The Shodan computer search engine [8] has been successfully tested to be able to index and identify Programmable Logic Controllers (PLCs). As those devices are standard components of industrial machines, several thousand devices can be found. As they are automatically tested on the running firmware and indexed accordingly, known vulnerabilities can be exploited easily.

In a 2015 overview, Sadeghi et al. [9] lists a couple of cyberattacks on IIoT (Industrial Internet of Things) and emphasize the fundamental difference between CPPS (Cyber-Physical Production System) compared to classical enterprise IT systems. In the tradeoff between security and availibility, the CPPS requirements are fundamentally different. They mention numerous possible attacks on intellectual property, product piracy. After providing an overview to different security architectures for CPS (Cyber-Physical System), the article concludes with the following statement: "However, existing security solutions are inappropriate since they do not scale to large networks of heterogeneous devices and cyber-physical systems with constrained resources and/or real-time requirements."

The book "Cybersecurity for Industry 4.0" [10] provides the technological foundations of cybersecurity for the production domain. It addresses existing threats caused by (A) humans, (B) technical insufficiencies, and (C) physical attacks of the actual IoT hardware. [11][12]

Recently, NIST published a draft with considerations for managing Internet of Things cybersecurity and privacy rights. [13] The main challenges are seen to protect device security, protect data security and protect individual's privacy. The publication focusses on "Internet of Things" in the sense explained above and does not cover specific production topics.

Are companies already aware of this topic? In the 2018 Global State of Information Security Survey (GSISS), 81 % of the companies judge IoT to be a critical part of at least some of their businesses. But only 39 % of survey respondents are confident that they have established "sufficient digital trust – security, privacy and data ethics– into their adoption of IoT". Furthermore, the replies from organisations using robotics or automation show that 40 % fear a disruption of operations due to a cyberattack on those systems.

II. The PLASMA Approach

To implement a holistic interactive support for service processes in production environments with the goal to reduce time- and resource-consuming error search and troubleshooting it is necessary to evaluate the following features:

1) Autonomous or automated event reporting in case of malfunction with digital communication tools like messengers or automated ticket systems,
2) Automated delivery of context-sensitive data sheets, videos, reports, statistics or other helpful stored information on a large variety of devices with different presentation models (textual, 2D, 3D, virtual, augmented, simulated, etc.)
3) An interactive remote support assistance with a far-off specialist,
4) A gateway to existing online-shop systems to automate the procurement of spare parts, and finally,
5) A complete connection to well-known ERP and Customer Relationship Management (CRM) systems.

With these features we aim to solve common use cases like a malfunctioning robot within an industrial plant. The goal is to find concrete solutions to elaborate a use case shown in Figure 2. The malfunction triggers the troubleshooting progress and tickets are created in an instant. A smart workflow manager can classify the incident and is able to suggests a solution depending on the severity of the error and archived data. The on-site worker gets useful information like data sheets, log files, instruction videos, virtual representations etc. to solve the issue by himself or receives remote support from a far-off specialist. All progress is documented and serves as new input for the smart workflow manager to sharpen its classification and support skills (cf. Figure 2).

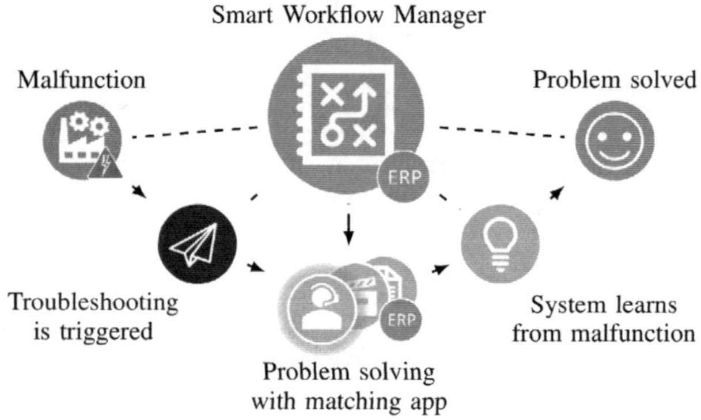

Figure 2. PLASMA workflow integrated in business processes

III. SECURITY CHALLENGES

The amount of information, as well as the aggregation of information makes a remote maintenance platform like PLASMA a high-value target for attackers. Because of the key knowledge on technologies, machines and algorithms stored in the system, economic espionage funded by competitors certainly is an issue. In case the attacker is not capable of extracting the desired information from the platform, for example, he could also try to bring the system down using a Distributed Denial of Service (DDoS) attack. This would lead to high financial losses for the providers of the platform and the customers relying on the system alike. Organised crime should also be taken into account because these attackers could also try to bring the system down and demand ransom money to be paid. Last but not least, secret services might become attackers, too, if the information stored in the platform is essential for companies or industrial branches in that country.

To put it in a nutshell: since the remote maintenance platform is intended to be hosted in the Cloud, all of the already known security issues of Cloud services, e.g., documented by the Cloud Security Alliance in [14], apply to PLASMA as well. The necessity to keep the platform available and accessible has already been stated. Considering additional security services, e.g., as recommended by CCITT X.800 [15], it can be stated that their importance for the system security of PLASMA is equally essential:

Authentication: It must be ensured that every entity communicating with the platform is properly authenticated. This means, the capability to perfectly identify users as well as attached machines is needed in order to prevent Spoofing or masquerading attacks.

Access Control: In addition to authentication it must be ensured that authenticated users and machines alike are only able to access data they are allowed to. Due to the involvement of many different companies and roles, Role-based Access Control (RBAC) systems that have been adapted for use in Cloud environments, as proposed by Tang et al. [16] or Balamurugan et al. [17], seem to meet this demand.

Confidentiality: For big remote maintenance platforms, it seems likely that they will have competing companies as customers. This means, all data must be kept confidential such that, for instance, one company cannot get access to data from its competitor. As stated before, a remote maintenance platform stores and aggregates different types of information, like algorithms, procedures, etc., from manufacturers and customers or machine data about outages and errors. The system potentially gathers data that is relevant concerning the EU General Data Protection Regulation (GDPR), like working hours of operators or maybe errors made by certain operators. If technicians or experts use smartglasses during the error searching process, it is possible that other personnel might get recorded as well. This must be considered when it comes to GDPR-compliant saving of the data.

Integrity: PLASMA is intended to learn from previous errors and outages and if a malfunction occurs it is supposed to automatically suggest the most suitable action to deal with this scenario. An attacker might want to tamper with data in a way that leads to wrong suggestions, either to derogate trust in the remote maintenance platform or to harm an affected company. Other targets might be stored sensor data that lead to wrong simulation results when modified or falsified documentation on machines or manuals which could mislead technicians in case of a malfunction and cause even greater (physical) damage to the machine. Weir, Aßmuth and Jäger have proposed strategies for intrusion monitoring in Cloud services and for managing forensic recovery in the Cloud. [19] It is planned to realise and evaluate these concepts for the remote maintenance platform.

Nonrepudiation: It must be ensured that no party is capable of denying its involvement in any communication with or in the system. One reason to keep track of all actions in the system is to monitor the security of the system itself. But, of course, the provider of a remote maintenance platform wants to earn money with the system, too. Depending on the chosen business model the amount of messages or communication in general could be a metric to measure the usage of the system by a certain company and this may be used for billing.

In order to emphasise the necessity for appropriate security measures in a Cloud-based remote maintenance platform, we revisit the use case described in Section II and depicted in

Figure 2. Obviously, the Cloud-based remote maintenance platform needs to be protected against DDoS attacks, otherwise the system would not take notice of the malfunctioning robot in one of the customer's industrial plants. The triggering of the troubleshooting process might be related to another security issue. Imagine the situation that there is no malfunctioning robot, but the troubleshooting is triggered by a manipulated sensor. The attacker might want to stop production in the industrial plant or learn how the maintenance platform deals with such problems. The adversary might also try to tamper with the smart workflow manager which could lead to inappropriate solutions for detected malfunctions and eventually cause even greater damage. In addition to that, if information about malfunctions and errors, manuals or machine data gets manipulated, the system will not be capable of learning properly how to handle such issues. Less knowing technicians working in the industrial plant but also specialists might be tricked into wrong actions. Security is essential for a system like PLASMA.

IV. Involved Partners

The project core team consists of four parties: two industrial partners and two partners from academia.

ESSERT GmbH provides its multi-user remote support system and large user base as an important starting point for the development. It already offers a detailed user and permission administration, generates service reports for further documentation and is available for iOS, Android devices and smartglasses. [18]

Awesome Technologies is involved in a couple of Industry 4.0 projects which use Augmented and Virtual Reality with actual off-the shelf head-mounted displays, which also involves localization issues.

The cooperative setting of remote support is a very interesting topic within the framework of human supervisory control of smart cyber-physical production systems (smart factory) at TU Delft.

The research group of Prof. Dr. Aßmuth at OTH Amberg-Weiden has been working on concepts and solutions to ward off cyber-attacks aimed specifically at production facilities or vehicles for many years. In cooperation with international colleagues, concepts for increasing the security of Cloud services and securing forensic data in the Cloud have been published as well. [19]

The mentioned partners are currently looking for additional partners and funding programs for a PLASMA funding proposal.

V. Conclusion and Future Work

To compete on Cloud service markets SMEs need to focus on security challenges. Launching a great idea on the market may fail due to insufficient data security or privacy issues. Meeting a customer's high expectations for security is essential and a great challenge for SMEs because there are no negotiation opportunities. The authors are convinced that a Cloud-based remote maintenance platform, like PLASMA, will be needed in future. Therefore, they plan to realise such a system in a funded research project as a collaboration of industrial partners and partners from academia.

References

[1] Y. Liao, F. Deschamps, E. de Freitas Rocha Loures and L. F. Pierin Ramos, "Past, present and future of industry 4.0 – A systematic literature review and research agenda proposal." International journal of production research, vol. 55, no. 12, pp. 3609–3629, 2017.

[2] D. Zuehlke, "Smartfactory – towards a factory-of-things." Annual Reviews in Control, vol. 34, no. 1, pp. 129–138, 2010.

[3] P. Mell and T. Grance, "The NIST definition of Cloud Computing." SP 800-145, 2011, URL: https://doi.org/10.6028/NIST.SP.800-145 [accessed: 2019.04.12]

[4] PwC, Ed., "Key findings from The Global State of Information Security Survey 2017." Technical Report, 2017, URL: https://www.pwc.com/gx/en/issues/assets/2017-gsisss-bold-steps-to-manage-geopolitical-threats-final.pdf [accessed: 2019.04.12]

[5] K. Kertysova, E. Frinking, K. van den Dool, A. Maričić and K. Bhattacharyya, "Cybersecurity: Ensuring awareness and resilience of the private sector across europe in face of mounting cyber risks – Study." Technical Report, European Economic and Social Committee, March 2018, URL: https://www.eesc.europa.eu/en/our-work/publications-other-work/publications/cybersecurity-ensuring-awareness-and-resilience-private-sector-across-europe-face-mounting-cyber-risks-study [accessed: 2019.04.12]

[6] R. Langner, "Stuxnet: Dissecting a cyberwarfare weapon." IEEE Security & Privacy, vol. 9, no. 3, pp. 49–51, 2011.

[7] R. Baxter, "Bluemix and the Internet of Things", 2014, URL: https://developer.ibm.com/bluemix/2014/07/16/bluemix-internet-things [accessed: 2019.04.12]

[8] R. Bodenheim, J. Butts, S. Dunlap and B. Mullins, "Evaluation of the ability of the Shodan search engine to identify Internet-facing industrial control devices." International Journal of Critical Infrastructure Protection, vol. 7, no. 2, pp. 114–123, 2014.

[9] A.-R. Sadeghi, C. Wachsmann and M. Waidner, "Security and privacy challenges in Industrial Internet of Things" in Proceedings of the 52nd Annual Design Automation Conference (DAC), June 07–11, 2015, San Francisco, USA. ACM, Article no. 54, ISBN: 978-1-4503-3520-1, 2015.

[10] L. Thames and D. Schaefer, Eds., "Cybersecurity for Industry 4.0. Analysis for Design and Manufacturing." Springer, ISBN: 978-3-319-50659-3, 2017.

[11] J. Dia and S. Smith, "A Hardware Threat Modeling Concept for Trustable Integrated Circuits" in Proceedings of the 2007 IEEE Region 5 Technical Conference, April 20–22, 2007, Fayetteville, USA. IEEE, Nov. 2007, pp. 354–357, ISBN: 978-1-4244-1279-2, 2007.

[12] A. B. Shahri and Z. Ismail, "A tree model for identification of threats as the first stage of risk assessment in HIS." Journal of Information Security, vol. 3, no. 2, pp. 169–176, 2012.

[13] K. Boeckl et. al, "Considerations for Managing Internet of Things (IoT) Cybersecurity and Privacy Risks." Draft NISTIR 8228, September 2018, URL: https://doi.org/10.6028/NIST.IR.8228-draft [accessed: 2019.04.12]

[14] Cloud Security Alliance, Ed., The Treacherous 12, Top Threats to Cloud Computing + Industry Insights, 2017.

[15] The International Telegraph and Telephone Consultative Committee (CCITT), Ed., Security Architecture for Open Systems Interconnection for CCITT Applications, Recommendation X.800, March 1991.

[16] B. Tang, Q. Li and R. Sandhu, "A multi-tenant RBAC model for collaborative cloud services" in Proceedings of the Eleventh Annual Conference on Privacy, Security and Trust, July 10–12, 2013, Tarragona, Spain. IEEE, Sep. 2013, pp. 229–238, ISBN: 978-1-4673-5839-2.

[17] B. Balamurugan, E. Durga Chowdary and S. Linkesh, "A Combined Architecture for RBAC and DAC for Inter-cloud Communication" in Proceedings of the 3rd International Conference on Eco-friendly Computing and Communication Systems, December 18–21, 2014, Mangalore, India. IEEE, Aug. 2015, pp. 167–171, ISBN: 978-1-4799-7002-5.

[18] ESSERT GmbH, Ed., "Augmented Support", 2019, URL: https://www.essert.com/en/digital-processes [accessed: 2019.04.12]

[19] G. Weir, A. Aßmuth and N. Jäger, "Managing Forensic Recovery in the Cloud", International Journal on Advances in Security, vol. 11, no. 3 & 4, pp. 264–273, 2018.

Risk Analysis of the Cloud Infrastructure of Smart Grid and Internet of Things

Katrin Neubauer
Dept. Computer Science and Mathematics
Ostbayerische Technische Hochschule
Regensburg, Germany
email:
katrin1.neubauer@oth-regensburg.de

Sebastian Fischer
Secure Systems Engineering
Fraunhofer AISEC
Berlin, Germany
email:
sebastian.fischer@aisec.fraunhofer.de

Rudolf Hackenberg
Dept. Computer Science and Mathematics
Ostbayerische Technische Hochschule
Regensburg, Germany
email:
rudolf.hackenberg@oth-regensburg.de

***Abstract*—Cloud Computing (CC), Internet of Thing (IoT) and Smart Grid (SG) are separate technologies. The digital transformation of the energy industry and the increasing digitalization in the private sector connect these technologies. At the moment, CC is used as a service provider for IoT. Currently in Germany, the SG is under construction and a cloud connection to the infrastructure has not been implemented yet. To build the SG cloud, the new laws for privacy must be implemented and therefore it's important to know which data can be stored and distributed over a cloud. In order to be able to use future innovative services, SG and IoT must be combined. For this, in the next step we connect the SG infrastructure with the IoT. A potential insecure device and network (IoT) should be able to transfer data to and from a critical infrastructure (SG). In detail, we focus on two different connections: the communication between the smart meter switching box and the IoT device and the data transferred between the IoT and SG cloud. In our example, a connected charging station with cloud services is connected with a SG infrastructure. To create a really smart service, the charging station needs a connection to the SG to get the current amount of renewable energy in the grid. Private data, such as name, address and payment details, should not be transferred to the IoT cloud. With these two connections, new threads emerge. In this case, availability, confidentiality and integrity must be ensured. A risk analysis over all the cloud connections, including the vulnerability and the ability of an attacker and the resulting risk are developed in this paper.**

Keywords*—*Smart Grid; Internet of Things; security analysis; safety-critical infrastructure; cloud computing

I. INTRODUCTION

The increasing use of digital systems is changing our world. This development is driven among other things by Internet of Things (IoT), Smart Grid (SG) and Cloud Computing (CC) technology. IoT, SG and Cloud are separate technologies. The digital transformation of the energy industry and the increasing digitalization in the private sector, connect these technologies. Future SG are highly networked systems. In order to be able to use future innovative services, IoT, SG and CC must be joined.

The integration of SG (intelligent energy supply system) is creating a new IT infrastructure in Germany for the transmission of data. For smart metering, an intelligent measuring system (iMSys) will be integrated in the future. The iMSys consists of a basic meter (smart meter) and the smart meter gateway (SMGW) [1]. The changeover is not only taking place in Germany, but also in other European countries. The pioneers are countries like Italy or Sweden. However, these roll-outs highlight the risks with regard to safety and security. Attacks on power grid control system via the internet represent a growing threat.

The increasing digitalization and networking of all kind of devices (charging station, sensors, household appliances, etc.) is known as IoT. The devices get a communication interface and are connected to the internet (directly or via a gateway). This increasing networking of different devices creates new challenges, like scalability. A service which until now had to manage only a few devices gets new users on a large scale. These new users are not always available or disappear just as quickly. It must be possible to react flexibly to this volatility.

Smart services are required for future application "SG and IoT". Cloud platforms are needed to use these services. The cloud platform can be described as a data hub. In this case, we have two cloud platforms. The IoT cloud from the IoT infrastructure and Smart Grid cloud (SG cloud) are used for data storage, analysis and new services.

In order to develop new innovative services in SG, such as value-added service, IoT, SG and must be combined. For this, we connect the SG infrastructure with the IoT. A potential insecure device and network (IoT) should be able to transfer data to and from a critical infrastructure (SG). By connecting the systems, new risks and attack vectors arise. These influence the security objectives - availability, confidentiality, integrity and, additional, privacy. In this case, more and more data is generated and more data accesses take place. This leads to new requirements for authentication and authorization.

This paper will explore the problems that arise in the networking of IoT, SG and CC. The aim is to identify new threats and problems and additional define technical and organizational requirements for future systems. The paper is structured as follows. Section II describes the related work. Section III introduces our architecture, while Section IV analyzes the security, followed by a conclusion in Section VI.

II. Related Work

IoT devices can be protected with known principles, but they also have to be implemented by the manufacturers. According to the current state, the most frequent security gaps can be closed with already known methods. It is important for research to respond to new challenges.

The first challenge is the scarce resources of IoT devices. Already known encryption algorithms need to be adapted or changed to work more effectively and operate acceptably with low-performance hardware (e.g. PRINCE [2]). Another possibility is to redevelop suitable algorithms (e.g. Secure IoT - SIT [3]).

At the moment, insecure devices are in use and therefore, solutions must be found to continue the operation. For example, several companies (including IBM) have developed a special DNS server (Quad9 DNS Privacy and Security Service), which should ensure the security as well as privacy of the IoT devices. Quad9 automatically blocks requests to infected sites. As a last challenge, manufacturers must be "forced" to improve IT security. This can be accomplished by guidelines and certifications.

The Smart Grid Architecture Model (SGAM) is a European architecture model that was developed in the context of the European standardization mandate M/490. It serves for the visualization, validation and structuring of SG projects from the beginning of the project as well as for the standardization of SG. In general, it is used for architecture development in the SG at different organizational levels. In this context, security is regarded as a cross-cutting topic and is not explicitly considered [4]. An analysis of the architecture in the SG shows that the architectural models of the countries differ in principle. The architecture models are mostly based on the SGAM. In Germany, the SG itself is regulated by the specifications of the Federal Office for Information Security (BSI) and is regarded as the state of the art (communication) [5]. The BSI was commissioned by the legislator to develop specifications for a SMGW in order to guarantee a secure infrastructure for intelligent measuring systems [6]. The intelligent measuring systems will be integrated into a communication network. The central element is the smart meter gateway as a communication unit [16]–[18]. In [14] and [15], there are the security and privacy considerations for IoT application on SG with a focus on survey and research challenges presented. It gives an overview about SG and IoT application on SG and identifies some of the remaining challenges and vulnerabilities related to security and privacy.

There are several publications [20]–[22] covering the subject security and privacy in SG and cloud applications. The focus of this publication is additionally the security and communication analysis of SG, IoT and CC in Germany.

Open questions with no related work, not exclusively in the scientific community, are the handling of data when they leave the "SG", requirements for authentication and authorisation in future SG-IoT-cloud application and how to deal with service provider who access data (service charging station) in critical infrastructures.

III. Architecture Challenges for Smart Grid and IoT

The SG reference architecture consist of the Local Metrological Network (LMN), the Wide Area Network (WAN) and the Home Area Network (HAN). The communication takes place through the SMGW. The SG infrastructure is extended with a SG cloud. This SG cloud enables additionally application for smart metering. For new applications and services, the existing architecture is extended with IoT devices. The IoT architecture consists of a device or sensor, connected via gateway to the router and the IoT cloud. The collected data is stored centrally on a server. This data is available to the user if rhequired. Figure 1 shows the unification of the architecture the cloud application on SG and IoT.

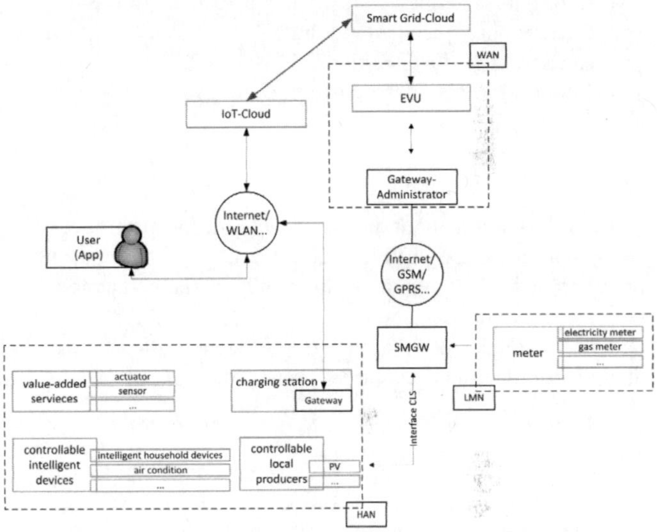

Figure 1. Architecture Cloud Application on Smart Grid with IoT

A. Application Example

In our example, a charging station with an IoT cloud is connected to a smart home. The home includes a smart meter, which is connected to the SG infrastructure and the corresponding SG cloud (Figure 1). To create a really smart service, the charging station needs a connection to the SG to get the current amount of renewable energy in the grid. This enables the possibility to load the car at the best times and supply the grid with stored energy from the car to stabilize it. The easiest way of getting these information is by connecting the two clouds (e.g. using predefined APIs).

B. Communication between Smart Grid and IoT

For a more detailed analysis, it is important to know, which data is stored on the IoT cloud and the SG cloud. In chapter "IV-C Communication between devices" this information is used to determine the risks of the communication between the two clouds.

1) Communications data Internet of Thing: The following data is stored in the IoT cloud:

- Connected car
- Sum of energy consumption
- Current energy consumption / supply
- History of energy consumption / supply
- Time to load the car
- User Data
  - Name
  - E-Mail

The connected car and the history can be used to create a profile of the user. This includes the times, the user is normally at home or at work. This data is private data and should be protected.

2) Communications data Smart Grid: The following data is generated and stored in the SG cloud:

- Information about the smart meter (ID, IP-Address)
- Current energy consumption
- Current price for electricity
- Information about the customer
  - Name
  - Address
  - Payment details

The information about the smart meter or the current energy consumption can be used to create a profile of the household (user). This is partly equal to the profile of the connected car, but can be extended to the whole household an therefore other people. In conclusion, like the connected car data, this data is also private data and should be protected.

IV. Security Analysis for Safety-critical Systems

The security analysis starts with the description of the attack vectors. From these vectors, the threads are derived. In the next step, the risk is shown for every thread, based on the ability of the attacker and the possible damage. Finally, two practical examples show the potential danger in our example architecture.

A. Attack vector Smart Grid and Internet of Thing

New attack vectors are emerging as a result of increasing networks (e.g. IoT and SG). IoT devices are potentially insecure. An attack is an unauthorized attempt to gain access [7]. If we analyze the previously described architecture with regard to potential attacks that influences the target of authenticity, current threats and gaps arise. Inspired by Hutle, the attack vector can be divided into the following categories (cf. Sichler 2014 [8] and Babar 2010 [9]).

1) Hardware manipulation attacks (physical attacks): With physical access to the device, the hardware and software can be changed. Malware installation is likely, which can lead to data manipulation and modification. At worst, a shutdown of the energy grid is possible or sensitive data (from the IoT cloud or SG cloud) can be manipulate. Furthermore, it is possible that, e.g. IoT services (IoT cloud), fail.

2) Software manipulation attacks: With integration of malware (on embedded software) or exploiting vulnerabilities (for example buffer overflow, code injection), the software can be changed. These attacks describe a targeted manipulation (energy supplier, user, etc.). At worst, a shutdown or manipulation of the energy grid or data manipulation and modification (energy supplier or at home) are possible. Additionally, the Cloud platforms (IoT cloud and SG cloud) can be manipulated and fail.

3) Network-based attacks: Identity theft, denial of service, cascading malware propagation (Business IT & Plant Control) and monitor, traffic analysis (passive attacks) are possible network-based attacks. At worst, personal damage to users, customers and the manipulation of the energy grid or the the cloud platforms are possible.

4) Privacy related attacks: Privacy related attacks can be, for example, collecting user-specific data (for example listening the communication). At worse, personal damage to customers or energy supplier are possible.

5) Conclusion: The analysis of the attack vectors shows us the following risks:

- manipulation of measured values and time
- manipulation of the communication between IoT cloud and SG cloud
- misuse of energy data and/or sensitive data
- sabotage of the power grid
- sabotage of mobility (example: charging station)

The IoT device, IoT infrastructure with an IoT cloud, smart meter, smart meter gateway, switching box, SG cloud and gateway administrator can be attacked in the architecture (cf. Figure 1). Summary, the security of the grid is dependent on the security of the information and communication from cloud application of IoT and SG.

B. Security threats: Infrastructure Smart Grid and Internet of Things

Table 1 covers a risk analysis for both, the IoT cloud and the SG cloud. It includes the ability of an attacker and potential damage. This leads to a risk for the associated attack. If an attacker needs a lower ability, it's more likely that someone uses the attack [10]. In the SG, the strict specifications lead to a high security and therefore the attacker must be advanced (high ability). If the attacker gets access to private data or can damage a big part of the SG, the damage is classified as high (e.g. DDoS attack on SG). For example, a medium ability and a high damage lead to a high risk [19].

The table shows that low to medium abilities are needed to attack an IoT device and its cloud. These vulnerabilities can have big impacts on the security of the SG (damage and risk). The IoT devices can be attacked easily to change the behaviour. Against wrong loading times (not much renewable energy is currently produced), the smart meter is completely exposed. It's not possible to prevent a device from loading, without limiting the comfort for the user. Other attacks, like

TABLE I. risk analysis for the IoT and SG cloud

DDoS Ability of an attacker: *low* A DDoS attack can be performed with a botnet at low cost. Damage: IoT: *medium*, SG: *high* If the SG is unable to broadcast the current amount of energy in the grid, all the connected cars start charging. In the worst case, this can lead to a shutdown of the grid. The damage is medium for the IoT because at the moment not much electric cars are available. Risk: *medium / high* The risk is medium to high because it's easy to attack and the damage is medium / high.
Malware Ability of an attacker: IoT: *low*, SG: *high* The attacker needs to find a vulnerability in the software to install a malware. In the insecure IoT, this is easily possible, because the most cheap devices never get an update. In the SG it's high because of the strict regularization. Damage: IoT: *medium*, SG: *high* The damage for the grid is medium if the IoT device is attacked (the reasons are similar to DDos). If an attacker gets access to the SG, the damage is high, because he can shutdown the critical infrastructure. Risk: IoT: *medium*, SG: *medium / high* For both IoT and SG, the risk is medium. In IoT, it's likely to happen, but the damage is similar to DDoS (medium) and in the SG, the ability of an attacker has to be high, so it's medium to high, because the damage can be high.
Broken Authentication Ability of an attacker: IoT: *low*, SG: *high* The broken authentication is similar to the malware. An IoT device is not secure at all and the SG is regulated. Damage: IoT: *medium*, SG: *high* Similar to malware. Risk: IoT: *medium*, SG: *medium / high* Similar to malware.
Broken Encryption Ability of an attacker: IoT: *low*, SG: *high* Similar to malware. Damage: *low / medium* The data, transferred to the network, is not critical for running the SG (low), but the privacy of an user can be exposed (medium). Risk: IoT: *medium*, SG: *low* Because it's easy to attack in the IoT and the privacy can be exposed, the risk is medium in the IoT. With nearly no damage, the risk is low in SG.
Data leakage The data leakage is similar to the broken encryption and therefore the same rating is used: Ability of an attacker: IoT: *low*, SG: *high* Damage: *low / medium* Risk: IoT: medium, SG: *low*
Data manipulation Ability of an attacker: IoT: *low*, SG: *high* Data manipulation can be performed easily in the IoT cloud and is difficult in the SG network (cf. broken authentication). Damage: IoT: *low*, SG: *medium* If an attacker can manipulate some data in the IoT cloud, the SG is nearly not affected. If it happens in the SG, the attack can lead to more damage, but only for a part of the user (the hacked ones). Risk: IoT: *low*, SG: *medium* This risk is low for IoT and medium for the SG.
Hardware manipulation Ability of an attacker: IoT: *medium*, SG: *high* To get on the hardware of the clouds, an attacker needs a lot ability, even in the IoT case. Damage: IoT: *medium*, SG: *high* The damage is medium in the IoT, because with the hardware attack, only one IoT manufacturer is affected. In the SG, it could lead to an shutdown of the grid. Risk: *medium* The risk is medium for the IoT and SG. The damage on the SG is high, but it's difficult to attack the SG cloud hardware.

a denial of service attack or a direct attack on the smart meter, can be detected and prevented by the right software (e.g. firewall or intrusion detection system). In conclusion, the communication between IoT devices and the smart meter should only be possible through a secure layer.

C. Communication between clouds

An IoT device and the IoT infrastructure are currently highly insecure [11]. The charging station or the IoT cloud can be hacked by an attacker (see risks above). The "SG device" is a secure device. For example, the SMGW is a certified device.

The communication between the two clouds should be transparent to the user and developed under the aspects of security and privacy by design. Both contain private data and only the user should allow an exchange. By default no data should be transferred.

Example 1: The user can register his IoT device in the IoT cloud only with a valid E-Mail address and a username. No further information is needed. The IoT provider only knows that this username has loaded his car 20 times per month. By exchanging data with the smart meter, detailed information (name, address) about the user can be transferred. Now it is possible to identify the user.

Example 2: The energy service provider doesn't need any information of the connected car of the user. But with additional information from the IoT charging station, it is possible to tell when the user is at home or if he gets visited by another person with an electric car. This part is very important. A third user can be tracked with his car, without knowing it.

The security analysis and the application example shows us problems and challenges of communication in cloud application on IoT and SG. A growing problem is the authentication and authorization. The analysis of the system shows that more and more data is being generated in the single systems, because they receive data from the other ones. This data differs in origin, need for protection, purpose, quality and volume. A further point is the constantly growing number of users who have access to the system or to the data. Users cannot only be individuals, but also devices, such as meters, sensors, etc. new risks, threats and attack patterns arise from the further development of the system. The question arises as to which requirements for authentication and authorization must be defined for future systems.

D. Requirements - authentication and authorization

The technical and organizational requirements can be derived from the application example and security analysis. The focus of the requirements is on authentication and authorisation. The security analysis shows us the weakness of communication. Future systems must be better protected against unauthorised access. The defined requirements are necessary for future development of authentication and authorization mechanism for cloud applications on SG and IoT.

The technical and organizational requirements of authentication and authorization mechanism for cloud applications on SG and IoT are defined as follows:

1) Availability: authentified and authorized users can access or use resources under defined conditions
2) Interoperability: user can be individuals and devices
3) Evidence: proof of access to the data or system to be protected
4) Performance: SG and IoT are a volatile systems
5) Scalability: SG and IoT are highly scalable systems
6) Device and user authentication: distinction should be made between device and user authentication
7) Data-Management: simple and cost-efficient management of authentication and authorisation information
8) Update-Management: ability to change information (e.g. device or device number)
9) Maintenance: simple and cost-efficient upkeep and maintenance of the system

Current authentication and authorization mechanisms are no longer sufficient for the defined requirements of authentication and authorization mechanism for cloud applications on SG and IoT. One important reason is the weakness of communication. Another reason is the increasing communication and data exchange. A new model is needed for authentication and authorization for cloud applications on SG and IoT. With this new model, the classical security model must also be reinterpreted. In the classical security model, the data is divided into two categories (secure and insecure).

V. CONCLUSION AND FUTURE WORK

We introduced an application example of a connection between SG and IoT. A charging station with an own cloud, connected to the smart meter gateway. These connection creates new attack vectors and threads. For example, an attacker can use an unsecured device like the charging station to get access to the highly secured SG network. This is critical, because of the different information stored on both clouds. The energy provider stores payment information and the amount of consumed energy, the IoT cloud information about the charging times. These private information should be strongly protected and not combined.

The application example and the security analysis shows us new attack vectors and threads and challenges of communication in IoT and SG. In this paper, we focus the problem with authentication and authorization mechanism for cloud applications on SG and IoT. Current authentication and authorization mechanisms are no longer sufficient for the defined requirements. The reason for this is the increasing communication and data exchange. This leads to an increased overhead in the classical security model. The question arises as to which framework can be used for the new requirements for authentication and authorization. An option is to develop a new role-based trust model for safety-critical systems. In order to develop a more flexible model, the new approach has to integrate several data categories. To protect the data, the different information need a classification and a clear mechanism to ensure that they are only accessed by authorized users. For this task, a new Role-based trust model for Safety-critical Systems should be implemented. With this model, the occurring problems, like data exchange, can be addressed. The different data, stored by the clouds, can be classified and secured by adding an extra layer for the access. The role-based access control model ensures an efficient administration of the rights. This model is still a work in progress and the next steps will be to implement and to evaluate it.

REFERENCES

[1] M. Irlbeck, Digitalisierung und Energie 4.0 Wie schaffen wir die digitale Energiewende?, Springer Fachmedien Wiesbaden GmbH, pp. 135-148, 2017.

[2] H. Kim and K. Kim, Toward an Inverse-free Lightweight Encryption Scheme for IoT, Conference on Information Security and Cryptography, 2014.

[3] M. Usman, I. Ahmed, M. I. Aslam, S. Khan, and U. A. Shah, SIT: A Lightweight Encryption Algorithm for Secure Internet of Things, CoRR abs/1704.08688, 2017.

[4] M. Uslar, C. Rosinger, and S. Schlegel, Application of the NISTIR 7628 for Information Security in the Smart Grid Architecture Model (SGAM), VDE Kongress, 2014.

[5] Bundesamt fuer Sicherheit in der Informationstechnik, Technische Richtlinie, BSI TR-03109, 2015.

[6] P. Peters and N. Mohr, Digitalisierung im Energiemarkt: Neue Chancen, neue Herausforderungen, Energiewirtschaftliche Tagesfragen, pp. 8-12, 2015.

[7] C. Eckert, IT-Sicherheit, Konzepte - Verfahren - Protokolle, Boston De Gruyter, 2012.

[8] R. Sichler, Smart und sicher geht das?, Springer Fachmedien Wiesbaden, pp. 463-494, 2014.

[9] S. Babar, A. Stango, N. Prasad, J. Sen, and R. Prasad, Proposed embedded security framework for Internet of Things (IoT), Electronic Systems Technology (Wireless VITAE), 2010.

[10] L. ben Othmane, H. Weffers, and M. Klabbers, Using Attacker Capabilities and Motivations in Estimating Security Risk, Symposium On Usable Privacy and Security, 2013.

[11] The OWASP Foundation, Internet of Things Project, IoT Vulnerabilities, 2019.

[12] M. Lipp, et al., Meltdown: Reading Kernel Memory from User Space, 27th USENIX Security Symposium, 2018.

[13] P. Kocher, et al., Spectre Attacks: Exploiting Speculative Execution, CoRR abs-1801-01203, 2019.

[14] F. Dalipi and S. Y. Yayilgan, Security and Privacy Considerations for IoT Application on Smart Grids. Survey and Research Challenges, IEEE 4th International Conference on Future Internet of Things and Cloud Workshops (FiCloudW), pp. 63-68, 2016.

[15] M. Yun and B. Yuxin, Research on the architecture and key technology of Internet of Things (IoT) applied on smart grid, International Conference on Advances in Energy Engineering, pp. 69-72, 2010.

[16] V. C. Gungor, et al., A Survey on Smart Grid Potential Applications and Communication Requirements, IEEE Trans. Ind. Inf. 9 (1), pp. 28-42, 2013.

[17] X. Li, et al., Securing smart grid. Cyber attacks, countermeasures, and challenges, IEEE Commun. Mag. 50 (8), pp. 38-45, 2012.

[18] C. Wietfeld, C. Muller, J. Schmutzler, S. Fries, and A. Heidenreich, ICT Reference Architecture Design Based on Requirements for Future Energy Marketplaces, 1st IEEE International Conference on Smart Grid Communications, pp. 315-320, 2010.

[19] The OWASP Foundation, OWASP Risk Rating Methodology, 2019.

[20] B. Genge, A. Beres, and P. Haller, A survey on cloud-based software platforms to implement secure smart grids, 49th International Universities Power Engineering Conference (UPEC),pp. 1-6, 2014.

[21] S. Bera, S. Misra, and J. Rodrigues, J.P.C: Cloud Computing Applications for Smart Grid. A Survey, IEEE Trans. Parallel Distrib. Syst. 26 (5), pp. 1477-1494, 2015.

[22] Y. Simmhan, A. G. Kumbhare, B. Cao, and V. Prasanna, An Analysis of Security and Privacy Issues in Smart Grid Software Architectures on Clouds, IEEE 4th USENIX International Conference on Cloud Computing (CLOUD), pp. 582-589, 2011.

Security of Cloud Services with Low-Performance Devices in Critical Infrastructures

Michael Molle[1], Ulrich Raithel[1], Dirk Kraemer[2], Norbert Graß[3], Matthias Söllner[4] and Andreas Aßmuth[4]

[1]SIPOS Aktorik GmbH, Altdorf, Germany, Email: {michael.molle | ulrich.raithel}@sipos.de
[2]AUMA Riester GmbH & Co. KG, Müllheim, Germany, Email: dirk.kraemer@auma.com
[3]Grass Power Electronics GmbH, Nuremberg, Germany, Email: norbert.grass@grass-pe.com
[4]Technical University of Applied Sciences OTH Amberg-Weiden, Amberg, Germany,
Email: {m.soellner | a.assmuth}@oth-aw.de

***Abstract*—As part of the Internet of Things (IoT) and Industry 4.0 Cloud services are increasingly interacting with low-performance devices that are used in automation. This results in security issues that will be presented in this paper. Particular attention is paid to so-called critical infrastructures. The authors intend to work on the addressed security challenges as part of a funded research project, using electrical actuators and battery storages as specific applications. The core ideas of this research project are also presented in this paper.**

Keywords–Low-performance devices; Cloud; automation.

I. Introduction

The increasing integration of the Internet of Things into industrial production has lead to the next industrial revolution called "Industry 4.0". [1] Increasing digitisation and automation leads to a greater number of systems being connected to the Cloud. This also means that in addition to traditional IT systems a growing number of Operational Technology (OT) systems is also connected to Cloud services. Nowadays, even Supervisory Control And Data Acquisition (SCADA) systems without a suitable built-in Industry 4.0 implementation will be hard to find. All of this leads to the so-called "Industrial Internet of Things" (IIoT) as a part of the IoT.

However, besides the big SCADA systems there is a great variety of embedded systems on devices like sensors, storage systems and actors running in physical processes. A power plant, for example, has only one process control system, but a couple of thousands of actuators to control the actual processes of energy generation. In recent years, many of these devices have been connected to Cloud services for advanced analytics that cannot be computed on the devices themselves because of their limited resources concerning computing power or memory. These embedded devices very often consist of a low-cost micro controller with low clock rate (usually in double-digit MHz range), using proprietary protocols on proprietary operating systems, while maintaining the real-time capability as topmost objective. This quite significant number of embedded devices incorporates a steadily growing part of the processes and infrastructure of whole branches of industrial production. It also means that industry and economy of whole countries more and more rely on such components.

The government of each individual country defines for itself which processes and infrastructures are especially important and which sectors of infrastructure have to be considered critical. In Germany, for instance, these critical infrastructures are devided into nine sectors, namely energy supply, information technology and communication, transportation and traffic, health, water supply and wastewater disposal, food provisions, finance and insurance industry, government and administration, and, finally, media and culture. [3] In the United States of America, a similar definition comprises even sixteen critical sectors. [4] Because of the high security requirements for

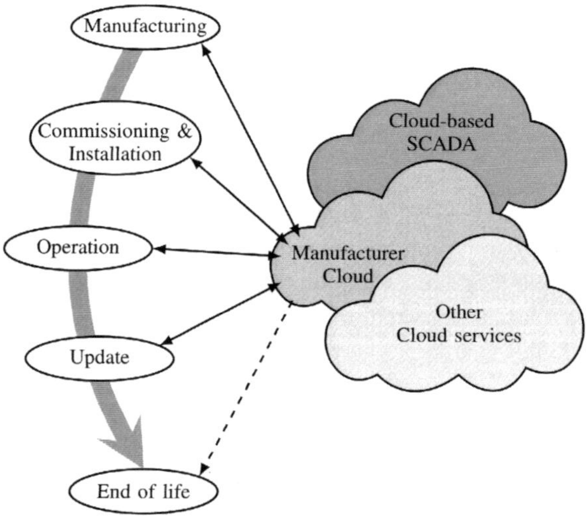

Figure 1. Lifecycle of a low-performance device and its connection to Cloud services. [2]

critical infrastructures, not only the operation of such a low-performance device must be taken into account, but all cross-relationships to Cloud services that occur during the life cycle of the device must be considered, too (cf. Figure 1). The manufacturer of the low-performance device stores specifications or maybe even initial versions of the device's firmware in their Cloud. When the device is installed in an industrial plant, it needs to be commissioned in order to communicate with the manufacturer's Cloud service. During operation, the device communicates with the Cloud service. It sends, for example, sensor data that is analysed maybe not only by the manufacturer, but also by one of the already mentioned Cloud-based SCADA systems. Therefore, an interface or gateway is needed to interconnect the manufacturer's Cloud service and the Cloud-based SCADA system. It can not be ruled out that the data is shared with other Cloud services, too. Because of known security issues or in case of new additional features, there might be updates for the software of the device. At the end of the lifecycle, e.g., when the device is broken or it no longer meets the requirements and therefore needs to be replaced, the manufacturer may wish to swipe all data and zeroise the device.

The paper is structured as follows: in Section II, we discuss threats and security challenges for Cloud-based SCADA systems as well as connected operational technology devices. In Section III, we review related work and present our own approach in Section IV. This approach is the subject of a current grant proposal by the authors, the different project partners are named in Section V. We conclude in Section VI with an outlook on future work.

II. Threats and Security Challenges

Most countries consider energy and water supply as critical sectors deserving special protection – and the increasing number of cyberattacks [5] confirm this assessment to be correct. In recent years, there have been numerous attacks, like the Ukrainian blackout in 2015, when 225,000 people were suffering for a number of hours from a power outage. [6] During this attack, not only Industrial Control System (ICS) but also the firmware of serial-to-Ethernet adapters was damaged in order to disconnect servers from their Uninterruptible Power Supply (UPS) to maximise the length of the blackout. In December 2016, there was another attack on the Ukrainian energy supply which again resulted in a blackout for 100,000 to 200,000 people over a period of several hours. [7] Such targeted attacks are no longer carried out by single attackers but by full groups with considerably different motivations. It is likely that groups of organised crime or intelligence services might be involved.

The lifecycle of such an embedded device used in critical infrastructures, as described above and depicted in Figure 1, can be used to identify many attack vectors. If the adversary has access to the manufacturer's Cloud service, he could attempt to install backdoors in the initial firmware while the device is being manufactured. In addition to that, the specifications stored in the Cloud would surely be interesting for competitors and also be helpful to the attacker to detect vulnerabilities that can be exploited later. During the on-site installation, an attacker could, in principle, redirect the connection to the manufacturer's cloud service via a computer controlled by him as a starting point for a man in the middle attack. Security issues during operation are discussed explicitly in the following sections. Based on the last two phases, "update" and "end of life", requirements for the protection of the manufacturer's intellectual property can be exemplified. For instance, suppose another manufacturer reproduces the embedded devices in order to sell them at a lower price. This competitor would certainly like to benefit from new features or security updates that the original device manufacturer rolls out. It must therefore be ensured that a manufacturer can distinguish their original devices from clones in order not to supply those with new firmware. Likewise, it must be ensured that at the end of an original device's lifecycle its identity cannot be copied or reused so that a cloned device can pretend to be an original one.

Due to these threats some operating companies start to prevent their devices from any kind of communication to outside their own network. But most of the manufacturers, however, do not want or cannot afford to dismiss the advantages of interconnectedness, e.g., for systems like energy storages in a Smart Grid. Because this development was discernible through recent years, developments ranging from classic SCADA up to Cloud-based SCADA solutions incorporate a growing number of security-critical functions. Additionally, the corresponding norms as well as legislation were pushed along, resulting, for example, in standards like IEC 62443. Legislation in Germany also has acknowledged the problem and demands – in accordance with requirements for Cloud operators stated by the Federal Office of Information Security [8] and along with a "CE-conformity label for IT security" for manufacturers of products for critical infrastructure applying similar rules. [9]

A. Security challenges for Cloud-based SCADA systems

In recent years, numerous Cloud-based ICS or SCADA systems have been developed and are now readily available. These systems interconnect on-site low-performance operational technology devices with Cloud services that run data acquisition and data analytics algorithms. The aggregation and analysis of these huge amounts of data is then used to optimise operation of the on-premise low-performance OT devices. This means that such Cloud-based SCADA systems are vulnerable against attacks targeting their Internet connection. A Distributed Denial of Service (DDoS) attack that prevents the above mentioned data acquisition and data analytics algorithms from being available for the on-premises devices certainly affects production in a non-beneficial way. In addition, data provided to these Cloud services might cause difficulties as well because of the loop back. If a sensor is hijacked and thus its data acquisition compromised, a control system today hardly has any chance at all to determine whether the data has been manipulated or not. At best, important data is provided redundantly which usually is true in plants only if the data emitting sensors are rated as safety critical. Manipulating a seemingly unimportant measurement often bears the potential of considerably interfering with a production plant's processes. Even worse are attacks on actors controlling these processes. If, for example, one of the couple of thousands actuators in a power plant can be compromised in a way that physically perturbs the process, the shutdown of the power plant – and so disconnecting it from the grid in order to reach a safe condition – is one of the more harmless scenarios imaginable.

Since OT networks benefit from having all data communication at precisely deterministic and thus predictable time slots, anomaly detection can be a means of locating interference caused by an attacker. However, direct manipulation of measurement within a sensor would not alter the sensor transmitting valid data using the proper protocol to its superior control system and anomaly detection would in most cases not recognise the data being counterfeit.

B. Security challenges for OT devices

For the development of low-performance devices which are deployed in critical infrastructures, security-related topics are usually the last on the list of requirements – if present at all. In most cases their importance is overruled by economic concerns, since they are neither really relevant for manufacturing issues nor (at least up till now) for the customers' purchasing decisions. In addition, the following fact is also in many cases unattended: a security level for low-performance systems that is comparable to traditional IT systems can only be achieved with great effort – if at all possible. For economic reasons these systems' soft- and hardware is usually designed to have exactly the performance to fulfil their main purpose – and nothing beyond. The deployment of higher performance or more complex security procedures, with respect to small profit margins and multiply optimized supply chains, quickly leads to unprofitable and uneconomic products.

Apart from such economic reasons several other factors may cause even partially secured systems to fail:

- insufficient communication security,
- lacking authentication of communication end points,
- faulty implementation of algorithms,
- faults at the protocol level,
- compatibility problems with applied protocols or
- problems with the initial key deployment.

All this increases the probability of security breaches which are either patched only infrequently or lead to a complete replacement of these devices. [9] While IT systems usually provide options to implement and install patches easily, big installations, like power plants, allow only precisely defined time slots for revisions during which systems may be patched without financial losses or penalties.

III. Related work

On a global scale, numerous institutions and companies are developing Cloud-based services for all kinds of devices, where they all have to consider security requirements.

As an example, the GE Predix service platform connects industrial assets (such as turbines, sensors, etc.) with a Cloud in order to collect and analyse operational and historical data to allow and improve predictive maintenance. [10] An additional application security service comprises two main features: a user account and authentication service using industry standards for identity management via whitelisting (amongst others), and an access control service using policy-driven authorisation for access restriction to resources programmed in a special policy language.

The AUMA Cloud is a free and secure Cloud-based solution for cost-effective asset management and predictive maintenance of AUMA actuators, promoting high plant availability. [11] It provides an easy-to-use interactive platform to collect and assess detailed device information on all the AUMA actuators in a plant. It allows plant operators to detect excessive loads or potential maintenance requirements at an early stage and take remedial action in time to prevent unexpected failures.

MindSphere is an open cloud platform developed by Siemens for applications in the context of the Internet of Things. [12] It stores operational data from all kinds of devices and makes it accessible through digital applications in order to allow industrial customers to make decisions based on factual information. Assets can be securely connected to MindSphere with auxiliary products (e.g., MindConnect IoT2040 or MindConnect Nano) that collect and transfer relevant machine and plant data.

IV. The iSEC approach

The authors have submitted a funding proposal entitled "Intelligent Security for Electric Actuators and Converters in Critical Infrastructures (iSEC)" in order to solve some of the security challenges mentioned above.

The technology, which is in the scope of the authors of this paper, like actuators from SIPOS and battery storage combined with electric vehicle chargers from GPE, belongs to such critical infrastructure due to the widely distributed type of the installation and remote operation of such systems. The idea behind the funding proposal is to develop an integrated data communication which facilitates both, a high internal computing performance for the processing of real-time control algorithms and secured communication.

Primarily, the untampered local operation of the equipment needs to be ensured at any time and therefore the local firmware needs to be secured from any unauthorised access. Additionally, the local equipment's data communication containing real-time signals to system wide controllers or Cloud services is essential for proper and stable plant or grid operation. For service purposes, local equipment needs to be accessible by service staff to integrate new features into the system. The confidentiality of data and signals needs to be considered and ensured.

As stated before, microcontroller-based systems usually provide only very limited computing power and memory. Because of that, the computation of state of the art cryptographic algorithms or key negotiation algorithms may take several minutes. Almost all of these systems are run in environments where real-time requirements demand response times in the range of milliseconds or even microseconds, e.g., frequency converters in energy smart grids. Thus, system performance represents a significant limitation to the effectiveness of cryptographic operations. A further limitation is restricted amount of system memory – cryptographic algorithms have to be tailored to fit into the available RAM and ROM. As an approach to solve this problem the research of "lightweight cryptography" for low-performance embedded systems is just at its beginnings. [14]

Energy storage systems in larger quantities are essential to integrate higher contents of renewable energy sources into public distribution grids. Fluctuating power generation of photovoltaic or wind power systems requires short term storage to match the exact value of power consumption at any time of the day. Stationary energy storage systems and electric vehicle chargers become more common and are currently being installed into industrial buildings which are connected to public distribution grids. With increasing numbers, storage devices contribute to grid stability and therefore, they become critical infrastructure for grid operation and grid reliability. Data security becomes an important issue, as these systems are equipped with fully digital control systems, which are connected to remote systems for control and service access functionality. Furthermore, firmware updates can be installed via remote access, which is a very useful and system-critical feature likewise. Therefore, such critical systems need to be able to verify the data they receive and to authenticate the sender of the data before starting any actions based on the data received. Additionally, the data requires confidentiality to protect the systems from competitors and invaders.

Figure 2 depicts the data communication architecture. The power converters, controlled by digital signal processors (Level 1) are connected via a local CAN network to a Linux-based system and communication controller (Level 2). The system controller has a TCP/IP interface which facilitates data communication to local or via Internet connected Level 3 devices for operation and service functionalities. While CAN communication is restricted to the local system, TCP/IP is critical as it can be accessed from outside the local system.

It is planned to perform a detailed investigation of how internal and external interfaces can be constructed in a verifiable secure design, and how in-situ tests can prove their efficacy in terms of security and usability.

Cloud services shall be used for mechanisms of identifi-

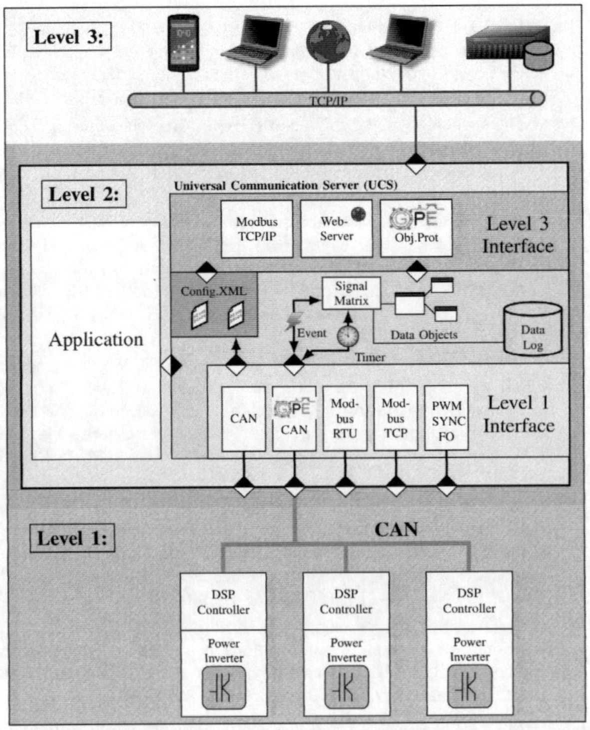

Figure 2. Data communication architecture. [13]

cation and authentication, for easing the task of performing necessary software patches and thus improving facilities' outage times and service intervals.

In addition, it is planned to investigate how Physical Unclonable Functions (PUF) can be used to secure communication between a Cloud server and (low-performance) sensor clients and to clearly identify a sensor client with a digital fingerprint. Hardware intrinsic deviations caused by the manufacturing process of semiconductors can be used to identify chips [15] and generate random encryption keys. The drawbacks of using non-volatile storage-mechanisms for storing encryption keys, can be overcome by using this relatively new approach. PUFs are a current subject of research, different approaches have yet been investigated. [16] [17] For example, with arbiter PUFs a race condition can be generated between two different digital paths on the same semiconductor. An arbiter circuit is used to measure which of the paths won the race. With different challenges the path can be configured and for every challenge, the winner is determined. Because of the manufacturing deviations every chip will give a different response, despite having the same hardware configuration and therefore, a digital fingerprint can be read out. As the response cannot be read out or predicted by an attacker it is called unclonable. Also, PUFs based on digital bistable storage elements, like SRAM cells, latches or flip flops, have been demonstrated. They are based on the principle of bringing them in, in an unstable state, and letting them settle in one of their stable states. Due to statistical variations during the manufacturing process, different chips cause different results despite the same hardware configuration. Many other solutions using deviations of the manufacturing process for identifying a chip are conceivable. [18] In this context, new protocols have also been investigated to secure lightweight communication based on PUFs. [19] [20] [21] Which lightweight PUF based protocols can be used for encryption of sensor data connected to a cloud-server is another topic of our studies. Just recently, first semiconductor devices with PUF-functionality are now readily available in order to identify hardware and implement a digital fingerprint, for example. [22] [23] [24] It has to be investigated whether these semiconductor devices can be used in order to help solving some of the security challenges mentioned before.

V. The Consortium

SIPOS Aktorik GmbH emanated in 1999 from the former actuator division of Siemens AG in Nuremberg, since 2008 situated at Altdorf. Main proprietor of SIPOS Aktorik GmbH is the AUMA Riester GmbH & Co KG, Muellheim, which as a holding also provides commercial services. Today, SIPOS Aktorik GmbH employs a staff of 85 people in the departments assembly, R&D, customer service and administration. During the last 20 years SIPOS Aktorik GmbH succeeded in positioning itself on the global market for electric actuators with an export quota of 80 %. Main customers are international plant engineering and construction companies, valve manufacturers, and operating companies of conventional and nuclear power plants in Europe and Asia.

Grass Power Electronics GmbH, Nuremberg, is working on grid conected stationary battery storage systems in the range of some hundreds of kilowatts. Core technology components are digital computer modules for real time power converter control and for system control, including TCP based data communication.

The security research group at the Technical University of Applied Sciences OTH Amberg-Weiden has already worked on funded research projects using lightweight cryptographic algorithms. They have also experience in developing security protocols using PUFs for authentication and device identification. [25]

VI. Conclusion and Future Work

In this paper, we showed that when it comes to combining low-performance embedded devices with Cloud services, all components must be secured to harden these systems against cyberattacks. Otherwise, compromised sensors can falsify computations and analytics performed in the cloud. And attacks against the Cloud services, e.g., a DDoS attack, has a direct impact on an ICS when it relies on a permanent connection to the cloud, too.

To master the challenges of IIoT and Industry 4.0, it is imperative to consider possible vulnerabilities and attack vectors when designing such systems ("security by design").

The authors hope that their submitted grant proposal iSEC will be approved to work on these security challenges.

References

[1] M. Hermann, T. Pentek and B. Otto, "Design Principles for Industrie 4.0 Scenarios," in Proceedings of the 49th Hawaii International Conference on System Sciences (HICSS), January 5–8, 2016, Koloa, USA. IEEE, Jan. 2016, pp. 3928–3937, T. X. Bui and R. H. Sprague, Jr., Eds., ISBN: 978-0-7695-5670-3, ISSN: 1530-1605, URL: https://doi.org/10.1109/HICSS.2016.488 [accessed: 2019.04.12]

[2] G.-J. Schrijen, G. Selimis, J.-J. Treurniet, "Secure Device Management for the Internet of Things" in Proceedings of the 2019 embeddedworld Exhibition & Conference, February 26–28, 2019, Nuremberg, Germany. To be published.

[3] Federal Ministry of the Interior, Building and Community, Ed., "Nationale Strategie zum Schutz Kritischer Infrastrukturen" (National Strategy for the Protection of Critical Infrastructures), 2009.

[4] Department of Homeland Security, Ed., "Critical Infrastructure Sectors", URL: https://www.dhs.gov/cisa/critical-infrastructure-sectors [accessed: 2019.04.12]

[5] Federal Office for Information Security, Ed., "Die Lage der IT-Sicherheit in Deutschland 2017" (The State of IT Security in Germany in 2017), No. BSI-LB17/506, August 2017.

[6] E-ISAC, Ed., "Analysis of the Cyber Attack on the Ukrainian Power Grid", Technical Report, March 18th, 2016, URL: https://ics.sans.org/media/E-ISAC_SANS_Ukraine_DUC_5.pdf [accessed: 2019.04.12]

[7] M. Strathmann, "Malware führte zum Blackout" (Malware led to Blackout), Zeit-Online, January 5th, 2016, URL: https://www.zeit.de/digital/internet/2016-01/stromausfall-hacker-ukraine-blackenergy [accessed: 2019.04.12]

[8] Federal Office for Information Security, Ed., "Anforderungskatalog Cloud Computing (C5)" (Cloud Computing Compliance Controls Catalogue), September 2017.

[9] UP KRITIS, Ed., "Empfehlungen zu Entwicklung und Einsatz von in Kritischen Infrastrukturen eingesetzten Produkten" (Recommendations for the Development and Deployment of Products used in Critical Infrastructures), Version 1.00, November 29th, 2018.

[10] General Electric Company, Ed., "Predix Architecture and Services", Technical Whitepaper, November 28th, 2016, URL: https://d154rjc49kgakj.cloudfront.net/GE_Predix_Architecture_and_Services.pdf [accessed: 2019.04.12]

[11] AUMA Riester GmbH & Co. KG, Ed., "The AUMA Cloud", 2019, URL: https://www.auma.com/en/service-support/digital-services/the-auma-cloud/ [accessed: 2019.04.12]

[12] S. Naujoks, "MindSphere – Siemens cloud for industry: What is it all about?", May 9th, 2016, URL: https://www.pac-online.com/mindsphere-siemens-cloud-industry-what-it-all-about [accessed: 2019.04.12]

[13] N. Grass, F. Ferner and F. Nickl, "Modular and Intelligent Battery Control System for Electric Vehicles and Stationary Storage Systems" in Proceedings of the 2016 IEEE International Telecommunications Energy Conference (INTELEC), October 23–27, 2016, Austin, USA. IEEE, Nov. 2016, pp. 1–7, ISBN: 978-1-5090-1877-2.

[14] "NIST Issues First Call for 'Lightweight Cryptography' to Protect Small Electronics", 2018, URL: https://www.nist.gov/news-events/news/2018/04/nist-issues-first-call-lightweight-cryptography-protect-small-electronics [accessed: 2019.04.12]

[15] S. Choi, D. Zage, Y. R. Choe and B. Wasilow, "Physically Unclonable Digital ID", in Proceedings of the 2015 IEEE International Conference on Mobile Services, June 2015, pp. 105–111.

[16] R. Maes and I. Verbauwhede, Physically Unclonable Functions: A Study on the State of the Art and Future Research Directions. Springer, Berlin; Heidelberg, 2010, chapter 1, pp. 3–37, in A.-R. Sadeghi, D. Naccache, Eds., Towards Hardware-Intrinsic Security, ISBN: 978-3-642-26578-5.

[17] H. Handschuh, G. J. Schrijen and P. Tuyls, Hardware Intrinsic Security from Physically Unclonable Functions. Springer, Berlin; Heidelberg, 2010, chapter 2, pp. 39–53, in A.-R. Sadeghi, D. Naccache, Eds., Towards Hardware-Intrinsic Security, ISBN: 978-3-642-26578-5.

[18] S. Katzenbeisser, Ü. Kocabaş, A.-R. Sadeghi, I. Verbauwhede and C. Wachsmann, PUFs: Myth, Fact or Busted? A Security Evaluation of Physically Unclonable Functions (PUFs) Cast in Silicon. Springer, Berlin; Heidelberg, 2012, pp. 283–301, in E. Prouff and P. Schaumont, Eds., Cryptographic Hardware and Embedded Systems – CHES 2012, ISBN: 978-3-642-33027-8.

[19] M. Majzoobi, M. Rostami, F. Koushanfar, D. S. Wallach and S. Devadas, "Slender PUF Protocol: A Lightweight, Robust, and Secure Authentication by Substring Matching" in Proceedings of the 2012 IEEE Symposium on Security and Privacy Workshops, May 24–25, 2012, San Francisco, USA. IEEE, Jul. 2012, pp. 33–44, ISBN: 978-1-4673-2157-0.

[20] T. Idriss and M. Bayoumi, "Lightweight highly secure PUF protocol for mutual authentication and secret message exchange" in Proceedings of the 2017 IEEE International Conference on RFID Technology Application (RFID-TA), September 20–22, 2017, Warsaw, Poland. IEEE, Nov. 2017, pp. 214–219, ISBN: 978-1-5386-1833-2.

[21] M. Delavar, S. Mirzakuchaki, M. H. Ameri and J. Mohajeri, "Puf-Based Solutions For Secure Communications In Advanced Metering Infrastructure (AMI)", IACR Cryptology ePrint Archive, Report 2016/009, https://eprint.iacr.org/2016/009, [accessed: 2019.04.12]

[22] Maxim Integrated, "ChipDNA", https://www.maximintegrated.com/en/design/partners-and-technology/design-technology/chipdna-puf-technology.html [accessed: 2019.04.12]

[23] INTRINSIC ID, "QuiddiKey", https://www.intrinsic-id.com/products/quiddikey/ [accessed: 2019.04.12]

[24] NXP, "Secure microcontroller family SmartMX2", https://www.nxp.com/docs/en/brochure/75017516.pdf [accessed: 2019.04.12]

[25] A. Aßmuth et al., "Improving Resilience by Deploying Permuted Code onto Physically Unclonable Unique Processors", in Proceedings of the 2016 Cybersecurity and Cyberforensics Conference (CCC), August 2–4, 2016, Amman, Jordan. IEEE, Oct. 2016, pp. 144–150, ISBN: 978-1-5090-2657-9.

Performance Comparision between Scaling of Virtual Machines and Containers using Cassandra NoSQL Database

Sogand Shirinbab, Lars Lundberg, Emiliano Casalicchio
Department of Computer Science
Blekinge Institute of Technology
Karlskrona, Sweden
email: {Sogand.Shirinbab, Lars.Lundberg, Emiliano.Casalicchio}@bth.se

***Abstract*—Cloud computing promises customers the on-demand ability to scale in face of workload variations. There are different ways to accomplish scaling, one is vertical scaling and the other is horizontal scaling. The vertical scaling refers to buying more power (CPU, RAM), buying a more expensive and robust server, which is less challenging to implement but exponentially expensive. While, the horizontal scaling refers to adding more servers with less processor and RAM, which is usually cheaper overall and can scale very well. The majority of cloud providers prefer the horizontal scaling approach, and for them would be very important to know about the advantages and disadvantages of both technologies from the perspective of the application performance at scale. In this paper, we compare performance differences caused by scaling of the different virtualization technologies in terms of CPU utilization, latency, and the number of transactions per second. The workload is Apache Cassandra, which is a leading Not Only Structured Query Language (NoSQL) distributed database for Big Data platforms. Our results show that running multiple instances of the Cassandra database concurrently, affected the performance of read and write operations differently; for both VMware and Docker, the maximum number of read operations was reduced when we ran several instances concurrently, whereas the maximum number of write operations increased when we ran instances concurrently.**

Keywords—Cassandra; Cloud computing; Docker container; Horizontal scaling; NoSQL database; Performance comparison; Virtualization; VMware virtual machine

I. INTRODUCTION

Today's modern data centers are increasingly virtualized where applications are hosted on one or more virtual servers that are then mapped onto physical servers in the data center. Virtualization provides a number of benefits, such as flexible allocation of resources and scaling of applications. Scalability corresponds to the ability of a system uniformly to handle an increasing amount of work [1]-[3]. Nowadays, there are two types of server virtualization technologies that are common in data center environments, hardware-level virtualization and operating system level virtualization. Hardware-level virtualization involves embedding virtual machine software (known as Hypervisor or Virtual Machine Monitor (VMM)) into the hardware component of a server. The hypervisor controls processor, memory, and other components by allowing several different operating systems to run on the same machine without the need for a source code. The operating system running on the machine will appear to have its own processor, memory, and other components. Virtual machines are extensively used in today's practice. However, during the last few years, much attention has been given to operating system level virtualization (also known as container-based virtualization or containerization). Operating system level virtualization refers to an operating system feature in which the kernel allows the existence of multiple isolated user-space instances (also known as partitions or containers) instead of just one. As it has been shown in Figure 1, containers are more light weight than virtual machines, various applications in container share the same operating system kernel rather than launching multiple virtual machines with separate operating system instances. Therefore, container-based virtualization provides better scalability than the hypervisor-based virtualization [4].

Currently, two concepts are used to scale virtualized systems, vertical and horizontal scaling [5]-[8]. The vertical scaling corresponds to the improvement of the hardware on which application is running, for example addition of memory, processors, and disk space. While the horizontal scaling corresponds to duplication of virtual servers to distribute the load of transactions. The horizontal scaling approach is almost always more desirable because of its advantages, such as no limit to hardware capacity, easy to upgrade, and easier to run fault-tolerance. In our previous study, we explored the performance of a real application, Cassandra NoSQL database, on the different environments. Our goal was to understand the overhead introduced by virtual machines (specifically VMware) and containers (specifically Docker) relative to non-virtualized Linux [9]. In this study, our goal is to provide an up-to-date comparison of containers and virtual machine environments using recent software versions.

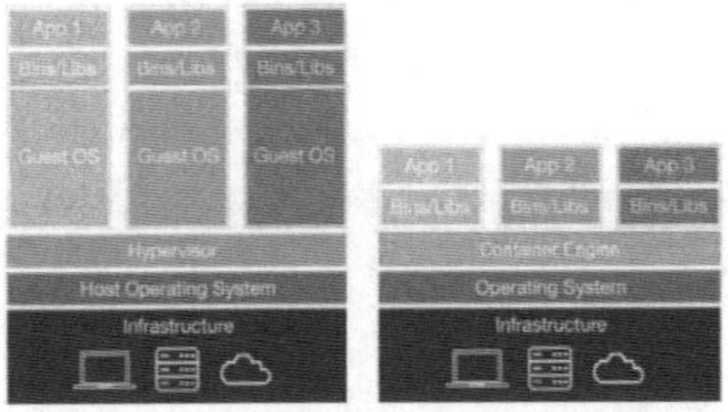

Figure 1. Difference between Virtual Machines and Containers Architecture

In addition, we explore how much horizontal scaling of virtual machines and containers will improve the performance in terms of the system CPU utilization, latency, and throughput. In this work, we have used multiple instances of the Cassandra running concurrently on the different environments.

The presented work is organized as follows: In Section II, we discuss related work. Section III describes the experimental setup and test cases. Section IV presents the experimental results, and we conclude our work in Section V.

II. RELATED WORK

Both container-based and virtual machine-based virtualization technologies have been growing at a rapid pace, and research work evaluating the performance aspects of these platforms provides an empirical basis for comparing their performance. Our previous research [9], has compared performance overheads of Docker containers, VMware virtual machines versus Non-virtualized. We have shown that, Docker had lower overhead compared to the VMware. In this paper, we try to expand our previous work and compare the two technologies; Container-based and Virtual Machine-based virtualization in terms of their scalabilities running Cassandra workload. There have not been many studies on both scalability and performance comparison between the two technologies. A comparison between Linux containers and AWS ec2 virtual machines is performed in [10]. According to their results, containers outperformed virtual machines in terms of both performance and scalability. In [13], the authors presented LightVM, which is a complete redesign of Xen. The authors made a comparison between the performance of LightVM and containers like Docker and LXC. According to their results VM could be as light as containers, however there is a development price to be paid. In our study, we used VMware because it has been used widely by the IT industry, hence VMware is more mature compared to LightVM.

In [11], the authors evaluated the performance differences caused by the different virtualization technologies in data center environments where multiple applications are running on the same servers (multi-tenancy). According to theirs study, containers may suffer from performance in multi-tenant scenarios, due to the lack of isolation. However, containers offer near bare-metal performance and low footprint. In addition, containers allow soft resource limits which can be useful in resource over-utilization scenarios. In [12], the authors studied performance implications on the NoSQL MongoDB during the horizontal scaling of virtual machines. According to their results, the horizontal scaling affects the average response time of the application by 40%.

III. EVALUATION

The goal of the experiment was that of comparing the performance scalability of the Cassandra while running it on multiple virtual machines versus on multiple containers concurrently.

A. Experimental Setup

All our tests were performed on three HP servers DL380 G7 with processors for a total of 16 cores (plus HyperThreading) and 64 GiB of RAM and disk of size 400 GB. Red Hat Enterprise Linux Server 7.3 (Maipo) (Kernel Linux 3.10.0-514.e17.x86_64) and Cassandra 3.11.0 are installed on all hosts as well as virtual machines. Same version of Cassandra used on the load generators. To test containers, Docker version 1.12.6 installed and in case of virtual machines VMware ESXi 6.0.0 installed. In total, 4 times the 3-node Cassandra clusters configured for this study (see Figure 2).

B. Workload

To generate the workload, we used Cassandra-stress tool. The Cassandra-stress tool is a Java-based stress utility for basic benchmarking and load testing of a Cassandra cluster. Creating the best data model requires significant load testing and multiple iterations. The Cassandra-stress tool helps us in this endeavor by populating our cluster and supporting stress testing of arbitrary Cassandra Query Language (CQL) tables and arbitrary queries on tables. The Cassandra package comes with a command-line stress tool (Cassandra-stress tool) to generate the load on the cluster of servers, the cqlsh utility, a python-based command line client for executing CQL commands and the nodetool utility for managing a cluster. These tools are used to stress the servers from the client and manage the data in the servers.

The Cassandra-stress tool creates a keyspace called keyspace1 and within that, tables named standard1 or counter1 in each of the nodes. These are automatically created the first time we run the stress test and are reused on subsequent runs unless we drop the keyspace using CQL. A write operation inserts data into the database and is done prior to the load testing of the database. Later, after the data are inserted into the database, we run the mix workload, and then split up the mix workload and run the write-only workload and the read-only workload. In [1] [9], we described in detail each workload as well as the commands we used for generating the workloads, in this paper we have used the same approach for generating the workload.

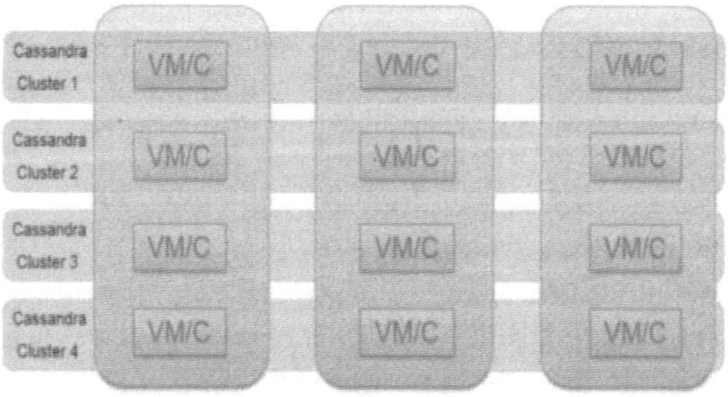

Figure 2. Experimental Setup

C. Performance Metrics

The performance of Docker containers and VMware virtual machines are measured using the following metrics:

- CPU Utilization (percentage),
- Maximum Transactions Per Second (TPS), and
- Mean Latency (milisecond).

The CPU utilization is measured directly on the server nodes by means of sar command. The latency and maximum

TPS are measured on the client side, that are measured by the stress test tool. The term transactions per second refers to the number of database transactions performed per second.

D. Test Cases

1) One-Cassandra-three-node-cluster: In this case, one virtual machine/container deployed on each host running Cassandra application. All virtual machines/containers configured as one 3-node cluster.

2) Two-Cassandra-three-node-clusters: In this case, two containers/virtual machines deployed on each host running Cassandra application. Each container/virtual machine on each host belongs to its own 3-node cluster, so in total two 3-node clusters configured to run concurrently.

3) Four-Cassandra-three-node-clusters: In this case, four containers/virtual machines deployed on each host running Cassandra application. Each container/virtual machine on each host belongs to its own 3-node cluster, so in total four 3-node clusters configured to run concurrently.

In this experiment, we compare the performance of virtual machines and containers running different Cassandra workload scenarios, Mix, Read and Write. However, unlike our previous study [9], here we decided to set the replication-factor as three. In our test environment with three-node clusters, replication factor three means that each node should have a copy of the input data splits.

IV. Performance and Scalability Comparison

A. Transactions per second (tps)

Figure 3 shows transactions per second (tps) during write, read and mixed load. In this figure, we summarized the total transactions per second from different number of Cassandra clusters running on Docker containers and VMware virtual machines. According to the results, overall in all cases Docker containers could handle higher number of database transactions per second than VMware virtual machines. In the case of the mixed load, Docker containers could handle around 25% more transactions per second than VMware virtual machines. In the case of only write load the difference is around 19% more for containers than virtual machines. While in the case of only read load, there is a huge difference of around 40% in the number of transactions per second between virtual machines and containers. Another aspect to consider according to the transactions per second results is that, running multiple instances of the Cassandra database concurrently, affected the performance of read and write operations differently; for both VMware and Docker, the maximum number of read operations was reduced when we ran several instances concurrently, whereas the maximum number of write operations increased when we ran instances concurrently. Note that increasing the number of Cassandra clusters did not have any significant impact on the number of transactions per second in the case of the mixed-load.

B. CPU utilization

Figure 4 shows the results of CPU utilization of multiple numbers of Cassandra clusters running on virtual machines and containers during write, read, and mix workloads. According to the results, in general CPU utilization of one cluster of virtual machines/containers are lower than two clusters and CPU utilization of two clusters is less than three clusters. It can be observed from the figures that, the overhead of running multiple clusters in terms of CPU utilization is around 10% for both containers and virtual machines. This overhead decreases as the load increases, one reason for this can be the background jobs that are running in Cassandra and as the load increases Cassandra by default delays these jobs since there are not enough resources available for executing the jobs. In addition, it can be observed from the figures that, the overall CPU utilization of containers is lower than virtual machines for all different workloads. Considering the mix workload CPU utilization of containers is around 15% lower than CPU utilization of virtual machines.

The difference between CPU utilization of containers and virtual machines is around 12% for the write workload which is very close to the difference that we saw for the mix workload case. However, this difference is significantly higher for the read workload up to around 40%. According to these results, read operations utilize more CPU cycles on virtual machines than on containers.

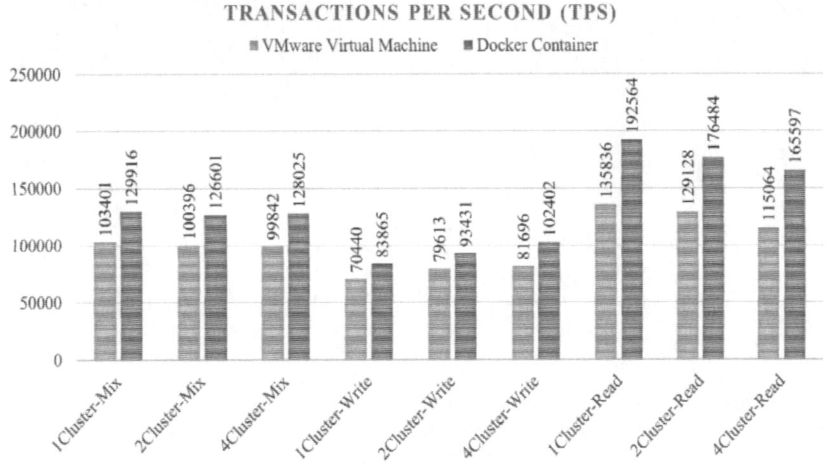

Figure 3. Transactions per second (tps)

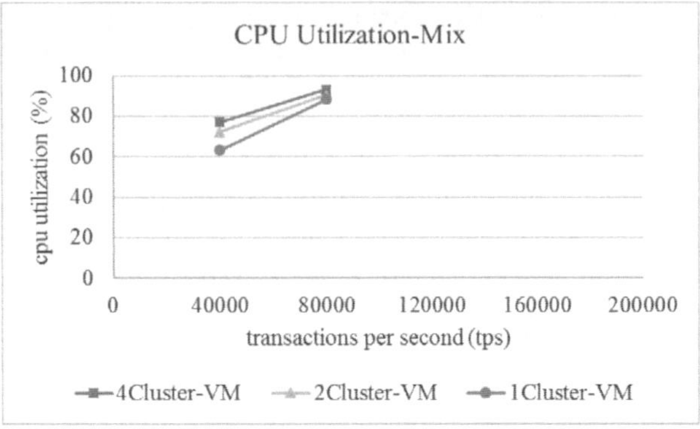

a.

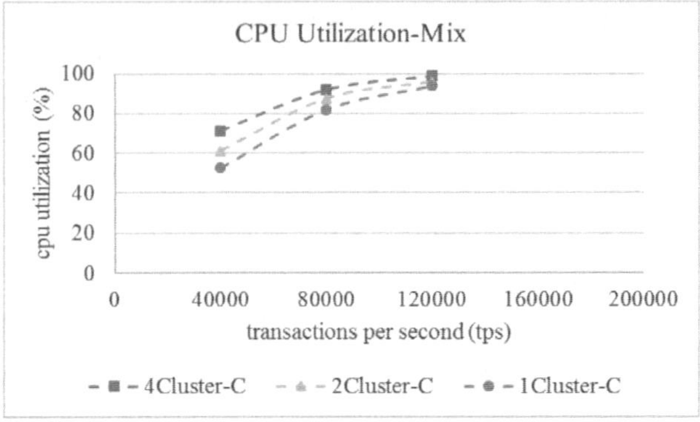

b.

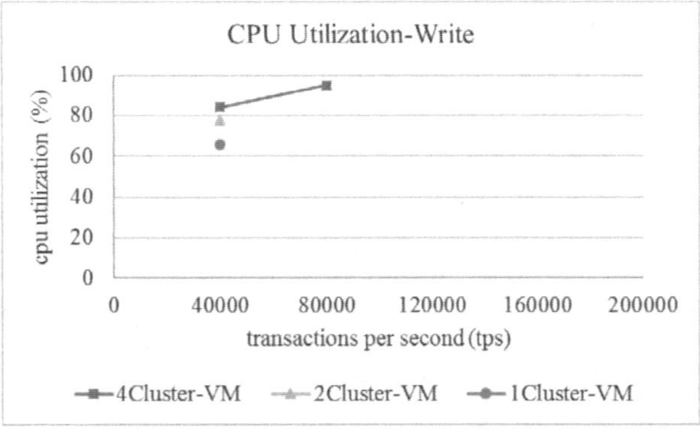

c.

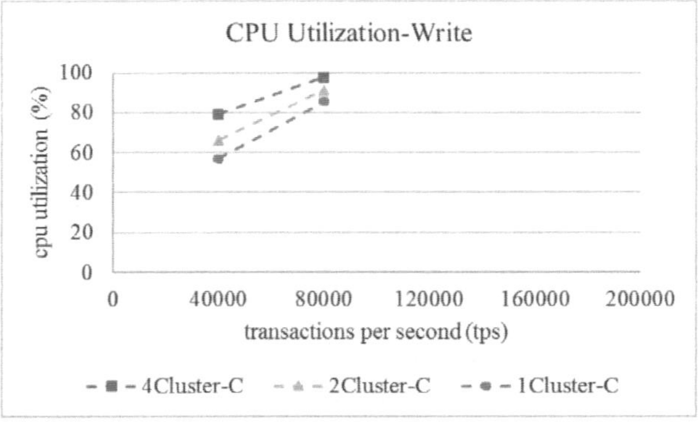

d.

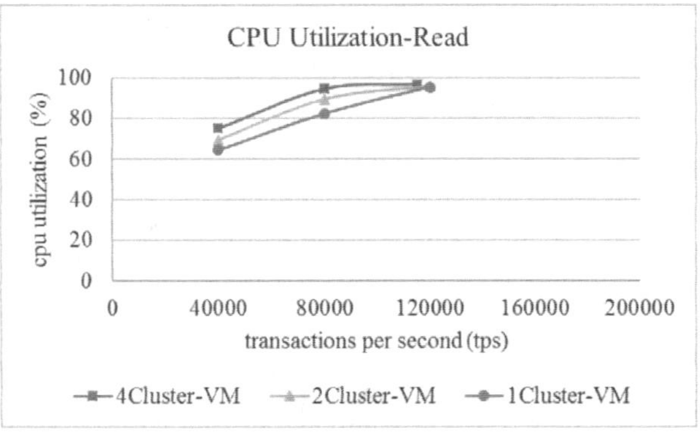

e.

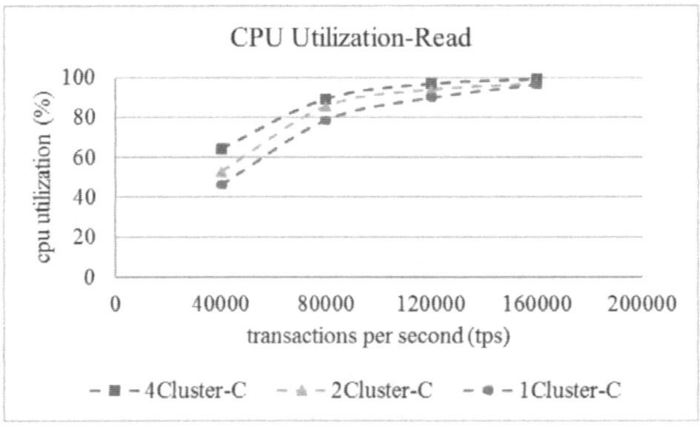

f.

Figure 4. CPU utilization results for Write, Read and Mix workload for multiple Cassandra clusters running on virtual machines and containers concurrently.

C. Latency

Figure 5 shows the results of latency mean of multiple numbers of Cassandra clusters running on virtual machines and containers during write, read, and mix workloads. As it can be observed from the figures, in general, the latency of containers is 50% lower than virtual machines as the load increases. In the case of the mixed workload, the latency difference between having one cluster and two clusters is negligible. However, the latency difference between having one or two clusters compared with four clusters is around 33%.

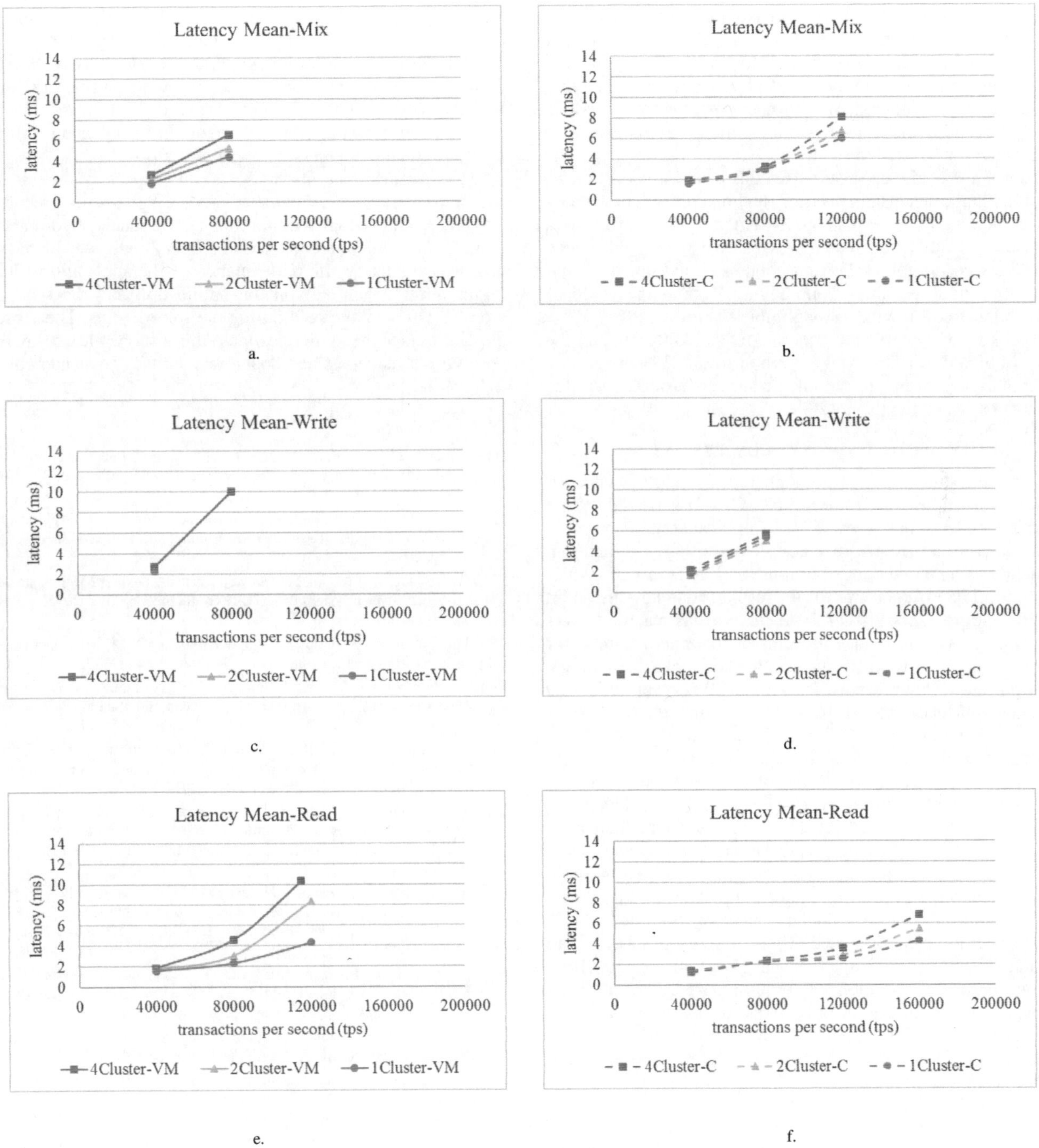

Figure 5. Latency mean results for Write, Read and Mix workload for multiple Cassandra clusters running on virtual machines and containers concurrently.

In the case of the write workload, the difference between having containers.

However, for virtual machines, the latency becomes around 10ms in the case of four clusters when the tps is only 80k. Also, in the case of two clusters and 1cluster, since the cluster did not handle the load of 80k tps the latency is only shown for 40k tps which is around 2-3 ms. In the case of the read workload, for the virtual machines the latency increases up to around 50% higher for the case with two clusters compared with one cluster. The latency increases up to around 20% for the case of four clusters compared with the case of two clusters and there is an increase of up to around 60%

compared to the case of only one cluster. According to these results scaling would be very expensive for virtual machines in terms of latency mean which will have a negative impact on the application performance. However, in the case of containers the cost in terms of latency difference for having multiple clusters compared with one cluster is up to around 23%. According to the results, running multiple clusters inside containers will have less impact on the latency and the performance of the application (in this case Cassandra) than running multiple clusters inside virtual machines. The latency difference increases exponentially as the number of clusters increases as well as the load increases. The latency difference increases up to around 23% on containers and up to around 60% on virtual machines while having 100% read workload. The latency difference is negligible in the case of write workload. Also, there is a moderate latency difference in the case of mixed workload which is up to around 20% for virtual machines when the tps is 80k and up to around 25% for containers when the tps is 120k.

V. Discussions and Conclusions

In this study, we have compared the performance of running multiple clusters of the NoSQL Cassandra database inside Docker containers and VMware virtual machines. We have measured the performance in terms of CPU utilization, Latency mean and the maximum number of Transactions Per Second (TPS). According to our results, running Cassandra inside multiple clusters of VMware virtual machines was showing less performance in terms of maximum number of transactions per second compared to the Docker containers. The performance difference was around 20% lower during the mixed workload, around 16% lower during the write-only workload and around 29% lower during read-only workload. One reason for this could be that containers are lighter-weight compared to virtual machines, therefore there is a less overhead of the virtualization layer and this helps the application to get more resources and performs better on containers than virtual machines. Another reason can be how a write and a read operation procedure works in Cassandra. In Cassandra, a write operation in general performs better than a read operation because it does not involve too much I/O. A write operation is completed when the data has been both written in the commit log (file) and in memory (memtable). However, a read operation may require more I/O for different reasons. A read operation first involves reading from a filter associated to sstable that might save I/O time saying that a data is surely not present in the associated sstable and then if filter returns a positive value, Cassandra starts seeking the sstable to look for data. In terms of CPU Utilization, the Cassandra application performs better on containers than on virtual machines. According to our results, the difference between CPU utilization on virtual machines is around 16% higher than containers during the mixed workload, around 8% higher during the write-only workload and around 32% higher during the read-only workload. In addition, the Cassandra application running inside virtual machines got up to around 50% higher latency than containers during the mixed workload. The difference became up to around 40% higher on virtual machines during the write-only workload compared to containers, also up to around 30% higher on virtual machines during the read-only workload compared to containers. As it has been discussed before, in general, the read-only workload is showing less performance than the write-only workload, and the impact of the different types of workloads on the performance in terms of CPU utilization is higher on virtual machines than containers.

However, considering the scalability aspects of the virtual machines and the containers, according to our results, containers scale better without loosing too much performance while virtual machines overhead is very high, and it has a negative impact on the performance of the application. This might differ depending on the application and the type of workload as we have seen during our experiments. Therefore, cloud providers need to investigate this issue while deploying both virtual machines and containers across data centers also at larger scale.

References

[1] Gaopan, Huang, et al. "Auto Scaling Virtual Machines for Web Applications with Queuing Theory," in ICSAI conference, pp. 433-438, 2017.

[2] Sijin, He, et al. "Elastic Application Container: A Lightweight Approach for Cloud Resource Provisioning," in AINA conference, pp. 15-22, 2012.

[3] A. Horiuchi and K. Saisho, "Development of Scaling Mechanism for Distributed Web System," in SNPD conference, pp. 1-6, 2015.

[4] Fan-Hsun, Tseng, et al. "A Lightweight Auto-Scaling Mechanism for Fog Computing in Industrial Applications," in IEEE Transactions on Industrial Informatics Journal, vol. PP, no. 99, pp. 1-1, 2018.

[5] W. Wenting, C. Haopeng, and C. Xi, "An Availability-Aware virtual Machine Placement Approach for Dynamic Scaling of Cloud Applications," in UIC/ATC conference, pp. 509-516, 2012.

[6] L. Chien-Yu, S. Meng-Ru, L. Yi-fang L. Yu-Chun, and L. Kuan-Chou, "Vertical/Horizontal Resource Scaling Mechanism for Federated Clouds," in ICISA conference, pp.1-4 , 2014.

[7] S. Sotiriadis, N. Bessis, C. Amza, and R. Buyya, "Vertical and Horizontal Elasticity for Dynamic Virtual Machine Reconfiguration," in IEEE Transactions on Services Computing Journal, vol. PP, no. 99, pp. 1-14, 2016.

[8] Y. Al-Dhuraibi, F. Paraiso, N. Djarallah, and P. Merie, "Elasticity in Cloud Computing: State of the Art and Research Challenges," in IEEE Transactions on Services Computing Journal, vol. PP, Issue. 99, pp 1-1, 2017.

[9] S. Shirinbab, L. Lundberg, and E. Casalicchio, "Performance Evaluation of Container and Virtual Machine Running Cassandra Workload, " in CloudTech conference, pp. 1-8, 2017.

[10] A.M. Joy, "Performance Comparison between Linux Containers and Virtual Machines," in ICACEA Conference, pp. 342-346, 2015.

[11] L. Chaufournier, P. Sharma, P. Shenoy, and Y.C. Tay, "Containers and Virtual Machines at scale: A Comparative Study," in Middleware Conference, pp. 1-13, 2016.

[12] Chao-Wen, Huang, et al. "The Improvement of Auto-Scaling Mechanism for distributed Database- A Case Study for MongoDB," in APNOMS conference, pp. 1-3, 2013.

[13] Manco, Filipe, et al. "My VM is Lighter (and Safer) than your Container," Proceedings of the 26th Symposium onOperating Systems Principles (SOSP 17). ACM, 2017.

BalloonJVM: Dynamically Resizable Heap for FaaS

Abraham Chan, Kai-Ting Amy Wang, Vineet Kumar
Huawei Technologies, Markham, Canada
Email: {abraham.chan, kai.ting.wang}@huawei.com, {vineet.kumar}@mail.mcgill.ca

Abstract—**Serverless computing, or more specifically, Function as a Service (FaaS), offers the ability for software developers to quickly deploy their applications to the public without worrying about custom server architecture. However, developers using FaaS services must be cautious not to exceed their container memory limits. For FaaS developers using Java, a spontaneous out of memory exception could terminate their application. This could prompt some developers to consider scalability rather than focusing on functionality, reducing the advantage of FaaS. In this paper, we present BalloonJVM, which applies ballooning, a memory reclamation technique, to dynamically resize the heap for Java FaaS applications, deployed on Huawei Cloud's FunctionStage system. We explore the challenges of configuring BalloonJVM for production and outline opportunities for improving both developer and service provider flexibility.**

Keywords–Ballooning; Function-as-a-Service; Serverless; Runtime environment; JVM Configuration.

I. INTRODUCTION

The Function as a Service (FaaS) programming model runs user-defined code in a process, typically a high-level language runtime, inside an operating-system-level container. FaaS is built upon the serverless architecture, which allows developers to deploy their applications on the public cloud in lieu of custom servers. A growing number of developers and companies are choosing to deploy their applications in this model to avoid the expenses of setting up and maintaining custom server infrastructure [1][2]. FaaS also offers the added advantage of billing developers only for the usage incurred.

Today, FaaS developers must carefully craft their functions so that its runtime memory usage is within the memory limit of its container, enforced through Linux's *cgroups* feature [3]. Exceeding the cgroups limit terminates the application abruptly. The developer must relaunch the application with the next large sized container. Such abrupt termination is unwarranted. Both the developer and service provider could benefit if it were possible to dynamically increase the heap size for a memory needy application while charging for the enlarged container.

Many service providers, including Huawei, use Oracle's Java Virtual Machine (JVM) to execute Java programs on FaaS. Oracle JVM contains a maximum heap option to control the application's memory usage, similar to the cgroups resource limit. Typically, a JVM running inside a 128MB container is started with a maximum heap setting of `-Xmx=128M`. Dynamically resizing the JVM heap is not supported in Oracle JDK. JVM throws an unrecoverable Out-Of-Memory (OOM) exception when the heap usage exceeds the maximum size.

If high memory limits were pre-allocated to applications, this could impact both the service provider and FaaS developers negatively. Higher pre-allocated memory for applications could diminish the number of FaaS applications runnable concurrently on a shared cloud infrastructure, reducing the service provider's profitability. On the other hand, FaaS developers could pay more for unused memory resources.

Ballooning is a memory reclamation technqiue, used by hypervisors to leverage unused memory by guest Virtual Machines (VMs) [4]. Each guest VM is allotted a large memory, but the guest only uses a portion of that memory in practice. The remaining memory space can be filled with balloons, which are pre-occupied memory spaces to an application (i.e., guest VM, JVM), but are actually empty memory spaces to the operating system (OS). This means the host OS is free to use the memory reclaimed through the balloons. When a guest VM requires more memory, the host can free the balloons inserted in that guest VM.

In this paper, we adopt ballooning for FaaS and expose it as a set of Java Application Programming Interfaces (APIs). We present *BalloonJVM*, a modified Java FaaS framework that calls ballooning APIs when invoking JVM to achieve dynamic memory adjustment. BalloonJVM is deployed on Huawei Cloud FunctionStage [5], a FaaS platform allowing user defined functions to be invoked on-demand. BalloonJVM is built on top of our prior work, ReplayableJVM [6], which features a checkpoint and restore framework that enables JVM to launch from an existing image to avoid its cold startup time. BalloonJVM can be launched with a larger maximum heap size than initially required (i.e., `-Xmx=512M` when only 128M is needed). Then, BalloonJVM inserts balloons at initialization and free balloons as additional runtime memory is required - creating the effect of dynamic memory resizing. This offers FaaS developers more flexibility over conventional fixed heap JVMs. Our approach does not modify JVM internals since maintaining a custom JVM build is expensive. The incorporation of BalloonJVM will provide an extra option to many FunctionStage users worldwide.

In summary, we make the following contributions in this paper.

- We present BalloonJVM, a FaaS framework with a resizable JVM heap, by developing a set of novel Java APIs that adapt ballooning for FaaS.
- We make recommendations of deployment configurations of BalloonJVM based on a runtime and memory analysis using eight representative FaaS applications.
- We ensure that BalloonJVM contains properly pinned balloons, such that no memory spikes occur as object memory is shifted around in the heap.

The remainder of the paper is organized as follows. In Section II, we offer a motivating example of how BalloonJVM helps FaaS developers. Then, in Section III, we outline our implementation of ballooning and while in Section IV, we describe GC principles that impact BalloonJVM. In Section V, we evaluate the feasibility of BalloonJVM using FaaS benchmarks, and in Section VI, we discuss the implications and limitations of our work. Later, we discuss related work in Section VII. Finally, in Section VIII, we conclude the paper.

II. Motivating Example

Consider a Java application on FaaS that provides a simple Key-Value (KV) store. Each request to the insertion function of the KV store allocates memory to insert a new object into an underlying hash map. Figure 1 shows the occupied heap memory compared to the total heap. Eventually, the memory allocated for objects in the KV store will reach the maximum heap size. In a regular JVM instance without ballooning, the application encounters an OOM exception. BalloonJVM ensures that a balloon, if one remains, is released before an OOM occurs. This increases the maximum heap available to the application, thus, evading the OOM.

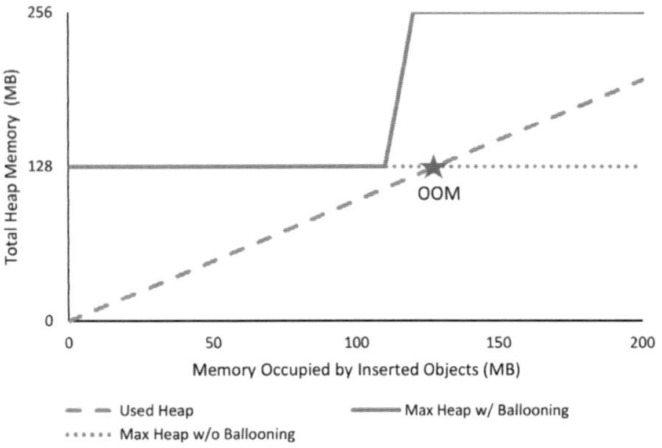

Figure 1. Avoiding an OOM exception with ballooning.

Without ballooning, the developer must ensure that the memory occupied by the KV store does not reach capacity in order to avoid a service disruption. To achieve this, the developer could either stop accepting new data, distribute insertions into another instance or write to a remote database. All of these options may prove to be more costly to the developer of a small upstart app than paying marginally more for dynamically increased heap space. BalloonJVM provides this latter option to developers, who wish to avoid infrastructure considerations for a simple deployment on FaaS.

III. Ballooning

BalloonJVM uses a variation of the memory ballooning technique, presented by OSv [7]. Unlike OSv, all of our ballooning features are exposed as a set of Java APIs, which are called by BalloonJVM to achieve ballooning. Our solution consists of two parts: *balloon insertion* and *balloon deletion*. BalloonJVM inserts balloons during the initialization of the JVM FaaS instance, while deleting balloons during the execution of JVM, between FaaS invocations.

A. Balloon Insertion

Balloon insertion is divided into two APIs: balloon *inflation* and *deflation*. Balloon inflation is the creation of the balloons in the JVM heap and unmapping them from the OS memory space. Balloon deflation involves the deallocation of OS memory occupied by balloons and returning it to the OS. Figure 2 shows balloon inflation in the first process, followed by balloon deflation in the second process. Balloons are implemented as a two dimensional Java byte array and are inflated and deflated natively through the Java Native Interface (JNI).

Balloon Inflation. Each balloon is created by allocating a single dimension array of a given balloon size in a 2D byte array. The memory held by the balloons is unmapped between JVM and the OS using the `munmap` system call, invoked through JNI. While the byte array represents used memory space to both JVM and the OS, JVM can no longer reference the balloon memory legally.

Balloon Deflation. After GC, each balloon is deallocated using the `madvise` system call with `MADV_DONTNEED` advice, through JNI. This advises the OS that the memory space occupied by the balloon is no longer needed in the near future. The OS has become aware that the balloon is free space.

After Balloon Insertion. At the end of balloon insertion, JVM holds references to inserted balloons and still thinks the balloon occupy their equivalent OS memory. However, through compacting, JVM will not touch the balloons during GC.

Compacting the Balloons. Once the balloons are inserted and deflated, it is important that the balloons are not moved by the Garbage Collector (GC) unless the corresponding JVM reference is also deleted. Otherwise, the mapped out pages may be mapped back in, resulting in a sudden jump in resident set size (RSS) and may lead to a JVM crash. To overcome this, we ensure that the balloons are inserted at the beginning of the old generation and compacted before deflation. We explicitly call GC multiple times to compact the inserted balloons and tenure them to the old generation. We verify that GC is actually invoked by analyzing the output of `jstat`, a JVM statistics monitoring tool. Additionally, the inflation and deflation of the balloons is implemented as a static block so that it executes before JVM runs `main()`, ensuring that the balloons are inserted before other objects are present. Note that our particular implementation is suitable for *Serial GC* and may not work for other garbage collectors.

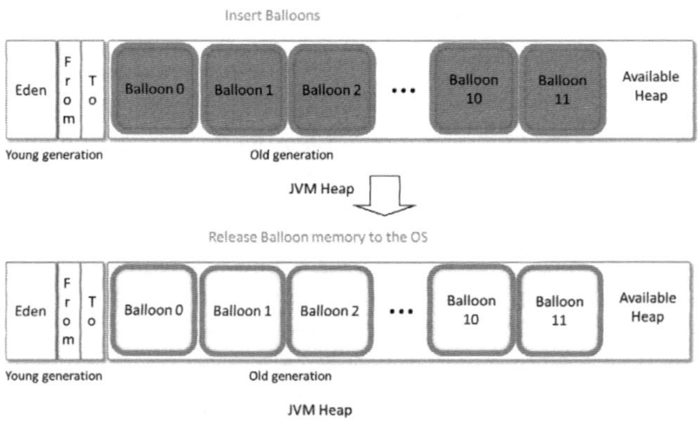

Figure 2. Balloon insertion.

B. Balloon Deletion

Our balloon deletion API calculates the amount of ballooned memory to release based on the size and number of balloons inserted. We also provide an option, Pre-Balloon Memory Utilization Ratio (PMUR), to control the memory used before balloons are deleted.

Implementation. The balloon deletion API is implemented by deleting the JVM reference to the balloon. This will trigger a GC, which frees up the Java heap space and allow JVM to reclaim memory from the OS. One shortcoming of balloon deletion, including our implementation, is the impact on JVM performance from the relative sizing of the old and young generation heap space [8]. In Section V, we empirically explore the feasibility of using different configurations on BalloonJVM to minimize this impact.

Size and Number of Balloons. Our insertion API provides options for the number of balloons to be inserted and the size of each balloon. We accept balloons of any size, as long as all balloons for a single configuration are equally sized. From this point onward, we refer to the current JVM maximum heap size as the container size in MB. We also represent this using the variable, C. For instance, we choose a balloon size of 128MB and insert 11 equally sized balloons in a max heap of 1.5GB. This sample configuration is aimed to support a container size of 128MB, with an eventual allowance to 1.5GB as heap usage grows. When JVM is initially started with a 128MB container, no balloons are deleted. When a 256MB container is needed, one balloon is deleted, and eventually for the 1.5GB container, all balloons are deleted.

Equation (1) determines the number of balloons for deletion, B_{del}, where C is the initial container size, H is the eventual max heap, B_{ins} is the number of balloons inserted, and S is the balloon size.

$$B_{del} = \max(\left\lceil \frac{C - (H - B_{ins} \times S)}{S} \right\rceil, 0) \quad (1)$$

Pre-Balloon Memory Utilization Ratio (PMUR). The PMUR is defined as the ratio between the memory used and the total heap memory available before a balloon is released, ranging from 0 to 1. If PMUR is close to 1, an OOM may occur before a balloon is released. If PMUR is too low, the developer will be forced to pay for a larger heap space, when free heap space is still available. We find that a value around 0.85 works best, through experimentation described in Section V-G.

IV. Garbage Collection (GC)

We observe that by tuning the generational heap, BalloonJVM can reduce time-consuming GCs, especially Full GCs.

Generation GC. Generational GC separates the heap into a new and old generation. Newly allocated objects that survive several rounds of GCs are tenured to the old generation [9]. Separate algorithms can be deployed for young and old objects to maximize the efficiency of the GC.

New Generation (NewGen). This section of heap is where all new objects are stored. It is further divided into the eden and survivor spaces. In this paper, we refer to the NewGen as the combination of the eden and survivor spaces. The eden space hosts the newly allocated objects before any GC occurs, while a pair of survivor spaces host objects that survive at least one GC, awaiting promotion to the old generation. BalloonJVM uses the parameters, `NewSize` and `MaxNewSize`, in Oracle JVM to control the NewGen size.

Old Generation (OldGen). This section of heap hosts objects that survived enough GCs to be considered old objects. GC events occur less frequently in the OldGen compared to the NewGen. BalloonJVM always ensures that balloons are tenured to the OldGen to exploit this property.

Young GC (YGC) and Full GC (FGC). *YGCs* clean up the new generation. Since objects in the new generation build up quickly, YGCs occur relatively frequently and its algorithms optimize for speed. *FGCs* clean up both the old and new generations. In contrast to YGCs, they occur infrequently - this allows its algorithms to optimize for space over speed. While both FGCs and YGCs consume execution time, FGCs typically take longer to run than YGCs.

GC Algorithm. There are several GC algorithms offered by Java 8, which BalloonJVM uses, but all of them are generational GCs. BalloonJVM uses Serial GC and we found that it compacts balloons sufficiently. Serial GC exhibits a stop-the-world behaviour, meaning it pauses the operation of the application. It is typically used for smaller heaps (i.e., heaps of 1.5GB or smaller) while faster algorithms like Parallel GC are used for large heaps [9]. Serial GC avoids synchronization overhead for tracking live objects, required in Parallel GC.

V. Evaluation

We evaluate BalloonJVM with respect to these questions.

1) Is it feasible for one configuration to support all containers?
2) How do we choose a NewGen size for BalloonJVM?
3) What is the feasibility of using two configurations?
4) Does BalloonJVM ensure that balloons are pinned?

A. Experimental Setup

The experiments are performed on an Intel Xeon CPU E5-2687W, which is a SandyBridge EP @ 3.0 GHz machine with 12 cores and with HyperThreading enabled. It has 30MB of L3 cache and 256GB of memory. Ubuntu 16.04 is used as the base OS together with Docker 1.12.6.

For the remainder of this paper, *DefaultJVM* refers to Oracle HotSpot 64-Bit Server VM version 1.8.0_151 with a fixed new to old generation heap ratio of 1:2, running on Huawei FunctionStage. We use DefaultJVM as our baseline as it is the most prevalent default configuration for JVM on the cloud [8]. *BalloonJVM* is DefaultJVM with ballooning enabled and a variable NewGen size. Both JVMs run in a cgroup, allowing the service provider to exploit namespace isolation, resource limitation, and checkpoint/restore [6]. Otherwise, a JVM in a cgroup behaves the same as a standalone JVM.

B. Benchmarks

We use eight different benchmarks that represent FaaS applications of varying workloads and domains [10]: `Allocation`, `DataFilter`, `Inverse`, `Sort`, `TF-IDF`, `ThumbNail`, `TimeStamp` and `Unzip`. We found a lack of benchmark suites for FaaS, so we manually adapted all of our benchmarks to lambda functions. Lambda functions for FaaS are typically self-contained, repetitive tasks that are triggered by external events and its execution cannot exceed a strict timeout. `Allocation` allocates 1MB of memory in a static array list for each service request. It represents the workload of memory intensive FaaS applications (i.e., a KV store). `DataFilter` filters an array of random words based on a search query, representing data querying. `Inverse` computes the inverse of a 9x9 matrix, used in machine learning. `Sort` sorts an array of random words alphabetically. `TF-IDF` computes the statistical importance of a word in relation to a document in a corpus. `Thumbnail` converts a JPEG photo into a thumbnail, representing multimedia processing applications. `TimeStamp` outputs the current datetime as a string. `Unzip` uncompresses a zip file, performing file I/O. `Inverse` and `ThumbNail` represent workload intensive applications while `TimeStamp` and `Unzip` represent light utility applications.

C. Metrics

We define a configuration as *feasible* if it has a low runtime overhead and a high *Actual Memory Utilization Ratio* (AMUR).

a) Runtime Overhead: We define this as the runtime performance overhead of BalloonJVM over DefaultJVM. FaaS functions deployed on BalloonJVM should not incur a high runtime overhead over a similar deployment in DefaultJVM. We measure the runtime duration of a benchmark function in nanoseconds, using `System.nanoTime()`. The runtime excludes the time taken for the FaaS framework to initialize since BalloonJVM uses a checkpoint and restore mechanism [6]. All of the runtime durations are averaged over 100 runs. The overhead is then computed by $(T_b - T_d)/T_d$, where T_b and T_d are the times taken to execute the same function in BalloonJVM and DefaultJVM, respectively.

b) Actual Memory Utilization Ratio (AMUR): The AMUR is defined as the percentage of actual used memory over the container memory size. The AMUR can help guide the selection of the PMUR, discussed in Section III-B. The actual used memory is measured by counting the maximum number of objects, with a size of 1MB each, which can be allocated before JVM throws an OOM exception. This metric provides an approximation of the total heap space utilization before either a balloon is freed or an OOM finally occurs when no further balloons can be freed. A larger AMUR frees fewer balloons, preserving server resources and allowing developers to be charged at a lower tier of memory usage.

D. Heap Flexibility at What Cost?

BalloonJVM provides memory benefits but at what overhead to DefaultJVM? To answer this, we measure the overhead of each request to `Allocation` until DefaultJVM reaches an OOM. We initialize BalloonJVM with a container size, C (MB) of 128, with a max heap of 512MB and DefaultJVM with a fixed heap of 128MB. We see in Figure 3 that the overhead is roughly 10% on average, but spikes at certain requests. We find that the spikes are correlated with GC events - the upwards spikes represent GCs invoked by BalloonJVM while the downward spikes represent GCs invoked by DefaultJVM. Hence, to improve the performance of BalloonJVM, we need to tune the heap parameters to reduce GCs. In this paper, we manually tune the heap using benchmark programs and determine the configuration's feasibility.

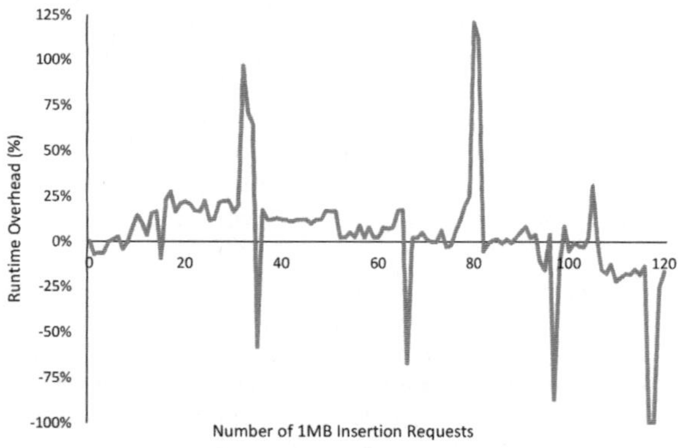

Figure 3. Overhead of BalloonJVM over DefaultJVM, at $C = 128$.

E. RQ1: Feasibility of a Single Configuration

In this section, we experimentally determine whether it is feasible to use a single max heap configuration, shown in Figure 4, to support C of 128, 256, 512, 1024 and 1536. To initialize our experiment, we allocate 110MB to the NewGen in order to maximize its use. In this single configuration, the eventual max heap size for BalloonJVM is 1536MB. The OldGen occupies the remainder of the heap, 1426MB, and is filled with 11 balloons of 128MB each. A NewGen of 110MB enables 18 MB of objects to be promoted to the OldGen for $C = 128$, while all 11 balloons remain. For $C = 256$, about 146MB of objects can be promoted to the OldGen with 10 balloons. Free OldGen space grows as balloons are released.

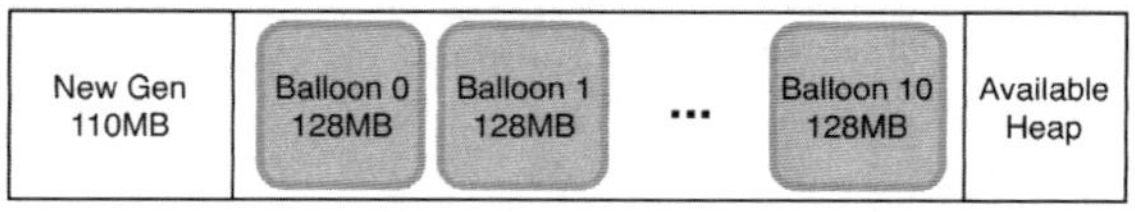

Figure 4. Single configuration, with an eventual max heap of 1.5GB.

We run the `Allocation` benchmark in DefaultJVM and BalloonJVM to measure the runtime overhead. As discussed in Section V-B, `Allocation` represents the most memory intensive application. As shown in Table I, the overheads for $C = 128, 1024, 1536$ exceed 10%. We then measure the YGC and FGC counts during the execution of the function in both JVMs using `jstat`. In Table I, we observe that `Allocation`, running in BalloonJVM, using $C = 1024$ and $C = 1536$, incur 9 and 15 extra YGCs respectively. $C = 128$ encounters an extra FGC. By inspecting the `jstat` output after each object inserted, we notice that the eden space is quickly exhausted. This is caused by insufficient memory for the NewGen, leading to frequent YGCs. Increasing the NewGen beyond 110MB is not practical to support the 128MB container, as there would be insufficient space for tenured objects and inserted balloons in the OldGen. Based on this observation, we conclude that a single configuration to support our range of container sizes is not feasible.

TABLE I. OVERHEADS AND GC COUNTS OF BALLOONJVM (B) VS DEFAULTJVM (D), USING `ALLOCATION` AND A SINGLE MAX HEAP.

C (MB)	Objs inserted	Overhead	YGC		FGC	
			D	B	D	B
128	100	13%	1	1	1	2
256	200	5%	2	2	1	1
512	400	6%	4	5	0	0
1024	800	21%	3	12	2	2
1536	1200	13%	3	18	4	2

F. RQ2: Choosing the NewGen Size

As shown in Figure 5, we partition the container sizes into two configuration groups, one for $C = 128, 256, 512$, and the other for $C = 1024, 1536$. For simplicity, we will refer to the former as Config A and the latter as Config B. Since a single configuration is not feasible, we wish to support the range of container sizes with as few partitions as possible, to reap the benefits of ballooning. It is important to note that the partition we made is only one possible combination - others may exist.

We explore the challenge of finding an appropriate NewGen size for the two configurations. For Config A, there is little leeway for choosing the NewGen size. A NewGen size of 110MB is feasible, as it provides just enough OldGen space for tenured objects. For Config B, there is an opportunity to increase the NewGen size in a max heap of 1.5GB. We measure the runtime overheads using three different NewGen sizes across eight benchmarks in Figure 6 for the 1024MB and Figure 7 for the 1536MB container sizes respectively. We observe that a 400MB NewGen size offers the lowest overhead for `Allocation`, while 200MB gives the lowest overhead for other benchmarks. `Allocation` contains a lambda class member variable, whose reference is retained between invocations. Other benchmarks contain mostly transient objects, which are deleted after an invocation. Benchmarks with many transient objects may benefit from a smaller NewGen as a YGC is triggered earlier, and tenured objects are subject to infrequent FGCs. Alternatively, a larger NewGen for such benchmarks can result in slower YGCs, by traversing objects that should be tenured. Despite this, the configuration overheads differ less than 10% in the worst case or 5% on average.

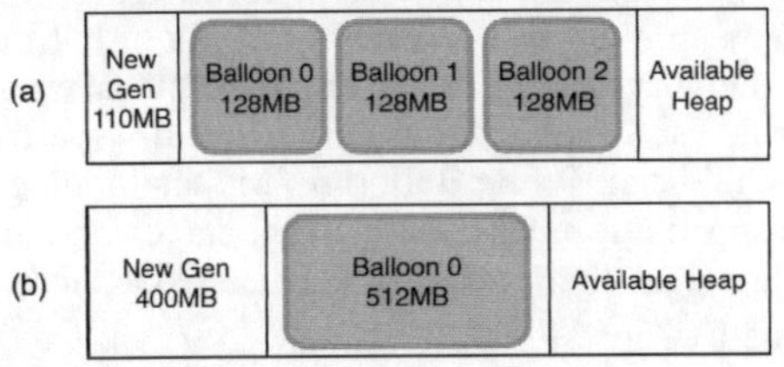

Figure 5. Two configurations approach. (a) Max heap of 512MB, with 3 balloons. (b) Max heap of 1.5GB, with 1 balloon.

TABLE II. NUMBER OF YGCS AND FGCS OF BALLOONJVM VS DEFAULTJVM, USING TWO CONFIGURATIONS.

Config	C (MB)	YGC		FGC	
		Default	Balloon	Default	Balloon
A	128	4	1	1	2
	256	4	3	3	2
	512	4	4	0	0
B	1024	3	3	2	2
	1536	3	4	4	3

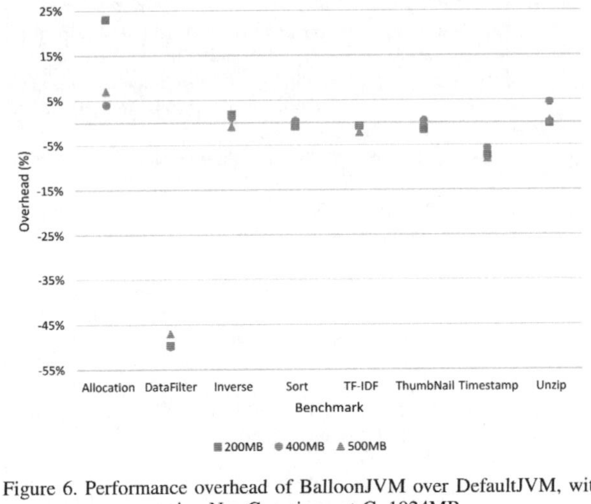

Figure 6. Performance overhead of BalloonJVM over DefaultJVM, with varying NewGen sizes, at C=1024MB.

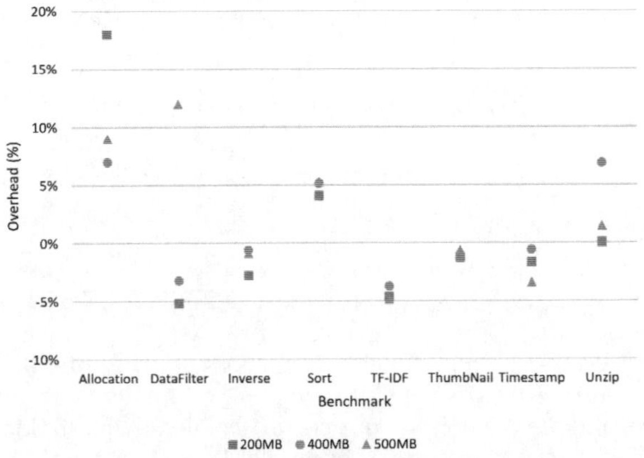

Figure 7. Performance overhead of BalloonJVM over DefaultJVM, with varying NewGen sizes, at C=1536MB.

G. RQ3: Feasibility of using Two Configurations

We evaluate the feasibility of using Config A and B with a NewGen of 400MB, for memory heavy workloads (i.e., `Allocation`).

First, we measure the AMURs of DefaultJVM and BalloonJVM as shown in Table III. We observe that BalloonJVM enables about the same amount of allocatable memory as DefaultJVM but the AMUR drops slightly in configurations with more balloons (i.e., $C = 128$ has 3 balloons vs. $C = 512$ has none). By analyzing the GC activity, we see that a FGC immediately follows a YGC whenever the OldGen is full, in this case, occupied by balloons. This bypasses the survivor space, reducing the overall usable heap memory.

Next, we measure the overhead of BalloonJVM against DefaultJVM across different container sizes using `Allocation`. To effectively evaluate BalloonJVM's performance, we condition `Allocation` to allocate a large number of objects, to approach its AMUR, and measure the overhead. As shown in Table IV, the overhead ranges from -56% to 14%. In some cases, benchmarks run faster in BalloonJVM than on DefaultJVM. In Table II, YGCs and FGCs drop sharply compared to the previous single configuration. Based on these observations, we conclude that this two configuration approach is feasible for allocation heavy workloads. However, the configuration feasibility does depend on the workload of the target applications.

TABLE III. AMUR OF BALLOONJVM AND DEFAULTJVM, USING TWO CONFIGURATIONS.

Config	C (MB)	Default	Balloon
A	128	94%	88%
	256	95%	93%
	512	97%	97%
B	1024	96%	95%
	1536	96%	97%

H. RQ4: Balloon Pinning

We evaluate BalloonJVM to determine whether the balloons inserted are properly pinned. If the balloons are not pinned, they may potentially move around the heap during GCs, causing the JVM RSS to jump abruptly. This will cause BalloonJVM to release balloons to compensate or crash JVM. We perform an experiment on only container sizes that have balloons. For Config A, this includes 128MB with 3

TABLE IV. OVERHEAD OF BALLOONJVM OVER DEFAULTJVM, USING TWO CONFIGURATIONS.

	C (MB)				
Config	A			B	
Benchmark	128	256	512	1024	1536
DataFilter	-56%	-11%	-11%	-50%	-3%
Inverse	-3%	-1%	-1%	1%	-1%
Sort	7%	5%	1%	0%	5%
TF-IDF	0%	-4%	-4%	-1%	-4%
ThumbNail	14%	-1%	1%	0%	-1%
Timestamp	4%	2%	5%	-6%	-1%
Unzip	4%	2%	2%	5%	7%

balloons and 256MB with 2 balloons. For Config B, this would be 1024MB with 1 balloon. For each eligible container, we allocate P MB of objects in the first request. In each subsequent request, we allocate A MB and randomly delete A MB of objects. The immediate allocation and deletion of large number of objects activates GC. We run the experiment on 128MB using $\{P = 95, A = 90\}$, 256MB using $\{P = 200, A = 150\}$, 1024MB using $\{P = 800, A = 500\}$ over 50k runs. We observe that the RSS remains consistent across all runs, showing that BalloonJVM's balloons are compact.

VI. DISCUSSION

A. Increased Flexibility

BalloonJVM offers increased flexibility to both the FaaS developer and cloud service provider. For the FaaS developer, BalloonJVM offers a safeguard when their application exceeds the initial maximum heap size. Developers may also deploy with a modest heap, and allow BalloonJVM to grow the heap as their application becomes more widely used. For the service provider, BalloonJVM allows improved resource sharing and adjustable price tiers. The memory occupied by balloons is directly returned to the OS, usable by other cloud applications. When multiple applications deployed on BalloonJVM release balloons, memory will be available on a first-come first-served basis. An OOM exception can occur if the actual memory is unavailable. Service providers can offer dynamic pricing where pricing jumps to the next tier when a balloon is freed.

B. Limitations

We identity three limitations to our work: the choice of GC algorithm, reinsertion of balloons, and the assumption of application functional correctness. We repeated our analysis by configuring both BalloonJVM and DefaultJVM to use Parallel GC, and found the runtime overheads to be feasible. However, we observe that RSS sharply increases as BalloonJVM fails to pin the balloons. This presents a challenge for deployment on large heaps where Parallel GC is desired over Serial GC. Secondly, BalloonJVM does not reinsert balloons after release, as we have not determined how to pin reinserted balloons when live data exists in the heap. Lastly, we assume that the FaaS application is functionally correct when requiring more memory. If the application erroneously consumes memory, BalloonJVM only delays its eventual failure through resizing.

VII. RELATED WORK

Ballooning is a widely used memory reclamation technique for VM memory management [4]. Ballooning to resize JVM's heap was first proposed in [7], which influenced the creation of BalloonJVM. However, our work differs in at least four major areas: we expose the features of ballooning as Java APIs rather than bundling it into an OS, we ensure that the inserted balloons are properly pinned by choosing a specific GC algorithm, we insert balloons before JVM is started without setting pressure criteria, and we implement ballooning for FaaS.

Salomie et al. [11] implement JVM ballooning by modifying the Parallel GC algorithm that is shipped with OpenJDK, requiring changes to the JVM internals. Hines et al. [12] present a framework called Ginkgo, which runs a background thread to monitor JVM heap usage and deletes or inserts balloons as needed. However, Java applications running on a Ginkgo resized JVM can experience high overhead as it does not consider the heap's generational nature.

VIII. CONCLUSION

Developers are choosing to deploy their applications on serverless architectures to avoid infrastructure costs. However, applications deployed on runtime environments like JVM are constrained by a maximum heap size. Developers either pay to overprovision or encounter a disruptive crash when the limit is exceeded. We present BalloonJVM, which utilizes ballooning, a memory reclamation technique, offering a dynamically resizable heap. Our results show that BalloonJVM can provide flexible memory benefits with less than 5% average overhead to typical FaaS applications, by carefully partitioning the generational heap. While BalloonJVM's ballooning implementation is specific for JVM, the concept can extend to other VM-based languages that constrain the heap size such as Node.js, another popular language for FaaS.

ACKNOWLEDGEMENT

We thank the anonymous reviewers and Tarek Abdelrahman for volunteering to provide feedback on our paper.

REFERENCES

[1] I. Baldini *et al.*, *Serverless Computing: Current Trends and Open Problems*. Springer, 2017, pp. 1–20.

[2] J. Jackson and L. Hecht, "TNS Guide to Serverless Technologies: The Best of FaaS and BaaS," http://thenewstack.io/guide-serverless-technologies-functions-backends-service, 2016, [Accessed: 21-Mar-2019].

[3] R. Buyya *et al.*, "A Manifesto for Future Generation Cloud Computing: Research Directions for the Next Decade," *CoRR*, pp. 105:1–105:38, 2017.

[4] C. A. Waldspurger, "Memory Resource Management in VMware ESX Server," *SIGOPS Oper. Syst. Rev.*, vol. 36, no. SI, pp. 181–194, 2002.

[5] Huawei, "Functionstage," https://www.huaweicloud.com/en-us/product/functionstage.html, [Accessed: 21-Mar-2019].

[6] K. Wang, R. Ho, and P. Wu, "Replayable Execution Optimized for Page Sharing for a Managed Runtime Environment," in *Proc. EuroSys'19*, 2019, pp. 39:1–39:16.

[7] A. Kivity *et al.*, "OSv: Optimizing the Operating System for Virtual Machines," in *Proc. USENIX ATC'14*, 2014, pp. 61–72.

[8] S. Sahin, W. Cao, Q. Zhang, and L. Liu, "JVM Configuration Management and Its Performance Impact for Big Data Applications," in *Proc. BigData Congress'16*, 2016, pp. 410–417.

[9] Sun Microsystems, "Memory Management in the Java HotSpot Virtual Machine," 2006.

[10] G. Fox, V. Ishakian, V. Muthusamy, and A. Slominski, "Status of Serverless Computing and Function-as-a-Service(FaaS) in Industry and Research," 2017.

[11] T. Salomie, G. Alonso, T. Roscoe, and K. Elphinstone, "Application Level Ballooning for Efficient Server Consolidation," in *Proc. EuroSys'13*, 2013, pp. 337–350.

[12] M. R. Hines, A. Gordon, M. Silva, D. D. Silva, K. Ryu, and M. Ben-Yehuda, "Applications Know Best: Performance-Driven Memory Overcommit with Ginkgo," in *Proc. CloudCom'11*, 2011, pp. 130–137.

Efficient Virtual Machine Consolidation Approach Based on User Inactivity Detection

Jan Fesl
Institute of Applied Informatics
Faculty of Science
University of South Bohemia
České Budějovice, Czech Republic
email: jfesl@prf.jcu.cz

Vineet Gokhale
Institute of Applied Informatics
Faculty of Science
University of South Bohemia
České Budějovice, Czech Republic
email: vgokhale@prf.jcu.cz

Marie Feslová
Institute of Applied Informatics
Faculty of Science
University of South Bohemia
České Budějovice, Czech Republic
email: dolezm05@prf.jcu.cz

***Abstract*—Large cloud architectures consist of numerous high-performance servers, each hosting a multitude of Virtual Machines (VMs). Naturally, the server resources for processing and storage are shared among VMs, which, in turn, could be simultaneously accessed by several authorized users. Resource reallocation takes place after a session terminates. However, failure of systematic session termination causes blockage of resources resulting in severe under-utilization. In order to mitigate such scenarios, one needs to efficiently detect user inactivity for timely release of the resources. This is a non-trivial task. To this end, we propose a hybrid resource-desktop monitoring technique, which involves capturing of user interaction with the client computer, in addition to monitoring the client-server network activity. The rationale behind this approach is that even in case of lightweight applications, the user interactions cause continuous changes in the visual contents being displayed. Periodic screenshots of the client screen and network activity between client and server provide crucial information about the user inactivity. Our preliminary investigation suggests that such self-organizing virtualization infrastructure is a promising direction for the design of modern cloud-based services.**

Keywords – cloud; consolidation; neural network.

I. INTRODUCTION

Cloud-based provisioning of memory and computational resources has proved to be one of the profound inventions of modern-day computer science. Such resources are typically available for usage to clients round the clock. One such example of cloud-based applications is Virtual Machine (VM). Entities known as virtualization servers host multiple VMs, hosted on, allowing multiple users to share the server resources simultaneously. Typically, the resources allocated to a VM are pre-configured by the system administrator. The degree of resource utilization of a VM depends solely on the type of applications being executed by its clients. Naturally, when the resources are underutilized it makes sense to re-allocate them to other VMs hosting more resource demanding applications. Moreover, very often, it is imperative to relocate certain VMs to another virtualization server with spare resources for optimization of power consumption. Such live migration of VMs, as well as re-allocation of resources across VMs in the same virtualization server is commonly referred to as *consolidation*.

After the completion of a virtual session, the virtualization server consolidates the resources tied to the *inactive* VMs to other VMs. However, in a vast majority of cases the human user leaves the session without properly terminating it, resulting in severe underutilization of the server resources. In order to mitigate such sub-optimal utilization of resources, one needs to monitor the utilization of VM, and be able to distinguish between durations of user activity and inactivity. In case of *active* VM, the resource configuration remains unchanged, whereas for instances of substantially long user inactivity, the VM can be characterized as inactive and subsequently subjected to the resource reallocation process.

Once a VM is characterized as inactive, it can be hibernated or powered off. Occasionally, if all the VMs in a virtualization server are relocated or powered off, the entire virtualization server itself can be hibernated. This step dramatically reduces the overall power consumption. In an earlier work, we proposed a novel consolidation technique [1]. However, literature also contains a fair volume of work in this domain; see, for example, [12]-[14].

The detection of state (active, inactive) of a VM is a non-trivial problem, since it is characterized by complex combinations of a gamut of parameters. The existing works take into account the parameters like memory and processor consumption of VM, network throughput of VM, login metadata, among others. Although the aforementioned works demonstrate that these parameters characterize the VM-state fairly well, we identify two more parameters that can be used for VM-state detection with higher efficiency and reliability - VM screenshot variations and VM-client network traffic profile. In this paper, we propose a novel scheme for reliable detection of VM-state that integrates the proposed new parameters with the existing ones in order to efficiently detect the current VM-state with high reliability. Our scheme treats VM as a black box, in the sense that no virtual machine introspection [2] needs to be done. All parameters used for VM-state detection are retrieved directly from hypervisors or external network devices. This simplifies the design considerations significantly.

The organization of the paper is as follows. In Section II, we provide an overview of the existing literature relevant to our work. In Section III, we describe in detail our approach for characterization of the VM state, and in Section IV, we explain our proposed approach for inactivity detection of VMs. We present preliminary measurements in Section V, and finally state our conclusions in Section VI.

II. RELATED WORK

VM-state detection is a topic that is actively being researched in the recent past; see, for example, [3]-[6]. Literature suggests that there exist primarily three main approaches of VM-state detection as follows.

A. Utilization-based approach: This approach is the most intuitive of all. The VM monitor, known as hypervisor, is able to provide certain information on the run-time behavior of a VM. The VM characteristics (VMC) are mostly represented as 4-D vector of items.

VMC = {CPU utilization [%], memory utilization [MB], network throughput [Mbit/s], and I/O operation count [number]}.

The existing works use a subset of VMC parameters for VM-state detection. Solution like Pulsar [7], which is a part of OpenStack-Nova, uses just only the CPU utilization. When the CPU utilization is below a specific threshold, the system marks the VM as "inactive". Another scheme [8] leverages CPU utilization, memory utilization, and network throughput for determining the state of a VM.

B. Rule-based approach: This approach means that the data center operators define some set of heuristics, which help to identify the unused virtual machine. Typical example of such approach implementation is the NetFlix service Janitor Monkey [9]. The similar approach is used in the next solution, which is called Poncho [10]. In Poncho, the rules are not defined as global, but only for a specific workload.

C. Graph-based approach: This approach has been inspired by some programming languages like Java, C# or Python. Such languages use virtual environment for the execution of byte code compiled applications. Their garbage collectors for automated memory management identify objects "to be cleaned" by examining object references. The resource dependencies are mostly represented by acyclic graphs. In many cases, standalone cloud resources – having no dependency on other cloud resources – cannot necessarily be identified as unused resources by only using resource dependencies. In other words, some VMs can cooperate with others, but this situation cannot be easily represented in the graph. Some graph-based systems are Pleco [4] and Garbo [5].

III. CHARACTERIZATION OF VM-STATE

In this section, we describe in detail the rationale behind the selection of important features for characterization of the VM-state and explain the VM-state detection metric for each feature.

A. Resource utilization of VM: Many existing works [7][8] in the literature have experimentally demonstrated that monitoring the local resources of VM like CPU and RAM usage, as well as the overall network activity can characterize the VM-state detection fairly accurately. In this work, we adopt the strategies proposed by the aforementioned prior works. Let C denote CPU usage of VM, M denote the ratio of memory currently being utilized to total memory capacity of VM. Let N denote the current network throughput related to maximal network throughput. The overall VM utilization (U) can then be expressed as shown Eq. (1).

$$U = \frac{1}{(1-C)(1-N)(1-M)} \tag{1}$$

B. Client-VM network activity: In order to optimally utilize the communication network between client and VM, any standard terminal service, like Remote Desktop Protocol (RDP) and Secure SHell (SSH), transfers only incremental information. For example, when the user continuously interacts with the VM, the contents to be displayed to the client change relentlessly, and hence large number of packets are exchanged. On the other hand, when the changes are insignificant, packets are transmitted occasionally. For instance, when the user is reading a document with negligible/less amount of mouse scrolling, the displayed contents remain predominantly unchanged. Since no significant information needs to be exchanged, the packet transmissions are sparse. On the other hand, if a multimedia file is being played at VM, irrespective of the display contents packets need to be constantly exchanged. Note that the overall network activity discussed previously subsumes the network activity between client and VM. However, it should be noted that some activities, like installation of software updates at VM that generate substantial network activity, may not be of interest from the client's perspective. Therefore, monitoring the network activity between client and VM, in addition to overall network activity, provides fine-grained network information which can be utilized in precisely characterizing the current state of VM. Terminal service activity can be expressed as follows. TR_h is an empirically set number of packets, which must be reached for flow activity detection. TR_h is an empirical value related to a specific time interval (t). The overall measurement time consists of K number t intervals. For each t interval, can be measured current count of packets C_t. If $C_t < TR_h$ then such TI is marked as "inactive". The total inactivity T [%] can be deduced as shown in Eq. (2).

$$T = \frac{\#\ of\ inactivity\ intervals}{\#\ of\text{total}\ intervals} \tag{2}$$

Necessary information about the traffic from network devices alike switches or routers can be provided via NETFLOW/IPFIX protocol, which does not affect the routers performance.

C. VM screenshot: We refer to the contents of the VM that are currently being displayed to the client. The Hypervisor creates a VM screenshot from the content of virtual graphic card memory. The idea behind using VM screenshot as an important parameter in VM-state detection is that whenever the user interacts actively with VM, the display contents keep changing continuously. Therefore, as a preliminary the differential information in consecutive screenshots can be utilized to detect the VM-state. Screenshots with same dimensions are generated periodically by the Hypervisor. Let S_k denote the kth screenshot. It is important to remark that our approach considers only the differential information in consecutive screenshots, and not the actual display contents themselves. This also reduces the computational load significantly. Let D_k denote the differential information between S_{k+1} and S_k as shown in Eq. (3).

$$DS(x,y) = C(x,y) - P(x,y) \tag{3}$$

An example of differential screenshot can be seen in Figure 1. From single differential screenshots, it is possible to assemble the sequence of differential screenshots.

We created a supervised learning-based classifier which is capable of analyzing if a screenshot change indicates the activity/inactivity of the user, as shown in Figure 2. For the analysis, we used deep convolutional network, which is able automatically to take into the account the position of change - for example clock on the desktop taskbar can cause the misinterpretation.

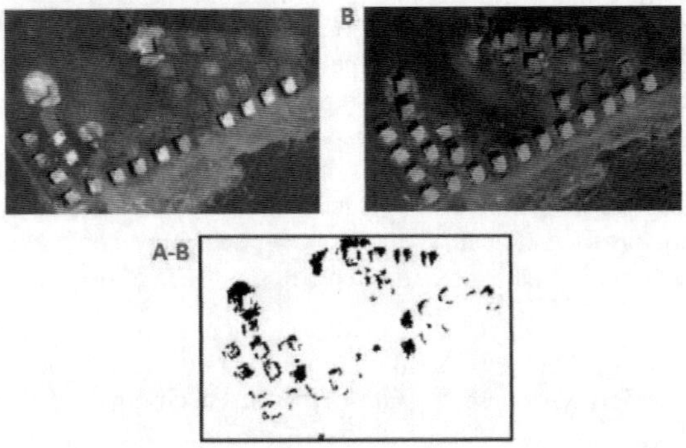

Fig. 1: Pixel differential image, which serves as an input for deep convolutional network. Such neural networks are able to detect the change and position of change as well.

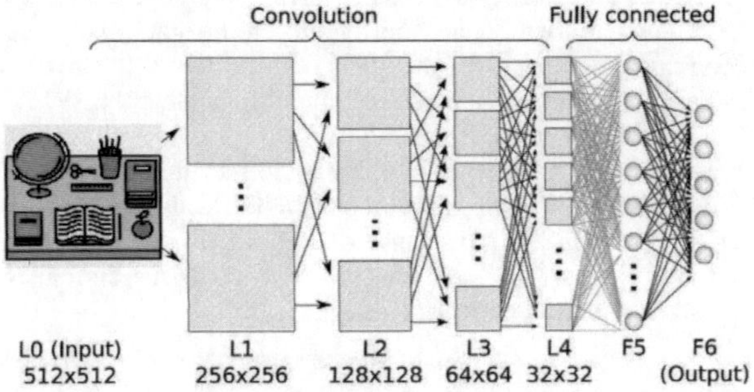

Fig. 2: Deep convolutional network used for image change classification is able to take into the account the position of change.

All differential screenshots from DS are being classified by the neural network. The result of classification is N-1 D vector of values, which expresses the probability (PI) of user inactivity for every screenshot as shown in Eq. (4).

$$PI = \{PI_1, PI_2, \ldots, PI_N\} \quad (4)$$

The average probability (P) for entire period can be computed as shown in Eq. (5).

$$P = \left(\frac{1}{N-1}\right) * \sum_{i=1}^{N-1} PI_i \quad (5)$$

P value is used in the decision three, which will be described in the next section.

IV. VM-STATE DETECTION

In this section, we present the description of the design and working principle of the proposed VM-state detection scheme.

In Figure 3, we present the architecture of a typical distributed virtualization infrastructure, along with the proposed VM-state detection elements. The clients connect to their respective VMs via a specific terminal service, like RDP or SSH. All these connections go via an IPFIX-enabled router and are monitored by a firewall. In order to relieve the VMs of monitoring the traffic stream from VM to clients, we use IPFIX [11] - a standard protocol for capturing network flows crossing the routers. The router can capture specific flow information, and subsequently report to VM Consolidator (VMC) - the principal component of the architecture. VMC coordinates with VMs and virtualization servers in order to receive vital parameters necessary for characterization of VM-state discussed in Section III. The possibility to see user screen must be supported by hypervisor.

As mentioned previously, we consider the following parameters for detection of the current state of VM: user-induced on-screen changes, network activity between client and VM, processing and memory resource consumption of VM, and overall network activity of VM. We now move to the characterization of VM-state based on the measurement of the aforementioned parameters. We propose a hierarchical VM state detection technique based on learning via ANN that classifies the current state of the VM through the aforementioned parameters using the decision tree shown in Figure 4.

Let p_n and p_{Tn} denote the decision metric and the corresponding threshold at the nth stage of the decision tree. In the first stage, we take the VM screenshot variation as the evaluation parameter for decision making. On-screen visual changes refer to the changes reflecting on the VM screen when the user interacts with the virtual computer. Therefore, if on-screen changes are significantly high, then the VM is in use with higher likelihood. If $p_1 < p_{T1}$ (indicating that VM screenshot variations are significant), we treat this as the sufficient condition to infer that the VM is active. Hence, further analysis is unnecessary, thereby relieving the monitoring node (MN) of resource-heavy computations. If $p_1 \geq p_{T1}$ (indicating negligible variations), we trigger subsequent stages of analysis.

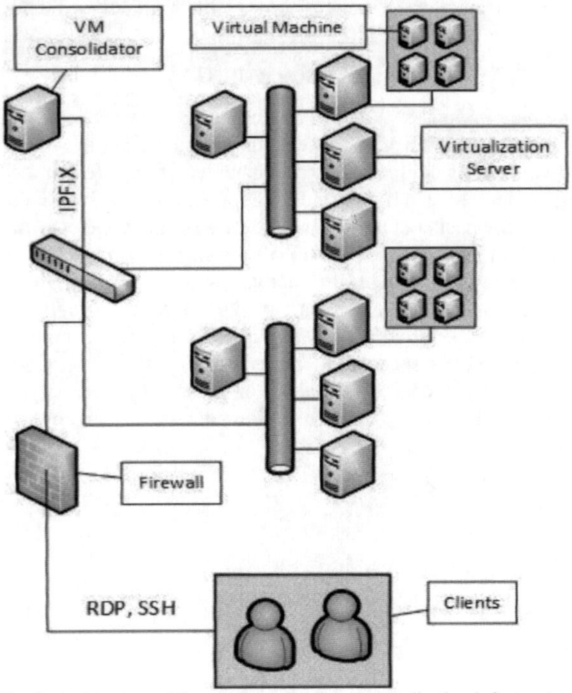

Fig. 3: Architecture of the proposed distributed virtualization infrastructure featuring clients, VMs, virtualization servers, VM consolidator, and IPFIX-enabled router.

In the second stage, we consider the client-VM network traffic profile, in addition to p_1 for characterizing the VM-state. If $p_2 < p_{T2}$ (indicating that the network activity is significant), then we infer that the VM is in active state. However, if $p_2 \geq p_{T2}$ (indicating negligible network activity), we move to the last stage of analysis.

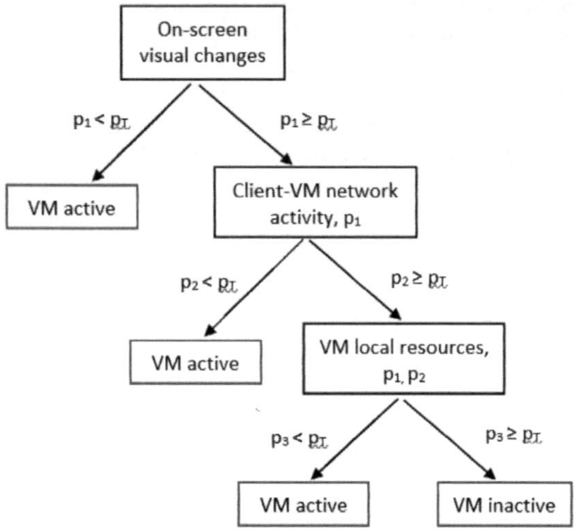

Fig. 4: Decision tree illustrating the working of proposed hierarchical VM state detection. p_n denotes the probability of VM being inactive as per the parameters considered in n^{th} stage.

In the last stage, we consider the resource utilization profile of VM for the decision making. If $p_3 < p_{T3}$ (indicating that the resource utilization is significant), then we infer that the VM is in active state. However, if $p_3 \geq p_{T3}$ (indicating negligible resource utilization), we conclude that the VM is in inactive state. This results in the hibernation of VM, and subsequent re-allocation of the resources across other VMs located in the virtualization server.

V. MEASUREMENTS

In this section, we report a preliminary measurement of packet count from VM to client for demonstrating the proof-of-concept of the proposed VM-state detection. We initiated a session between a VM and a client. In order to be able to notice the packet count variation between client and VM, we divide the user interaction into three types - *active*, *semi-active*, and *passive*. In active interaction, the user continuously performs certain tasks on VM through I/O devices. In semi-active interaction, the user only plays a multimedia content in VM, but performs no other interaction through input devices. Finally, tin passive interaction, the user simply reads a document without scrolling through it. Figure 5 presents the histogram of transmitted packets recorded during the session.

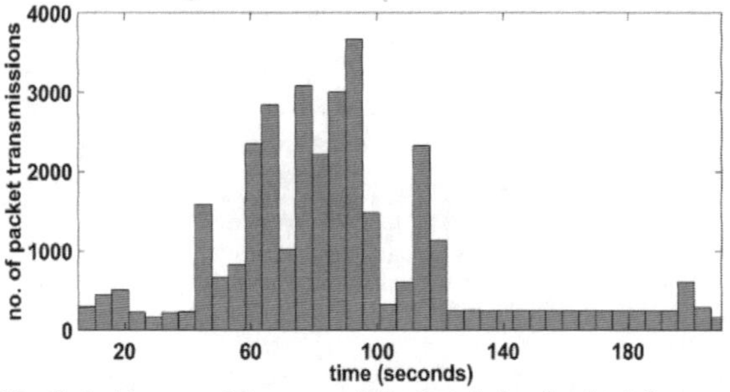

Fig. 5: Architecture of the proposed distributed virtualization infrastructure featuring clients, VMs, virtualization servers, VM consolidator, and IPFIX-enabled router.

We ask the user to perform active, semi-active, and passive interactions sequentially. In the first part of the plot, it can be seen that the packet count is significantly high indicating dense packet transmissions between VM and client during active interaction. Next, the packet transmissions are relatively sparse but non-negligible, indicating considerable traffic during semi-active interaction. Finally, the packet transmissions are near-zero indicating negligible traffic during passive interaction. This suggests that monitoring the traffic profile between VM and client could play a crucial role in accurately and efficiently determining the VM-state.

As a next step of this work, we plan to implement the proposed scheme on a real cloud infrastructure and compare its performance with state-of-the-art techniques in the domain.

VI. CONCLUSIONS

In this paper, we proposed a novel VM-state detection strategy in which two new parameters were introduced - VM screenshot and VM-client traffic profile. We described how these new parameters can improve up on the state-of-the-art techniques. We proposed the architecture of our scheme, and also proposed the usage of deep convolutional neural network for classification of VM-state. Through preliminary measurements, we demonstrated that monitoring the network activity between VM and client could lead to efficient performance. In the next phase of the project, we intend to perform extensive verification of our proposal and also improve the neural network classifier.

ACKNOWLEDGEMENT

The authors would like to thank the Technological Agency of Czech Republic for financing the current research, and Mr. Jiří Cehák for his assistance in system administration and management.

REFERENCES

[1] J. Fesl, J. Cehák, M. Doležalová, and J. Janeček, "New approach for virtual machines consolidation in heterogeneous computing systems", International Journal of Hybrid Information Technology, vol. 9, pp. 321–332, 2016.

[2] K. Nance, B. Hay, and M. Bishop., "Virtual Machine Introspection: Observation or Interference?", IEEE Security & Privacy, 6(5), pp. 32–37, September 2008.

[3] K. Kim, S. Zeng, Ch. Young, J. Hwang, and M. Humphre, "iCSI: A Cloud Garbage VM Collector for Addressing Inactive VMs with Machine Learning", IEEE International Conference on Cloud Engineering, 2017.

[4] Z. Shen, Ch. C. Young, S. Zeng, K. Murthy, and K. Bai, "Identifying Resources for Cloud Garbage Collection", 12th International Conference on Network and Service Management (CNSM), Montreal, 2016.

[5] B. Zhang, Y. Al-Dhuraibi, R. Rouvoy, F. Paraiso, and L. Seinturier "CloudGC: Recycling Idle Virtual Machines in the Cloud", IEEE International Conference on Cloud Engineering (IC2E), Vancouver, 2017.

[6] N. Cohen and A. Bremler-Barr., "Garbo: Graph-based Cloud Resource Cleanup", ACM Symposium on Cloud Computing (SoCC '15), Kohala Coast, Hawaii, USA, August 2015.

[7] D. Breitgand et al. "An Adaptive Utilisation Accelerator for Virtualized Environments", 2nd IEEE International Conference on Cloud Engineering (IC2E '14), Boston, MA, USA, March 2014.

[8] T. Wood, P. Shenoy, A. Venkataramani, and M. Yousif, "Black-box and Gray-box Strategies for Virtual Machine Migration", 4th USENIX Symposium on Networked Systems Design and Implementation (NSDI '07), Cambridge, MA, USA, April 2007.

[9] Netflix, Janitor Monkey, https://github.com/Netflix/SimianArmy/wiki/Janitor-Home, available online, Jan. 2015.

[10] S. Devoid, N. Desai, and L Hochstein, "Poncho: Enabling Smart Administration of Full Private Cloud", 27th USENIX Large Installation System Administration Conference (LISA '13), Washington D.C., USA, November 2013.

[11] IPFIX protocol specification, https://tools.ietf.org/html/rfc7011, available online, Sep. 2013.

[12] F. Farahnakian, P. Liljeberg, and J. Plosila, "Energy-Efficient Virtual Machines Consolidation in Cloud Data Centers using Reinforcement Learning", 22nd Euromicro International Conference on Parallel, Distributed, and Network-Based Processing, 2014.

[13] Z. Cao and S. Dong, "An energy-aware heuristic framework for virtual machine consolidation in Cloud computing", The Journal of Supercomputing, Volume 69, Issue 1, pp 429–451, Springer, 2014.

[14] E. Feller, L. Rilling, C. Morin, "Energy-aware ant colony-based workload placement in Clouds", Proceeding GRID'11 proceedings of the 2011 IEEE/ACM 12th international conference on grid computing. IEEE Computer Society, Washington, DC, pp 26–33, 2011.

Anomaly Detection and Analysis for Clustered Cloud Computing Reliability

Areeg Samir
Faculty of Computer Science
Free University of Bozen-Bolzano
Bolzano, Italy
Email: areegsamir@unibz.it

Claus Pahl
Faculty of Computer Science
Free University of Bozen-Bolzano
Bolzano, Italy
Email: Claus.Pahl@unibz.it

***Abstract*—Cloud and edge computing allow applications to be deployed and managed through third-party provided services that typically make virtualised resources available. However, often there is no direct insight into execution parameters at resource level, and only some quality factors can be directly observed while others remain hidden from the consumer. We investigate a framework for autonomous anomaly analysis for clustered cloud or edge resources. The framework determines possible causes of consumer-observed anomalies in an underlying provider-controlled infrastructure. We use Hidden Markov Models to map observed performance anomalies to hidden resources, and to identify the root causes of the observed anomalies in order to improve reliability. We apply the model to clustered hierarchically organised cloud computing resources.**

***Index Terms*—Cloud Computing; Edge Computing; Container Cluster; Hidden Markov Model; Anomaly; Performance.**

I. Introduction

Cloud and edge computing allow applications to be deployed and managed by third parties based on provided virtualised resources [2],[3]. Due to the dynamicity of computation in cloud and edge computing, consumers may experience anomalies in performance caused by the distributed nature of clusters, heterogeneity, or scale of computation on underlying resources that may lead to performance degradation and application failure: (1) change in cluster node workload demand or configuration updates may cause dynamic changes, (2) reallocation or removal of resources may affect the workload of system components. Recent works on anomaly detection [1],[4],[5] have looked at resource usage, rejuvenation or analyzing the correlation between resource consumption and abnormal behaviour of applications. However, more work is needed on identifying the reason behind observed resource performance degradations.

In a shared virtualised environment, some factors can be directly observed (e.g., application performance) while others remain hidden from the consumer (e.g., reason behind the workload changes, the possibility of predicting the future load, dependencies between affected nodes and their load). In this paper, we investigate the possible causes of performance anomalies in an underlying provider-controlled cloud infrastructure. We propose an anomaly detection and analysis framework for clustered cloud and edge environments that aims at automatically detecting possibly workload-induced performance fluctuations, thus improving the reliability of these architectures. We assume a clustered, hierarchically organised environment with containers as loads on the individual nodes, similar to container cluster solutions like Docker Swarm or Kubernetes.

System workload states that might be hidden from the consumer may represent anomalous or faulty behaviour that occurs at a point in time or lasts for a period of time. An anomaly may represent undesired behaviour such as overload or also appreciated positive behaviour like underload (the latter can be used to reduce the load from overloaded resources in the cluster). Emissions from those states (i.e., observations) indicate the possible occurrence of failure resulting from a hidden anomalous state (e.g., high response time). In order to link observations and the hidden states, we use Hierarchical Hidden Markov Models (HHMMs) [8] to map the observed failure behaviour of a system resource to its hidden anomaly causes (e.g., overload) in a hierarchically organised clustered resource configuration. Hierarchies emerge as a consequence of a layered cluster architecture that we assume based on a clustered cloud computing environment. We aim to investigate, how to analyse anomalous resource behaviour in clusters consisting of nodes with application containers as their load from a sequence of observations emitted by the resource.

This paper is organized as follows. Section II provided the related work. Section III explores our wider anomaly management framework. Section IV details the anomaly detection and fault analysis. Section V discusses evaluation concerns, followed by conclusions an future work.

II. Related Work

Several studies [9] and [5] have addressed workload analysis in dynamic environments. Sorkunlu et al. [10] identified system performance anomalies through analyzing the correlations in the resource usage data. Peiris et al. [11] analyzed the root causes of performance anomalies by combining the correlation and comparative analysis techniques in distributed environments. Dullmann et al. [12] provided an online performance anomaly detection approach that detects anomalies in performance data based on discrete time series analysis. Wang et al. [5] proposed to model the correlation between workload and the resource utilization of applications to characterize the system status. However, the technique neither classifies the different types of workloads, or recovers the anomalous behaviour. Maurya and Ahmad [14] proposed an algorithm that dynamically estimates the load of each node and migrates the task on the basis of predefined constraint. However, the algorithm migrates the jobs from the overloaded nodes to the underloaded one through working on pair of nodes, it uses a server node as a hub to transfer the load information in the network which may result in overhead at the node.

Many literatures used HMM, and its derivations to detect anomaly. In [15], the author proposed various techniques implemented for the detection of anomalies and intrusions in the network using HMM. Ge et al. [17] detected faults in real-time embedded systems using HMM through describe the healthy and faulty states of a system's hardware components. In [20] HMM is used to find which anomaly is part of the same anomaly injection scenarios.

III. Self-Adaptive Fault Management

Our ultimate goal is a self-adaptive fault management framework [7],[6],[21] for cloud and edge computing that automatically identifies anomalies by locating the reasons for degradations of performance, and making explicit the dependency between observed failures and possible faults cause by the underlying cloud resources.

A. The Fault Management Framework

Our complete framework consists of two models: (1) Fault management model that detects and identifies anomalies within the cloud system. (2) Recovery model that applies a recovery mechanism considering the type of the detected anomaly and the resource capacity. Figure 1 presents the overall approach. The focus in this paper is on the Fault management model.

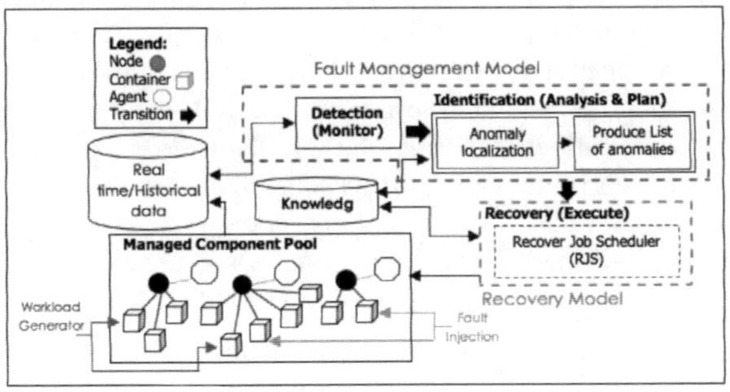

FIGURE 1. THE PROPOSED FAULT MANAGEMENT FRAMEWORK.

The cloud resources consist of a cluster, which composed of a set of nodes that host application containers as loads deployed on them. Each node has an agent that can deploy containers and discover container properties. We use the container notion to embody some basic principles of container cluster solutions [13] such as Docker Swarm or Kubernetes, to which we aim to apply our framework ultimately.

We align the framework with the Monitor Analysis, Plan, Execute based on the anomaly detection Knowledge (MAPE-K) feedback control loop. Monitor, collects data regarding the performance of the system as the observable state of each resource [16]. This can later be used to compare the detected status with the currently observed one. Each anomalous state has a weight (probability of occurrence). An identification step is followed by the detection to locate the root cause of anomaly (Analysis and Plan). The identified anomalous state is added to a queue that is ordered based on its assigned weight to signify urgency of healing. Knowledge about anomalous states are kept on record. Different recovery strategies (Execute) can mitigate the detected anomalies. Different pre-defined thresholds for recovery activities are assigned to each anomaly category based on observed response time failures.

The detection of an anomaly is based on using historical performance data to determine probabilities. We classify system data into two categories. The first one reflects observed system failures (essentially regarding permitted response time), and the second one indicates the (hidden) system faults related to workload fluctuations (e.g., by containers consuming a resource). We further annotate each behavioural category to reflect the severity of anomalous behaviour within the system, and the probability of its occurrence. The response time behaviour captures the amount of time taken from sending a request until receiving the response (e.g., creating container(s) within a node). For example, observed response time can fluctuate. The classified response time should be linked to the failure behaviour within system resources (i.e., CPU) to address unreliable behaviour. We can also classify the resource workload into normal (NL), overload (OL), underload (UL) categories to capture workload fluctuations.

B. Anomaly Detection and Identification

Anomaly detection, the Monitoring stage in MAPE-K, collects and classifies system data. It compares new collected data with previous observations based on the specified rules in the Knowledge component. Fault identification, the Analysis and Plan stages in MAPE-K, identifies the fault type and its root cause to explain the anomalous behaviour. The main aim of this step is specifying the dependency between faults (the proliferation of an anomaly within the managed resources), e.g., an inactive container can cause another container to wait for input. We use Hierarchical Hidden Markov models (HHMM) [8], a doubly stochastic model for hierarchical structures of data to identify the source of anomalies.

Based on the response time emissions, we track the path of the observed states in each observation window. Once we diagnose anomalous behaviour, the affected nodes will be annotated with a weight, which is a probability of fault occurrence for an observed performance anomaly. Nodes that have a high workload will be prioritised in the later fault handling based on the assigned weight. Nodes with the same weight can be addressed based on a first-detected-first-healed basis. In order to illustrate the usefulness of this analysis, we will also discuss the fault handling and recovery in the next subsection. Afterwards, we define the HHMM model structure and the analysis process in detail.

C. Fault Handling and Recovery

After detecting and identifying faults, a recovery mechanism, the Execute stage in MAPE-K, is applied to carry out load balancing or other suitable remedial actions, aiming to improve resource utilization. Based on the type of the fault, we apply a recovery mechanism that considers the dependency between nodes and containers. The recovery mechanism is based on current and historic observations of response time for a container as well as knowledge about hidden states (containers or nodes) that might have been learned. The objective of this step is to self-heal the affected resource. The recovery step receives an ordered weighted list of faulty states. The assigned probability of each state based on a predefined threshold is used to identify the right healing mechanism, e.g., to achieve fair workload distribution.

We specify the recovery mechanism using the following aspects: **Analysis**: relies on e.g., current observation, historic observation. **Observation**: indicates the type of observed failure (e.g., low response time). **Anomaly**: reflects the kind of fault (e.g., overload). **Reason**: explains the root causes of the problem. **Remedial Action**: explains the solution that can be applied to solve the problem. **Requirements**: steps and constraints that should be considered to apply the action(s). We will apply this to two sample strategies below.

D. Motivating Failure/Fault Cases and Recovery Strategies

In the following, we present two samples failure-fault situations, and suitable recovery strategies. The recovery strategies are applied based on the observed response time (current and historic observations), and its related hidden fault states. We illustrate two sample cases–overloaded neighbouring container and node overload.

1) Container Neighbour Overload (external dependency)

Analysis: based on current/historic observations, hidden states
Observation: low response time at the connected containers (overall failure to need performance targets).
Anomaly: overload in one or more containers results in underload for another container at different node.
Reason: heavily loaded container with external dependent one (communication)
Remedial Actions: *Option 1*: Separate the overloaded container and the external one depending on it from their nodes. Then, create a new node containing the separated containers considering the cluster capacity. Redirect other containers that in communication to these 2 containers in the new node. Connect current nodes with the new one, and calculate the probability of the whole model to know the number of transitions (to avoid the occurrence of overload), and to predict the future behaviour. *Option 2*: For the anomalous container, add a new one to the node that has the anomalous container to provide fair workload distribution among containers considering the node resource limits. Or, if the node does not yet reach the resource limits available, move the overloaded container to another node with free resource limits. At the end, update the node. *Option 3*: create another node within the node with anomalous container behaviour. Next, direct the communication of current containers to this node. We need to redetermine the probability of the whole model to redistribute the load between containers. Finally, update the cluster and the nodes. *Option 4*: distribute load. *Option 5*: rescale node. *Option 6*: do nothing, if the observed failure relates to regular system maintenance/update, then no recovery is applied.
Requirements: need to consider node capacity.

2) Node overload (self-dependency)

Analysis: current and historic observations
Observation: low response time at node level (a failure).
Anomaly: overloaded node.
Reason: limited node capacity.
Remedial Actions: *Option 1*: distribute load. *Option 2*: rescale node. *Option 3*: do nothing.
Requirements: collect information regarding containers and nodes, consider node capacity and rescale node(s).

IV. ANOMALY DETECTION AND ANALYSIS

A failure is the inability of a system to perform its required functions within specified performance requirements. Faults (or anomalies) describe an exceptional condition occurring in the system operation that may cause one or more failures. It is a manifestation of an error in system [22]. We assume that a failure is an undesired response time observed during system component runtime (i.e., observation). For example, fluctuations in workload are faults that may cause a slowdown in system response time (observed failure).

A. Motivation

As an example, Figure 2 shows several observed failures and related resource faults in a test environment. These failures occurred either at a specific time (e.g., F_1, F_9) or over a period of time (e.g., $F_2 - F_8$). These failures result from fluctuations in resource utilization (e.g., CPU). Utilization measures a resource's capacity that is in use. It aids us in knowing the resource workload, and aid us in reducing the amount of jobs from the overloaded resources, e.g., a resource is saturated when its usage is at over 50% of its maximum capacity.

The response time varies between high, low and normal categories. It is associated with (or caused by) resource workload fluctuations (e.g., overload, underload or normal load). The fluctuations in workload shall be categorised into states that reflect faults. The anomalous response time is the observed failure that we use initially to identify the type of workload that causes the anomalies. In more concrete terms, we can classify the response time by the severity of a usage anomaly on a resource: low response time (L) varies from $501 - 1000ms$, normal response time (N) reflects the normal operation time of a resource and varies from $201 - 500ms$, and high response time (H) occurs when a response time is less than or equal $200ms$, which can be used to transfer the workload from the heavy loaded resources to the underloaded resources.

As a result, the recovery strategy will differ based on the type of observed failure and hidden fault. The period of recovery, which is the amount of time taken to recover, differs based on: (1) the number of observed failures, (2) the volume of transferred data (nodes with many tasks require longer recovery time), and (3) network capacity.

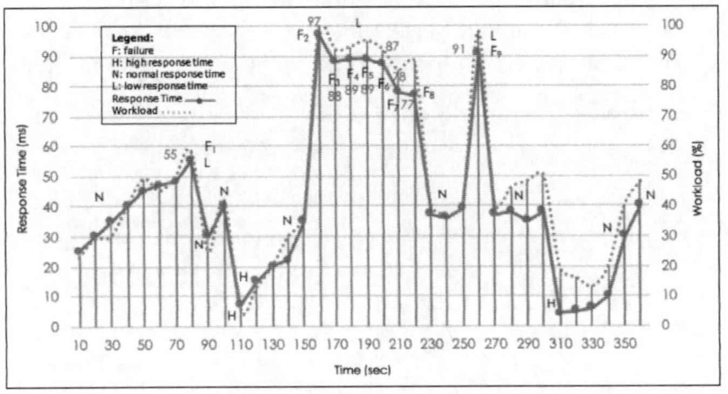

FIGURE 2. RESPONSE TIME AND WORKLOAD FLUCTUATIONS.

B. Observed Failure to Fault Mapping

The first problem is the association of underlying hidden faults to the observed failures. For the chosen metrics (e.g., resource utilization, response time), we can assume prior knowledge regarding (1) the dependency between containers, nodes and clusters; (2) past response time fluctuations for the executable containers; and (3) workload fluctuations that cause changes in response time. These can help us in identifying the mapping between anomalies and failures. An additional difficulty is the hierarchical organisation of clusters consisting of nodes, which themselves consist of containers. We associate an observed container response time to its cause at container, node, or cluster level, where for instance also a neighbouring container can cause a container to slow down. We define a mapping based on an analysis of possible scenarios.

The interaction between the cluster, node and container components in our architecture is based on the following assumptions. A cluster, which is the root node, is consisted of multiple nodes, and it is responsible for managing the nodes. A node, which is a virtual machine, has a capacity (e.g., resources available on the node such as memory or CPU). The main job of the node is to submit requests to its underlying substates (containers). Containers are self-contained, executable software packages. Multiple containers can run on the same node, and share the operating environment with other containers. Observations include the emission of failure from a state (e.g., high, low, or normal response time may emit from one or more states). Observation probabilities express the probability of an observation being generated from a resource state. We need to estimate the observation probabilities in order to know under which workloads large response time fluctuations occur and therefore to efficiently utilize a system resource while achieving good performance.

We need a mechanism that dynamically detects the type of anomaly and identifies its causes using this mapping. We identified different cases that may occur at container, node or cluster levels as illustrated in Figure 3. These detected cases will serve as a mapping between observable and hidden states, each annotated with a probability of occurrence that can be learned from a running system as a cause will often not be identifiable with certainty.

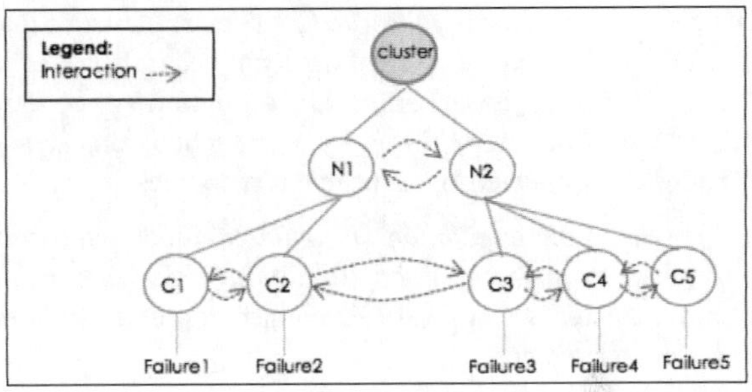

FIGURE 3. THE INTERACTION BETWEEN CLUSTER, NODES AND CONTAINER.

1) Low Response Time Observed at Container Level: There are different reasons that may cause this:

- *Case 1.1. Container overload (self-dependency)*: means that a container is busy, causing low response times, e.g., c_1 in N_1 has entered into load loop as it tries to execute its processes while N_1 keeps sending requests to it, ignoring its limited capacity.
- *Case 1.2. Container sibling overloaded (internal container dependency)*: this indicates another container c_2 in N_1 is overloaded. This overloaded container indirectly affects the other container c_1 as there is a communication between them. For example, c_2 has an application that almost consumes its whole resource operation. The container has a communication with c_1. At such situation, when c_2 is overloaded, c_1 will go into underload, because c_2 and c_1 share the resources of the same node.
- *Case 1.3. Container neighbour overload (external container dependency)*: this happens when a container c_3 in N_2 is linked to another container c_2 in another node N_1. In another case, some containers c_3, and c_4 in N_2 dependent on each other and container c_2 in N_1 depends on c_3. In both cases c_2 in N_1 is badly affected once c_3 or c_4 in N_2 are heavily loaded. This results in low response time observed from those containers.

2) Low Response Time Observed at Node Level: There are different reasons that cause such observations:

- *Case 2.1. Node overload (self-dependency)*: generally node overload happens when a node has low capacity, many jobs waited to be processed, or problem in network. Example, N_2 has entered into self load due to its limited capacity, which causes an overload at the container level as well c_3 and c_4.

- *Case 2.2. External node dependency*: occurs when low response time is observed at node neighbour level, e.g., when N_2 is overloaded due to low capacity or network problem, and N_1 depends on N_2. Such overload may cause low response time observed at the node level, which slow the whole operation of a cluster because of the communication between the two nodes. The reason behind that is N_1 and N_2 share the resources of the same cluster. Thus, when N_1 shows a heavier load, it would affect the performance of N_2.

3) Low Response Time Observed at Cluster Level (Cluster Dependency): If a cluster coordinates between all nodes and containers, we may observe low response time at container and node levels that cause difficulty at the whole cluster level, e.g., nodes disconnected or insufficient resources.

- *Case 3.1. Communication disconnection* may happen due to problem in the node configuration, e.g., when a node in the cluster is stopped or disconnected due to failure or a user disconnect.
- *Case 3.2. Resource limitation* happens if we create a cluster with too low capacity which causing low response time observed at the system level.

This mapping between anomalies and failures across the three hierarchy layers of the architecture needs to be formalised in a model that distinguishes observations and hidden states, and that allows weight to be attached. Thus, HHMMs are used to reflect the system topology.

C. Hierarchical Hidden Markov Model

Hierarchical Hidden Markov Model (HHMM) is a generalization of the Hidden Markov Model (HMM) that is used to model domains with hierarchical structure (e.g., intrusion detection, plan recognition, visual action recognition). HHMM can characterize the dependency of the workload (e.g., when at least one of the states is heavy loaded). The states (cluster, node, container) in HHMM are hidden from the observer, and only the observation space is visible (response time). The states of HHMM emit sequences rather than a single observation by a recursive activation of one of the substates (nodes) of a state (cluster). This substate might also be hierarchically composed of substates (containers). Each container has an application that runs on it. In case a node or a container emit observation, it will be considered a production state. The states that do not emit observations directly are called internal states. The activation of a substate by an internal state is a vertical transition that reflects the dependency between states. The states at the same level have horizontal transitions. Once the transition reaches to the End state, the control returns to the root state of the chain as shown in Figure 4. The edge direction indicates the dependency between states.

HHMM is identified by $HHMM =< \lambda, \theta, \pi >$. The λ is a set of parameters consisted of horizontal ζ and vertical χ transitions between states q^d, state transition probability A, observation probability distribution B, initial transition π; d specifies the number of vertical levels, i the horizontal level index, the state space SP at each level and the hierarchical parent-child relationship q_i^d, q_i^{d+1}. The Σ consists of all possible observations O. γ_{in} is the transition to q_j^d from any q_i^d. γ_{out} is the transition of leaving q_j^d from any q_i^d.

We choose HHMM as every state can be represented as a multi-levels HMM in order to:

1) show communication between nodes and containers,
2) demonstrate impact of workloads on the resources,
3) track the anomaly cause,
4) represent the response time variations that emit from nodes and containers.

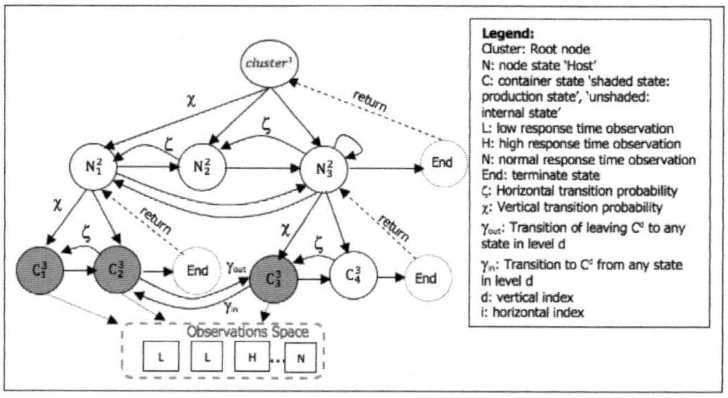

FIGURE 4. HHMM FOR WORKLOAD.

D. Detection and Root Cause Identification using HHMM

Each state may show an overload, underload or normal load state. Each workload is correlated to the resource utilization such as CPU, and it is associated with response time observations that are emitted from container or node through the above case mapping. The existence of anomalous workload in one state not only affects the current state, but it may also affect the other states in the same level or across the levels. The vertical transitions in Figure 4 trace the fault and identify the fault-failures relation. The horizontal transitions show the request/reply transfered between states.

The observation O is denoted by $F_i = \{f_1, f_2, ..., f_n\}$ to refer to the response time observations sequence (failures). The substate and production states are denoted by N and C respectively. A node space SP containing a set of containers, $N_1^2 = \{C_1^3, C_2^3\}$, $N_3^2 = \{C_3^3, C_4^3\}$. Each container produces an observation that reflects the response time fluctuation, $C_1^3 = \{f_1\}$, $C_2^3 = \{f_1\}$, $C_3^3 = \{f_2\}$. A state C starts operation at time t if the observation sequence $(f_1, f_2, ..., f_{n-1})$ was generated before the activation of its parent state N. A state ends its operation at time t if the F_t was the last observation generated by any of the production states C reached from N, and the control returned to N from C_{end}. The state transition probability $A_{ij}^{N_i^d} = (a_{ij}^{N^d})$, $a_{ij}^{N^d} = P(N_j^{d+1}|N_i^{d+1})$ indicates the probability of making a horizontal transition from N_i^d to N_j^d. Both states are substates of $cluster^1$.

An observed low response time might reflect some overload (OL). This overload can occur for a period of time or at a specific time before the state might return to normal load (NL) or underload (UL). This fluctuation in workload is associated with a probability that reflects the state transition status from OL to NL ($PF_{OL \rightarrow NL}$) at a failure rate $\Re$, which indicates the number of failures for a N, C or $cluster$ over a period of time. Sometimes, a system resource remains OL/UL without returning to its NL. We reflect this type of fault as a self-transition overload/underload with probability PF_{OL} (PF_{UL}). Further, a self-transition is applied on normal load PF_{NL} to refer to continuous normal behaviour. In order to address the reliability of the proposed fault analysis, we define a fault rate based on the number of faults occurring during system execution $\Re(FN)$ and the length of failure occurrences $\Re(FL)$ as depicted in "(1)" and "(2)".

$$\Re(FN) = \frac{No\ of\ Detected\ Faults}{Total\ No\ of\ Faults\ of\ Resource} \quad (1)$$

$$\Re(FL) = \frac{Total\ Time\ of\ Observed\ Failures}{Total\ Time\ of\ Execution\ of\ Resource} \quad (2)$$

As failure varies over different periods of time, we can also determine the $Average\ Failure\ Length\ (AFL)$. These metrics feed later into a proactive recovery mechanism. Possible observable events can be linked to each state (e.g., low response time may occur for an overload state or normal load) to determine the likely number of failures observed for each state, and to estimate the total failures numbers for all the states. To estimate the probability of a sequence of failures (e.g., probability of observing low response time for a given state). Its sum is based on the probabilities of all failure sequences that generated by (q^{d-1}), and where (q_i^d) is the last node activated by (q^{d-1}) and ending at End state. This is done by moving vertically and horizontally through the model to detect faulty states. Once the model reaches the end state, it has recursively moved upward until it reaches the state that triggered the substates. Then, we sum all possible starting states called by the $cluster$ and estimate the probability.

We used the generalized Baum-Welch algorithm [8] to train the model by calculating the probabilities of the model parameters. As shown in "(3)" and "(4)", first, we calculate the number of horizontal transitions from a state to another, which are substates from q^{d-1}, using ξ as depicted in "(3)". The γ_{in} refers to the probability that the O is started to be emitted for $state_i^d$ at t. $state_i^d$ refers to container, node, or cluster. The γ_{out} refers to the O of $state_i^d$ were emitted and finished at t. Second, as in "(4)", $\chi(t, C_i^d, N_l)$ is calculated to obtain the probability that $state^{d-1}$ is entered at t before O_t to activate state $state_i^d$. The α, and β denote the forward and backward transition from bottom-up.

$$\xi(t, C_i^d, C_{End}^d, N_l) = \frac{1}{P(O|\lambda)} \left[\sum_{s=1}^{t} \gamma_{in}(N_l, cluster)\ \alpha(t, C_i^d, N_l)\right] a_{End}^{C_l} \gamma_{out}(t, C_l, cluster) \quad (3)$$

$$\chi(t, C_i^d, N_l) = \frac{\gamma_{in}(t, N_l, cluster)\pi^{N_l}(C_i^d)}{P(O|\lambda)} \left[\sum_{e=t}^{T} \beta(t, e, C_i^d, N_l)\gamma_{out}(e, N_l, cluster)\right] \quad (4)$$

The output of algorithm will be used to train Viterbi algorithm to find the anomalous hierarchy of the detected anomalous states. As shown in "(5)-(7)", we recursively calculate $\Im$ which is the ψ for a time set ($\bar{t} = \psi(t, t+k, C_i^d, C^{d-1})$), where ψ is a state list, which is the index of the most probable production state to be activated by C^{d-1} before activating C_i^d. $\bar{t}$ is the time when C_i^d was activated by C^{d-1}. The δ is the likelihood of the most probable state sequence generating $(O_t, \cdots, O_{(t+k)})$ by a recursive activation. The τ is the transition time at which C_i^d was called by C^{d-1}. Once all the recursive transitions are finished and returned to $cluster$, we get the most probable hierarchies starting from $cluster$ to the production states at T period through scanning the sate list ψ, the states likelihood δ, and transition time τ.

$$L = \max_{(1 \le r \le N_i^d)} \left\{\delta(\bar{t}, t+k, N_r^{d+1}, N_i^d)\, a_{End}^{N_i^d}\right\} \quad (5)$$

$$\Im = \max_{(1 \le y \le N^{j-1})} \left\{\delta(t, \bar{t}-1, N_i^d, N^{d-1}) a_{End}^{N^{d-1}}\ L\right\} \quad (6)$$

$$stSeq = \max_{cluster} \left\{\delta(T, cluster), \tau(T, cluster), \psi(T, cluster)\right\} \quad (7)$$

Once we have trained the model, we compare the detected hierarchies against the observed one to detect and identify the type of workload. If the observed hierarchies and detected one are similar, and within the specified threshold, then the status of the observed component will be declared as 'Anomaly Free', and the framework will return to gather more data for further investigation. Otherwise, the hierarchies with the lowest probabilities will be considered anomaly. Once we detected and identified the workload type (e.g., OL), a path of faulty states (e.g., $cluster$, N_1^2, C_2^3 and C_3^3) is obtained that reflects observed failures. We repeat these steps until the probability of the model states become fixed. Each state is correlated with time that indicates: the time of it's activation, it's activated substates, and the time at which the control returns to the calling state. This aid us in the recovery procedure as the anomalous state will be recovered first come-first heal.

E. Workload and Resource Utilization Correlation

To check if the anomaly at cluster, node, container resource due to workload, we calculated the correlation between the workload (user transactions), and resource utilization to specify thresholds for each resource. The user transactions refer to the request rate per second. Thus, we used spearman's rank correlation coefficient to generate threshold to indicate the occurrence of fault at the monitored metric in multiple layers.

Our target is to group similar workload for all containers that run the same application in the same period. So that the workloads in the same period have the similar user transactions and resource demand. We added a unique workload identifier to the group of workloads in the same period to achieve traceability through the entire system. We utilized the probabilities of states transitions that we obtained from the HHMM to describes workload during T period. We transformed the obtained probabilities to get a workload behavior vector ω to characterize user transactions behaviors as in "(8)".

$$\omega = \{C_{i=1}^{d=3}, \cdots, C_{j=m}^{d=n}, \cdots, N_{i=1}^{d=2}, \cdots, N_{j=m}^{d=n}, \cdots, cluster\} \quad (8)$$

The correlation between the workload and resource utilization metric is calculated in the normal load behaviour to be a baseline. In case the correlation breaks down, then this refers to the existence of anomalous behaviour (e.g., OL).

V. EVALUATION

The proposed framework is run on Kubernetes and docker containers. We deployed TPC-W[1] benchmark on the containers to validate the framework. We focused on three types of faults CPU hog, Network packet loss/latency, and performance anomaly caused by workload congestion.

A. Environment Set-Up

To evaluate the effectiveness of the proposed framework, the experiment environment consists three VMs. Each VM is equipped with LinuxOS, 3VCPU, 2GB VRAM, Xen 4.11 [2], and an agent. Agents are installed on each VM to collect the monitoring data from the system (e.g., host metrics, container, performance metrics, and workloads), and send them to the storage to be processed. The VMs are connected through a 100 Mbps network. For each VM, we deployed two containers, and we run into them TPC-W benchmark.

TPC-W benchmark is used for resource provisioning, scalability, and capacity planning for e-commerce websites. TPC-W emulates an online bookstore that consists of 3 tiers: client application, web server, and database. Each tier is installed on VM. We didn't considered the database tier in the anomaly detection and identification, as a powerful VM should be dedicated to the database. The CPU and Memory utilization are gathered from the web server, while the Response time is measured from client's end. We ran TPC-W for 300 min. The number of records that we obtained from TPC-W was 2000.

We used docker $stats$ command to obtain a live data stream for running containers. SignalFX Smart Agent[3] monitoring tool is used and configured to observe the runtime performance of components and their resources. We also used Heapster[4] to group the collected data, and store them in a time series database using InfluxDB[5]. The data from the monitoring and from datasets are stored in the Real-Time/Historical Data storage to enhance the future anomaly detection. The gathered datasets are classified into training and testing datasets 50% for each. The model training lasted 150 minutes.

[1] http://www.tpc.org/tpcw/
[2] https://xenproject.org/
[3] https://www.signalfx.com/
[4] https://github.com/kubernetes-retired/heapster
[5] https://www.influxdata.com/

B. Fault Scenarios

To simulate real anomalies of the system, script is written to inject different types of anomalies into nodes and containers. The anomaly injection for each component last 5 minutes to be in total 30 minutes for all the system components. The starting and end time of each anomaly is logged.

- CPU Hog: such anomaly is injected to consume all CPU cycles by employing infinite loops. The stress[6] tool is used to create pressure on CPU
- Network packet loss/latency: the components are injected with anomalies to send or accept a large amount of requests in network. Pumba[7] is used to cause network latency and package loss
- Workload contention: web server is emulated using client application, which generates workload (using Remote Browser Emulator) by simulating a number of user requests that is increased iteratively. Since the workload is always described by the access behavior, we consider the container is gradually workloaded within [30-2000] emulated users requests, and the number of requests is changed periodically. The client application reports response time metric, and the web server reports CPU and Memory utilization. To measure the number of requests and response (latency), HTTPing[8] is installed on each node. Also AWS X-Ray[9] is used to trace of the request through the system.

C. Fault-Failure Mapping Detection and Identification

To address the fault-failure cases, the fault injection (CPU Hog and Network packet loss/latency) is done at two phases: (1) the system level (nodes), (2) components such as nodes and containers, one component at a time. The detection and identification will be differed as the injection time is varied from one component to another. The injection pause time between each injected fault is 180 sec.

a) Low Response Time Observed at Container Level: Case 1.1. Container overload (self-dependency): here, we added a new container C_5^3 in N_1^2, and we injected it by one anomaly at a time. For the CPU Hog, the anomaly was injected at 910 sec. It took from the model 30 sec to detect the anomaly and 15 sec to localize it. For the Network packet loss/latency, the injection of anomaly happened at 1135 sec, and the model detected and identified anomaly at 1145 and 1163 sec respectively.

Case 1.2. Container sibling overloaded (internal container dependency): in this case, the injection occurred at C_3^3 which in relation with C_4^3. The CPU injection began at 700 sec for C_3^3, the model detected the anomalous behaviour at 710 sec and localized it at 725 sec. For Network packet loss/latency, the injection of anomaly occurred at 905 sec. The model

[6] https://linux.die.net/man/1/stress
[7] https://alexei-led.github.io/post/pumba_docker_netem/
[8] https://www.vanheusden.com/httping/
[9] https://aws.amazon.com/xray/

needed 46 sec for the detection and 19 sec for the identification. For the C_4^3 the detection happened 34 sec later the detection of C_3^3 for the CPU Hog and the anomaly was identified at 754 sec. For the Network, the detection and identification occurred at 903 and 990 sec respectively.

Case 1.3. Container neighbour overload (external container dependency): at this case, a CPU Hog was injected at C_1^3 which in relation with C_3^3. The injection began at 210 sec. After training the HHMM, the model detected and localized the anomalous behaviour for C_1^3 at 225 and 230 sec. For Network fault, the injection occurred at 415 sec for C_1^3. The model took 429 sec for the detection and 450 sec for the identification. While for C_3^3, the CPU and Network faults were detected at 215/423 sec and identified at 240/429 sec.

b) Low Response Time Observed at Node Level: Case 2.1. Node overload (self-dependency): at this case we created a new node N_4^2 with small application and we injected the node by one anomaly at a time. For the CPU Hog, the anomaly was injected at N_4^2. The injection began at 413 sec. After training the HHMM, the model detected the anomalous behaviour at 443 sec and localized it at 461 sec. For the Network packet loss/latency, the injection of anomaly happened at 1210 sec, and the model detected and identified anomaly at 1260 and 1275 sec respectively.

Case 2.2. External node dependency: at such situation, a CPU Hog anomaly was injected at N_1^2. The injection began at 813 sec. After training the HHMM, the model detected the anomalous behaviour at 846 sec and localize it at 862 sec. For Network packet loss/latency, the injection of anomaly occurred at 1024 sec. The model needed 1084 sec for the detection and 1115 sec for the identification.

c) Low Response Time Observed at Cluster Level (Cluster Dependency): Case 3.1. Communication disconnection: at this case, we terminated N_1^2 and N_2^2, and we injected N_3^2 once with CPU Hog at 290 sec, and once with Network fault 525 sec. The detection and identification for each anomaly was: for CPU 335 and 345 sec respectively, and for Network was 585 sec for the detection and 610 sec for the identification.

Case 3.2. Resource limitation: at this case, we injected N_1^2, and N_3^2 at the same time with the CPU Hog fault to exhaustive the nodes capacity. The injection, detection, and identification were 1120, 1181, and 1192 sec. For the Network fault, the injection happened at 1372 sec, and the detection, and identification were at 1387, and 1392 sec.

D. Detection and Identification of Workload Contention

For the workload, to show the Influence of workload on CPU utilization monitored metric, we measured the response time (i.e., the time required to process requests), and throughput (i.e., the number of transactions processed during a period). We first generated gradual requests/sec at the container level. The number of users requests increases from 30 to 2000 with a pace of 10 users incrementally, and each workload lasts for 10 min. As shown in Figure 5, the results show that the throughput increases when the number of requests increases, then it remains constant once the number of requests reached 220 request/sec. This means that when the number of users requests is reached 220 request/sec, the utilization of CPU reached a bottleneck at 90%, and the performance degrades. On the other hand, the response time keep increasing with the increasing number of requests as shown in Figure 6. The result demonstrated that dynamic workloads has a noticeable impact on the container metrics as the monitored container was unable to process more than those requests. We also noticed that there is a linear relationship between the number of concurrent users and CPU utilization before resource contention in each user transaction behavior pattern. We calculated the correlation between the monitored metric, and the number of user requests. We obtained a strong correlation between the two measured variables reached 0.25775 for two variables. The result concludes that the number of requests influences the performance of the monitored metrics.

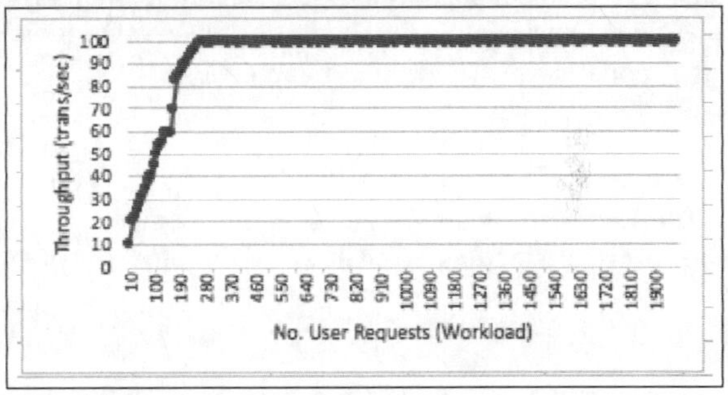

FIGURE 5. WORKLOAD - THROUGHPUT AND NO. OF USER REQUESTS.

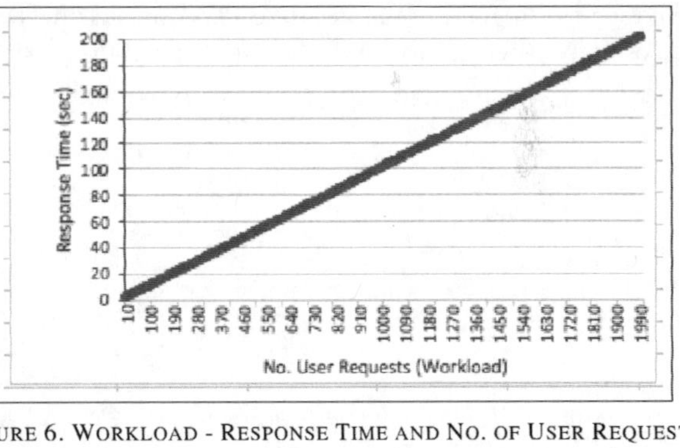

FIGURE 6. WORKLOAD - RESPONSE TIME AND NO. OF USER REQUESTS.

E. Assessment of Detection and Identification

The model performance is compared with other techniques such as Dynamic Bayesian Network (DBN), and Hierarchical Temporal Memory (HTM). To evaluate the effectiveness of anomaly detection, common measures in anomaly detection are used:

Root Mean Square Error (RMSE) measures the differences between detected and observed value by the model. A smaller RMSE value indicates a more effective detection scheme.

Mean Absolute Percentage Error (MAPE) measures the detection accuracy of a model. Both RMSE and MAPE are negatively-oriented scores, i.e., lower values are better.

Number of Correctly Detected Anomaly (CDA) It measures percentage of the correctly detected anomalies to the total number of detected anomalies in a given dataset. High CDA indicates the model is correctly detected anomalous behaviour.

Recall It measures the completeness of the correctly detected anomalies to the total number of anomalies in a given dataset. Higher recall means that fewer anomaly cases are undetected.

Number of Correctly Identified Anomaly (CIA) CIA is the number of correct identified anomaly (NCIA) out of the total set of identification, which is the number of correct Identification (NCIA) + the number of incorrect Identification (NICI)). The higher value indicates the model is correctly identified anomalous component.

$$CIA = \frac{NCIA}{NCIA + NICI} \quad (9)$$

Number of Incorrectly Identified Anomaly (IIA) is the number of identified components which represents an anomaly but misidentified as normal by the model. A lower value indicates that the model correctly identified anomalies.

$$IIA = \frac{FN}{FN + TP} \quad (10)$$

FAR The number of the normal identified component which has been misclassified as anomalous by the model.

$$FAR = \frac{FP}{TN + FP} \quad (11)$$

The false positive (FP) means the detection/identification of anomaly is incorrect as the model detects/identifies the normal behaviour as anomaly. True negative (TN) means the model can correctly detect and identify normal behaviour as normal.

TABLE I. VALIDATION RESULTS.

Metrics	HHMM	DBN	HTM
RMSE	0.23	0.31	0.26
MAPE	0.14	0.27	0.16
CDA	96.12%	91.38%	94.64%
Recall	0.94	0.84	0.91
CIA	94.73%	87.67%	93.94%
IIA	4.56%	12.33%	6.07%
FAR	0.12	0.26	0.17

The results in Table I depicted that both HHMM and HTM achieved good results for the detection and identification. While the results of the DBN a little bit decayed for the CDA with approximately 5% than HHMM and 3% than HTM. The three algorithms can detect obvious anomalies in the datasets. Both HHMM and HTM showed higher detection accuracy as they are able to detect temporal anomalies in the dataset. The result interferes that the HHMM is able to link the observed failure to its hidden workload.

VI. CONCLUSION AND FUTURE WORK

This paper presented a framework for the detection and identification of anomalies in clustered computing environments. The key objective was to provide an analysis feature that maps observable quality concerns onto hierarchical hidden resources in a clustered environment and their operation in order to identify the reason for performance degradations and other anomalies. We used hidden hierarchical Markov models (HHMM) to reflect the hierarchical nature of the unobservable resources. We have analysed mappings between observations and resource usage based on a clustered container scenario. To evaluate the performance of proposed framework, HHMM is compared with other machine learning algorithms such as Dynamic Bayesian Network (DBN), and Hierarchical Temporal Memory (HTM). The results show that the proposed framework is able to detect and identify anomalous behavior with more than 96%.

In the future, we aim to fully implement the framework, and carry out further experimental evaluations to fully confirm these conclusions. Further, we will provide a self-healing mechanism to recover the localized anomaly. More practical concerns from microservices and container architectures shall also be investigated [19],[18]

REFERENCES

[1] X. Chen, C.-D. Lu, and K. Pattabiraman, "Failure Prediction of Jobs in Compute Clouds: A Google Cluster Case Study," *International Symposium on Software Reliability Engineering, ISSRE*, pp. 167–177, 2014.

[2] C. Pahl, P. Jamshidi, O. Zimmermann, "Architectural principles for cloud software," ACM Transactions on Internet Technology (TOIT) 18 (2), 17, 2018.

[3] D. von Leon, L. Miori, J. Sanin, N. El Ioini, S. Helmer, C. Pahl, "A Lightweight Container Middleware for Edge Cloud Architectures," Fog and Edge Computing: Principles and Paradigms, 145-170, 2019.

[4] G. C. Durelli, M. D. Santambrogio, D. Sciuto, and A. Bonarini, "On the Design of Autonomic Techniques for Runtime Resource Management in Heterogeneous Systems," PhD dissertation, Politecnico di Milano, 2016.

[5] T. Wang, J. Xu, W. Zhang, Z. Gu, and H. Zhong, "Self-adaptive cloud monitoring with online anomaly detection," *Future Generation Computer Systems*, vol. 80, pp. 89–101, 2018.

[6] P. Jamshidi, A. Sharifloo, C. Pahl, H. Arabnejad, A. Metzger, G. Estrada, "Fuzzy self-learning controllers for elasticity management in dynamic cloud architectures," Intl Conf on Quality of Software Architectures, 2016.

[7] P. Jamshidi, A. Sharifloo, C. Pahl, A. Metzger, G. Estrada, "Self-learning cloud controllers: Fuzzy q-learning for knowledge evolution," Intl Conference on Cloud and Autonomic Computing, 208-211, 2015.

[8] S. Fine, Y. Singer, and N. Tishby, "The hierarchical hidden Markov model: Analysis and applications," *Machine Learning*, vol. 32, no. 1, pp. 41–62, 1998.

[9] R. N. Calheiros, E. Masoumi, R. Ranjan, and R. Buyya, "Workload Prediction Using ARIMA Model and Its Impact on Cloud Applications," *IEEE Transactions on Cloud Computing*, vol. 3, no. 4, pp. 449–458, oct 2015.

[10] N. Sorkunlu, V. Chandola, and A. Patra, "Tracking System Behavior from Resource Usage Data," in *Pro-*

ceedings - IEEE International Conference on Cluster Computing, ICCC, 2017, pp. 410–418.

[11] M. Peiris, J. H. Hill, J. Thelin, S. Bykov, G. Kliot, and C. Konig, "PAD: Performance anomaly detection in multi-server distributed systems," in *Intl Conference on Cloud Computing, CLOUD*, 2014.

[12] T. F. Düllmann, "Performance Anomaly Detection in Microservice Architectures Under Continuous Change," Master, University of Stuttgart, 2016.

[13] C. Pahl, A. Brogi, J. Soldani, P. Jamshidi, "Cloud container technologies: a state-of-the-art review," IEEE Transactions on Cloud Computing, 2018.

[14] S. Maurya and K. Ahmad, "Load Balancing in Distributed System using Genetic Algorithm," *Intl Jrnl of Engineering and Technology*, vol. 5, no. 2, 2013.

[15] H. Sukhwani, "A Survey of Anomaly Detection Techniques and Hidden Markov Model," *Intl Jrnl of Computer Applications*, vol. 93, no. 18, pp. 975–8887, 2014.

[16] R. Heinrich, A. van Hoorn, H. Knoche, F. Li, L.E. Lwakatare, C. Pahl, S. Schulte, J. Wettinger, "Performance engineering for microservices: research challenges and directions," ACM, 2017.

[17] N. Ge, S. Nakajima, and M. Pantel, "Online diagnosis of accidental faults for real-time embedded systems using a hidden Markov model," *SIMULATION*, pp. 0 037 549 715 590 598—-, 2015.

[18] R. Scolati, I. Fronza, N. El Ioini, A. Samir, C. Pahl, "A Containerized Big Data Streaming Architecture for Edge Cloud Computing on Clustered Single-Board Devices," CLOSER, 2019.

[19] D. Taibi, V. Lenarduzzi, C. Pahl, "Architecture Patterns for a Microservice Architectural Style," Springer, 2019.

[20] G. Brogi, "Real-time detection of Advanced Persistent Threats using Information Flow Tracking and Hidden Markov," Doctoral dissertation, 2018.

[21] A. Samir, C. Pahl, "A Controller Architecture for Anomaly Detection, Root Cause Analysis and Self-Adaptation for Cluster Architectures," Intl Conf on Adaptive and Self-Adaptive Systems and Applications, 2019.

[22] IEEE, "IEEE Standard Classification for Software Anomalies (IEEE 1044 - 2009)," pp. 1–4, 2009.

Relational Algebra for Heterogeneous Cloud Data Sources

Aspen Olmsted
Fisher College
Department of Computer Science, Boston, MA 02116
e-mail: aolmsted@fisher.edu

Abstract— **Cloud computing has changed the way commonly used data is stored. Before the adoption of the cloud, most data was preserved in proprietary relational databases. Cloud services provide native storage for several complex data types including contacts, calendar events, tasks and form responses. Along with the cloud services the user is delivered mobile application synchronization, web application interfaces and guarantees of availability. Unfortunately, along with all the benefits of the native cloud data types comes complexity that leads to several difficulties. One difficulty is data queries that relate data from different heterogeneous data sources. In this paper, we develop a relational algebra that operates on two-dimensional data stored in many heterogeneous cloud formats. The relation algebra is exposed via web-services and allows a user to combine data from different data types and across domains.**

Keywords-Relational Algebra; Cloud Computing; Heterogeneous Data

I. INTRODUCTION

Relational algebra is a mathematical notation used for modeling the data stored in two-dimensional tables. Edgar F. Codd [1] created relational algebra to express the operations and operators used with relational databases to query data. Since its original inception, relational algebra has been extended to model query operations on many different data source structures from the original relational model. Two examples of extensions to the original relational algebra specification is an extension that allows operations on hierarchical data [2] and an extension that allows operations on semantic data [3].

In the same work [1], Codd also developed algorithms for reducing redundancy in the data model to ensure that data was kept correct and not lost from the update and deletion anomalies. At the time of Codd's work, access to computers to store databases was rare, and access to applications that manage data was even rarer. In today's world, most individuals carry at least one device with several databases on it. The same data is often stored on different machines in their office and their home. The redundant copies of the data lead to problems Codd could not have anticipated with his single data store where he applied his relational algebra operations.

Keeping the distributed data updated across all the diverse devices has been improved by the cloud. Often the data is stored in the cloud and changes made on mobile devices or desktops are bi-directionally synchronized with the cloud. Unfortunately, the data tends to be stored in different heterogeneous databases that are specialized for the type of data the application handles. An example of the diverse data source problem in the cloud is seen when looking at the three major cloud productivity app providers. Google G Suite [4], Microsoft Office 365 [5], and Zoho Docs [6] each have different data formats and application programmer interfaces (API) for emails, form data, calendar data. Each of these cloud office suites also provides the ability to store diverse two-dimensional data in spreadsheet files.

The organization of the paper is as follows. Section II describes the related work and the limitations of current methods. In Section III, we describe the relational algebra operators, we implemented for the cloud data sources. Section IV describes the different data sources we allowed as operands in our work. Section V describes some motivating examples of queries we developed using our relational algebra. Section VI drills into some specific details on how we programmed the relational algebra query engine and how data can be returned from the engine. In section VII, we talk about using the relational algebra to enforce consistency in the distributed data source. We conclude and discuss future work in Section VIII.

II. RELATED WORK

Garcia-Molina, Ullman, and Widom [6] spend several chapters in their database textbook discussing algebra on relations. The authors build upon the work originally developed by Codd [1]. They contribute several expressive additions to Relational Algebra in their book. One addition allows for a linear sequence of operations. The second addition utilizes relation algebra to express constraints on relations. We utilize their work to develop our cloud heterogeneous data source constraints.

Agrawal [2] extended relational algebra to handle hierarchical data. In Codd's original work and our work, we assume the data sources are two-dimensional tables where a column, or set of columns, of the table, relates to a column or set of columns, in a different two-dimensional table. Agrawal's work adds an operator to express hierarchical relationships and query the transitive closure of those relationships.

Cyganiak [3] took relation algebra and applied the operators to Resource Description Framework (RDF) triples. An RDF triple is a 3 part notation for expressing the subject object and predicate. An interesting piece of Cyganiak work is in a subsection of the paper that looks at extensions to relational algebra that would allow the operators to work on full RDF datasets. RDF datasets are collections of RDF graphs that would be distributed across the internet. Our work uses distributed data sources but does not limit the format to the same data structure as he did with RDF graphs.

III. CLOUD RELATIONAL ALGEBRA OPERATORS

Relational algebra is a set based mathematical model that provides a notation for performing operations on sets and producing sets as results of the operations. In this work, our cloud-based relational algebra includes the same operators as traditional relational algebra, but instead of operating on sets, our algebra operates on bags or multisets. A bag or multiset is a generalization of a set that allows duplicate instances of elements in the bag. We choose to work with bags for performance reasons as we do not have control of the data sources in the cloud and they may contain duplicate elements. We also use bag operations for performance reason. The deduplication process of a bag is at best a $N\log_2 N$ operation.

Table I shows our relational cloud algebra operators mapped from the original relational algebra. Our implementation was developed as functions in Google App Script. The signature of each function contained the same number of arguments as the original relational algebra but implemented as parameters to the function. Each function also returns a two-dimensional relational structure that can be passed into any of the other cloud relational functions as an input for the relation. The consistent return type allows the operators to be combined to produce complicated queries.

A. *Selection*

The cloud selection function is called by passing in a condition as a string and a relation. The algorithm iterates over the tuples in the relation and returns all the tuples where the condition evaluates to true.

B. *Projection*

The cloud projection function is called by passing in a comma-delimited list of columns in the first argument as a string. The second argument is the original relation data source that holds the data columns. The result is a new table with just the columns specified.

TABLE I
RA CLOUD OPERATORS

Relational Operator	Example	Name	Cloud Function
Σ	R1 := σ_C (R2)	selection	R1 = ra_select(c,R2)
Π	R1 := π_L (R2)	projection	R1 = ra_project(L,R2)
⋈	R3 := R1 $\bowtie_C$ R2	theta join	R3 = ra_theta(R1,c,R2)
⋈	R3 := R1 ⋈ R2	natural join	R3 = ra_natural(R1,R2)
Ρ	R1 := ρ_L (R2)	rename	R1 = ra_rename(L,R2)
X	R3 := R1 X R2	product	R3 = ra_product(R1,R2)
∩	R3 := R1 ∩ R2	intersection	R3 = ra_intersect(R1,R2)
∪	R3 := R1 ∪ R2	union	R3 = ra_union(R1,R2)
—	R3 := R1 —R2	difference	R3 = ra_diff(R1,R2)

C. *Product*

The cloud production function takes the two arguments passed in and creates a cartesian product of the tuples in the first argument and the tuples in the second argument. The result is a new two-dimensional multiset with the schema made up of the combination of the columns from the two input datasets. The multiplicity of the result relation is the number of tuples in the first argument data source multiplied by the number of tuples in the second argument data source.

D. *Theta Join*

The cloud theta join function is invoked by passing in three arguments. A new data source is passed out of the function with the same schema as if the first and third arguments were passed to the product function. The multiplicity is reduced by applying a filter to the product. The filter condition is specified in the second argument to the function.

E. *Natural Join*

The cloud natural join function is similar to the theta join function except no condition is specified. The caller specifies the two input sources and the data is joined based on equal column names between the two sources.

F. *Rename*

The cloud rename function is used to change the names of the columns in the data source. The primary purpose of the operator is to ensure as a predecessor to a natural join or an intersection, union or difference operation.

G. *Intersection*

The intersection cloud function takes two data sources as arguments and finds the tuples that exist in both data sources. The schema of both data sources needs to match so that the tuples can be compared. The result relation has the columns of one of the input data sources and the tuples that were in common between the two data sources. Often in bag relational operations, the intersection operator produces a set. Our implementation produces a bag for the performance reasons given earlier.

H. *Union*

The union cloud function takes two data sources as arguments and combines the dataset. The schema of both data sources needs to be identical so that the tuples can be combined. The result relation has the schema of one of the input data sources and all the tuples that were in both of the two input data sources. Often in bag relational operations, the union operator produces a set. Our implementation produces a bag for the performance reasons given earlier.

TABLE II
RA CLOUD DATA SOURCES

Data Source	schema	Ownership
Spreadsheets	Dynamic	Distributed
Forms	Dynamic	Personal
Contacts	Static	Personal
Events	Static	Distributed
RSS Feeds	Static	Distributed
RESTful data	Dynamic	Distributed

TABLE IV
EVENTS SCHEMA

Field	Data Type
Id	String
Title	String
Description	String
StartTime	Date
EndTime	Date
AllDay	Boolean
Recurring	Boolean
Location	String

I. Difference

The cloud difference function takes two data sources as arguments and finds the tuples that exist in the first data source but not in the second data source. The schema of both data sources needs to be identical so that the tuples can be compared. The result relation has the columns of one of the input data sources and the tuples that were in the first data sources but not the second data source. Often in implementations of relational operations on bags, the difference operator produces a set. Our implementation produces a bag for the performance reasons given earlier.

IV. CLOUD HETEROGENEOUS DATA SOURCES

Cloud service providers offer native storage for many different sources of data a user may want to query. In our implementation, we supported several different types of data sources. The data sources either had a fixed static schema or the schema was dynamic based on the configuration of the data source. Some examples of fixed static schemas are Rich Site Summary (RSS) feeds, events and contacts. With other data sources, the schema varies based on the specific relation queried. These sources include spreadsheet data, form data, and web services. Table II shows the breakdown of the schema types for the different cloud data sources.

Some of the schemas for the different data types are fixed while others are pulled from the metadata of the data. The data sources that cross domains require the unique address of the data source. RSS Feeds are a data source that can cross domains and have a fixed schema. When an RSS data source is used as the operand of an operation, we prepend a string of "rss=" followed by the feed URL. An example operand of type RSS would be expressed as "rss=http://today.cofc.edu/category/news-briefs/feed/." Table III shows the fixed schema for all tuples in a relation of type RSS. Each RSS tuple has a title, date of publication and description, which are the typically displayed by an RSS reader. There is also a link field returned by an RSS feed. We parse the link into four parts: scheme, host, the path and query string. The scheme is the protocol that is used to reference the link. The host is the website where the link is hosted. The path identifies a specific resource at the website, and the query string is a set of key-value pairs that are sent as parameters to the resource. We parse URL into the separate components so that each component can be easily joined to other data sources in relational algebra queries.

TABLE III
RSS SCHEMA

Field	Data Type
Title	String
LinkScheme	String
LinkHost	String
LinkPath	String
LinkQueryString	String
PubDate	String
Description	String
GUID	String

The Calendar datasource is a fixed schema source that reads data that is stored in the Google GSuite. The calendar data source is broken into two different relations. The first relation has the primary event details for events on the calendar. The second relation has the guests that are linked to the event. Table IV displays the schema for the event component of the data source, and TABLE V shows the schema for the event guest data. We separated the calendar data into two sources to normalize the guest email addresses. The email address is often a unique identifier in cloud data sources. Having the email addresses in a normalized relation will allow for easy joining to other data sources. When a calendar data source is used as an operand, the operand is passed as a string with a prefix of "calendar=" followed by

TABLE V
EVENT GUEST SCHEMA

Field	Data Type
EventId	String
Name	String
Email	String

TABLE VI
CONTACTS SCHEMA

Field	Data Type
Id	String
FullName	String
GivenName	String
MiddleName	String
FamilyName	String
Initials	String
Prefix	String
Suffix	String
MaddenName	String
NickName	String
ShortName	String
HomeAddress	String
HomeAddressIsPrimary	Boolean
WorkAddress	String
WorkAddressIsPrimary	Boolean
Company	String
JobTitle	String
AssistantPhone	String
CallBackPhone	String
HomePhone	String
WorkPhone	String
MobilePhone	String
Page	String
HomeFax	String
WorkFax	String
HomePage	String

the name of the calendar. The events data source allows data to come from different ownership. To access a calendar owned by a different user B, user A would need to share the calendar with user B. An example operand of type event would be expressed as "calendar=US Holidays." To query the guests of an event, you would prefix the relation with "calendarguests=." An example operand of type event would be expressed as "calendarguests=US Holidays."

The contacts data source is a large schema with many de-normalized columns. We chose to leave the table mostly de-normalized except pulling out the contact emails into their own relation. Table VI shows the schema for the contact relation. In the schema, addresses and phone number types are represented by distinct attributes. The phone and address fields were not used in any of our test cases that involved join operations. For simplicity, we left the phone and address fields de-normalized. A future version may add additional cloud data sources where the address or phone number is a

TABLE VII
CONTACT EMAILS SCHEMA

Field	Data Type
ContactId	String
Type	String
Email	String
Primary	Boolean

primary key, and we will want to normalize this data. Table VII shows the schema for the contact emails. When a reference to a contacts data source is used as an operand in a relational algebra operation, the operand is expressed with a fixed string of "contacts." The primary cloud providers of contact services do not support distributed contacts, so there is one single relation that holds the contacts. If the relational algebra operation should operate on the contact emails, then the operand is expressed as the fixed string of "contactemails."

The spreadsheets data source use the first row of the data range to specify the schema to be used. In our experimental implementation, we assume the data range starts in cell A1 on the first tab of the spreadsheet. Future implementations could enhance the spreadsheet functionality to specify specific tabs and specific cell ranges. As you will see in our example distributed queries our primary goal with spreadsheet queries was to allow queries across ownership. So in the relational algebra operations, the operand can specify wildcards to include many spreadsheets stored in the same folder. With the Google GSuite, each spreadsheet can be owned by a different user. The user executing the relational algebra can locate the shared files into their own folder.

Form data behaves almost identically to spreadsheet data in our implementation. The Google GSuite stores form data as spreadsheet data so when a form is queried in a relational algebra operation the first row in the spreadsheet is the form questions. Again our implementation assumes all questions are included in the data set by starting the data from cell A1 in the backend spreadsheet.

```
[ { country: 'China',         population: 1379510000 },
  { country: 'India',         population: 1330780000 },
  { country: 'United States', population:  324788000 },
  { country: 'Indonesia',     population:  260581000 },
  { country: 'Brazil',        population:  206855000 }]
  ];
```

Figure 1. Example REST data

TABLE VIII
SAMPLE POS

Semester	Class	Area
Fall 17	CSIS602	Core
Fall 17	CSIS603	Core
Fall 17	CSIS614	Cybersecurity
Spring 17	CSIS601	Core
Spring 17	CSIS604	Core
Spring 17	CSIS631	Cybersecurity
Summer 18	CSIS638	Elective
Summer 18	CSIS649	Elective
Fall 18	CSIS632	Cybersecurity
Fall 18	CSIS641	Cybersecurity
Fall 18	CSIS618	Elective

Our implementation of restful web-services made some simple assumptions to ensure success in the first version. The first assumption is that there is no authentication. The second assumption was that data is returned in JavaScript Object Notation (JSON) format. The data returned from the web-service must be an array of JavaScript objects, each with the same properties. In the industrial world, these restrictions are too high to successfully include data from many 3rd party vendors, but it was good enough for our implementation to prove that web-service data could be included in the relational algebra operations. Figure 1 shows a sample JSON array of countries along with its population that can be processed by our relational algebra.

V. EXAMPLE DISTRIBUTED QUERIES

The first example query we tested with our cloud relational algebra was querying of graduate student program of study (POS) plans that were stored in individually owned spreadsheets in the cloud. Each student in the graduate program keeps a spreadsheet they have shared with the program director. The MS degree requires each student to take eleven classes to complete their degree. Four of the classes are core classes, so all students are required to take these classes. There are some additional four classes to represent the focus area, so students choose a focus area and have a set of classes to choose from to meet the focus requirement. The final three courses are electives that can be taken as a thesis option. Table VIII shows a sample POS for a typical student with a focus on cybersecurity. The shared links are stored in a single cloud directory named "GradSchool." Each spreadsheet is given a name that starts with the student's name followed by the letters "POS." The spreadsheets have three columns. The semester a student plans to take a course is the first column. The course they plan to take is the second column. The third column holds the POS category the course is fulfilling.

To determine the demand for a specific course, we can write a relational algebra expression that uses a combination of the selection and projection operations. Figure 2 shows the cloud relation algebra that will return a two-dimensional array of the student's email address and the class they want to take in the "Summer 18" semester. Once the result data is returned to a cloud spreadsheet, a pivot table can be used to display the course demand.

Figure 3 extends this example by performing a theta join operation on the students taking summer classes with their contact information. For the implementation, two theta joins are applied. The first join is done by the owner of the spreadsheet to the email of the contacts. The second join is completed from the contact email id to the contact id. This query is only possible because the normalization that was performed on the contact data described earlier. A student may have both a home and work email address, and it is not known which email is the owner of the spreadsheet data.

The second example query we wanted to handle with our cloud relational algebra was also related to student data. In this example, we want to combine the results from a student survey on happiness in the program with the events the student attended and the classes they took during the semester. Figure 4 shows a part of our final query. We start by extracting the classes from the program of study spreadsheets with the selection operation on the semester = "Fall 17". We apply a theta join to the results of the selection operation with the cloud form named "SpringStudentSurvey." The results of the join operation are then theta joined to the event guests in the "studentevents" calendar. In the final step, the guest is theta joined with the event they attended. Normally, the attributes would be

```
ra_project("owner, class",ra_select("semester=Summer 18","Spreadsheet=GradSchool/*POS"))
```

Figure 2. RA to retrieve students taking summer classes

```
ra_theta(ra_theta(ra_project("owner, class",ra_select("semester=Summer 18","Spreadsheet=GradSchool/*POS")),"owner=email",contactemails),"contact_id=id",contacts)
```

Figure 3. RA to retrieve student summer contact info

```
ra_theta(ra_theta(ra_select("semester=Fall 17","Spreadsheet=GradSchool/*POS"),"owner=username", ra_project("opinion", "Form=SpringStudentSurvey")),"email=username","calendarguests=studentevents"),"eventid=id","calendar= studentevents")
```

Figure 4. RA to retrieve student survey and student data

TABLE IX
Sample Form Constraint Table

Field	RA	Invalid	Message
1	ra_select("semester=*Field1*","Spreadsheet=Rooms")	Empty	Please choose a valid room
2	ra_select("semester=*Field2*","Spreadsheet=Resources")	Empty	Please choose a valid resource

minimized with another projection operation, but for simplicity, we left projection out of Figure 4.

The three queries presented in this section are just a small representation of the types of queries that can be performed with the heterogeneous data.

VI. IMPLEMENTATION

As discussed in the earlier sections we developed our solution using Google Application Script (GAS) [7]. The GAS environment was designed to allow a developer to extend G Suite [4], Google's suite of cloud office applications. The programming environment concepts are similar to the Microsoft VBA programming functionality included in Microsoft Office [8]. At the time of our experimentation, Microsoft did not offer a similar programming environment for their cloud office suite Office 365 [5].

We felt the best storage location for the result of the cloud relational algebra operations was in Google spreadsheets. Google spreadsheets can be enhanced with GAS to allow custom functions. Unfortunately, for security reasons, Google does not allow spreadsheet custom functions to access external data. We decided to implement our solution as a web-service that could be called from any programming language but also imported into a Google cloud spreadsheet using the "importdata" function.

VII. CONSTRAINTS ON HETEROGENEOUS DATA SOURCES

In this section, we build on the work previously described to query data using relational algebra. We extend the work to guarantee consistency in data entry in the cloud by expressing constraints utilizing the heterogeneous data. The general idea is that we want to express a constraint that evaluates to true before allowing new data to be saved.

Since the heterogeneous data is entered into the different native cloud applications directly, we have limited ability to intercept the request and execute our relational algebra queries. Google has exposed some Triggers in the GAS framework that do allow us to intercept the save request we can use for validation.

Google Forms and Calendars are the two applications that currently provide triggers that allow us to intercept the data save and validate that the relational algebra evaluates to true. We are hopeful that more triggers will be exposed via the API and we can extend our constraint work.

With Google Forms a trigger can intercept the post and run the related relational algebra constraint. Since all the relational algebra operators return a two dimensional set of data, we assume an empty set is false and any data returned is true. If an empty set is returned, then the form is not submitted. Instead, the user is redirected to a new URL with the fields of the form prefilled. The field with the error is replaced with an error message stored in the constraint setup. TABLE IX shows our implementations simple constraint setup for form submissions. The first column in the table identifies the field in the form that is checked. The second column holds the relational algebra. The third column specifies how validity is identified. The validity column is expressed as invalidity to simplify the rule definition as it is often expressed as an empty set on the return of the relational algebra. The fourth column holds the message that is to be displayed in the pre-filled form the user is redirected to if there is a constraint violation. TABLE IX was used with a simple example form for event booking that ensured that the room specified in field 1 and the resource specified in field two where valid. To be valid, they had to exist in specific cloud spreadsheets.

The calendar triggers were designed to solve the problem of synchronization of events between multiple calendars. Because of this design, there is not a way to intercept a call before the data is persisted. Several of the Google cloud products support time-driven triggers. Time-Driven trigger functions are similar to a CRON [10] job that runs a script based on a specific time. Time-driven triggers let scripts execute at a particular time or on a recurring interval, as frequently as every minute or as infrequently as once per month. The challenge with a time-driven trigger is how to know what data has changed since the last time the trigger fired. The calendar triggers solve this problem by passing a list of events that have changed since the last trigger fired. We decided not to implement relational algebra constraints that based on the calendar triggers or the time-driven triggers because it would require human interaction after the data is persisted to fix the constraint issue.

VIII. CONCLUSIONS AND FUTURE WORK

Based on our research, we believe the use of native heterogeneous cloud data sources will continue to grow and replace the proprietary relational data sources that people and organizations have come to rely upon for joining data into queries for analysis and constraints. This work demonstrates a successful implementation of the low-level relational algebra operations and provides some successful use cases of our tool. The hooks available to enforce constraints based on the relational algebra are inadequate at this point as demonstrated in our discussion. We hope the cloud vendors can be enticed to provide programmatic hooks before all data persistence operations in the future. Our future work will expand our use cases and provide a native front end to the relational algebra web-services we provided.

REFERENCES

[1] E. F., "A relational model of data for large shared data banks," *Communications of the ACM,* vol. 13, no. 6, pp. 377-387 , 1970.

[2] R. Agrawal, "Alpha: an extension of relational algebra to express a class of recursive queries," *IEEE Transactions on Software Engineering,* vol. 14, no. 7, pp. 879 - 885, 1988.

[3] R. Cyganiak, "A Relational Algebra for SPARQL," HP Labs, Bristol, UK, 2005.

[4] Google, "Get Gmail, Docs, Drive, and Calendar for business.," [Online]. Available: https://gsuite.google.com/. [Accessed 18 September 2018].

[5] Microsoft, Inc., "Modernize the workplace with Office 365," [Online]. Available: https://www.microsoft.com/en-us/CloudandHosting/office365.aspx. [Accessed 18 September 2018].

[6] Zoho, Inc, "Your personal file manager," [Online]. Available: https://www.zoho.com/docs/. [Accessed 18 September 2018].

[7] H. Garcia-Molina, J. Ullman and J. Widom, Database Systems: The Complete Book, Pearson, 2008.

[8] Google, "Google Apps Script," [Online]. Available: https://developers.google.com/apps-script/. [Accessed 18 September 2018].

[9] Microsoft, Inc., "Getting Started with VBA in Office," 7 June 2017. [Online]. Available: https://docs.microsoft.com/en-us/office/vba/library-reference/concepts/getting-started-with-vba-in-office. [Accessed 18 September 2018].

[10] Wikipedia Foundation, Inc., "Cron," [Online]. Available: https://en.wikipedia.org/wiki/Cron. [Accessed 24 September 2018].

Building Trust in Cloud Computing – Isolation in Container Based Virtualisation

Ibrahim Alobaidan
Department of computer science
Liverpool John Moores University
Liverpool, UK
i.m.alobaidan@2012.ljmu.ac.uk

Michael Mackay
Department of computer science
Liverpool John Moores University
Liverpool, UK
M.I.Mackay @ljmu.ac.uk

Nathan Shone
Department of computer science
Liverpool John Moores University
Liverpool, UK
N.Shone @ljmu.ac.uk

Abstract— Cloud computing is now a mature technology that provides a wide variety of services. However, a challenging issue that remains for many users is choosing the best cloud service for a specific application and in many cases, one of the key factors to consider is security and trust. For example, ensuring data privacy is still a main factor in building trust relationships between cloud service providers and cloud users. In this paper, we propose a security system to address the weak isolation in container-based virtualisation that is based on shared kernel OS and system components. We address the isolation issue in containers through the addition of a Role Based Access Control model and the provision of strict data protection and security.

Keywords-Cloud computing; Container isolation; RBAC.

I. INTRODUCTION

Adding new resources and services in a highly scalbe shared tenancy environment is a key feature of cloud computing [1], which has now become a ubiquitous technology in all areas of computing. However, one constant issue faced in cloud computing is that of data security, which has long limited the adoption of the approach in certain areas. It has always been the responsibility of the cloud user to ensure that the selected cloud enviroment provides a reliable data privacy, integrity and trust model through its data storage security framework. However, there has also always been a corresponding trade-off to be made by the Cloud Service Provider (CSP) in the need for security versus the performance overheads this introduces on the system. One example of this trade-off is in the move away from traditional full-stack virtualization towards Containers. Performance, isolation, security, networking, and storage are five factors that are commonly used to compare between Virtual Machines (VM) and Containers [2]. In the Virtual Machines (VM) each guest VM has its own operating system and kernel built on top of the virtualized hardware, while container-based systems share the kernel OS and virtualize the environment above it.

Containers provide better performance compared with Virtual Machines because of this reduced overhead compared to full virtualization but may provide less isolation, and therefore be less trustworthy, as a result. The isolation aspect is increasingly important in cloud computing to ensure the users' data privacy and integrity. Due to shared tenancy, which is a central feature of virtualised infrastructures, providers need to enforce strong mechanisms to ensure that virtual services running on the same physical server do not interfere with or impede each other, and that users cannot break out of their allocated virtual machine (VM). As a result, in this paper we propose a system to improve the isolation of users in container-based virtualisation with the aim of improving privacy of these services and therefore the trustworthiness of the whole infrastructure.

In the remainder of this paper, we first describe some of the related work on trust in cloud computing, an evaluation of hypervisor vs container isolation, and an overview of container security mechanisms in section 2. In Section 3, we then present our proposed approach that would help to build trust relationships between CSPs and users by solving the isolation issue in container-based virtualisation. Next, we present our system architecture that focuses on provider a Docker plugin using Role Based Access Control (RBAC) in Section 4. We briefly present the current implementation of our proposed system in Section 5 and finally, we conclude in Section 6.

II. RELATED WORK

In Cloud Computing the cloud service provider (CSP) is responsible for providing a trusted computing platform to guarantee privacy and security for the users [3]. This has been an active research area since the inception of Cloud Computing and many works in academia and industry have aimed to address this issue. We will first discuss this in the context of full stack virtualisation before analysing the changed introduced with containers.

A. Cloud Security

CSPs typically deploy strong security mechanisms to protect their infrastructure and by default use, encryption to secure the remote connection to the user, but limited external accountability has led to a lack of trust in the safety of data and services entrusted to the Cloud by users. A few critical issues for building trust in cloud computing were identified by The Cloud Security Alliance [4] where different levels of security are required in public and private clouds. Data integrity and confidentially and building trust between providers and users were the critical security issues identified in every case. Another study [5]reported that trust was a vital component to be combined into cloud systems, and security is one of the key factors that many users and providers are often concerned about.

Fundamentally, the fact that clouds use a remotely administered shared virtual infrastructure often requires a higher level of trust to exist between the CSP and the cloud user. Therefore, having authorization as a form of security measure is not only useful, but also highly necessary in order for trust to exist between these two parties. For example, the provider could use some approaches to limiting system access to authorized users, such as through Role Based Access Control (RBAC). Another mechanism to build up trust is through a formal Trusted Computing Platform (TCP), which can be used to ensure that only the customers can access their data and the administrator has no access to any of the customer's secured data and cannot damage its contents. This also provides assurances that user's computations are running on a trusted platform by validating whether the VM is operating on a trusted implementation or not.

B. Container vs hypevisor based isolation

Container-based virtualisation differs from that in VM based virtualisation in that the latter is applied comprehensively down to the hardware, whereas containers use shared Operating System components. As such, the hypervisor approach provides inclusively complete isolation of the user applications and services, but incurs a comparatively large performance overhead through the additional management. In contrast, containers have become very popular due to their improved performance and relatively low overheads, but may offer less isolation to users as a result. Some work has been done to measure the difference in isolation between containers and hypervisors.

A study by IBM provided a comparison of isolation in Linux containers and full Virtual Machines (VM) [6] where the goal was to evaluate efficient methods of resource control using the two different methodologies. The level of resource isolation was evaluated between traditional VMs and Linux containers when handling various workloads that were particularly CPU, memory, and network intensive. The results concluded that container-based technologies did offer reduced isolation in some cases but ultimately provided a superior alternative for cloud-based solutions because of their better performance and easier deployment.

The authors in [7] also present results from testing the isolation properties of VMWare, Xen, and OpenVZ through various performance stress tests. Here, both VMware and Xen operated perfectly in isolating the VMs in all the tests with little resource degradation. However, OpenVZ containers displayed a significant impact in comparison, particularly where no resource-sharing controls are applied. The results showed that the networking tests resulted in the biggest impact in container isolation and therefore provided the weakest isolation between virtual instances. This could be a result of the network-oriented measurements using SPECWeb, which were the benchmarking tools used. There was also some impact on the disk intensive tests, especially given the limited load the test introduced in the normal servers. However, a significant shortcoming of the testing was that it only considered a single type of container virtualisation For example; Docker provides a much more lightweight environment then OpenVZ and is still the default solution for this type of virtualisation.

To evaluate the isolation performance of Docker in this context, we replicated the test above to evaluate the performance impact on a HTTP server in one container while the other ran the above-mentioned isolation benchmarking tests [2]. In this case we used Httperf for our testing because it is a more open and flexible approach. In this test, we created two Raspberry PI hosts connected via a local Ethernet connection running at 1GBps, one as a client and the other as a server; both are running Raspbian OS and Docker. The client is running Httperf in a single container while the server is configured with two containers, one with an Apache2 webserver and another with the isolation-benchmarking suite. The isolation benchmark tests were compared to the Httperf-only test to highlight any discrepancies. In particular, the fork bomb intensive results showed significant degradation in the presence of the stress tests and demonstrates that Docker containers are also susceptible to the same weaker isolation and performance.

C. Container security features

When reviewing Docker security, the Kernel namespace, control groups and the Docker daemon itself are the three major areas to consider. This is because Docker shares access to the underlying Linux Kernel between the host and the containers and therefore the responsibility of enforcing isolation is also shared between the host and the platform. Figure 1 shows the location of the main Dockers security features.

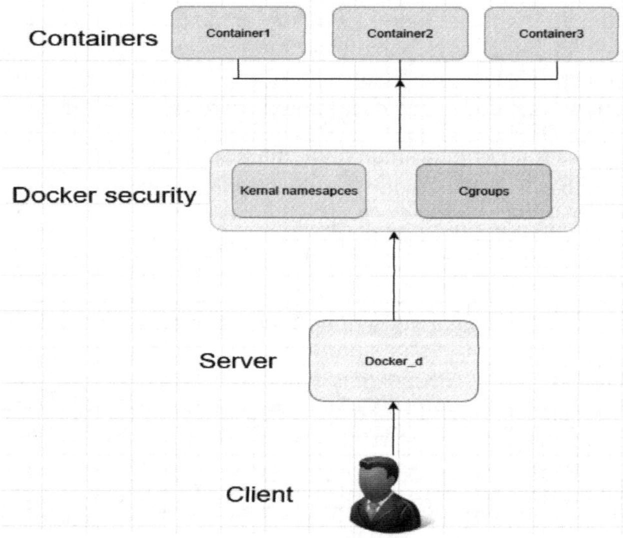

Figure 1. Kernel Namespaces and Cgroups

The Linux Kernel has Namespaces features, which is a fundamental aspect of containers on Linux [8]. Layer isolation is provided by these namespaces, which ensure that Docker users can only access particular containers. Docker creates these namespaces when the container is started, which then isolates processes running within the container from other containers and the host [2]. Each container has a separate process ID (PID), network artefacts (e.g. routing table, iptables and loopback Interface), and Inter-Process Communication (IPC) mechanisms namely semaphores, message queues and shared memory segments. Each container also has its own mountpoint, which is provided by the mnt namespace. Finally, hostnames for different containers could be supported by the Unix Time Sharing (UTS) namespace. Cgroups also provide many useful metrics for container isolation [2]. Access to memory, CPU, disk I/O and other system resources can be equally distributed on the host, which aims to prevent a container from crashing the system by exhausting its resources.

However, the focal point of all communication to and from containers is the Docker daemon itself [9]. This program runs on the host machine and provides a central point of interaction between the system and the containers. The users do not directly interact with the Docker daemon, instead this is done through the Docker client, which provides access to the daemon through sockets or a REST API.

III. PROPOSED APPROACH

Given this reliance on the underlying Linux mechanisms in Container-based virtualisation, and the limitations in isolation this introduces, this paper proposes the development of an enhanced security system to address the issue by using Role Based Access Control (RBAC). RBAC policies will be configured for each container using an authorisation plugin running within the Docker daemon with the not only to isolate each container from the other and the underlying systems but also to isolate user resources in the same container from each other.

In our proposed system, the containers trust the host to make and enforce authorisation decisions as an extension of the existing system without the need to introduce additional components in the architecture. The plugin will be registered as part of the Docker daemon, which resides on the host and the containers have no access to this. Therefore, access can be granted only to resources when authorised by the plugin. The Docker daemon obtains this request through the CLI or via the Engine API as before, which passes the request to the authorisation plugin. The authorisation plugin will obtain the user request data and provide a decision according to the user policy. Figure 2 shows a typical authorisation scenario for a user request.

A user request should contain information on the username, policy, container ID, the object path, and action. Then, the authorisation plugin will make a decision whether to accept or deny the user request. For example, user Bob is part of the HR user group. Bob wants to access the employee database that is stored in a HR container that has the ID 495ad09fc530. A typical request in this case would include the following information:

Subject: = "Bob" // the user that wants to access an employee database.
Object: = "495ad09fc530" // the container that is going to be accessed.
Path: = "/H/employee-database" // the path for the resources within the containers that is going to be accessed.
Action: = "read" // the action that the Bob performs on the employee database.

The benefits of this centralised approach are that it reduces complexity and resource usage, as only one security mechanism will be required per host. Further, due to the centralised nature of data stored in cloud infrastructures, our proposed design would minimise data leakage and improve monitoring. Developers can already add access control in the Docker daemon through a number of existing authorisation plugins. However, this authorisation is currently performed on a very coarse level and does not support the centralised management of this process across the entire cloud infrastructure.

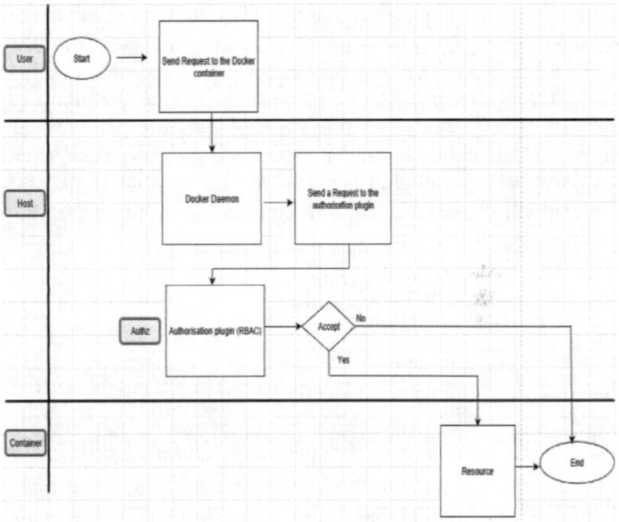

Figure 2. Authorisation Scenario

The system we propose includes the ability to allow or restrict access to specific containers, or the resources contained within those containers on a per-user basis using RBAC. The RBAC model has been the standard authorisation approach for more than two decades [10]. However, RBAC has been deemed unsuitable for further use, according to the continuously evolving access control requirements of emerging computing paradigms. These RBAC drawbacks have been addressed by Attribute Based Access Control (ABAC), which has appeared as a powerful alternative to RBAC. As such, it is necessary to explain why we have not adopted this approach in our work. In our analysis, we can determine that each container image will be created in advance of deployment and so an appropriate set of policies will be developed as part of this process. Then, whenever an image is deployed in a container, these policies can simply be imported into the authorisation plugin in the host. This makes RBAC more scalable in situations where large numbers of containers are expected to be deployed and more performant with fewer overheads in resource-constrained environments.

IV. SYSTEM DESIGN

We have created a first design of our security system based on the approach outlined above. We first describe the system architecture before focussing specifically on the design of the plugin.

A. System architecture:

In the cloud datacentre, each Docker host is configured with the authorisation plugin such that any container that is deployed on is subject to the same process. Now, users who utilise the datacentre can specify user authorisation policies and associate them with any container images that they configure on the system. This will provide a consistent model of access that determines which users can access which resources within that specific image. Thereafter, any time an image is deployed into a container on any host with the datacentre, the associated policies will be deployed into the authorisation plugin alongside the image to control access, as shown in figure 3. This system provides a scalable point of control, such that the user roles and access can be administered centrally and dynamically applied with each update. Once a container is removed, the associated policies are also simply deleted from the authorisation plugin on the host.

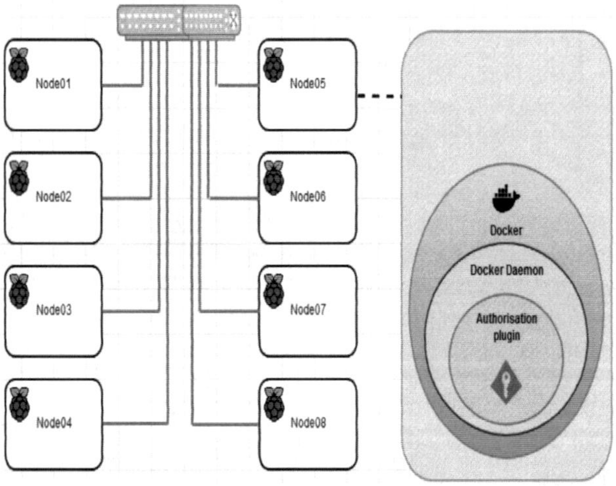

Figure 3. System Architecture

In this approach, the authorisation plugin in the host does not require any knowledge of the resources inside the container, but the administrator of the account can control which users (or roles) can access which data, files or services. The advantages of this is that only one authorisation plugin has responsibility for each host, which may be running a number of containers from many users. Moreover, regardless of how the user resources are deployed in the data centre, the policies that control user access are consistent and controlled by the account administrator. Finally, the underlying CSP does not need to understand how these policies are configured to control access to resources, only that the mapping between the image and policy is maintained.

The users can then request access to specific applications within a Docker container, which is approved or denied utilising the RBAC-based authorisation plugin. Each user has a unique username that is used to access any host in the data centre and the RBAC policies governs what actions users can perform based on their assigned roles. The authorisation process is shown in Figure 4 below. As outlined in the previous section, the user accesses the deployed container via a client, which will provide access to the Docker daemon. The daemon will pass the request on to the authorisation plugin which will process the request against the current policy base. If a positive match is found then the request is granted or, as shown below, the request is denied if no matching policy is in place.

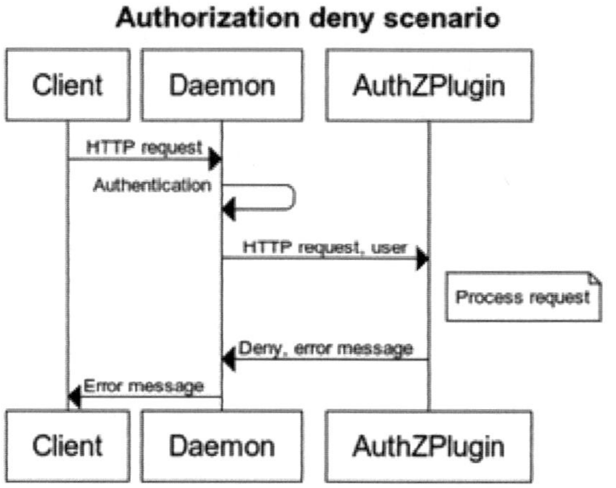

Figure 4. User Authentication via the plugin [11]

B. Authorisation plugin

The authorisation plugin runs directly on the Docker framework and makes use of the intrinsic plugin support offered by the daemon. The authorisation plugin is registered as part of the Docker daemon at start-up and contains a user policy file, which allows the administrator to set specific permissions for the users. For example, a container might have three objects groups that can be labelled objectgroup1, which starts with /H in the file system, objectgroup2, which stars with /W and objectgroup3, which starts with /F. Now, user (Bob) belongs to usergroup1 that has some policies to access objectgroup1 resources within a container. A policy should be defined that ensures that usergroup1 has access to all resources that have paths that start with /H in the file system on the specific container. In this case, a typical policy for the system would be as follows:

P, /v1.38/usergroup1/container/id//H/start, POST
P, /v1.38/usergroup1/container/id//H/attach, POST

The policy file contains rules that are specified according to the following format. P is the policy type that is the first field in each line. This project has one policy type, which is P (policy_definition) that contain subject, object, path, action) but it is possible to add more than one policy type in the model such as P, P1and P2. For example:

[policy_definition]
P = subject, object, path, action
P1 = subject, object, action
P2 = object, action

The policy definition is matched by policy type so, for the following policy definition:

P,/v1.38/usergroup2/container/495ad09fc530//W/start, POST

P is the policy type and v1.38 is the Docker API version. The subject is usergroup2 and the object is the container that has ID 495ad09fc530. The path is /W and the action is start. All rules in the policy file should follow the Docker API references. For example, /containers/id/start, POST is to start a particular container. Request data from containers is provided by GET. Send data to server to stop, start or attach containers is provided by POST.

The plugin model consists of a *request definition*, *policy definition*, *role definition*, *policy effect* and *matchers*. Role definition is represented by the letter G in the trust model, which is based on the definition for RBAC role inheritance relations. Each user will have one or more roles in the predefined RBAC policy file. For example, the system has a role named Role1 that is related to usergroup1, which allows all users who are related to HR to access HR resources. If user Ibrahim is part of the HR user group then we can define the following policies:

P,/v1.38/Role1/container/495ad09fc530//H/start, POST
G, Ibrahim, Role1

In the first policy, the subject will allow all users who are part of Role1 to access all resources that begins with /H within the container that has ID 495ad09fc530. In the second policy we simply add the user Ibrahim to Role1 which means that he can access the resource. The action is set to read only here because in container virtualisation, users should not have permission to delete or edit the Docker image that contains all the user data. In practice, this can be overcome through the use of local caches that can be committed back to the image over time. However, this functionality goes beyond the scope of our work at this stage.

V. IMPLMENTATION

The trust architecture is designed to be run in a Cloud Data Centre (CDC) cluster, which may be comprised of a large cluster of servers. As such, the first stage of implementing our work was to build a realistic data center cluster by using Raspberry PI devices. This allows us to develop our solution in a realistic, scalable, and cost-effective environment. The Raspberry PI cluster is created using the MPI (Messaging Passing Interface) library for communication [12]. MPI is a communication mechanism used in parallel computing environments to allow clustered nodes to interact seamlessly. The Raspberry PI devices will communicate without username or password through configured SSH [13]. The three main capabilities provided by secure SSH are secure command-shell, secure file transfer and Port forwarding. Raspberry PI cluster has a master node that has IP addresses for all cluster nodes and one or more Docker hosts which can run containers as shown in figure 5. Each Docker host is configured with our authorisation plugin as part of the daemon, which has policies for each deployed container. All containers in the system should be accessed by users through the master node.

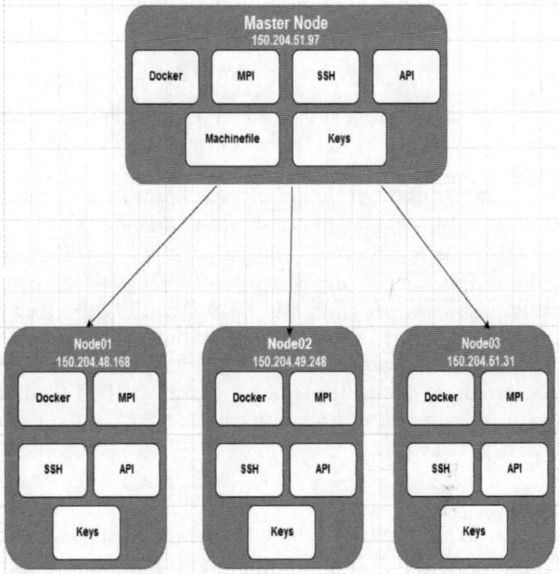

Figure 5. Trusted container PiCloud implementation

The authorization plugin is being created using the GO language because this was used by Google in the development of Docker and includes support for RBAC. GO has many libraries including one for RBAC and so we can easily extend the existing Docker plugin support framework to develop our system.

The trust plugin model is made up of the *request definition*, the *policy definition*, the *role definition*, the *policy effect* and *matchers*. As explained in the previous sections, the request definition has four factors, which are subject, object, path and action. Our implementation has three Roles (Role1, Role2 and Role3), which are related to Usergroup1, Usergroup2 and Usergroup3 respectively. The policy definitions are based on the four factors explained in the previous section, so a policy file in the authorisation plugin might typically comprise of the following policies:

A. Usergroup1

p, /v1.38/Role1/container/495ad09fc530//H/json, GET
p, /v1.38/ Role1/container/495ad09fc530//H/start, POST
p, /v1.38/ Role1/container/495ad09fc530//H/stop, POST
p, /v1.38/ Role1/container/495ad09fc530//H/attach, POST
g, usergroup1, Role1

B. Usergroup2

p, /v1.38/Role2/container/495ad09fc530//W/json, GET
p, /v1.38/ Role2/container/495ad09fc530//W/start, POST
p, /v1.38/ Role2/container/495ad09fc530//W/stop, POST
p, /v1.38/ Role2/container/495ad09fc530//W/attach, POST
g, usergroup2, Role2

C. usergroup3

p, /v1.38/Role3/container/495ad09fc530//F/json, GET
p, /v1.38/ Role3/container/495ad09fc530//F/start, POST
p, /v1.38/ Role3/container/495ad09fc530//F/stop, POST
p, /v1.38/ Role3/container/495ad09fc530//F/attach, POST
g, usergroup3, Role3

The policy file above specifies that Usergroup1 can access all resources that start with /H, Usergroup2 can access all resources that start with /W, and usergroup3 can access all resources that start with /F within a single container that has ID 495ad09fc530. The role definition maps users to a specific usergroup to allow them to access the containers.

Finally, the matcher will compare the policy rule against the request based on the subject, object, path or action. Specifically, the matcher will compare r.sub (request definition subject) to p.sub (policy definition subject), r.obj (request definition object) to p.obj (policy definition object) and so on for the path and action. A match will be found only when there is an exact correlation between each of the request and policy parameters:

[matchers]
m = g(r.sub, p.sub) && r.path == p.path && r.obj == p.obj && r.act == p.act

VI. CONCLUSION

This paper has addressed the isolation issue in container-based virtualisation. We have developed a security system to enhance access control policies and provide data protection and security for users within each container. This security system can protect container guests from malicious users and improves the integrity of container data, applications and resources by adding a Role Based Access Control model.

In our system, the containers rely on the host to make the access decision through an authorisation plugin. This helps to address scalability issues because just one security model is required in the host instead of within each container. Moreover, each Docker image is defined along with a set of user groups and policies, which define how access should be granted to the resources it contains. Each time a new image is deployed in a container on the host, the authorisation plugin retrieves and applies the policy.

We are in the process of developing a proof of concept implementation of the authorisation plugin as part of our future work. Once completed, we will deploy and test it in our PiCloud CDC testbed to evaluate its suitability to provide fine-grained access control.

REFERENCES

[1] P. Sirohi and A. Agarwal, "Cloud computing data storage security framework relating to data integrity, privacy and trust," in *2015 1st International Conference on Next Generation Computing Technologies (NGCT)*, 2015, pp. 115-118.

[2] R. Dua, A. R. Raja, and D. Kakadia, "Virtualization vs Containerization to Support PaaS," in *2014 IEEE International Conference on Cloud Engineering*, 2014, pp. 610-614.

[3] P. Sen, P. Saha, and S. Khatua, "A distributed approach towards trusted cloud computing platform," in *2015 Applications and Innovations in Mobile Computing (AIMoC)*, 2015, pp. 146-151.

[4] K. Hwang and D. Li, "Trusted Cloud Computing with Secure Resources and Data Coloring," *IEEE Internet Computing,* vol. 14, no. 5, pp. 14-22, 2010.

[5] Z. Shen and Q. Tong, "The security of cloud computing system enabled by trusted computing technology," in *2010 2nd International Conference on Signal Processing Systems*, 2010, vol. 2, pp. V2-11-V2-15.

[6] W. Felter, A. Ferreira, R. Rajamony, and J. Rubio, "An updated performance comparison of virtual machines and Linux containers," in *2015 IEEE International Symposium on Performance Analysis of Systems and Software (ISPASS)*, 2015, pp. 171-172.

[7] J. N. Matthews *et al.*, "Quantifying the performance isolation properties of virtualization systems," in *Proceedings of the 2007 workshop on Experimental computer science*, 2007, p. 6: ACM.

[8] D. docs. (2019). *Isolate containers with a user namespace*. Available: https://docs.docker.com/engine/security/userns-remap/

[9] B. Kelley, J. J. Prevost, P. Rad, and A. Fatima, "Securing Cloud Containers Using Quantum Networking Channels," in *2016 IEEE International Conference on Smart Cloud (SmartCloud)*, 2016, pp. 103-111.

[10] I. Alobaidan, M. Mackay, and P. Tso, "Build Trust in the Cloud Computing - Isolation in Container Based Virtualisation," in *2016 9th International Conference on Developments in eSystems Engineering (DeSE)*, 2016, pp. 143-148.

[11] D. docs. (2019). *Access authorization plugin*. Available: https://docs.docker.com/engine/extend/plugins_authorization/

[12] X. Wei, H. Li, and D. Li, "MPICH-G-DM: An Enhanced MPICH-G with Supporting Dynamic Job Migration," in *2009 Fourth ChinaGrid Annual Conference*, 2009, pp. 67-76.

[13] V. software. (2008). *An Overview of the Secure Shell (SSH)*. Available: https://www.vandyke.com/solutions/ssh_overview/ssh_overview.pdf

Cloud-RAIR: A Cloud Redundant Array of Independent Resources

Abdelhamid Khiat

Research Center on Scientific and Technical Information
CERIST - Algiers- Algeria
Email: a.khiat@dtri.cerist.dz

***Abstract*—Cloud computing is considered as a dynamic distributed environment composed of a large number of resources. The Physical Machines (PM) and Virtual Machines (VM) are two main Cloud components. They collaborate together with other Cloud resources to provide a set of services to the end user, who must be satisfied as soon as possible. Unfortunately, the risk of a PM or VM failure is still inevitable in a Cloud environment. To ensure the end user satisfaction, a power fault tolerance technique must be used to avoid the service failures. In this paper, a new VM and PM fault tolerance management mechanism called Cloud Redundant Array of Independent Resources (Cloud-RAIR) is proposed. The *Cloud-RAIR* solution is based on Redundant Array of Independent Disks (RAID).**

Keywords–Cloud Computing; Fault Tolerance; Redundant Array of Independent Disks.

I. INTRODUCTION

The use of Cloud technology has increased enormously in these last few years. Given the benefits offered by this technology, a significant number of services have been migrated to the Cloud environment, which implies a huge need of used resources, including storage space. With this increase in the amount of used resources in the Cloud environment, the probability to get a PM or VM failure also increases, possibly causing a service interruption. The recovery of such a failed PM or VM can be achieved by using a fault tolerance management solution. The latter must avoid any risk of inability to recover the data after a VM or PM crash. One of the most important parameters to take into account in any fault tolerance solution is the used space storage, which should be minimized as much as possible. Such minimization can also help in optimizing other important parameters like cost and consumed energy .

In this work, we propose *Cloud-RAIR*, a reactive fault tolerance management policy based on the powerful concept known as Redundant Array of Independent Disks (RAID) solution. The latter is widely used by most open source operating systems and usually provided as hardware solutions. *Cloud-RAIR* allows to discover and repair the PM and VM failures. The major contribution of the proposed solution lies in the space storage optimization using a specific level of RAID, namely RAID 6.

The rest of this paper is organized as follows. Section II summarizes the related work. In Section III, the proposed solution is described in detail. An evaluation of our solution is presented in Section V. Finally, a conclusion and future work are given in Section VI.

II. RELATED WORK

Two main standards of fault tolerance are defined for Cloud environments, namely Proactive Fault Tolerance Policy and Reactive Fault Tolerant Policy [1]. The first one envisages to avoid failures, while the second one aims to reduce the effects of occurring faults. Considering the nature of our proposed policy, only some Reactive Fault Tolerant policies will be presented in the rest of this section.

In [2], the authors have discussed some reactive fault tolerance approaches, among which we mention:

- Task Resubmission: this technique is based on task resubmission when a fault is detected. The resubmission processes must be done without interrupting the system workflow.
- Check-pointing/Restart: this technique allows to restart the failed Cloud component (application, VM or PM) from a saved state called checkpoint. It is considered as an efficient fault tolerance technique for high computation intensive applications hosted in the Cloud.
- Replication: this technique consists to keep multiple copies of data or object, which will be used when a fault occurrs. According to [2], the replication technique is a popular solution with many varieties.

A collaborative fault tolerance method based on the Checkpointing technique was proposed in [3]. In this technique, both the service consumer and provider participate to ensure the fault tolerance management. According to authors, application faults can be detected and repaired at the customer level, while VM and hardware faults can be detected and repaired at the Cloud provider level.

In [4], the authors exploit the virtualisation by adding a service layer which acts as a Fault Tolerance Middleware (FTM). The added service is inserted between the computing infrastructure and the applications. Then, the proposed FTM can offer fault tolerance support to each application individually.

A Self-tuning Fault Detection system (SFD) was proposed in [5]. It detects faults in the Cloud computing environment. According to authors, SFD has the advantage of ensuring a better fault detection by adjusting fault detecting control parameters.

A framework called *BFTCloud* was proposed by Yilei Zhang et al. in [6]. The authors have used the dynamic replication technique, in which voluntary nodes are selected based on QoS characteristics and reliability performance. Extensive experiments on various types of Cloud environments show that *BFTCloud* guarantees robustness of systems when f resources out of a total of $3f+1$ resource providers are faulty.

Redundant Array of Independent Disks (RAID) [7], is the standardized scheme for the design of redundant multi-unit systems. The RAID systems can be provided either as software solutions or as hardware solutions integrated into the computing system. A RAID system allows to enhance fault tolerance through redundancy. A number of standard schemes (levels) have evolved over the years. In our case, we are interested into the RAID 6 level, which consists in block-level striping with double distributed parity. RAID 6 requires a minimum of four disks and provides fault tolerance up to two simultaneously failed drives.

In [8], the authors have combined DRBD [9] and heartbeat [10] solutions to enhance the high availability of the system in the case of resource failure. The proposed architecture was designed for an OpenNebula [11] based Cloud. DRBD was used to ensure distributed replicated storage, whereas heartbeat was used as a high-availability solution.

A typical replication method called K-fault tolerance strategy was proposed in [12]. According to the authors, the service is not largely affected when no more than k nodes fail. In [13], the authors propose an (m,n)-fault tolerance strategy that can ensure (m,n)-fault tolerance and investigate the optimal virtual machine placement strategy.

In order to minimize the number of QoS violations in a fat-tree data center and continue to support the QoS requirement of an application after data corruption, an optimal data replication approach was proposed in [14]. The solution aims to preserve the quality of service requirements after each data crash.

III. PROPOSED CLOUD-RAIR

The main objective of *Cloud-RAIR* consists to ensure the service continuity by detecting and repairing the physical and virtual machine failures. A failure can be a hard one like a storage disk crash, or a soft one like an operating system crash. Note that an application crash is not considered by the *Cloud-RAIR* solution, the latter reacts only when the fault affects VM, or PM components. *Cloud-RAIR* aims to optimize the total used space storage, taking inspiration from RAID, a powerful technique used in a large number of Open-Source operating systems and in hard storage solutions. Among the set of different RAID levels, the RAID level 6 was chosen, given its optimization of the total space storage used to save the data, and its ability to recover data in case of two simultaneous resource (PM, or VM) failure.

The RAID 6 technique recommends to use disks of same size with a total number of used disks that must be at least four. This recommendation is taken into account in our architecture, by dividing the set of VM and PM into sub-sets of the same size, where a VM or PM is the equivalent of a disk in the basic RAID solution. Two types of resources are considered in the *Cloud-RAIR* architecture. The first one is the VM resource type, while the second one is the PM resource type. The set of resources of a given sub-set must be independent; Two resources of type VM are independent if they are not hosted on the same PM, hence the use of the term *Independent Resources* in the name *Cloud-RAIR* (Cloud Redundant Array of Independent Resources). Note that all the resources of the PM type are independent.

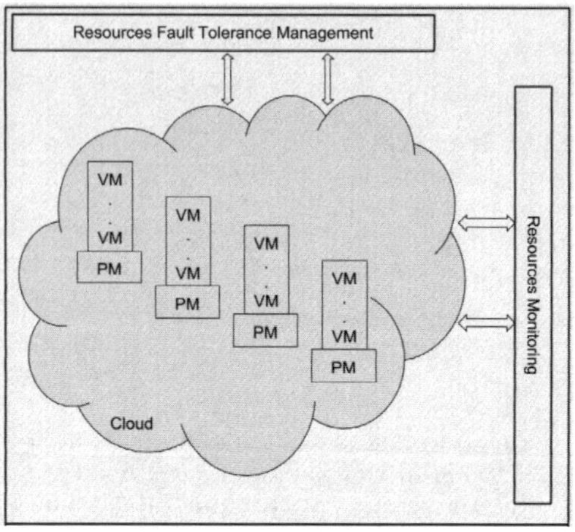

Figure 1. Cloud-RAIR global architecture

As described in Figure 1, *Cloud-RAIR* is composed of two modules that work in parallel and in coordination. The first one ensures a real time Cloud monitoring, in order to detect any event, like resource leaving/joining. The second one ensures the backup management by repairing any resource fault.

From a practical point of view, the two modules can be deployed on any host related to the Cloud. Those modules interact with Cloud components using a Cloud service. Two types of Cloud services are used by the *Cloud-RAIR* solution. The first one is dedicated to provide the informations about the status of a resource, the latter being used by the *Monitoring Resource* module to monitor the status of the resources. Meanwhile, the second one is used to manage the Cloud resources through operations like additions and deletions. This service is used by the *Resource Fault Tolerance Management* module to reconstruct the failed resource.

The global processes of *Cloud-RAIR* are described in the rest of this section.

When a new VM or PM is added to the set of Cloud resources, the addition event is detected by the *Monitoring Resource* module, and an automatic script is triggered by the module, in order to notify the *Resource Fault Tolerance Management* module (RFTM) of their creation. Afterwards, the RFTM module starts by attributing a unique R_id to the new resource and saves all informations about the new added resource. It then uses all saved informations in order to find the best suitable sub-set (SS_id), and subsequently integrates the new resource into that sub-set. Finally, a tuple (R_Type, R_id, SS_id) is constructed as follows:

R_Type: Represents the resource type with several possible values. For example, a type value can be PM to represent PM, VM_Small to represent a Small VM, or VM_Large to represent a Large VM, etc. R_id: Represents a unique id that allows to identify a resource in the system.

SS_id: Represents a unique id used to identify the sub-set that includes R_Id.

VM or PM deletion is another event that can appear. Like a VM/PM addition event, the VM/PM deletion event is detected by the *Monitoring Resource* module, which subsequently launches an automatic script, in order to inform the RFTM module that a component has been deleted. Then, the RFTM module identifies the deleted resource by its id, removes it from its sub-set and checks if the size of the sub-set after the removal is smaller than four. If that is the case, it deletes the whole sub-set and adds the remaining resources of the sub-set one bye one as new resources without modifying their id.

The third event that can appear is the resource failure. When a resource failed to continue its service, the *Monitoring Resource* module detects the event and notifies the RFTM module to start the process that allows to recover the failed resource. A resource is considered as a failed resource when it does not respond to user requests, which can usually happen if the resource is not reachable.

The proposed *Cloud-RAIR* approach follows the RAID concept. Whenever the Resource Monitoring module detects a PM_i or VM_j failure, *Cloud-RAIR* will not look for a full copy of the lost PM/VM. It will instead reconstruct the lost resource from the sub-set that contains VM_i/PM_j.

In *Cloud-RAIR*, VM and PM are internally coded by a sequence of bits representing an operating system with the users data. Assuming that a sub-set SS_i contains p resources of same size noted $(R_1, R_2, ..., R_p)$, with p equal or greater than four and R_{p-1}, R_p represent the parity values as shown in (1). According to the RAID 6 level, the parity sequences of bits R_{p-1} and R_p represent the data used to recover failed resources and are computed using Formula 1.

$$\begin{cases} R_{p-1} = R_1 \oplus R_2 \oplus ... \oplus R_{p-2} \\ R_p = R_1 \oplus SH^1(R_2) \oplus ... \oplus SH^{p-1}(R_{p-2}) \end{cases} \quad (1)$$

In the formulaes, SH represents the $shift$ function, and a resource R_i is coded as a sequence of bits $R_i = r_0 r_1 r_2 ... r_x$. The corresponding SH function is computed as follows:

$SH^1 = r_1 r_2 ... r_x r_0$, $SH^2 = r_2 r_3 ... r_x r_0 r_1$, etc.

The formulaes 1 and 2 are valid only if $x \geq p$, otherwise, other functions must be applied. In general, $SH^x(R_i)$ represents the shift of R_i by x positions.

For the reconstruction phase, two cases are possible. The first case considers a single resource failure, while the second considers two simultaneous resource failures. In the first case, the reconstruction is done with a simple XOR between all the resources that compose the corresponding sub-set except R_p. Meanwhile, in the second case, the function 2 is applied. In the formulae of the function where k l represent the failed resources. The results of Formula 2 represent a system of $2x$ equations with $2x$ unknowns which uniquely determine the two failed resources R_k and R_l.

$$\begin{cases} R_k \oplus R_l = \bigoplus_{i=0,i!=k,l,p}^{p} R_i \\ SH^{k-1}(R_k) \oplus SH^{l-1}(R_l) = \bigoplus_{i=0,i!=k,l,p-1}^{p} SH^{i-1}(R_i) \end{cases} \quad (2)$$

IV. DESCRIPTION OF THE ALGORITHMS

Two algorithms can ensure the *Cloud-RAIR* proper system functioning. The first one allows to manage the sub-sets (Figure 2). The second one (Figure 3) allows to recover the failed resource.

```
Input : VM_i, PM_j
Output: SS_id
Order SS according to Size;
for SS_i ∈ SS do
    SB: for VM ∈ SS_i do
        if VM hosted on PM_j then
            break SB ;
        else
        end
    end
end
if found SS_i then
    Add(VM_i to SS_i)
else
    Create new SS;
    migrate two others VM to the new SS;
    add VM_i to new SS;
end
```

Figure 2. Resource addition algorithm

The algorithm presented in Figure 2 allows to manage the sub-sets over two main setups. In the first setup, the set of sub-sets is sorted in ascending order according to their size, aiming to insert the new VM into the smallest possible sub-set in terms of size. The second setup consists to search the sub-set that does not contain any VM hosted in the same PM with the new VM; if no sub-set is found, a new sub-set is created and two VM are randomly chosen and migrated to the new created sub-set, provided that these two VM are not hosted in the same PM as the new VM. Finally the backup of the new sub-set and the two other altered sub-sets are restarted.

```
Input : R_1, R_2, ...., R_p
Output: R_failed
if R_failed is PM then
    for R_i ∈ PM do
        Reconstruct(R_i)
    end
else
    Reconstruct(R_failed)
end
function Reconstruct (R_failed)
find SS_id with R_failed in SS_id
Reconstruct R_failed
end function
```

Figure 3. Resource recovering algorithm

Figure 3 presents the algorithm used to recover the failed VM or PM once the failure has occurred. Two cases of failure can appear, the first one consists into a VM failure (VM_{failed}), while the second one consists into a PM failure. In the first case, *Cloud-RAIR* has to identify the sub-set that contains VM_{failed}, then, VM_{failed} is reconstructed using the recovery process defined in Section 1. For the second case, all the VM that have been hosted on the failed PM are identified and the set of VM are reconstructed, similarly to the case of VM failure.

V. EVALUATION

For the evaluation phase, the JAVA, SHELL and R languages were used to develop a simulator designed to make our experiments. The different experiments have been done by simulation on a personal computer equipped with an Intel Core i5 processor and 6 GB of RAM, using Ubuntu 16.04 as an operating system. *Cloud-RAIR* was implemented using the JAVA programming language, and evaluated by simulation. Our approach was compared with the replication policy.

The replication technique used in the evaluation phase was also implemented in JAVA and deployed with *Cloud-RAIR* in the developed simulator. The implementation of the used replication technique was done as follows: assuming that we have a set of n VM hosted under a set of m PM, the replication consists to make only one copy of each VM (VM_i) on a PM different from the PM that hosts VM_i. Then the OS and data of each PM are copied on another PM.

The following Cloud model was used for the evaluation phase: assuming that the Cloud is composed of a set of m PM and n VM. The whole set of resources (VM and VM) is connected by a private network. The term R is used as a common term to denote a PM or a PM. Each VM is characterized by a tuple ($TypeVM_i$, $SizePM_j$).

A table called $Type\_VM$ = $["Type1", "Type2", ..., "Typek"]$ contains the different types that can be taken by a VM. The variable denoted $TypeVM_i$ is used to designate the type of VM_i, and $TypeVM_i$ is defined at the creation of VM_i and can not be changed during the VM_i life cycle. An associative table denoted $Size\_VM = ["Type_1" => Size_1, ..., "Type_p" => Size_p]$ contains the sizes of the different VM types, where the size of a VM_i is calculated as follows: $SizeVM_i = Size\_VM[TypeVM_i]$.

The variable $CStorageSize$ denotes the total space consumed by the Cloud excluding the storage space used for the backup. Meanwhile, the variable $CBackupSize$ represents the space used for the backup. The variable $CTotalSize$ represents the total space used by the Cloud ($CTotalSize$=$CStorageSize$ + $CBackupSize$).

For the replication technique, the storage size consumed by the backup ($CBackupSize$) is equal to $CStorageSize$, since, each VM has exactly one copy. Subsequently, the size of each copy of VM_i is exactly equal to $SizeVM_i$. Similarly to VM, each PM haw only one copy, and the PM_j copy size is exactly equal to $SizePM_j$. The total space consumed by the Cloud ($CTotalSize$) is equal to $2 * CStoeageSize$.

Cloud-RAIR assumes that we have p sub-sets denoted SS_i. Following to the concept of *Cloud-RAIR*, all resources of the same SS_i have the same size denoted $RSize_i$. Then the total size of the Cloud is computed using Formula 3.

$$CStorageSize = CStorageSize + (2 * \sum_{i=1}^{p} RSize_i) \quad (3)$$

In order to evaluate and compare *Cloud-RAIR* with the replication policy described above, we assume that we have 5 types of VM according to their size, which are tiny, small, medium, large, and xlarge VM. It is considered that there is no constraint on the available storage space on the PM, that is, the space is sufficient for all VM and backup. For evaluation purpose, the number of PM is varied inside the following set $\{5, 10, 50, 100, 250, 500, 1000, 2500, 5000, 10000, 20000\}$. The number of hosted VM on each PM is randomly generated, and each PM can host between 1 and 20 VM. The evaluation metrics are, the storage space consumed by each policy and the percent of space saved by the *Cloud-RAIR* approach compared with the replication policy.

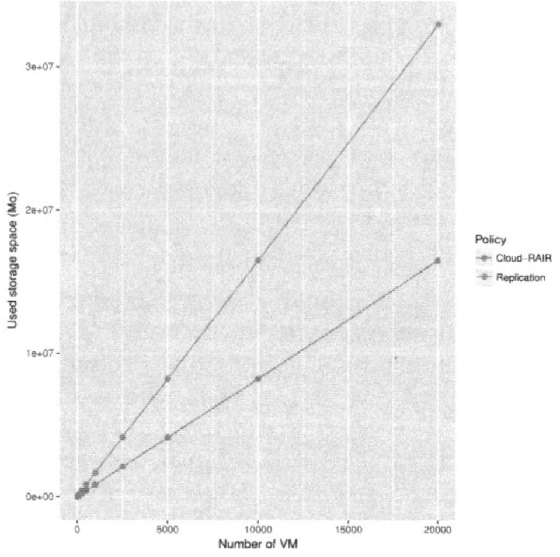

Figure 4. Used space comparison

As previously explained, for the replication approach, the total size of space used for VM backup equals exactly the sum of the sizes of all VM. In contrast, for *Cloud-RAIR*, the storage space depends on the total number of VM and PM, as well as on the way in which VM are distributed on PM. The total space used for backup storage is calculated for each case, as shown in Figure 4.

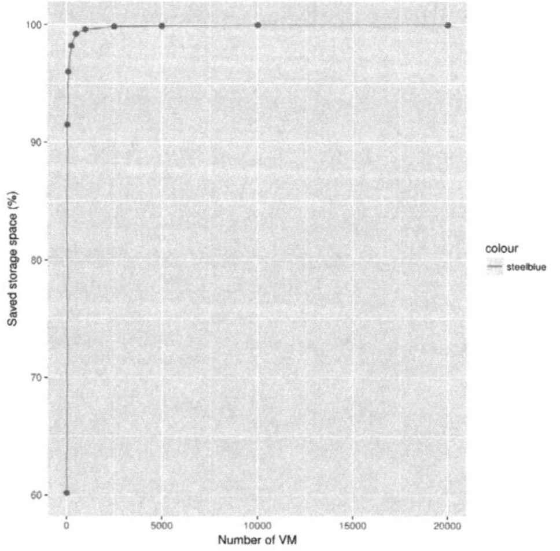

Figure 5. Cloud-RAIR saved backup storage space

Figure 5 shows the percentage of backup space saved using *Cloud-RAIR* compared with the replication method. The saving becomes more important when the Cloud size in terms of total number of PM and VM becomes large enough. The space saved using *Cloud-RAIR* compared with the replication policy peaks around 99%, where the Cloud size becomes more important. This shows the usefulness of *Cloud-RAIR* when the Cloud is large.

The overall results show the good properties of *Cloud-RAIR* from a theoretical point of view, when the different times taken by the operations are not considered. However, in practice, it is necessary to take into account other parameters, such as communication time. These parameters can potentially have an impact on *Cloud-RAIR* efficiency, particularly when the number of resources is large.

VI. Conclusion and Future Work

In this paper, a new fault-tolerance policy for managing both virtual and physical machine failures in a Cloud environment has been proposed. As described in this paper, *Cloud-RAIR* inherits its concepts from the RAID 6 technique, consequently, inheriting the advantages provided by RAID 6, particularly, in terms of storage space optimization compared with the standard backup systems, and in terms of the number of simultaneous failures that can be recovered. *Cloud-RAIR* being based on RAID 6 level, it can be useful to adapt the policy of sub-set management defined in this paper with other RAID levels, in order to study the impact of *Cloud-RAIR* solution on the consumed storage space when changing the RAID level.

It will also be useful to introduce the communication time between resources, in order to compute the minimum allowed time between two successive failures. This will allow to predict the maximum allowed failures per unit time. It can also be useful to study the efficiency of *Cloud-RAIR* if the sub-set size is limited, (although this will increase the backup storage size, it will probably allow to reduce the repairing time). Another potential future work to consider, consists in making a real implementation of the *Cloud-RAIR* solution on a real Cloud environment and study its performance in terms of cost and energy consumption. In the proposed solution, the VM and PM failures are considered, but not the application crashes. It could be useful to consider adding the fault management of application level faults.

References

[1] K. Ganga and S. Karthik, "A fault tolerent approach in scientific workflow systems based on cloud computing," in Pattern Recognition, Informatics and Mobile Engineering (PRIME), 2013 International Conference on. IEEE, 2013, pp. 387–390.

[2] A. Ganesh, M. Sandhya, and S. Shankar, "A study on fault tolerance methods in cloud computing," in Advance Computing Conference (IACC), 2014 IEEE International. IEEE, 2014, pp. 844–849.

[3] A. Tchana, L. Broto, and D. Hagimont, "Approaches to cloud computing fault tolerance," in Computer, Information and Telecommunication Systems (CITS), 2012 International Conference on. IEEE, 2012, pp. 1–6.

[4] R. Jhawar, V. Piuri, and M. Santambrogio, "A comprehensive conceptual system-level approach to fault tolerance in cloud computing," in Systems Conference (SysCon), 2012 IEEE International. IEEE, 2012, pp. 1–5.

[5] N. Xiong, A. V. Vasilakos, J. Wu, Y. R. Yang, A. Rindos, Y. Zhou, W. Song, and Y. Pan, "A self-tuning failure detection scheme for cloud computing service," in 2012 IEEE 26th International Parallel and Distributed Processing Symposium, May 2012, pp. 668–679.

[6] Y. Zhang, Z. Zheng, and M. R. Lyu, "Bftcloud: A byzantine fault tolerance framework for voluntary-resource cloud computing," in 2011 IEEE 4th International Conference on Cloud Computing. IEEE, 2011, pp. 444–451.

[7] D. A. Patterson, G. Gibson, and R. H. Katz, A case for redundant arrays of inexpensive disks (RAID). ACM, 1988, vol. 17, no. 3.

[8] C.-T. Yang, J.-C. Liu, C.-H. Hsu, and W.-L. Chou, "On improvement of cloud virtual machine availability with virtualization fault tolerance mechanism," The Journal of Supercomputing, vol. 69, no. 3, 2014, pp. 1103–1122.

[9] P. Pla, "Drbd in a heartbeat," Linux Journal, vol. 2006, no. 149, 2006, p. 3.

[10] D. Bartholomew, "Getting started with heartbeat," Linux Journal, vol. 2007, no. 163, 2007, p. 2.

[11] D. Milojičić, I. M. Llorente, and R. S. Montero, "Opennebula: A cloud management tool," IEEE Internet Computing, vol. 15, no. 2, 2011, pp. 11–14.

[12] F. Machida, M. Kawato, and Y. Maeno, "Redundant virtual machine placement for fault-tolerant consolidated server clusters," in Network Operations and Management Symposium (NOMS), 2010 IEEE. IEEE, 2010, pp. 32–39.

[13] A. Zhou, S. Wang, C.-H. Hsu, M. H. Kim, and K.-s. Wong, "Virtual machine placement with (m, n)-fault tolerance in cloud data center," Cluster Computing, 2017, pp. 1–13.

[14] J. Lin, C. Chen, and J. M. Chang, "Qos-aware data replication for data-intensive applications in cloud computing systems," IEEE Transactions on Cloud Computing, vol. 1, no. 1, Jan 2013, pp. 101–115.